"JOHN O'BRIEN"
AND THE BOREE LOG

ANGUS & ROBERTSON PUBLISHERS
London • Sydney • Melbourne • Singapore • Manila

First published by Angus & Robertson Publishers, Australia, 1981

© Rev Frank Mecham, 1981

National Library of Australia
Cataloguing-in-publication data.

Mecham, F.A. (Francis A.).
   John O'Brien and the boree log.

   Bibliography.
   Includes index.
   ISBN 0 207 14745 0.

   1. O'Brien, John. 2. Poets, Australian — Biography.
   I. Title.

A821′ .2

Typeset in 10 pt Trump Mediaeval by Setrite Typesetters
Printed in Hong Kong

"JOHN O'BRIEN"
AND THE BOREE LOG

FRANK MECHAM

ANGUS & ROBERTSON PUBLISHERS

THE HARTIGAN

Patrick Hartigan = Ann Cleary

John Sullivan = Anne

Mary = John Collins

Mary b. 1877 — Bridget = Pat Mooney — Susan (Sister of Mercy) — John = Mary Hoase — Tom = Ruby Summerhayes — Edmund = Dolly

Mary = Pat Sullivan (South Coast N.S.W Gundagai Independent) — Katherine Margaret (both died in childhood) — Anne (Sister Imelda) — Honorah (Dolly)

Mary

Catherine Vera — Tony Howard = Mary John Pat Imelda Bede — Bob = Iris Wells — Tom

Molly Pat = Madge McCormack (Gundagai Independent) — Jim Nance Kathleen Carmel = Eric Rusconi

Patricia Mary Kathleen Michael Jim Judith John

Carmel (still-born) — Patricia = Neville Scott — John = Lorraine Eccleston — Jim = Patricia Jacobs

John Patrick = Colleen Pigram (Gundagai Independent) — Bernadette = Keith Turner — Margaret = Brian Lidden

FAMILY TREE

Michael Townsell = Elizabeth Flynn
(or Trousdell)

Patrick = Mary | Bridget | Catherine | Patrick | Willie | Mathew = | Michael =
1842–1940 | 1846–1934 | 1845–1930 | b. 1840 | | (emigrated | Kate Keane | Miss
| | (Sister Patrick) | | | to America) | | Bradley

John | Bridget | Patrick | Joseph | Annie = Dick Mecham | Frank | Matt = | Matt =
b.1872 | 1875–1943 | 1878–1952 | | 1882–1956 | 1878–1952 | 1888–1924 | Mary | Minnie
died in | (Sister | | | | | | Mangan | Landers
infancy) | Ignatius) | | | | | |

Lily | Jane | Minnie | | Michael = Irene Costello
1873–1928 | 1877–1911 | 1881–1968 | | 1884–1948 | 1893–1979
(Sister Gonzaga) | (Sister Michael) | (Sister Peter) |

Willie
1921–1952

Frank | Jean | Bernie = Cecily | Nance | Desmond = | Gerald | Patricia = | Bessie = Albert
| | Merle Daniel | | Gwyn | (died in | Mark | O'Dea
| | | | Henderson | childhood) | Gilchrist |

Peter

Elizabeth | Jennie | Marie | Linda | Rosalie | Jill = John Curtin | Paul | Kevin | Mary Ann
| | | | | | | | Bernadette

MECHAM

Walter | Fred | Dick = Annie Hartigan | Harriet | Mary = Cliff Mecham
| | | (Sister Lutgarde) |

Paul d'Arton = Mary | Peter | Cliff

Michael | Peter | Anne | Damian | Anthony | Helen | Maria

Contents

Acknowledgements   1

Foreword   3

1   Origins   5
     Address on Yass
     Story of Sisters of Mercy coming to
        Yass

2   Training for the Priesthood   23
     Tribute to Bishop John Gallagher
     Story of Father Tom Ryan

3   First Years as a Priest   52
     'A Plea for Australian Literature'

4   Inspector of Schools   80
     'The Man from Snowy River'

5   Parish Priest of Berrigan   107

6   Early Years at Narrandera   115
     The Ligouri Case

7   The Publishing of *Around the Boree Log*   133
     Some unpublished poems
     Jubilee address for Mgr Tim
        O'Connell

8   Trip to Europe   160

9   'The Girls'   169

10   Later Years at Narrandera   179
     'Father Brendan's Christmas Day'
     Panegyrics for Fathers Hanrahan and
        Reidy
     Father Percy's jubilee
     Addresses at opening of North
        Goulburn Chapel and Bombala
        Church

11 Switch to Historical Writing   218
        The Church of the south-west
        Jubilee of the diocese of Wagga
        Seventy years of St Patrick's
            College, Goulburn

12 Decision to Leave Narrandera   260

13 Years at Rose Bay   274
        Addresses for Christian Brothers,
            Holy Name Society, conferring
            of the pallium on Archbishop
            Terry McGuire, Legion of Catholic Women,
            diamond jubilee of Manly
            College

14 Final Illness and Death   312
        Publishing of *On Darlinghurst Hill*
        Tributes from Cardinal Freeman,
            Father Owen Cosgriff and Rev
            Dr John Harper

    Epilogue   330

    Bibliography   336

    Index   338

Acknowledgements

Material for a biography comes from many sources, and when the work is spread over several years it is a hard task to give due credit to all who have helped.

Let me begin by recalling the places where I was warmly received and encouraged. In Ireland, Mannix Joyce of Limerick and the librarians at the city library in Ennis helped me in researching the family names of Hartigan and Townsell.

At Yass, Father Hartigan's birthplace, the parish priest, Dermot O'Hurley, and the Sisters of Mercy made their records available; Adrian Roche of the Yass Historical Society gave special help.

At St Patrick's College, Manly, I was the guest of the President and staff and the Sisters of Our Lady Help of Christians. At Goulburn the Christian Brothers at St Patrick's College, particularly Brother Marzorini, gave me every help, as did the Administrator of the Cathedral, Father Michael O'Brien, the Sisters of Mercy and the Sisters of St Joseph.

I was the guest of the sisters at the Mercy Hospital, Albury, and at the convent and elsewhere in the district I benefited from the reminiscences of contemporaries of Father Hartigan. Miss G.E. Harris made available the family's treasured scrapbook of 'Joker' Byrne.

At Berrigan and Narrandera many of the friends of 'John O'Brien' rallied around, in particular Fathers Dick O'Donovan and Tom Desmond, the priest-poet's only surviving curates. The Sisters of St Joseph, with Sister M. Dolores to the fore, provided many delightful memories.

On the Wagga scene, Bishop Frank Carroll, the Presentation Sisters at Mt Erin, Mrs Sylvia Walsh and Sheila Tearle (now at Hurstville) provided valuable material. In Canberra the late Archbishop Thomas Cahill gave me access to the archives, Father Bill Kennedy provided valuable photographs and John Bartley hosted me at his presbytery while he regaled me with priceless yarns about 'Paddy' Hartigan, and these were supplemented at the nearby convent with precious memories from Sisters Alexius and Oliver who knew him so well at Narrandera.

The religious of the Sacred Heart, Rose Bay, provided valuable historical and photographic material and my special thanks go to Mother Golden, the sister of my great friend, the late Father Jerry Golden S.J. The Sisters of Mercy of Parramatta provided interesting facts about Father Hartigan's two sisters who entered their congregation.

His Eminence Cardinal James Freeman, a friend of Father Hartigan for

ACKNOWLEDGEMENTS

many years, was a constant encourager. The lovely tribute he wrote at the time of Father Hartigan's death is, with his permission, reproduced here, and it is a precious jewel.

Father Owen Cosgriff also has authorised the use of his reminiscences, published in the *Messenger of the Sacred Heart*, and the piece is a brightly written insight into the man and his poetry.

Fathers Tom Linane of Torquay (Victoria) and Michael Donlon of Redcliffe (Queensland) — friends from our days together at St Patrick's College, Manly — read the whole work in typescript and made valuable suggestions which have been incorporated in the text. I am very grateful to them both. I am further indebted to Father Linane for his Foreword and his advice on matters of history.

Monsignori John Harper and Tom Wallace provided valuable impressions of the man they knew and loved so well.

Pat Kavanagh, the producer of the Australian Broadcasting Commission's documentary on 'John O'Brien', was one who urged me strongly to undertake this biography and I am grateful for this and other help he gave.

Librarians, staff of newspaper offices, and many others co-operated generously with their expertise. *The Catholic Weekly* has backed the venture handsomely and I pay tribute to the staff there.

Typists Vera Reilly, Marie Waldie, Betty Burke and Barbara Tallis had a part in the many rewritings and I thank them for their patience.

I remain conscious of the impossibility of mentioning all my helpers — so many of them close friends of Father Hartigan and myself. To one and all, a sincere thanks.

Frank Mecham

Foreword

Pride in seminary of training, now less characteristic of priests on the Australian scene than in the past, motivates the writing of this Foreword.

My passing acquaintance with the tall figure of Father Pat Hartigan goes back fifty years, and since then I have continued delving into his writings under the 'John O'Brien' disguise.

With fellow students at St Columba's Springwood I listened in awe to his after-dinner fare on at least two occasions. His words were a blend of the very serious and the very humorous, and had the effect of making us read his *Boree Log* poems. As one who had been toasted at mallee log fires in the icy Ballarat climate I found it difficult to agree with the footnote on the first page of the *Log* theme song that the boree and the gidgee were the best firewood for homely kitchen comfort. But this was only a passing thought of an eighteen-year-old as I memorised the racy words of 'Tangmalangaloo'.

Volunteering to recite the piece at an impromptu concert of students, I found my confidence waxed and suddenly waned. To bring out the bishop's part in questioning the 'overgrown two-storey lad', I ventured to imitate the squeaky voice of the reigning archbishop and under the stress of heckling was just declaiming 'come, tell me now, and what is Christmas Day', when the bulky frame of the rector, Monsignor Brauer, appeared at the hall door. Fearing and expecting a reprimand, I later received instead a commendation for daring to copy the episcopal squeak. Later still when walking through Megalong Valley, the benign Brauer administered the medicine of encouragement: 'Have you been learning any more of John O'Brien's poems?' My response was to sing the first verse of 'The Little Irish Mother'.

No writer has better described in verse and prose (in fact nobody else has tried) the generic Irish-Australian build-up of the faith than Father Hartigan, under the pseudonym of 'John O'Brien'. Is it too much to claim that the versifying resembles and compares with that of Lawson and Paterson?

My association with his nephew and biographer has been consistent, since our days together at St Patrick's Manly in 1934. In 1973 an invitation was extended to me to collaborate in editing the 'In Diebus Illis' series, published in the *Australasian Catholic Record* in the early 1940s. The subject of these essays, pioneer planters of the faith in the countryside, happened to correspond with a lifelong research interest of mine. The new name of *The Men of '38* resulted, in book form. Sales were not spectacular, but the production did contribute to a revival of interest in the priest-poet and his works.

Our collaboration continues. Now Father Mecham has asked me to check historical detail and style of presentation. I have gladly complied, with the single proviso that the complete O'Brien-Hartigan record—sermons, addresses, anecdotes—should be embodied in the text of the life story.

This biography is simple in style yet gripping in its content; in fact, touching, when it recounts the sad events of the Mecham sisters, Father Hartigan's nieces and the biographer's sisters.

May the life story, thoughts and writings of 'John O'Brien' be a better option and provide more enjoyment for discerning readers than peering into the 'box'.

Father T.J. Linane
Co-editor of *The Men of '38*
Editor of *Footprints*

1 Origins

The Irish are great leg-pullers, and, as likely as not, they may tell you that Tom Graney is courting Lizzy Casey. Tuamgraney is the name of a village in East Clare, and Lissycasey another village, just a few kilometres from Ennis in the west of the county. Here, in the late summer of 1925, came Patrick Joseph Hartigan, parish priest of Narrandera, New South Wales, seeking traces of his forebears. No Hartigans were to be found; a search of the records there and at the parish of Ballynacally, to which Lissycasey belongs, revealed only a bevy of Hartigan girls who lost the name at marriage.

In seeking out Hartigans the priest-poet was on the track of one of the old Irish families. The name comes from a diminutive form of the Christian name Art. One of the family, Duntaing Hartigan, was a hero at Clontarf in 1014 when Brian Boru drove the Vikings out of Ireland. Another, Cineth Hartigan, appropriately enough, was a Gaelic poet who died in 975. The name is found in both Clare and Limerick.

Father Hartigan's search brought him to an old man who knew his father, and who gave Father Hartigan this bit of Irish whimsy that he loved to relate: 'I knew your father; a fine man he was too. Tell me, did he ever marry?' Be that the old man's tale or a 'trimmin' of 'John O'Brien' is for conjecture, but we do have an account of the meeting at Lissycasey from Monsignor Patrick Tuomey of Sydney who was present. Monsignor wrote to Father Hartigan many years later[1] and began by recalling that occasion:

> My Dear Paddy,
>   'There was a Pat Hartigan who left here for Australia about sixty years ago. I well remember him. He held the best pen in the school.'
>   Do you remember the rainy evening at Lisicasey[2] when bending low over the half-door you elicited this information from an old man whose day-dreams by the cosy hob you had interrupted?

'The best pen in the school'—whether it meant calligraphy or creative writing—fits in well with the fact that Patrick Hartigan wanted to be a

---

1. 1 March 1943.
2. One of the many ways the name is written.

5

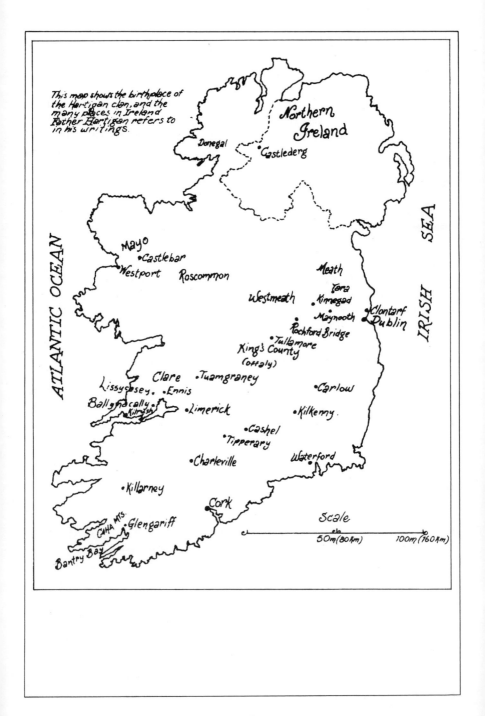

This map shows the birthplace of
the Hartigan clan, and the
many places in Ireland
Father Hartigan refers to
in his writings.

Northern
Ireland

Donegal
Castlederg

ATLANTIC OCEAN

Mayo
•Castlebar
Westport   Roscommon

Meath
Tara
Westmeath   •Kinnegad
             •Maynooth   •Clontarf
            Rochford Bridge   Dublin
                •Tullamore
King's County
(Offaly)

Clare   •Tuamgraney
Lissycasey. •Ennis   •Carlow
Ballynacally.
    Kilrush   •Limerick   •Kilkenny .

                    •Cashel
                  •Tipperary
              •Charleville   Waterford

    •Killarney
                Cork
CAHA MTS.
    •Glengariff
Bantry Bay

IRISH SEA

Scale

50m(80km)   100m(160km)

schoolteacher but in the oppressed Ireland of last century he had perforce to give up that dream.

The other link Father Hartigan found in Lissycasey was his mother's home, a thatched cottage standing a little back from the road that links Ennis and Kilrush, roughly half-way along those forty-four kilometres. He found there a first cousin, Matt Trousdell, his wife Minnie and their son Willie. It was as Mary Townsell that Father Hartigan's mother had left Ireland, and in the sixty years the name had changed to Trousdell. An examination of the parish registers shows many variations over a hundred years—Townsend, Trounsele etc. Names are often anglicised from the Gaelic in different forms; further, the Irish were not particularly anxious to be helpful to their English overlords and were in fact often quite happy that they should have the wrong name. Townsend may well have been the original: some of the Irish took English names after the siege of Limerick.

My own first link with these cousins was twenty-five years after Father Hartigan's visit. At our meeting then Matt and Willie stood there, quite perplexed at my Australian way of speaking. Minnie came to my rescue with a smile: 'Never you mind, Father, I was in California as a young girl and I am used to all kinds of strange accents.'

Willie, in a fall from his bicycle, was killed on Christmas Day 1952 on the Ennis Road; Matt also is dead. Minnie was for some years in the care of the Sisters of St John of God at Ennis. She died there in 1976 and the old home is now deserted. A cousin, Bessie O'Dea (née Trousdell), and her family live further along the road to Kilrush and always have a warm welcome for the wanderer with 'the strange accent'.

There are Hartigans to be found all over Australia. The only one known to belong to the Lissycasey branch of the family is Desmond of Northwood, New South Wales, a son of Father Hartigan's brother, Michael.

When a Tom Hartigan became the Commissioner of Railways in the 1930s a newspaper report made him the brother of 'John O'Brien'. It was the time of the Depression and Father Hartigan had a pile of letters from people asking him to recommend them for a job with the New South Wales Railways. Only once did these two Hartigans meet, at a dinner in Sydney arranged by Stan O'Keefe of Yamma station, near Narrandera. It was in the years of Father Hartigan's chaplaincy at Rose Bay, and I made the fourth at the table. By a strange coincidence, Mary Townsell and Ellen Cusack, the future wives of Patrick Hartigan, Father Hartigan's father, and Michael Hartigan, Tom's father, travelled out from Ireland on the same ship, the **John Temperley.**

Two sisters of Patrick Hartigan also came to Australia: Mary married

John Collins of Yass and their son was Tom Collins, federal Member for Hume and Postmaster-General in the Menzies Ministry of 1940-41; Anne married John Sullivan of Caha, Coolac, New South Wales. The Sullivans came from Glengariff, at the head of Bantry Bay, County Cork, with the Caha Mountains in the background. A daughter of this marriage, Mary, married Patrick Sullivan whose family had settled earlier on the south coast of New South Wales. These Sullivans gave the country press of Australia the **Gundagai Independent,** now in the hands of the third generation of this family.

Patrick Hartigan emigrated to Australia in 1864 when he was twenty-two years old. He came to a Sydney that had been declared a city twenty years earlier; its population of 100 000 was a little over a quarter of that of New South Wales. Archbishop Polding and a dozen or so priests ministered to the Catholic population in the three churches of the city and the half dozen in the suburbs. It was old St Mary's Pat Hartigan knew; he used to speak of the grief of the Catholic people when it was burnt down the year after his arrival.

The greater part of the Catholics of Sydney were Irish and so were three quarters of the priests of the colony. It was almost the end of Archbishop Polding's dream of a Benedictine abbey-diocese. His greatest friend and ally, his vicar-general, Dr Gregory, had been recalled by the Holy See in 1860 in the hope that his going might make peace between the Benedictine and the Irish element in the Australian Church. The next few years were to see the establishment of an Irish hierarchy in Australia. The **Freeman's Journal** of those years was in the forefront of the lay movement for greater participation in the running of the affairs of the Church.

As a youngster in the west of Ireland, Patrick Hartigan had the impatient boyhood yearning to see one day a 'horseless carriage'. Now he had arrived in a city lit by gas for twenty years and where the lamplighters were to ply their trade until the end of the century. It was over ten years since the P & O Line had inaugurated a passenger service between Sydney and London, an eighty-day voyage with S.S. **Chusan.** Telegraphic communication with Melbourne had been achieved six years before.

The railway had gone south as far as Campbelltown and west to Penrith. It was to take four years to get to the top of the Blue Mountains at Mount Victoria using the first zig-zag. Another eight years were to pass before it descended the other side by means of the second or Lithgow Zig-Zag and reached Bathurst.

The main streets of Sydney were by this time well established. There was a horse tram between Redfern Railway Station and Circular Quay via Pitt Street. From the city a road went out to the lighthouse at South

Head, another to Botany, one to the Cooks River and the principal one out to Parramatta and the west, with its branch through Liverpool on to the Port Phillip Track.

The previous decade had seen tremendous changes following the discovery of gold: the cities at first denuded of people flocking to the gold fields, then the influx of migrants attracted by the lure of gold. There was a new wave of bushrangers in the sixties, hardly a week going by without some new atrocity. It was to this lively scene that Patrick Hartigan was introduced in 1864.

The young man set out for Yass where in October of that year Henry O'Brien on Douro station was advertising for a bookkeeper: 'A good active man to keep accounts on an establishment and to make himself otherwise useful. Douro, 18 Oct. 1864'.[3] The family tradition is that Patrick was a bookkeeper at Douro and also at Hardwicke[4] nearby, two properties on the outskirts of Yass.

Yass was the original parish of the south-west and its conditions were described by Dr Morgan O'Connor in 1861:

The ecclesiastical district of Yass is, in its extreme length, at least four hundred miles [644 km], extending from the dividing mountainous range, five miles [8 km] on the Goulburn side of Gunning, to the junction of the Lachlan and Murrumbidgee rivers; and in the greatest width is one hundred and twenty miles [193 km]. The average width of the district is sixty miles [97 km], and the area may be put down, in lowest numbers, at twenty-four thousand square miles [62 000 km²]. The Catholics are in number at least five thousand scattered over hill and vale, along the banks of the rivers, and amidst vast wastes or sparsely populated plains. Many hundreds, in addition to the settled inhabitants, lead a nomadic life, wandering from gold-field to gold-field and exposed to the thousand perils from temptations of very eventful careers.

One priest is always in the saddle; no matter whether an almost tropical sun pours down its fiercest rays, or rain descends in torrents, rendering creeks either utterly impassable or dangerous to man and beast. The Priests ministering for the last four years in the district have ridden every day, on an average, at least twenty-four miles [38 km], or perhaps thirty [48 km].[5]

---

3. Yass Courier, *22 and 29 October 1864.*
4. Sands Directory of N.S.W. *for 1867 lists Patrick Hartigan as a general hand at Hardwicke.*
5. Dr Morgan O'Connor, A Sketch of the Rise and Progress of the Yass Mission, *Goulburn*, Chronicle Office, *1861, p.14.*

The year before Patrick arrived, that immense region had been reduced a little by forming a separate parish for the Catholics of the Tumut district and those on the goldfields of the Adelong. At that time Father James Hanly[6] was the pastor of the parent parish.

Father Hartigan himself in a sermon in St Augustine's, Yass, at the Golden Jubilee of Mother M. De Sales and Sister Bridget of Mount Carmel Convent on 11 August 1942, describes early Yass:

When Hamilton Hume discovered Yass Plains in 1821 Father Therry had just begun his lonely but effective mission in Sydney. Settlement had been slow to spread inland from the coast, but it is on record that the intrepid missionary visited Goulburn Plains in 1824. In 1833 he made a visitation of families who had taken up land in this district. Names mentioned in his diary are Davis, Henry O'Brien of Douro to whose memory the window behind the high altar in this church is dedicated, Manton of Manton's Creek. Father Therry was then the Parish Priest of the whole of Australia.

The first Bishop, Dr Polding came to Australia in 1835; when he was able to gather a few priests around him he set about erecting parishes outside Sydney wherever settlement was springing up. One of the first of these was Yass. In 1838 two priests were stationed here, Fathers Michael Brennan and John Fitzpatrick. There was then no town or village of any kind between here and Melbourne. These two priests began the first collection for St Augustine's but transferring their activities to Goulburn, they left the work to their successor, the venerated Father Charles Lovat ...

Dr John Dunmore Lang says in his Memoirs that on a trip he made in 1843 to Port Phillip, St Augustine's, Yass, was the only church in the Murrumbidgee District. In 1859 that great man, Dr Michael McAlroy, who has well been called 'The Apostle of the South', added thirty-seven feet [9 m] to the building left by Father Lovat, and built the spire. And here it stands today on its little hill, watching the world go by as it has watched it for one hundred years. It has seen every page of our history written.

It was here when the chain-gangs cut the stone for the massive culverts still standing; when ticket-of-leave men were shepherds on

---

6. *Father Hartigan tells a story about him in* The Men of '38, *page 112; the writer has this recollection among many others of old St Augustine's, Yass, where he said his phonetic prayers as a child. One evening at Benediction he saw in the sanctuary an aged man with a long white beard. He had never in all his life seen an unshaven face inside those altar rails, and his faith tottered. Wishing to discuss the scandal when the family gathered round the kitchen fire, he was silenced with a 'Sh, sh, sh, shuuh—that was dear old Dean Hanly, who was stationed here when your father came'.*

Douro. It saw adventurers go by furtively seeking land out-back, when the English Government had forbidden settlement to spread beyond two hundred miles [320 km] from Sydney and the boundary was a line drawn across the track at Bowning Hill.

When a wise Governor saw fit to ignore that regulation, it saw the bullock drays go lumbering down the old Port Phillip Track and Conroy's Gap and Cooney's Creek have seen their early camp-fires that later lit the overlander's track across Australia.

In crumbling ledgers and age-stained title deeds in many a western lands office, Yass names are still legible among those who went with splendid daring to win the land another mile. Broughton, who with Hume discovered these plains in 1821, was the original holder of stations between Urana and Jerilderie: George Mair, manager for O'Brien in 1838 and manager again for the widow till 1892, was one of the first to take up land on the Upper Murray. Jimmy Tyson, a station-hand on Douro, went out west to make himself a millionaire.

Again, this church has seen their wool teams making back from shearing sheds five hundred miles [800 km] from Sydney wharves. It saw Her Majesty's mail come in a fortnight out from Melbourne when a letter cost one shilling to deliver ten years before Rowland Hill introduced the adhesive postage stamp in England. It saw the first bishop of Melbourne go by with four-in-hand—the first time the overland trip was made by buggy. It saw the venerable Dr Polding go down the old Port Phillip Track with Father Bermingham to lay the foundation-stones of churches at Jugiong, Gundagai, Tumut and Albury. It saw the selectors, the farmers go out west round Bowning Hill when John Robertson's Land Act: 'Free selection before survey' in 1861 put an end to the sky-line boundaries of the squatters. It saw the coaches come and go—Roberts and Crane, The Sheehans, the Barrys, Cobb & Co—to be put off the road by the railway, itself to be challenged by the motor-car and the aeroplane. There is not one phase of development or change that St Augustine's has not seen: the gold rushes, the coming of Nationhood, elected Councils, Responsible Government, Federation, and through the shifting scene its tapering spire like a slender finger has pointed upwards, an eloquent reminder that one thing alone is necessary. Other things are transient. They have their season for a year or for a day, but they shall pass.

'Yes, they shall pass, nor deem it strange,
They come and go, as comes and goes the sea;
But let them come and go; Thou through all change

Keep thy firm gaze on virtue and on me'.[7]

All this then was the world of Patrick Hartigan as he began his long life in Australia.

After a few years working on these properties, Patrick decided to set up as a hay and corn merchant with a shop on the south-eastern corner of Cooma and Lead Streets. He secured an agency for Wright, Heaton & Co. and was later a carrier between the railway station and the town.

In July 1871 he went to Sydney to claim his bride, Mary Townsell, who with two elder sisters, Catherine and Brigid, had arrived in Sydney on the **John Temperley** on 1 August 1863 and obtained employment in domestic service in the city.

They were married in St Mary's Cathedral on the 25th of the month. The record is sparse enough, the birthplace of both entered as Ireland (it was Lissycasey, County Clare), his place of abode Yass, hers Sydney; his father Patrick, his mother Ann (née Cleary), her parents Michael and Elizabeth (née Flynn). In those days only the men had occupations; both their fathers were farmers and Patrick junior was a storekeeper. He was twenty-eight and she was twenty-four. They were destined to celebrate the diamond jubilee of their wedding and he was to miss his century of living by only two years.

He brought his bride back to a home he had acquired at 29 De Mestre Street, O'Connell Town, Yass. That house is still standing, well preserved and in use.

His bride soon had the home running sweetly and it was always renowned for its hospitality. Sunday afternoons were often spent on a drive out into the country with friends brought to share their enjoyment. Mary Hartigan always had great notions of the heights to which the family should aspire. Her strong character had a great influence on the children, particularly Father Pat.

She was well known for her concern and kindnesses toward the poor. Her lively faith and her solid piety were an edification for her fellow Catholics in the parish and indeed for many other people of the town. In the afternoon she would make a visit to the Blessed Sacrament and while at the church she made the Stations of the Cross with evident devotion. The family rosary was her concern each evening and much that Father Pat wrote about the rosary in his verse was thus inculcated in his own home.

In those early years things prospered for Patrick Hartigan and his name

---

7. *From the original typescript of the sermon which was printed (with the change of a word here and there) in* Our Cathedral Chimes, *Goulburn, 6 September 1942, pp.1 and 2.*

Top: *Father Hartigan's parents, Mary and Patrick, photographed in 1908. They were destined to celebrate the diamond jubilee of their wedding, and Patrick died only two years before his 100th birthday.*

Bottom left: *An example of the kind of carrying business that Patrick Hartigan senior established in Yass.*

Bottom right: *Father Hartigan's birthplace in Yass.*

appeared prominently in lists of parishioners; so it was appended to the church accounts for 1880, and it figured in subscription lists, though again more noticeably in earlier than in later years.

In 1874 Father (afterwards Dean) O'Keefe replaced Dean Hanly as parish priest and was there for all the remaining years the Hartigans were in Yass. Patrick Francis Capistran O'Keefe, O.F.M., was not a man to brook opposition and Patrick Hartigan, usually easy-going, crossed swords with him more than once.

The Dean left an intriguing comment behind him at Yass; when in 1875 Jugiong was given to the newly formed parish of Gundagai, the Dean noted that he regretted losing the people of Jugiong: 'They were always generous, and, in things reasonable, obedient'.

He has left us also an interesting record of the visit made by Dean Fitzpatrick—one of the first two priests stationed at Yass—who returned there to celebrate Mass on 8 December 1880: 'Father Fitzpatrick told me he superintended the Yass presbytery during its erection and [superintended also] a portion of the present church. It was forty-two years since the Presbytery was built. He appeared as if he came to see the old place once more before his death.'[8]

Again it is 'John O'Brien', in the sermon mentioned above, who, in describing the arrival of the Sisters of Mercy at Yass, gives us a colourful story of Dean O'Keefe:

The Sisters were driven from Goulburn where the railway then terminated, accompanied by Dr Lanigan and Father Pierce Bourke of St Patrick's College (who, by the way, was afterwards in charge of Tumut parish). Four miles from Yass at five in the afternoon at what was known as O'Brien's toll-bar bridge the party was met by Father O'Keefe and Father Dunne of Burrowa (later first Bishop of Wilcannia) and a large calvalcade of parishioners in vehicles and on horseback. The procession half-a-mile long escorted the nuns into Yass.

The old paper says that many eyes were moist with emotion, and in that I well believe the reporter did not exaggerate. They were all from the Old Land,—welcomers and welcomed; and who would blame an exile from Tullamore or Kinnegad, or a lad from Donegal or Clare or any part, if his eyes grew dim as he gazed upon the latest link with Faith and Fatherland.

At O'Brien's Hill, so runs the report, the cortege was met by the

---

8. *These comments are found in a diary of Dean O'Keefe's kept at the presbytery at Yass. It was made available to the author by the courtesy of the parish priest, Father Dermot O'Hurley.*

rest of the population of Yass on foot and headed by the band—the crowd marched down Cooma Street with banners flying to the tune of all the Irish airs they knew: 'The Harp that Once Through Tara's Halls', 'Where the Grass Grows Green', 'The Rose Tree'. Tunes that meant nothing yet meant everything—'St Patrick's Day in the Morning'—though it was six o'clock in the evening! What matter! Round the Royal Hotel to St Augustine's where the band came off the fighting note and, as the Sisters walked into the old Church over a path strewn with flowers, played 'Home, Sweet Home'. Well, whatever it may have seemed at the time to hearts that yearned for Tullamore and Kinnegad and Rochfort Bridge, Mt Carmel has been a sweet, sweet home to the Sisters, Irish and Australian-born, for nearly seventy years.

An Address was read by Dr Blake signed on behalf of the parishioners by I.M. Blake, P. Brennan, M. Cassidy, P. Hartigan, M. Conlon, James Fitzgerald, Owen Ryan, Thomas Townsend, Thomas Comins, William Comins, P. Sheeky, R. McJennett. Of that list not one is left today and descendants only of Thomas Comins and P. Sheeky remain in Yass. That was before the Coens came here, otherwise the name of Coen would have been first on that list, as it has been first on every list since 1879.

The Sisters made a temporary home of the old Presbytery till the Convent was completed two years afterwards by Father O'Keefe. He was not 'Dean' then—that came about twelve years later and I was present when he explained to us, with illustrations, the true signification of that exalted title. He was here for more than thirty years and the buildings and equipment of the early schools were done by him. He did much good work at St Augustine's and usually did it with a flourish, and I recall one flourish particularly which brought him a measure of publicity which was almost fame.

Soon after the arrival of the nuns at Yass the children of the aborigines were refused admittance to the State Schools. Father O'Keefe immediately set aside some rooms behind the Convent and arranged with these Sisters to teach the aborigines and with the congregation to feed them. This was, I think, the first, and perhaps only, school of its kind established in Australia. The Bulletin, *which was young and very fresh at the time, came out with a full-page cartoon which pictured Sir Henry Parkes with an outsize in brooms sweeping the aboriginal kiddies out of his way, and the piccaninnies swarming round the figure of a priest and climbing all over him as high as his tall hat. Underneath were these lines:*

'Oh, what inanity, base inhumanity, spurning the sons of our soil:
Are they not national? Are they not national? or is it our lot to despoil?
But there is charity, aye, liberality in the good Soggarth O'Keefe,
The downtrodden race clung to his embrace, and he gave them Christian
relief.'

Whatever may be thought of the poetry, there is this to be said. The
Bulletin, though at times we have called it 'The Pink Infidel' and
other unkind names[9] has always been ready to give us full marks
when we deserved it. It has never forgotten its birth ties. The first
edition was set up in the office of the old Freeman's Journal.

After this digression on the Sisters of Mercy and their pastor, Dean
O'Keefe, let us take up again the fortunes of the Hartigan family. There
were nine children born to Patrick and Mary Hartigan. The first, John
Patrick, born 20 May 1872 and baptised six days later with his aunt, Anne
Hartigan, as godmother, died in infancy.

The eldest girl was Elizabeth Catherine, known as Lily, born 28 July
1873. At the baptism were an uncle and aunt as sponsors, Patrick and
Bridget Townsend;[10] Patrick appeared mysteriously from Ireland and
then drifted off into the mists. Bridget lived with the Hartigans and
helped to rear the earlier children. In 1880 she entered the Convent of
Mercy at Yass where she appears in the records as Sister Patrick
(Townsell). She chose to be a lay sister and gave a half-century of prayer
and service. She visited us at Haberfield and was known and loved as
Aunty B. She never adjusted to short dresses and years before miniskirts
she spoke with disapproval about my sisters' dresses. 'Annie,' she
complained to my mother, 'those children's dresses are too short, and
your own is too short, too.'

Lily Hartigan, after doing her schooling at the local convent, entered in
1891 the Sisters of Mercy at Parramatta, being known as Sister Mary

9. The preacher may have been thinking back to its early years when cartoons unflattering to the
Catholic Church—to say the least—appeared in its pages; a typical example was in the issue of 14
November 1885. In this there is a drawing of Pope Leo lying awake in bed, studying the gold yields
from Australia. The title to this picture was: 'How it was according to Dr Moran'. 'The Cardinal,
in sincerely thanking the deputation for their congratulations, said Pope Leo had ever taken the
deepest interest in his Australian children and had honoured them by calling him to Rome for the
express purpose of conferring on him the dignity of a Prince of the Church.' Below this is a picture
of Irishmen interviewing Pope Leo. It is entitled: 'How it really was', and depicts the spokesman of
the Irish Landleaguers (who don't think much of Dr Moran and have come to the Eternal City to
say so): 'Faith, yer holiness it's no use. The Gazette that makes him Cardinal Archbishop of
Dublin will knock the bottom out of the bag that holds the Irish Peter's Pence.' Leo: 'But I brought
him all the way from Sydney to give him Dublin.' Spokesman: 'Thin make him a Kyardinal, and
sind him back again. You can say it was done to show you love Australia.' (And Leo did.)

10. Here again, as in the Irish records, there are variations in the spelling of the name.

Gonzaga. (In those times a girl often went into the convent in a town other than her own—this was thought a greater sacrifice and dedication.) Highly successful as a teacher of English, she is remembered also as an artist. The Sisters still treasure at Parramatta an exquisitely painted dinner set, a fine example of her artistic achievement. She was regarded as a most saintly person and suffered a lingering death from tuberculosis, dying in 1928.

Bridget Agnes was born on 30 April 1875 and baptised a week later. She entered the Sisters of Mercy at Yass and was professed in 1895 as Sister M. Ignatius. She stands out as one before her time, and her flexibility was remarkable in an age when religious life was tightly constructed. In her vision of religious life she anticipated, as far as she could, many of the more humane reforms of the convents of today. Her sympathy went out to Sisters who were worrying about aged parents and she would find all kinds of ways of relieving the situation. Superior in almost all the branch houses of the Yass Sisters of Mercy, she finally became Superior at Yass.

Joanna Maria was born on 16 April 1877 and was known in the family as Jane. She entered the Mercy Convent at Albury on 8 September 1896 and was professed there on 5 April 1899 as Sister M. Michael. She taught very successfully but was to succumb early to tuberculosis, dying in Albury on 14 March 1911.

Sister Regis (O'Brien), ninety-seven-year-old Presentation Sister at Domremy, Five Dock, with her mind still clear and keen, recalls her days as a boarder at the Mercy Convent, Albury. As a lonely bush girl she looked forward to her music lessons from Sister M. Michael. She remembers also the day of her profession. Mr and Mrs Hartigan and their youngest daughter, Annie, came for the occasion. The father was a fine figure of a man, bearded, and the mother was beautifully dressed in a simple way. Annie had long black hair down to her waist. On another occasion Mary Ellen (afterwards Sister M. Peter, R.S.M. Parramatta) came to see her sister and the two of them were full of laughter and stories. Even on her death bed, Jane retained her sense of humour. At one stage the Sisters with candles lit were saying the prayers for the dying; Jane rallied and with a smile told them to blow out the candles; 'You will want them again' was her comment!

Patrick Joseph Hartigan was born on 13 October 1878[11] and baptised on 20 October, with John Collins and Mary Hartigan as godparents.

---

11. *He himself and the family always celebrated his birthday on 12 October, and that date appeared on his documents, such as his driver's licence. Were his parents superstitious? As I knew them in their old age, they gave no evidence of being so. He himself was the last person to take any notice of superstitions. Both the baptismal register at Yass Church and the Registrar-General's records at Sydney give 13 October as the date of his birth.*

Seven of the nine Hartigan children, photographed about 1888. From left, Mary Ellen, Jane, Lily, Annie (in front), Bridget, Michael and Patrick.

The fourth daughter was born on 31 January 1881, baptised Maria Helena and known as Mary Ellen or Minnie. She followed Lily to Parramatta, entering the convent there in 1899 and being professed on 14 January 1902. She had a long life, dying in 1968. As Sister Mary Peter, she was loved by her pupils, parishioners and above all by her own community. The Parramatta Sisters of Mercy were her world—their communities, schools, relatives of the sisters, parishes where the sisters had foundations, and the priests in those places—these were the interests that fascinated her and she was full of stories about them. She had tremendous loyalty to her congregation and was meticulously faithful to her rule. Stationed for seventeen years continuously at Surry Hills, she there prepared with great success the first class for the state bursary. Before that time, state bursaries for the five years of secondary education were not tenable at Catholic schools.

She started the Cronulla foundation in 1924, and we as youngsters were enthralled at the steam-tram ride from Sutherland. Golden Grove, Holy Cross Woollahra, Stanmore and Harris Park were successive appointments, but it was at Port Hacking that her hospitality, joyousness and kindness had its full scope. The Port Hacking house doubled as both the convent for the sisters teaching at Caringbah and, during vacations, as a holiday home for sisters from other convents. Sister Peter greatly enjoyed the constant stream of visitors and did everything to make them welcome. Death came to her after a short time in retirement at the Sisters of Mercy hospital in Cronulla at the beautiful site on the ocean esplanade where she had opened the convent almost a half century earlier.

It was always an interesting encounter when Minnie and Pat met—the kind of friendly tussle that so often goes on between brother and sister close to each other in the family.

Next came the youngest girl, known always as Annie. The baptismal record gives her as Anna Martha, born 31 July 1882. She flits through the memories of friends, like the Coens, as a bright girl full of humour. Her secondary schooling was done at Our Lady of Mercy College, Parramatta. She had two sisters there as Sisters of Mercy and remembered how her pranks and misdemeanours were magnified on that account. She had always a great love for O.L.M.C. and for the friends she made there. Many thought she would follow her sisters into the convent and it was Mother Ignatius who sensibly told her not to be swayed by the expectations of others and to enter only if she saw clearly that it was her vocation. She taught with the Sisters at Ryde for a couple of years. When she returned to Yass she found the family business in a bad way. The Yass 'tram' had started between Yass Junction and the town; it was made up of a couple of wagons and a passenger car pulled by a small locomotive. Pat Hartigan senior was unable to compete with it in the carrying business. It was Annie's difficult task to convince her parents to sell up and go to Sydney. This they did in 1905 and settled in Summer Hill, at that time in the Lewisham parish. Annie taught art and other subjects for some years with the Sisters of Charity at Bethlehem College, Ashfield.

Michael was born on 18 October 1884; he had his secondary education at St Patrick's College, Goulburn, where he did well and then joined the Public Service, first in the Lands Department and later in that of the Master of Lunacy. After a period in Sydney where he lived with his parents at Summer Hill, he was stationed on the north coast where he met his wife, Irene Costello of Lismore. He was also at Bathurst and in these country places he was most happy. He was a good judge of cattle and had 'green fingers'. After he moved to Sydney he was successively at Balgowlah, Manly and Mosman where he died in 1948. His widow survived him by over thirty years, living at Beauty Point with her daughter Pat Gilchrist and her family.

Youngest of the Hartigans was Francis William, born on 19 May 1888 and baptised two days later. He was educated at Yass Convent School and St Patrick's College, Goulburn. He then joined the Missionaries of the Sacred Heart and was at Douglas Park and Kensington preparing for the priesthood.

During his years with this congregation there were rumblings of dissatisfaction on the kind of training that was given. Frank himself told the story of expressing the opinion as a novice that a tree he was watering had no hope of surviving. He was told to plant a broom stick and water that regularly as an exercise in blind obedience. Reports of these happenings reached Bishop Gallagher of Goulburn who told Father Hartigan that a visitation to the Missionaries of the Sacred Heart was contemplated and suggested that he would be willing to accept Frank for the diocese if he applied before the visitation took place—it might not be so simple afterwards.

Following on this advice, Father Pat wrote to Manly about his brother:

The Presbytery, Albury,
May 28 1909.

Dear Father McDermott,
I am writing re my brother who you may remember entered
Kensington some time ago. The time for taking his final vows will come
around next April, and for many reasons I would think it better for him to
slip out of the order before then. He is in a somewhat confused state of

*mind himself on the matter. He rather likes the order, but the personnel
does not appeal to him. Anyway, I think he realizes he would be better
somewhere else. I was speaking to Dr Gallagher, and he told me that if
arrangements could be made he would adopt him for the diocese of
Goulburn and would consider him entitled to the usual privileges of his
subjects—referring of course to the part payment of the premium. When
speaking to you last you gave me to understand, if I remember rightly, that
there was an objection to one placed such as he is entering Manly. I would
be very thankful if you would be kind enough to give me some information
on the matter, as I would prefer that he should go to Manly than
elsewhere. Also, I would esteem it a favour if you would say how he stands
as regards his vows. They expire next April or thereabouts. Of course if he
decides to leave, it will be of his own accord.*

*Well, I often think of Manly by the Sea; and the longer grows the
string of years that lengthens day by day between it and me the more I am
convinced that life has nothing to show that I would not gladly
exchange for a place again in the old home with the old hopes and the old
friends. I trust things are going smoothly with you. You deserve it. Please
remember me to Father Hayden and the professors.*

and believe me dear Father McDermott

Yours most affectionately,

P.J. Hartigan[12]

Frank entered Manly the following year and did theology there for three
and a half years. He was ordained a priest in July 1913.

He had a keen mind and was interested especially in theology and
social justice. As a hobby he used to mend clocks; everyone in the district
brought them to him till the presbytery was chock-full. His gaiety was
infectious; light-hearted, he would take any risk, as on that occasion
when criticism was voiced at the parish football team in Harden playing
on Sundays. He published in the local paper a poem about his critics.
They threatened a libel case and Frank's friends collected £50 to settle
out of court.

The Hartigan children all attended the convent school in Yass and
'John O'Brien' in 1942 paid this beautiful tribute to the Sisters and their
work:

*I am the only priest living who knew every member of the little
band who came from Rochfort Bridge. I am the oldest priest living*

---

12. *McDermott papers, St Patrick's College, Manly, Archives.*

who was trained in their schools. *Father Alphonsus Coen of cherished memory was before me but he has long gone to receive the reward of a saintly life. I am therefore thankful to the Sisters for remembering me and for giving me the opportunity to stand here once more among you—my ain folk so to speak—to pay a genuine tribute of affection and esteem.*

I have always believed that I owe my priesthood to the prayers they said for me, supplemented in secret by those of a little Irish Mother who takes her long last sleep afar. I recall that when forty years ago, with the road before me, I came to say my first public Mass in the Old Mother Church, I wore a set of vestments that were given me by my old teachers whose eyes were bright with joy to see me where I stood.

I have these vestments still, but when I wear them now, with most of the road behind me, I march with a slower step, for the names of almost all of those I knew and loved when the world was young have been transferred from the Commemoration of the Living to the Memento for the Dead. Paul the Foundress—like her patron a convert and an Apostle too—sleeps in a little cemetery on the banks of the Darling; Alacoque, the genial little Reverend Mother; Bernard, with a hatred of even a venial sin like that which characterised her great namesake of Clairvaux; Xavier, the exact religious; Stanislaus, with the big warm Irish welcome in her voice; Joseph, the gifted teacher, the first of the band from Rochfort Bridge to be called away; Augustine, her sister; Poor old Berchmans, with her Rosary Beads; if more things are done by prayer than this world dreams of, her work was not the least; Patrick, my mother's sister; the little Sister Clare who taught the music and who died so young; a gentle minstrel from the Land of the Bards. God rest her patient soul, she tried to teach me the piano, but where she failed no one else succeeded.[13]

13. Our Cathedral Chimes, *Goulburn*, 6 September 1942, p.4.

2 Training for the Priesthood

In 1859 the New South Wales government, through Sir John Robertson, Minister for Lands, made a grant of land at Manly[1] to John Bede Polding, the first Catholic archbishop. The conditions were that it would be used as an archiepiscopal residence, and that a building would be raised within twenty-five years. Its location alongside the Quarantine Station and its great distance in those times from the city took from the attractiveness of the grant, but the Archbishop, realising the possibilities of the site, accepted and erected a cross on a rocky outcrop overlooking the Pacific.

The grant remained unused until Archbishop Moran arrived in September 1884. Within a week of his arrival the Hon Bede Dalley, who lived at Manly, brought to the new Archbishop's attention the magnificent property facing the Pacific that was lying unused and pointed out that it would be lost if not built upon quickly. The very next day the Archbishop accompanied by his secretary, Very Rev Dean Denis Francis O'Haran, joined Dalley in an inspection of the property. He decided to build on it immediately, and began with his own residence.

In March 1885 he approved plans for a seminary on the site. These were the work of architects John Hennessy and Joseph Sheerin and followed the general lines of St Joseph's College, Hunter's Hill, which they had designed two years earlier.

In May the Archbishop set out for Rome and the construction of the seminary began the following month. W.J. Jennings was the builder, the contract price was £60 000 and the final price was to rise by another £10 000.[2]

In September the Archbishop returned to Sydney as a cardinal. He immediately presided at the first Plenary Council of Australia, and

---

1. *In 1856—just three years before the grant was sought for an episcopal residence—there were but three cottages along the Corso, and only twelve families lived in the district. But visitors had learned the way, and Gilbert Smith built a hotel at the Pier and ran the S.S. The Brothers occasionally for their benefit. Later still a more or less regular steamer service took up the running when the boats so used were not engaged in towing operations. The fare charged was 3s and the journey took an hour. Not until 1866 did anything like a daily service begin, and then there were only three trips a day! Rev. J.J. McGovern, 'The Making of Manly', Australasian Catholic Record VIII, 1, 1931, p.31. Father McGovern in an interesting account in three issues of the ACR of 1931 (January pp.24-35, April pp.117-28, July pp.198-206) traces also earlier attempts to obtain a grant at Camperdown, Coogee and Cabarita.*
2. *See K.T. Livingston, The Emergence of an Australian Catholic Priesthood 1835-1915, Catholic Theological Faculty, Sydney, 1977, pp.111-13.*

invited the prelates attending to be present at the laying of the foundation stone of Manly College which took place in November. At this function the ceremonies were directed by Dean O'Haran and Father Vincent Dwyer, who was to be the first Australian to be appointed a bishop when twelve years later he was made Coadjutor of Maitland.

Manly College opened on 23 January 1889 under the presidency of Rev Dr Michael Verdon. There were two other professors, Father Hugh McDermott and Mr James Leonard. The former was to spend many years at Manly and become its third president; the latter was there until 1893 and died half a dozen years later.[3]

There were five students when the college opened, and the total for the year reached thirteen. Nine were in the Grammar class, three in Humanity, and there was an Irish student (Louis Flynn) for the diocese of Meath. He was described as 'delicate for some years previously'; he spent some months at the college doing philosophy but returned to Ireland before the end of the year and died there. He took up residence at the college at the same time as Dr Verdon, on the Feast of the Immaculate Conception 1888, so he may be considered Manly's first student.

As he had left before the arrival of the last entrant for the year, the number did not go over the dozen—the 'twelve apostles', they were called, and the sceptics spoke of the beautiful building with so few students as the 'Cardinal's folly'. Of the twelve who finished the first year, seven were eventually ordained.

The year 1890 began with fifteen students, eleven of them from the previous year's enrolment (Patrick Kelly of Adelaide did not front up again). This year saw the advent of Father Thomas Hayden to the staff. He arrived on Christmas Day 1889, and few men have made such a notable impact on the college. A great favourite with the students of those early years, he was to be there longer than anyone else and was to become its fourth rector, a position he held from 1915 for the next fifteen years.

He was one of Father Hartigan's heroes. When writing back to Manly on business, Father Hartigan made it a point to include greetings to Father Hayden, and Father Hayden was proud of his protégé who early earned his commendation because of the solid grounding in Greek he had received from 'Johnny' Gallagher. We have on record Father Hartigan's tribute to Monsignor Thomas Hayden:

---

3. One of 'John O'Brien's' stories about him was that on one occasion he asked a student in mathematics at what hour of the day the hands of the clock would make a certain angle. 'Let x equal both hands' said the hopeful student. 'Let x equal the whole damn clock' was Leonard's rejoinder.

An oil painting by E.M. Smith of Father Thomas Hayden, one of Father Hartigan's heroes, and a professor at St Patrick's College, Manly, for forty years.

*He was a professor at St Patrick's College, Manly for forty years,
during fifteen of which he was its President. He was unique among
his fellows for his learning, and he was unique among scholars in
the way he handled it. He was really a simple-minded man, simple
in dress and tastes, at times he looked simple, but in the field of
knowledge he was a thoroughbred, and herein again he was unique
in the way he hated vincible ignorance. That is to say, while being
all on the side of the genuine tryer, he despised the fraud and the
humbug and regarded them as desecrators of the Temple. The talker
with nothing to say, the cheap-jack with all his wares on view, and
with nothing in reserve, the mountebank camouflaging his
shallowness with oddments of information and pilfered pedantic
phrases—these were anathema to him, and he loved nothing better
than to deflate their wind-bag of verbiage with a seemingly artless
and semi-nonsensical quip. His orbit embraced Theology in all its
branches, Sacred Scripture, History, Ancient and Modern Language,
even Music, but it was in Scholastic Philosophy that he excelled.
His scholarship was profound, his mind unerringly logical and when
he mounted the rostrum he was supreme. The notes which he
propounded in his class, mostly in extempore Latin, were models of
condensation. He could put into a sentence what authors, noted for
succinctness, would take a paragraph to express, and his statements
were invariably the clearer. In making an abstruse idea
understandable to minds of moderate acumen he had few equals
anywhere. He spent fourteen years in the Parish of the Sacred
Heart, (Darlinghurst) but while giving himself over to his pastoral
duties, he was a schoolman all the time. The pity is that he wrote
little. What little he wrote he valued not at all. Had he left behind
him on the printed page the results of his vast learning and keen
reasoning, his reputation would be established far beyond the
confines of his College and his Country. Likely, his faculty and life-
long habit of scorching criticism when turned in upon himself dried
the ink on his pen. His death at eighty removed a great scholar and a
faithful priest from the ranks.*[4]

To return to the year 1890, it saw such innovations as time set
aside on Thursdays after the morning walk for the reading of literature.
From July onwards the philosophers and students of other classes who
were over twenty-one went to study in their rooms, the rest remaining in

4. 'John O'Brien', On Darlinghurst Hill, *Ure Smith*, Sydney, 1952, pp.81-2.

the study halls. In November arrived Father Reginald Bridge, an Australian ordained from the Irish College in Rome. He became the first Dean of Discipline and, with Very Rev P. McCarthy who had come earlier in the year, brought the staff to six. The student total at the end of 1890 was twenty-six.

The early months of the scholastic year of 1891 saw thirty-one students in residence. Two more arrived in April, Frank Burton of Brisbane and Matt Brodie, a New Zealander destined to be the first of Manly's sons to be raised to the episcopate, while John Egan from Redfern came in May. This year there was no First Philosophy class. It may be that it was realised that with the number of youthful students enrolling there was need for further consolidation of their preliminary studies. In each of these first three years the average age of the students was only seventeen. In 1891 there were four in Second Philosophy class, and the remainder were divided into Latin I, II, and III.

This then was the story of the first three years of Manly to which young Patrick Hartigan came in 1892.[5]

As the fourth year was about to begin, Sister Bernard of Yass wrote to Dr Verdon as follows:

> *Convent of Mercy,*
> *Mt Carmel, Yass*
> *20.1.92*
>
> *Dear Revd Father,*
>
> *There is a very good smart little boy in Yass who is going to some College to complete his studies. His name is Hartigan. I have requested his Mother to send him, if she possibly could, to Manly. She has asked me to write and learn for her particulars as to pension, outfit etc. It is best your reply be addressed to Mr 'P. Hartigan, O'Connell Town' Yass; he is Father of the boy. He has a large family and no one to earn for him yet. If any little reduction is made in college fees at Manly, the charity will not be misplaced here. I see the family has to go in for much economy to let the boy away. His sisters with us are giving up music so as to make ends meet. I hope to be excused for the liberty I take in sending this letter. I only do it for the sake of charity and on account of hopes I entertain for the future of this little man.*
>
> *Dear Revd Father,*
> *Very respectfully yours in Xt,*
> *Sr Mary Bernard[6]*

5. *Details of the early years at Manly are from the college archives which were made available through the courtesy of the presidents of the college, the late Father Neil Collins and Bishop Patrick Murphy.*
6. *Verdon papers, Manly Archives.*

Satisfactory arrangements were made and young Patrick, thirteen years old, arrived on the steps of the college in February, to be greeted by Dr Verdon with the words: 'So you want to be a priest, young man.' 'I haven't made up my mind' was young Patrick's reply. 'Oh, you will,' said the Monsignor, and accepted him. He was enrolled in the Grammar class.

When Patrick began as number 51 on the roll of students at Manly he was by no means alone in his youthfulness as fifteen of those enrolled ahead of him were fifteen years of age or less at the time of their entry, and indeed, half a dozen of these were only twelve. The distinction of being the youngest ever to enter Manly belongs to James Liston who in 1893 came to Manly from New Zealand at eleven years of age. He was to become the oldest living Manly priest, seventy-two years a priest and a bishop for fifty-six.

The young age of those entering Manly is understandable in the light of the Irish practice of having seminaries or colleges which offer an education through secondary classes without demanding that each student be already decided on his vocation to the priesthood. Sister Bernard's letter about young Patrick Hartigan brings out this point: 'a very good smart little boy . . . who is going to some College to complete his studies . . . I have requested his Mother to send him, if she possibly could, to Manly'.

It is clear from his case and others that there was no intention on the part of the authorities to allow this viewpoint to develop, and the insistence was on Manly being seen as an ecclesiastical college. So the names of these classes, Latin I, II and III, were dropped and eventually Grammar also disappeared. Instead, they were called Humanity and Rhetoric and the emphasis was on their being preparatory classes for the studies towards the priesthood.

In that year 1892 in which young Patrick enrolled there were four students in First Theology: Michael Flemming, destined to be the first Manly student ordained for the archdiocese of Sydney, Michael Dolan of Melbourne, who was to see forty years as a priest, Charles White, also of Melbourne, who was to die as a deacon—student folklore had his ghost haunting an upstairs altar, reaching out as it were for the celebration of the Mass that eluded him—and James McManamy of Ballarat who went to the Capranica College in Rome and was the first Manly priest to gain a doctorate. He died early, in July 1909, and Michael Flemming followed him to the grave six months later.

There were no students in Second Philosophy, but fifteen in First Philosophy; these the previous year had been in Latin I, except James Sweeney of Longford, Ireland, who would seem to have studied some philosophy the year before, and Joseph Darby who arrived from New Zealand already qualified to begin in philosophy.

There were twelve in Rhetoric, six of whom were new, and the rest were from the previous year's Latin II. The remaining seventeen of the total forty-eight students attained by midwinter that year were in the classes of Humanity and Grammar. Patrick Hartigan, enrolled in Grammar, began his secondary studies.

Two priests from Ireland were added to the teaching staff, Father John Brosnan who patronised and remodelled the debating society and Father James Whyte, later to be Bishop of Dunedin. He was gazetted for Manly but did not take up his appointment until the following year. James Leonard severed his connection with the college this year, and Mr Harry Leston gave lessons in elocution and put on a scene from Shakespeare which was creditably performed.

The parish church in the village of Manly—so the annalist describes it—was opened this year, and the students were present. The ceremony was performed by His Eminence Cardinal Moran, and Father John Gallagher, parish priest of Wagga, preached an eloquent sermon. We may speculate that this may have been the first time young Patrick met the priest who later, as President of St Patrick's College, Goulburn, and also Bishop of Goulburn, was to have such an influence on him.

In June tonsure was given at St Mary's to the four theologians—the rest of the college had classes and the new clerics were back from the city in time to take their places at third class.

For recreation and relief from the grind of studies, a billiard table was installed on the northern wing of the top floor, above what was known to later students as 'Balmy Lane', and such was the interest it stimulated that the committee, to provide cue-room for the contestants, was forced to bring in the rule demanding non-players to stand 1.2 metres from the table. Cricket was so popular that expert wielders of the willow had to absent themselves every second day to allow the college 'McDougalls' to acquire some knowledge of the game. That year football replaced hockey as the approved winter game. Dr Verdon presented the students with a football, putting an end to speculation as to whether he would allow the game, and Australian Rules took a place in student life. Rugby was to prevail later on.

The year 1893 saw Patrick in Humanity, and the college total moved up to fifty-five. One of the new arrivals was Edward O'Brien, an Australian from Braidwood, then in the archdiocese of Sydney, who had been studying at the Irish College, Rome. He was added to the four students of Second Theology. Two others started in First Philosophy, another in Humanity and the remaining seven new faces were in

Top: *Father Hartigan aged about fifteen and then a student at St Patrick's.*

Bottom: *St Patrick's College, Manly, in 1920.*

Grammar. Dunedin student James Delaney of the Second Philosophy class departed for Rome in mid-year. An able student, interested in literary matters, he was something of a hero to young Patrick Hartigan. With him from First Philosophy went John O'Mahony of Port Augusta and these were the first two of a long line of Manly students to go off to Rome. Most went to Propaganda, some few to the Irish College or elsewhere.

On 4 December Cardinal Moran returned from Europe and the Manly students on the **Midget** joined the other sixteen boats greeting the Cardinal's ship. He appeared on deck in his cardinal's robes and then transferred to the boat containing the priests. A hundred thousand people awaited him at Circular Quay, and marched to the cathedral, which was packed. Afterwards the students had a picnic at Clark Island.

In 1894 Patrick and his classmates were in Rhetoric. There were only six of them, and one, Timothy O'Sullivan of Melbourne, was new that year. He was to remain a life-long friend of Patrick Hartigan, wonderfully hospitable with the table of his presbytery at Kyneton always set ready for visitors. He was to be sixty-two years a priest. That same year Terence McGuire arrived for the diocese of Grafton, thirteen years old, starting in the Grammar class. Harry O'Grady of Melbourne, another life-long friend, started in Humanity, and over the years he was to host Father Hartigan and many other men of Manly visiting Melbourne. The total of students for the year was fifty-five, eighteen of them theologians, twenty-one philosophers and the remainder in the three junior classes.

On the professorial staff were the same six priests as in the previous year, Dr Verdon and Fathers McDermott, Hayden, Bridge, Brosnan and Whyte. The student annals tell us that 'after Midwinter the Rev James Whyte relinquished his professorial chair, to the keen regret of the students'. He was to go to St Benedict's, to become Inspector of Schools and in 1920 Bishop of Dunedin, dying in his ninetieth year in 1957. Numbered then on Manly's staff in those years were two future bishops of Dunedin as Michael Verdon also was to go to that see.

We can form a picture of the daily program that young Patrick Hartigan followed at Manly from the diary of James Aloysius Kenny of Melbourne.[7] The rising bell was at 6 a.m., morning prayer at 6.30 and meditation with Mass at 7. There was a study period of forty minutes before breakfast at 8.15. There were two classes at 9 and 10, recreation at 11, study at 11.15 for an hour and a half, another class, particular examen, at 2 p.m. and dinner at 2.05 followed by an hour's recreation. At

7. *Quoted by K. Livingston,* The Emergence of an Australian Priesthood *(Catholic Theological Faculty), Sydney, 1977, pp.137 et seq.*

3.30 spiritual reading and a visit to the Blessed Sacrament, another class followed by recreation for an hour and a half, study from 6 till 7.45, then rosary and tea and recreation till night prayers at 9. Repose was at 9.30. The time from after night prayers till after Holy Mass was to be spent as in retreat. It was the **Summum Silentium**, the great Silence, usually abbreviated as the **Summum.**

That program lasted at Manly for more than fifty years. The only changes made were to bring dinner forward an hour, to combine the two afternoon recreation periods into one and provide a cup of coffee at 5.30. It rejoiced in the Latin name **merendula**, a little snack, and was commonly known as 'dooley'. It was later called **frustulum**, and then there was the obvious student change to **crustulum.**

The rules of the college likewise had a long currency. They were quite restrictive by modern standards. Trips outside the college were few and far between—to St Mary's Cathedral sometimes for ceremonies, walks 'in crocodile' around Manly and an occasional picnic on the Harbour and elsewhere.

One of the occasions when young Patrick Hartigan visited the city was not quite what the authorities envisaged. He had a great love of things nautical, and he and Patrick O'Neill from Dunedin resolved to run away to sea. When the ship came into port on which young Patrick O'Neill had come to Sydney and met the captain, they resolved to try their luck. Paddy Hartigan had talked boldly about going to sea and now felt he could not back down. His courage evaporated rapidly as the moment of meeting came. To his relief the captain told them to get back to college as quickly as they could. Had it been a tramp steamer, the story might have been quite different.

It was in this year 1894 that young Patrick Hartigan gained admittance into the debating club, which at that time was reserved for the seniors. The minute book of the club for the Wednesday evening, 4 August, tells the story:

An opportunity of enlarging the institution was offered in the proposed admittance of three new members. Considering that the members have for some time been complaining of the continually increasing number in the club, it would be inconsistent were they too easily to admit the junior students of the house, for such indeed were the aspirants, Messrs Hartigan, Cotter and Liston. In the ballot opposition was indeed evinced, for Mr Hartigan alone was received as a member. The others were rejected by a large majority.[8]

8. *Volume for the years 1893-97, p.85.*

Alongside Patrick Hartigan's name in the register kept by Dr Verdon is the note that he went to St Patrick's College, Goulburn, at the end of 1894.

In 1866 Father Michael McAlroy had purchased land in Goulburn for a college for boys. Dr Lanigan, first bishop of Goulburn, went ahead with the scheme but not on the site bought by McAlroy.[9] St Patrick's College was opened in 1874 and Father Patrick Dunne became its first president.[10] The following year it was placed under the care of Father John Gallagher.

Dr Badham, Professor of Classics and Logic at the University of Sydney and described by Cardinal Newman as 'the first Greek scholar of the day'[11] noticed the brilliant passes from the college in Goulburn, and on inquiry found that Father Gallagher was responsible. Not long afterwards in a letter to his 'dear Dalley' he said he had discovered 'in a modest Irish priest who was hiding his light in a country town one of our best classical scholars'. 'Father Gallagher', he added, 'should be helping us. They will make him a Bishop and higher education in New South Wales will then go into mourning. This Goulburn priest would be more at home in a Chair of Classics than on the throne of a Bishop, with nothing but Church Latin all the year round'.[12]

Father Hartigan has given us his own beautiful tribute to Dr Gallagher, written shortly after the bishop's death in 1923:

> Though not the founder, he took charge of St Patrick's College, Goulburn, in the early days of its career, and since then its progress has been closely associated with his name. Though Dr Gallagher was renowned as a priest and as a Bishop, it was as president of a school that he was most remarkable, and in this he came near to greatness. He may be said to have been the originator of the secondary schools as we know them today. A great deal of their success is due to the influence which he began to exert nearly fifty years ago, and every high school in the Commonwealth should have been represented at his funeral. The domain of learning knows no barriers, and one institution at least rose to the occasion. As the cortege was passing the Goulburn High School, the pupils, under their headmaster, Mr

9. See 'John O'Brien', The Men of '38, Lowden, Kilmore, Vic., 1975, pp.211 et seq.
10. Ibid., pp.145-7.
11. Quoted in the article on Badham, Australian Encyclopedia, Angus & Robertson, Sydney, 1925, vol. 1, p.119
12. Freeman's Journal, Sydney, 20 May 1920, p.31, in an article on the occasion of the death of Professor Badham's daughter. There too is it noted that it was Badham who composed the Latin inscription on the gold salver presented to Cardinal Newman by the Catholics of Sydney. The cardinal wrote to William Bede Dalley asking him to thank his eminent Anglican friend for the inscription.

Blumer, M.A., stood at attention, as a tribute to the old scholar who had closed his books for ever. Goulburn was not the first college of its kind in the country, but with Dr Gallagher at its head, it quickly took a leading place. After he left in '87 it went back and nearly dropped out of sight, only to be saved by himself when he took charge again for a brief period before his consecration in '95. Through his instrumentality it was handed over to the Christian Brothers in '98, and under them it has been restored to what it was in its palmy days.

As President, the late Bishop was widely known as a man of vast learning. It would have been difficult to find his superior in Greek, Latin, French or English. A neat turn of construction or a striking phrase gave him genuine delight. He would lecture for half an hour on the shade of difference of meaning made by the presence and position of the article in a difficult line of Greek. Like a child with a wonderful toy, he would gloat over a word for which his class could find no adequate substitution in English. And with what a loving lilt would he roll out those splendid lines of Homer and Virgil, whose mighty measures were enhanced by the fine light of enthusiasm in his eye, and enriched by his broad, natural accent.

No one could juggle with the classics like he could: he would sum up a situation, humorous or otherwise, by some neat quotation from them, and in this respect, as an after-dinner speaker, he stood alone. Of English he was no less a master. He had the poets at his fingertips, and revelled in sonorous prose.

His own style was fine. Balanced and ornate, it belonged like himself to a bygone period. His addresses to the boys were masterpieces in their way, and it is a pity that they have not been preserved. A wide reader and a thinker always, it is possible, had he not been made a Bishop, that he would have left behind him something that would have made his name enduring in a literary sense. As it is, the writer believes that several manuscripts are still in existence. These are mainly sermons and addresses, but include some essays and a few lectures, and should most certainly be rescued from obscurity.

As a teacher of more advanced boys he was unrivalled, but his methods were all his own. He was of a severe type who gave his scholars no rest, and certainly never flattered them. No call in the classics seemed to satisfy him. 'Right enough, but it could be better', was the highest praise which even the best could hope to receive. Only on a single occasion did anyone get full marks, and it was when a certain plodder, driven to desperation, procured a translation—'cog', as we understood it—and read page after page under the old man's very eyes.

Though his pupils were invariably successful in the examinations of the time, he cared little for such tests. 'Not for school, but for life we learn', was his motto. Walking about among the trees in the grounds of old St Patrick's, he taught his class, and referred to them as his 'peripatetic philosophers'. Of a Sunday afternoon he would don a familiar ancient biretta, with a hole in the top of it where the tassel used to be, and take the boys for a walk along one of the Goulburn roads. Always on such occasions he would make the seniors bring with them their Plato or their Horace, and those old, wheel-worn tracks are still musical in their memories with the ring of the splendid language of the past.

After he was made Co-adjutor Bishop he would utilise any odd moments he could spare in 'putting them through' the classics. Up and down the cricket pitch he tramped them of an evening till the stars came peeping out, and their hands grew too numbed to hold the book. 'Thoroughness' was his watchword. 'Age quod agis'. 'If a thing is worth doing, it is worth doing well'.

He was a man of high ideals in education, and he kept them untarnished to the end. He strove to make Goulburn a great seat of learning, and afterwards as Bishop he saw that schools were built in every part of his vast diocese.

Many years ago his name was submitted as a candidate for the Rectorship of St John's within the University but when he saw that he had no chance he withdrew it. This he often referred to as one of the greatest disappointments of his life.

It is not easy to put one's finger on the real reason for the wonderful influence he exerted over his boys, even in their afterlife. It must be sought in the whole man, for he was like no other. He never pandered to them, and took little interest in their sport. Occasionally when an important football match was being played with old rivals, the battered biretta might be seen bobbing about among the barrackers on the boundary, while an unique brogue called excitedly. 'Go on, aye' 'Attack him, aye' 'You're fitted only to be a herdsman of geese', or some other well-phrased equivalents for the modern 'Put in the boot'.

To the students in their every-day life he always showed a sterner side, and their many misdemeanours invariably brought down upon their heads slabs of earnest and eloquent abuse. 'You're a boor, and I kick boors'. 'I'll lick you into shape as the bear licks her cub', were some of the uncomplimentary epithets with which he regaled them, but strangely enough whatever grievances might be remembered against other teachers, no one ever nurtured resentment against 'Old Johnnie'. It was the evident sincerity of the man that won through.

The mention of the name by which they always knew him in his absence, brings back a host of memories. More stories have been told about him than any other schoolmaster. The Australian boy usually manifests his appreciation or disapproval of a superior by a nick-name, and it is safe to say that no title—be it 'Father', 'Doctor', or 'My Lord', by which the late Bishop of Goulburn was known, was ever pronounced with more reverence, affection and love than that which his boys gave him. He was 'Old Johnnie' nearly fifty years ago. He was 'Old Johnnie' to the end.

He never forgot a name or a face. Hundreds of lads passed through St Patrick's during his presidency; some of them left no record behind, except a name roughly carved on the desk or painted in uneven letters in the ball alley; still meeting them, even after a lapse of many years, he remembered them without hesitation and was right glad to see them.

It was a touching thing to see him at the college re-unions surrounded by his boys. Boys no longer—the serious things of life were showing the silver in their hair, and in the wrinkle on their cheek, but they were still his 'boys', and he was still their old master. They flocked around him—doctors, lawyers, men in every walk of life—as ready to be guided by him as they were when their hearts were fresh and young, and willing to be led. This was a splendid tribute to the man, and in all the annals of Australian school life and its sequel the writer has not seen anything quite like it.

The next muster was to have been in March, at the celebration of the golden jubilee of the college—and how the old man looked forward to it! In the lonely days that came before the end he often spoke of it, and it was clear that he hoped to shake again the hands of many whom he had not met for years, and then happily chant his Nunc dimittis. They would all have been there; but it was not to be. The reunion was held at Sts Peter and Paul's Cathedral.

At the Requiem several seats near the coffin were filled with ex-students and though 30, 40, 50 years had passed over the heads of some since they were associated with him, their eyes were wet, and they mourned him as they would have mourned a father. Six of them bore him to his grave—Austin DeLauret of Goulburn; Fred Tietyens of Albury; Monks and Walsh of Wagga; Mick Coen of Yass; Jack Hennessey of Sydney—and if the old Bishop could have chosen *he would have had it thus. No more reverent hands could have been found to place him where he lies. Perhaps he thought of it when he felt the world was slipping from him and the end was near. Who knows? In the hearts of his old boys he is living still.*[13]

Before Bishop Gallagher left Goulburn in 1887 the college had reached a peak of over seventy students.[14] It is interesting that Sister Bernard of Yass, when thinking in 1892 of a college for young Patrick Hartigan, passed over Goulburn and advised Manly. She may, of course, have thought in terms of a vocation for the priesthood. But the Goulburn College of the early 1890s as a place of learning was not of high repute and its numbers dropped each year to under thirty at the end of 1894.[15]

It can hardly be a coincidence that young Patrick Hartigan left Manly for Goulburn at the very time that Father Gallagher was going back to his presidential post. They would have met at Manly as we saw and while Dr Gallagher was not yet coadjutor, he was undoubtedly in a position to suggest the changeover of the student for Goulburn diocese from Manly to the local college. Moreover, Dr Verdon used to write in the Manly register 'A.V.S.' (**ad vota saecularia,** 'to secular pursuits') after the names of those leaving with no intention of continuing their studies for the priesthood. Against Hartigan's name is the simple recording of his going to Goulburn.

Very early in his stay at Goulburn young Patrick won the affection of his famous schoolmaster. It is recorded that Father Gallagher asked the class for a translation of **absens amatur.** 'The girl I left behind me' was young Patrick's punt and it won him full marks. He kept that high place in 'Johnnie's' esteem so that at his ordination the Yass **Courier Mail** could report: 'He is only twenty-five years of age and is a great favourite with Dr Gallagher, Bishop of Goulburn'.[16]

To come back again to the year 1895, Father Gallagher returning to his old position of president of St Patrick's College, remained as parish priest of Wagga until his nomination as coadjutor bishop in April. With him on the teaching staff of the college were three laymen and four priests, including Rev Dr Dick Daly, an Australian educated abroad (an erratic genius, so brilliant that he was teaching the Gaels of Ireland their Gaelic and discovering links with their tongue and the Basques of Spain; he was something of an escapologist and some of the most delightful of 'John O'Brien's' stories were about this picturesque character); Rev Patrick

---

13. Freeman's Journal, *Sydney, 13 December 1923.*
14. Official Catholic Directory *for 1886.*
15. *Ibid., 1895.*
16. *Quoted by the* Daily News, *Albury, 29 January 1903. He was in fact twenty-four years of age.*

Hickey as Bursar; Rev Joseph Dwyer, the only other Australian priest in
the diocese (he was to be with Father Hartigan later on in the parish of
Albury and ultimately to be his bishop when Wagga was made a diocese);
and Rev Patrick Dowling, a newly ordained Irish priest on loan from
Sydney, making the fourth of the priests. Rev John O'Donoghue was
added to the teaching staff the following year.

Foremost among young Patrick's friends at Goulburn was Tom Ryan
from Barnawartha on the Victorian side of the Murray. They were to
spend three years together at Goulburn and five at Manly, and be
ordained together at Sts Peter and Paul's Cathedral and spend many years
as priests of Goulburn diocese. As students they spent part of their
seminary holidays together, Pat going to Barnawartha and Tom returning
the compliment by spending some time at Yass. When the diocese of
Wagga was cut off from Goulburn they became incardinated in the new
diocese. Not long afterwards Tom died unexpectedly after a simple
operation. It was Father Hartigan who preached the panegyric at the
Month's Mind (the Requiem Mass said a month after death) at Wagga on
11 March 1926. He had this to say of his deceased friend:

> To those who knew his early life it was clear that most of his
> goodness was born in him, the rest of it was due to the
> wholesomeness of his early environment. He was the child of a good
> Catholic home presided over by a wise excellent Irish father of that
> splendid band who were apostles as well as pioneers, ably helped by
> an Irish mother than whom the great God has never given a finer
> influence to mould the noble instincts in a man.
>
> It was my privilege to have been in that home many times and if
> happiness ever finds a place in this vale of tears it found it there.
> Days of work which brought success were lightened by happy nights
> in the family circle where the merry jest went round, but never an
> unbecoming word was heard and never an uncharitable thing was
> said. And then before we retired to rest we all knelt down to say the
> Rosary. Through the mist of years I can see that kneeling circle now,
> young men, young women and children grouped around the grey-
> haired father—priest for the time being among his family as he gave
> out the decades of that glorious prayer which the Irish boys and girls
> brought from the old land to strengthen them in their trials and
> sweeten their home life in the new.
>
> That old home passed into other hands. Of the ten children who
> were cradled there only three survive and the old couple are sleeping
> side by side in the bush cemetery where the old, old, friends are
> gathering one by one.

Father Ryan was a creature of his early environment. Right through life he was true to the simple lesson he had learned at his saintly mother's knee. Though manhood had broadened his outlook and responsibility had stiffened him into a strong and capable business man, there was much of the simple boy about him to the end with his delight for the bright world and his love of nature and on his lips that quaint Australian humour which amused but never left a sting. Nobody ever heard him say an unkind word, and boy or man, I never heard anyone say an unkind thing of him. I believe he never made an enemy.

And when in the fulness of time he became a priest, God's grace, working on a nature that was particularly suited for the exalted office, made of him a priest of whom the school that trained him and the land that bore him might well feel proud. He did well and thoroughly the simple things that lay around him and when his Bishop called upon him for greater efforts none could have acquitted himself better than he. He was a most efficient administrator of this Cathedral parish at a time when a strong hand and a wise head was needed, and when during His Lordship's absence the care of the diocese practically devolved upon him, his broad shoulders carried the burden in a way which won the admiration of everybody and especially of his chief.

But all these things are well known to you. They augured greater things for the future and in loud tones proclaim the loss the whole Diocese of Wagga has suffered in the cutting off at noonday of a truly valuable life, but there are other things I would like to mention, simpler things if you measure them by the standards of the world but which have already pleaded trumpet tones before the Judgement Seat for his departed soul. I refer to the everyday duties of his sacred calling. The Masses he said, the hours he spent in the confessional, the consolation he brought to those in sorrow, the sick calls when some poor soul about to set out on that long and terrifying journey grew strong at the absolution given with lifted hands.

He was a priest for twenty-three years, and throughout that long span he was ever the good and faithful servant. He was never found wanting when duty called, I know no one who did good more quietly. He made no parade of it, it was the work to which he had set his heart and he did it without complaint and without any thought of reward, at least in this life. Good deeds of the nature of which I speak have a lustre all their own if done in secret. Noblest worth works ever humbly, often is unseen. 'Take heed that you do not your justice before men, that you may be seen by them . . . And when you pray, you shall not be as the hypocrites who love to pray standing in the synagogues and at the corners of the streets, that they may be seen by men. Amen I say to you, they have received their reward'.

None obeyed this precept more carefully than the late Father Ryan. In the old diocese of Goulburn and in the diocese of Wagga during the twenty-three years of his ministry how many splendid things stood to his credit, known only to His Maker and one or two individuals besides.

For the last six years his field of labour was here and how many in the congregation could bear testimony to what I say. When sorrow and trouble flung their pall upon your lives, who was it came to you? Who was it cheered you like the grip of a strong hand in the dark? When you knelt beside the bed where parting life was laid, whose welcome step was it that came unbidden to your door, and when you watched beside your dead, who was it poured into your gaping wound the oil and wine of Christian consolation? But he is dead and charity and kindness stand with drooping wings beside his early grave.

Since the formation of the diocese of Wagga some eight or nine years ago, death has been busy among its ranks, but there has never been such a blow as this. The people of this parish have lost one whom it will be very hard to replace. His fellow labourers in the vineyard stare aghast at their thinning ranks and in their morning Mass another name is transferred from the Memento of the Living to the Memento of the Dead.

To me—if I may be pardoned for referring to a personal grief in a loss in which so many share—his passing leaves the world very empty. We were so closely associated in the old days, that I cannot think I shall not meet him any more. I have not realised that I shall not see him somewhere round the presbytery with his cheery word, and on his lips that quaint humour in which he bade me welcome.

On the same day over thirty years ago we went to Goulburn College, then presided over by the late Dr Gallagher, the present Bishop of Wagga being on the teaching staff. Three years later, we went together to St Patrick's Seminary, Manly, and then for five years we sat side by side and learned those noble principles which were to be the guide of our priesthood—and one, he at least, was very true to them. The billows still croon the old, old melody, another generation fills our places and dreams mayhap the self-same dreams we dreamt beside the sea.

40

Twenty-three years ago we were ordained by Dr Gallagher and since then his path and mine have lain apart. Just now and then we met to talk of those sweet associations which were so closely entwined around the lives of both of us. Only two short years ago we met at Galong. He talked in the old way. We spoke of the passing of the years, and how swiftly they have gone. It seemed only yesterday since he and I were boys together; we promised to see more of each other in the years to be, and how eagerly I looked forward to the honour of having him around my winter fire and the privilege of acting the willing host to my early friend. But it was not to be.

The firelight mingles with the moonlight and round me flock pale forms of things I knew and loved—just shadows of the past. The grey dawn creeps in on feet of pain. All, all are gone and I am musing still beside the ashes of a treasured friendship.

To him the future was full of golden promise. He had the highest hopes of the possibilites of this great town, and an unbounded confidence in its affectionate and generous people. He had done great things in his short life but he looked forward to greater things still. At our last meeting he spoke of his plans to me. He looked so well and as I beheld him in his strength I thought that no one was better fitted than he to bring these plans to a successful termination. How little we thought that the black-robed messenger was on his way, and he would have to go and leave his work unfinished. How little I thought that we would be gathered here so soon and I would be weaving a poor frail wreath of words and offering them as a token to the sacredness of his memory.

But such is human life. No one knows how long or how short it will be. No one knows who will be next. He has been taken in his prime, but he has left an example to those who remain. He kept his priesthood untarnished to the end. He kept the bright flame of his manliness burning clear for all the world to see. He was a true priest.

I am thankful to the Bishop for the opportunity given me this morning of placing this 'tender leaf of my regard' upon his grave. May the turf rest lightly on his bed. May he rest in peace.

I have only one more word to say and my task is done. Pray for his soul. Nothing else avails him now. He may have had imperfections to atone for, and only your prayers can help him. Nothing is at rest in the world of change. The passing of the years shall tramp flat that grave upon the hillside. We shall follow him in God's good time. Another congregation shall gather within these Cathedral walls and the splendour that surrounds his name today shall grow dim. Other cares and other sorrows shall take men's minds from him and he may slumber on forgotten, waiting still for the prayers that shall release him from the place of purgation where the soul must tarry till the last farthing is paid. Pray for him now. Pray for him every day. In your private prayers at Mass remember him; he prayed for you so often. You loved him in life, do not forget him now that he is dead, may he rest in peace. Eternal rest grant unto him, O Lord, and let perpetual light shine upon him.[17]

The end of the year 1897 signalled the closing of an era at St Patrick's College, Goulburn—that of the diocesan priests in control of the college. They had begun twenty-four years before and had their good years and their lean ones. The Christian Brothers who took over from them guaranteed an even continuity and almost immediately this confidence in the future was reflected in the support they got—within half a dozen years the number of students doubled, reaching almost a hundred, and that success has continued in many ways down the years.

The year 1897 marked also the completion of secondary studies for Patrick Hartigan and Tom Ryan. Today at St Patrick's College, Goulburn, they point to the name P. Hartigan chipped laboriously into the stone window-ledge of the north-western corner of the Villa. There has been talk of setting up a poets' corner there to mark:

> *where at least I left a name*
> *Carved in agricultural letters—'twas my only bid for fame.*[18]

At the beginning of the scholastic year 1898 Patrick Hartigan and Tom Ryan were enrolled in the Logic class at St Patrick's College, Manly, as students for the diocese of Goulburn.

While Pat Hartigan was away in Goulburn, Dr Verdon left the position of president of Manly. In 1895 he had been selected by the First Plenary Council to represent the Australian bishops at Rome. He got as far as Adelaide when news came of his elevation to the bishopric of Dunedin. There for many years—his death took place a few days after the end of the First World War—he gave evidence as a bishop of the same sterling qualities that he manifested at Manly and which helped so much to give the college the excellent start it had. Always afterwards he was interested

---

17. From a typescript amongst Father Hartigan's papers.
18. 'John O'Brien', 'The Old Bush School', in Around the Boree Log, Angus & Robertson, Sydney, 1921, p.23.

in Manly, sending students and doing all he could to further its progress, though naturally after Mosgiel was founded in 1900 as the National Seminary for New Zealand much of his attention was necessarily focused there.

His place at Manly was taken by Dr Patrick Murphy, originally from Kilkenny. He had been administrator of St Mary's Cathedral and for a short time parish priest of Concord. With Dr Murphy in 1898 were five professors, Fathers McDermott, Hayden, Brosnan, Burke and Dowling. (The last named had been brought back from Goulburn where, with the advent of the Christian Brothers, he was no longer needed at St Patrick's College there.) The students totalled sixty-five, about half of whom were theologians.

Dr Murphy was not able to fire young Patrick with any enthusiasm. He hardly ever spoke of him in after years except to remark that he was a 'foosterer'[19] and the young man seems to have made his life at Manly almost independently of the president. The ideals of the priesthood that he set himself, his studies, the companionship of his fellow students, a moderate interest in sport—these were the things that filled his life at Manly and the shortcomings of the president were remote from him.

Already he was giving his attention to writing and Jim Kelleher, editor of **The Catholic Weekly**, had this story from an interview with him:

> It happened that the President of St Patrick's was a stern
> disciplinarian with very set ideas about the type of literature that
> should not find its way into a major seminary.
>
> High on the list of 'outlawed' magazines at the time was the
> Sydney Bulletin, but some of the more daring students managed
> to smuggle it in from time to time.
>
> Fortunately it had the same red-coloured cover as the
> Messenger of the Sacred Heart and was invariably referred to in
> conversation as the 'Messenger'. So, its devotees were able to escape
> detection.
>
> Noting the Bulletin's encouragement of Australian writers,
> Patrick Hartigan decided to send a contribution in verse. For obvious
> reasons, he could not use his own name, so he chose a nom-de-
> plume and foolishly revealed it to a few close friends who, he
> imagined, could keep a secret. The pen-name was 'Mary Ann'.
>
> The poem was about an old race-horse, and Monsignor Hartigan
> chuckles today as he recalls some of the stanzas. The last one read

19. For Dr Murphy's term as president of the college, records are almost non-existent.

like this:

'Then bury me 'neath the shade of the box,
Where the magpie will welcome the morn,
Place a cross on my grave to show I expect
A land where no protests annoy,
Where cheating ne'er harms the Almighty's elect,
Nor bitterness adds to their joy'.

The 'Messenger' was eagerly sought for the next few weeks, but
no trace of the poem could be found. Then a 'friend' found the
following item in the famous 'Answers to Correspondents' column
(of the Red Page):
'MARY ANN—the blanky bush person has been killed in these
columns in all manner of ways, by horses falling on him, calves
kicking him in the stomach and by an overdose of religion, and
everything from dead wattle boughs to bad poetry has been strewn
on his tomb. See if you can kill him in a new way and add
something fresh.'
It did not take many minutes for the whole student body to hear
of the sad fate of 'Mary Ann' but many months were to pass before
they forgot it.[20] Pat Hartigan ceased to take any interest in the
Bulletin for the next few months, but surreptitiously he continued
to write verse.
On one occasion he wrote a skit about some of the personalities at
the college, and unwittingly wounded some tender feelings. The
matter was reported to Dr Murphy who, like Queen Victoria, 'was
not amused'. He even threatened the budding satirist with expulsion
for a second offence. Fortunately there was no second offence, or if
there was, Dr Murphy never heard of it.[21]

---

20. *Father Arthur Vaughan of Kensington, Victoria, writing to Father Hartigan in September 1918, was
still able to quote a verse of this disastrous poem:*
    Ah, hang up the saddle, the bridle and whip
    Let the cobwebs around them be spun
    No more with the sweat of old Trojan they'll drip
    For the horse and his rider are done.
21. The Catholic Weekly, 8 May 1952. Bishop John Cullinane, when a student at Manly in 1944, asked
    the late Father Peter Murphy (ordained 1904 and then parish priest of Clifton Gardens) for his
    recollections of the early years of the college Literary and Debating Society. In his reply he had
    these references to 'John O'Brien': 'Even in those days Father Pat Hartigan was good to listen to
    . . . The most pleasant recollection of the Society was the Manuscript Magazine. Two editors
    were appointed and all articles were anonymous, and these editors were expected to keep all
    personalities out of the items and they would read the productions. Pat Hartigan was the editor on
    one occasion and it was only afterwards that we realised that he was giving us his own verse. Our
    head-prefect those days was a bit strait-laced—he is now in heaven—and he reported Hartigan to
    the president for being vulgar. Paddy did not write any more verses till he was ordained.'

Father Frank Flynn of Wodonga, Victoria, in a piece written for **Manly** entitled 'Pioneer Days of Manly', tells us of a further diversion that occupied the young student:

> In diebus illis *there was a young student at Manly College—he was good at his classwork—he was a budding poet—he was a good sketcher—he was mechanically inclined.*
>
> *He designed a magnificent ship and executed the design in every sense of the word. Like Noah's Ark, it was made of wood, like Noah's Ark, it was not a steamship, not an oil ship, nor a turbine nor a windjammer. But unlike Noah's Ark, it was a clockwork ship.*
>
> *He said: 'I will make me an Auto Ship'. So he secured an old box of small dimensions into which he placed the works of an old clock and, when the ship was fit to go to sea (adstante A. Vaughan), he prepared to float her on St Patrick's lake; he held the craft in his left hand while he wound it up with his right, and great was his joy when the ship was launched successfully.*
>
> *Having encountered no obstacle at the beginning he felt encouraged and said, 'I shall go further and a gunboat she shall be'.*
>
> *So his friends secured for him two bungers and, having installed these on his Dreadnought, he again put her to sea, and at the moment the order 'Fire' was given she discharged her shells. But alas! the recoil was more than she could stand. She trembled, turned in different directions, swayed, tail-spun, nose dived, and floundered. Down went the 'Royal George' with all her crew complete.*

> *Pat launched his boat upon the deep and let the clockwork spin*
> *And slowly it began to creep along with grinding din.*
> *His craft he watched eyes full of glee, across the lake career*
> *And e'en the ranks of Tuscany could scarce forbear to cheer.*
> *But as the ship to port returned from this first trip to sea,*
> *A new resolve within him burned—a gunboat she shall be.*

> *Ere long the boat was launched again—a cruiser all complete*
> *Armed fore and aft with bungers twin with shirt of mail replete*
> *But when the guns began to rain their shells upon the sea,*
> *Both submarine and aeroplane she showed herself to be,*
> *With frenzied whirr, she spun around and like a sea horse reared*
> *Then with a final frantic bound, she dived and disappeared.*[22]

22. Manly 5, 4, 1939, pp. 21-9, at p.25. Manly, *usually published yearly, is a journal produced by the Manly Union, the association of priests who studied at Springwood and/or Manly.*

Patrick on his return to Manly in 1898 had found his previous classmates in Third Theology, and early in the year those who originally had been in the class above him came up for ordination as priests. Harry Bakker, a late vocation, was the first. His ordination in March was in Sydney, though he came from Melbourne and was ordained for that archdiocese. Most of the other ordinations that year were also in Sydney, so insistent was the Cardinal on ordaining the students of Manly.

It must have been quite an experience for those young Australians to witness the making of a priest. Apart from a few isolated instances, mostly of students from St Charles' Seminary, Bathurst, all the clergy of their acquaintance had come to the country already priests.

At the end of the year Patrick Hartigan's name appeared in the prize list, second in Logic and Metaphysics and honourable mention in Mathematics, Natural Philosophy and English Elocution.

The year 1899 did not bring many changes, though the number of students dropped down to fifty. The annalist noted as a most important event the introduction of rugby. Hitherto Australian Rules held sway; now rugby was played on alternate days. The pioneers were J. Ellis, P. Doherty, T. Ryan, P. Hartigan, P. Ellis, F. Lloyd, W. Mullins, P. Murphy, T. Nolan and J. Kelly.

The debating society minute book tells us that on 5 September Arthur Hogan speaking on his ordination and impending departure confessed that 'he never thought he would be sorry to leave Manly. He realised as he had never realised before that his best friends were in St Patrick's College and his affections would ever remain with them.' (The annalist adds: 'Here the tremor in the reverend gentleman's voice bespoke how keenly he felt the parting; it was noticeable also that some of his hearers were much affected.')

The prize list this year again featured Patrick Hartigan in Philosophy, second to Denis Conaghan, and a mention again in English Elocution.

Denis Conaghan, nicknamed the Fenian because he was born in Ireland, was held back for ordination—no one was quite sure whether it was because of his boisterousness or his youth or a combination of both—and missed his golden jubilee of priesthood on that account. Father Hartigan wrote about him without revealing his identity:

There was a room in it [the Darlinghurst presbytery] in which was preserved the bed on which the Old Archbishop [Dr Polding] had breathed his last. But even this was not sacrosanct. Early in this century, and not yet thirty years after the Prelate's death, there was appointed to the parish a young curate with the clerical garb still looking awkward on him. He was of the modern cult, caring nothing

*for the past and its glories. He was given the room in which was the
treasured bed in which Dr Polding died. He was not impressed. As a
relic it had its points, but as a couch to induce dreamless slumber,
the only place or state in which a curate can forget he is a curate, it
was a failure, so after fighting it and 'wrestling' with it into the
small hours, he rose, and with suitable anathemas, heaved it
through the window to the pavement below where he considered it
belonged. One would have supporters in surmising that that Curate's
life was short and beset with woes. How else but through a broken
heart can such as he be made to think. Yet the Handmaiden Truth,
who has guided this faltering pen through these veracious pages, bids
it write that neither pain nor ache, nor any ecclesiastical censure has
ever come to him. And there is nothing likely now—that is humanly
speaking—to blur the pastel shades of a mellow afternoon. Through
a long and useful life he has come, from unpromising beginnings, to
be a notable and respectable clergyman, and a Dignitary of his
Church withal.*[23]

We might add that he lived to see a nephew, Pat Dougherty, ordained
and two others, John and Bill, enter the seminary—they have since been
ordained and all three continue his fine work. Further, the year 1976 saw
the eldest, Pat, ordained as an auxiliary bishop for the archdiocese of
Canberra and Goulburn.

The year 1900 found Patrick Hartigan beginning Theology.[24] On 28
February the senior debating society admitted students from the junior
club, namely O'Hanlin, Dunne, Denny, Conaghan, Gurry, Hartigan and
Ryan.

Patrick Hartigan's name occurs half a dozen times in the minute book
that year. He gave an original 'storyette', took part in a dramatic scene,
and in a discussion on 'How to safeguard the interest of Catholic Youth'
pointed out that as young fellows are committed to the care of a young
curate, he should gain their confidence and esteem. Later on he
enumerated all the qualifications which entitled Yass to become the
federal capital. At 'A Night with Longfellow' he read 'The Day is Done',
and 'The Footsteps of Angels'. On an elocutionary night he read an
extract from Boswell's **Life of Johnson.**

In the prizes at the end of the year, Patrick Hartigan did moderately
well in each of the four subjects taken by the theologians.

---

23. *'John O'Brien', On Darlinghurst Hill, Ure Smith, Sydney, 1952, p.75.*
24. *In that same year 1900 the editors of the annals were Terry McGuire, Dick Denny of Adelaide and Pat Hartigan.*

The debating club's minute book for 13 March 1901 records that Mr Hartigan was elected vice-president, and the president, chosen as usual by Dr Murphy, was Mr Bourke. As vice-president Patrick Hartigan occupied the chair at alternate meetings of the debating club.

There is an interesting note on 2 April when Patrick was occupying the chair: 'Owing to members being too excited over the unanimous verdict of the jury in the Coningham case, the meeting was adjourned.' This case had begun in the previous December. Coningham, a well-known cricketer, was seeking a divorce on the grounds that his wife had repeatedly committed adultery with Rev Dr Denis O'Haran in St Mary's Cathedral and adjacent buildings. Coningham claimed £5000 damages from the co-respondent. It was a bitter sectarian conflict. The first jury disagreed, but the second, after less than two hours' retirement, returned a unanimous verdict for O'Haran.

On 4 September Messrs Hartigan and Mangan were elected as editors of the **Manuscript Journal.**[25] Billy Mangan was afterwards to control the Melbourne Catholic paper, the **Tribune,** and to cross swords with the redoubtable Archbishop Mannix. Father Hartigan's favourite story about him concerned his role as a military chaplain in World War I. He returned from Europe on a ship bringing back the wounded which was to leave again with troops almost immediately. The chaplain approached the Archbishop for leave for a few weeks. Dr Mannix turned down the request with the words: 'Father if that ship went down and you weren't on it, I would never forgive myself'.

In the examinations this year Pat Hartigan did very well: first in Moral Theology, second in Dogma, third in Scripture and a **proxime accedit** in History.

The year 1902 saw Patrick relinquishing his post as vice-president of the debating club, merely holding the fort until April when Jimmy Lawless, the new president, took over from him. Jimmy was nicknamed Cracka-Dookie, as he came from the town of Dookie in north-eastern Victoria. He spent many years as parish priest of Rutherglen, and his presbytery was a half-way house on Father Pat's trips from Narrandera to Melbourne. Jimmy established the reputation as most consistent in attending priests' jubilees, funerals etc. In the days when this was done by train, it was nothing for him to travel to Melbourne and Sydney in the one week.

At the end of May Pat Hartigan was in a debate but his name does not appear in the Literary and Debating Society's records after that date. This

---

25. *See above, fn. 21. It was referred to both as a journal and a magazine.*

may have been because of Dr Murphy's warning mentioned earlier.[26] Whether or not it was a case of **post hoc, ergo propter hoc**, the prize list at the end of the year records brilliant successes for him: first prize for Moral and Dogmatic Theology, second in Church History and third in Scripture.

His course of studies at Manly was brought to an abrupt end by the decision of his bishop to ordain him after he had completed only three years of theology. Dr Gallagher was due to make his **ad limina** visit to Rome—bishops are required to give regularly a report on their diocese, in the case of bishops in Australia usually every ten years. Dr Gallagher was leaving early in 1903 and was to be away a good part of the year. He resolved to ordain Pat Hartigan and Tom Ryan before he left and fixed January as the month.

The years at Manly were happy times for young Patrick Hartigan and they provided him with stories which were perennial favourites. Father Hugh McDermott taught Latin and, perhaps because of his Christian name, wanted the use of 'one'. To the questioner: 'How would you translate this line?' he said: 'Don't say "you", sir'. 'Well', was the reply, 'how would I translate it?'.

On one occasion the students were allowed to take part in the parish fête at Manly. An attractive girl was selling tickets for a pair of silver-eyed sparrows and none of the students could refuse. Next day Dr Steve Burke discoursed eloquently on philosophy. He finished his lecture a few minutes before the bell and asked: 'Any questions?' 'Yes', said a country lad, 'who won them silver spadgers?'

Among the many friends Pat Hartigan made at Manly, Terry McGuire would perhaps have been the closest. On the day Terry became the first bishop of Townsville, it was Paddy who preached at Pontifical Benediction in the evening. He spoke beautifully of devotion to Our Lady and of the history of the feast of Our Lady, Help of Christians, and has this to say of Townsville and its bishop:

Only a hundred and sixty years ago an English ship threading a sinuous course past reef and sound paused like a weary bird on the shimmering waters of Cleveland Bay. Today that lone horizon is smeared with the smoke of the messengers of commerce. Less than seventy years ago the first impetus was given to activities along this seaboard; today this noble city, the Metropolis of the North, reigns like a queen in State enthroned upon her magic hills.

26. See fn. 21.

If the future holds in its keeping the fulfilment of the promise of today, if the development of present activities and the promotion of new ones dot these empty spaces with settlement, and spread a population over this immense area it will be necessary for religion to expand side by side with material things.

Today provision has been made that the Eternal should guard the temporal when this big country comes into its own. Today provision has been made that the pillar of cloud by day and the pillar of fire by night shall lead us ever, lest allured by phantom lights along the way we turn aside from God and worship idols. Without religion, there can be no true progress. Nations have fallen in the past, Empires have wilted from the earth because in the wild pursuit of this world's goods men have forgotten the saving lessons that were taught by the shelving shores of Galilee.

The forward step taken today was made possible by the work of three priests whose names will ever be associated with this episcopal city. Two of them came from that little island far away from which have come those pioneer priests who have laid the foundation of our Faith so broad and deep and strong: the third was among the first fruits of their example. They sleep in hallowed graves tonight but their gentle spirits linger near to bless, to hail a leader who has come to continue in a higher sphere the work they did so well.

It is a matter of consolation to us all that there has been chosen as your first Bishop one in whose fitness for the task we confidently put our trust. He comes to you in the fulness of his manhood, with a mind richly stored, with a judgement that can be trusted in all things, with an outlook that is big. He has the genius to plan and the courage to dare. He has:—

> *An eye to guide and a hand to rule*
> *and a calm and a kingly head.*
> *And a heart from which, like a holy*
> *well, the souls of his flock are fed.*

If anyone be worthy, he is worthy, and we who knew his worth in the old days and watched his advancement since, saw him take the shepherd's staff this morning with a feeling of affectionate pride which somehow trembles on the lip and catches strangely at the heart. He is not one of those who think that his own efforts, unaided by Divine Grace, are sufficient for the task that lies before him. Only too well he knows that it has been said by Divine Wisdom: 'Without me you can do nothing'. And confidently, too, he

50

remembers what has been spoken by inspired lips: 'I can do all things in Him that strengthens me'.[27]

Tom King, army chaplain, diplomat, raconteur, was another of Father Hartigan's very close friends from Manly days. When Tom was overseas with the Forces in World War I he wrote to Paddy, addressing him as 'My Dear Hartigan', telling him that shortly he would have circumstances of danger surrounding him and detailing what he wanted Paddy to do 'if death overtakes me during the time of my military service'. He was in fact to outlive his beloved Paddy by a year or so.

One of Father Hartigan's treasures was a clock that came from Tom. On a visit to Sydney, he had expressed his admiration for the chimes of a clock in the presbytery at Stanmore. A few days after he returned to Narrandera the clock arrived there as a gift from Tom. It has been with our family since Father Hartigan's death and now in Holy Family Church, Lindfield, it signals the time for Mass.

27. *From a typescript of the sermon. It was published in* Manly 4, 1, 1930, pp. 38-45.

3 First Years as a Priest

Pat Hartigan, along with his friend and seminary confrère Tom Ryan, was ordained a priest in the Cathedral of Sts Peter and Paul, Goulburn, on Sunday 18 January 1903, and next day celebrated his first Mass. His cousin Anne Sullivan (Sister M. Imelda) was a novice at the time; she loved to recall that the newly ordained priest had given her Holy Communion first in the Sister's Chapel before ministering to his parents and family. The following Sunday his Mass was at St Augustine's Yass and there in the church of his baptism he preached his first sermon. The vestments he wore and treasured ever afterwards were the gift of the Sisters of Mercy who had taught him at the convent school.

He was appointed immediately to Albury. The letter of appointment ran as follows:

Bishop's House
Goulburn
Jan. 22 1903

Dear Father Hartigan,

I hereby appoint you as junior assistant to Rev. D. Griffin in the important and gradually increasing parish of Albury. As Albury is an old established parish in which all ecclesiastical functions have been carried out in full and regular order for many years, I have only to add that you are to be guided in all your duties by the customs of the Parish in accordance with the directions of its Pastor, Father Griffin.

Wishing you God's best blessing in discharging worthily all the varied duties of your sacred office, I am, Dear Father Hartigan, yours sincerely

† *John Gallagher*

Rev. P. Hartigan
Albury

P.S. As I am likely to be absent during most of the year, I should perhaps exhort you to make a supreme effort to meet the obligation quam primum *in regard to the Mission Fund. You could, when able, give it to Father Slattery, explaining to him why you do so. This will not only bring a blessing but enhance one's character for upright manly adherence to principle and obligation at the beginning of one's career.*

J.G.

N.B. You should be in Albury in time to be ready for full discharge of all duties on Sunday, February 1.[1]

The Albury **Daily News** of 26 January had the news of his appointment, and the baptismal book of St Patrick's Church shows his first baptism there as on 12 February. He signed it flamboyantly Patrick J. Hartigan, but after this initial tribute to new importance he settled down to the P.J. Hartigan he was to use ever afterwards. He had fond memories of Father Dan Griffin who was his parish priest for his first four years in Albury. During the first twelve months he had the company of Father Peter Mulligan who had arrived from Young at the same time as Father Pat came to Albury. The departing priest was Father Peter Paul McAlroy who, as the senior curate of the diocese, got his first appointment in charge of a parish, which was Jerilderie. Father Hartigan's arrival meant that for the first time there were three priests in the parish of Albury.

The postscript to the Bishop's letter referred to the fees owing for his education at Manly. Bishop Lanigan had granted young Patrick a half-bursary at Manly, which was the usual arrangement for Australian students. In his later years at Manly his father's business was going badly and he was unable to meet his half share of the fees. Bishop Lanigan decreed that young Patrick should pay off the debt after his ordination. The young priest found this a heavy burden and in after years he would joke about it saying that he used to rush to the presbytery front door at the sound of the bell in the hope that it might be someone with an offering for a Mass! Finally he went to Bishop Gallagher and told him the family situation—his parents eking out a precarious existence in Sydney, and a younger brother studying for the priesthood, also in need of help.

The Bishop, once he knew the real position, was all sympathy. Referring to Bishop Lanigan's requirement that the young man should pay off the debt, he burst out in his Northern Ireland brogue: 'By Gud, I was coadjutor bishup then and by Gud, I am bishup now and you shall not pay a penny more of that debt'.

In the archives of Manly College there are three letters from Father Hartigan concerning the promotion of young men to the priesthood; all of them touched on this problem of finance. We have seen already his letter about his younger brother Frank.[2]

In his early years at Albury he wrote about William Percy:

---

1. *Letter amongst Father Hartigan's papers.*
2. *See pp. 20 and 21.*

> *St Patrick's Presbytery*
> *Albury*
> *January 17, 1906*

Dear Father McDermott,
   I am writing to you about a young man of this town who would like to go on for the Church. He would be, I fancy, about twenty-five years of age, comes of a good Catholic family, and in addition bears the best reputation. For the last few years he has been working at the 'Carrying business'. Of course he knows nothing of Latin but is steady and very anxious to learn. Would there be a class for him at Manly if matters with the Bishop can be settled? I would be very thankful if you could manage to drop me a line giving the information: also a little advice re the wisdom of his going on at that age etc.
   This is the first time I have had the pleasure of writing to you. I intended doing so once or twice when a few little difficulties cropped up: but knowing you are kept busy, I did not care to trouble you.
> *With kindest regards dear Fr McDermott*
> *I am,*
> *Yours sincerely,*
> *P.J. Hartigan.*[3]

Percy was accepted at Manly and was ordained a priest in Goulburn in July 1913 along with Father Hartigan's brother Frank. Father Percy gave sterling service to the dioceses of Goulburn and Wagga for many years until his death in Albury in June 1964.

The third letter concerns Harold Devine, an outstanding late vocation:

> *Albury*
> *March 8, 1910*

Dear Father McDermott,
   I take the liberty of writing to you re a young man, Harold Devine, who is anxious to be a priest. His difficulty is the usual one,—want of means. He can see his way clear, I am led to believe, should he get philosophy. But in the event of his not getting that, he says he must stay away and work at his trade and attend a night-school etc. and present himself next year and so on. He is also thinking of trying New Zealand. I told him, however, to call on you, assuring that you would give him every chance. Of course, Dear Fr McDermott, you understand the reason for my writing this, it is not to ask you to change your rules for Devine, it is

3. McDermott papers, Manly Archives.

simply to give you a strong recommendation for him in every way as a
most deserving man: He has passed the Junior Matriculation, I think, in
latin etc., and fitted himself for it by attending what school he could and
paying for it out of his earnings. He is a hardworker, and a splendid
character, and I would be sorry if he went elsewhere without seeing you.
Hoping you are all well and wishing you a successful year,

I am, dear Fr McDermott,
Yours sincerely,
P.J. Hartigan.[4]

When in the first decades of this century the priests from Manly set
about encouraging Australian vocations, they formed an association
known as the Manly Union. Through this association bursaries were
established by which Australian young men were assured that there
would be no bar financially to their becoming priests. No one did more to
establish these bursaries than Father Harold Devine.

To return now to Father Hartigan's beginnings in Albury, there is an
amusing account of his first visit to the parish school; it comes from the
recollections of one of the pupils of that time, John (better known as
'Joker') Byrne:

Welcome, Father to Our School

For the preceding three days Mother Theresa, at frequent intervals,
had rehearsed us.

At a given signal every child in the Class Room was to rise and
make what was by some a graceful, but by most an agricultural bow,
and repeat, whilst bowing, or bending, or stumbling, 'Welcome,
Father to our School'.

The occasion was the appointment of a new Curate to the Parish
and his first visit to our little 'Country School'.

She had impressed upon us—he was young—only recently
ordained—and, an Australian. An Australian Priest, Australian! Our
young minds found difficulty in believing that there were such
things.

We had lots of warning as to time, and day of visit; had been

4. Ibid.

instructed the previous afternoon to attend on the morrow in our best raiment. So the class assembled, the best dressed placed in the front desks, but all bathed, dressed and polished in our 'Go to Mass Suits' arranged to welcome our young New Curate.

Punctually he arrived and he was certainly something new in Priests. We'd never seen anything like him before. He was very tall. He was very thin; he wore a long frock coat, which accentuated his length and his height was extended by the tallest, shiniest 'bell-topper' hat that our young eyes had beheld. Till then we only knew two frock coats, the two bell-topper hats. They were worn by our Bishop, Dr Gallagher, on his visits, and our Parliamentary Representative, Sir William Lyon, but neither hat could compete in sheen, height, or style with that of our 'newest inhabitant'. His frock coat could button, whilst theirs seemed incapable of doing so. We queried whether the said coats were shy or shrinking from the importance, or whether the importance of the importance was increasing too much for the coats, but this new one was different, it buttoned.

He thanked us for the welcome. Made a short and simple speech, cracked some jokes at our expense, which Sister enjoyed and more at Sister's expense which we enjoyed; an extended play hour was granted, and so was born our affection for the New Curate.[5]

At Albury, Father Pat came in contact again with Father Joe Dwyer who had been on the teaching staff of St Patrick's College, Goulburn, when he studied there. For the first five years Father Dwyer was Inspector of Schools, with residence at Thurgoona or Newtown on the outskirts of Albury. Then in 1906 when Father Griffin left to take charge of the parish of Ganmain, Father Dwyer took his place as administrator of the parish of Albury. It was a good relationship and contributed in no small way to the happiness of Father Hartigan's years in Albury.

Soon after his arrival he founded the Catholic Young Men's Society, the C.Y.M.S. as it was called. Its members met weekly and one night of each month was given to a manuscript journal at which papers written by members were read and discussed. He developed amongst its members a deep love for Australia and Australian literature.

Again it is Joker Byrne who is our informant:

I recall how we would sit and listen in wonderment fascinated by his

5. *From a typescript among the Hartigan papers.*

extraordinary fund of knowledge on such a variety of subjects and all so racy of Australia. The development of the Merino Sheep: the Blood Horse: the Snowden strain: the Bruce Lowe System: Federation wheat: the Bushrangers: the families and localities immortalised by Banjo . . . and then his marvellous memory . . . his fund of quotation: his capacity as a reciter: his characterisation, his powers of description and mimicry: his stories, and his delightful humour.[6]

All this time he was writing poetry, some pieces for the manuscript journal, others, mostly under a **nom-de-plume,** for local papers and the metropolitan press.

One of these was linked with a tragic occasion. Father Daniel Griffin was being transferred to Ganmain, and the after-dinner speaker was John Maclure, a Presbyterian and chieftain of the local Caledonian Society. He quoted the lines:

> *Lives of great men all remind us*
> *That we should make our lives sublime*
> *And departing leave behind us*
> *Footprints on the sands of time.*

Then glancing down at the feet of Father Griffin—who was a big man of splendid physique—he said 'and where our guest has stood, he has certainly left a footprint'. Continuing he said 'But those footprints were ever deepest around the doorsteps of the poor'. Then taking the reverend guest by the hand he said: 'If we should never meet again'. As he uttered those words he staggered, collapsed and fell. All was commotion, the curtain was lowered, then silence broken by the announcement that John Maclure had passed away.

The next day the following verses appeared in the local paper:

The Last Good-Bye

The last! Ah yes, he'll take thy hand no more
That he, last night in unfeigned friendship pressed.

---

6. *Ibid.*

> The last full tide was ebbing from the shore,
> He sank upon its breast.
>
> We thought the sun was high above its bed;
> Its hopeful rays were still upon the plain.
> 'We've met each other oft through life' he said,
> 'We may not meet again'.
>
> We did not think the shadow was the night's;
> We wept and laughed, we laughed and wept with him
> We sat beneath the clustered golden lights,
> And one grew quickly dim.
>
> We watched it flicker—watched in hope, in doubt
> We saw the gloom was deepening on the wall
> A whispered word—we knew the light was out,
> We saw the curtain fall.
>
> No mimic veil, no mimic actor gone;
> A tragedy that needs no gloss of art.
> He bowed his exit from Life's stage, whereon
> He played a hero's part.
>
> A silent throng is moving down the street;
> The tears are falling like the autumn rain.
> In life we meet to part; we part to meet;
> 'We shall not meet again'.
>
> A weeping throng is standing round the bier,
> Along the street is borne the heartfelt sigh;
> A silent, well-loved face is smiling near,
> He said the last good-bye.[7]

A few months earlier in this same year 1906 Father Hartigan's deep knowledge and love of Australian literature had become more widely known locally through a lecture he gave on the subject before 'a large and eager audience', as the local paper described it, noting: 'It is to the credit of the fair sex that they were present in preponderating numbers'. In all there were two full-page closely printed columns of sustained eulogy and these paragraphs are typical:

> In all he spoke for an hour and forty minutes, and the attention of the audience was held absolutely from beginning to end, and when he had resumed his seat the spell of his clever and interesting narrative and criticism was still upon his hearers to such an extent that they would have preferred him to continue. It would be difficult to find any one better equipped for the task of reviewing the history

7. Daily News, *Albury*, 9 October 1906.

—personal and impersonal—of Australian poetry than Father Hartigan, with his exceptional insight, acute and independent judgment, his fine analytical power, literary instinct, extraordinary retentiveness of memory, and command of beautiful poetic language. While he is capable of bestowing upon the whole of the Australian poets an abundant appreciation, Father Hartigan never descends to the level of the mere flamboyant panegyrist. He criticises as keenly as need be, and throws an enlightening ray of light here and there upon the relative values of words, the utter impossibility of some of them when used in poetry; and substantially his judgment may be said to be that of the whole of those competent to place the Australian poets in the order of merit in which they must ever stand in the settled literature of the country now or in the future ...

The lecture was interspersed with racy and humorous anecdotes of an apt character; and the fine imagery and delicate poetic phrases in which he presented most of his serious passages, revealed the fact to those who do not know of Father Hartigan's literary faculty that they were in the presence not only of one who could appreciate and criticise the work of the poets, but who has no small measure of the 'divine afflatus' in his own entity. As he resumed his seat Father Hartigan was greeted with prolonged applause, the general view being that he had afforded the audience a rare treat indeed ...

Father Hartigan has a memory like Macaulay. He can at will quote voluminous passages from the old world and Australian poets, and that without mislaying a single comma.

It is said that the public has no taste for poetry. This can scarcely be said to apply to a very large section of the people of Albury. We have never seen an audience held in such rapt attention as that last night, the only interruptions being laughter (evoked by some humorous side-light), or spontaneous applause.[8]

For a wider audience he wrote an article on this same subject in the **Australasian Catholic Record.**[9] He begins thus:

At the idea of claiming for Australia a literature of its own ... the superior person is apt to smile long and complacently.

Father Hartigan conceded that our literature had at that stage chiefly a local interest, but he considered that we certainly have what Longfellow

---

8. Daily News, *Albury, 2 August 1906.*
9. '*A Plea for Australian Literature'*, Australasian Catholic Record, *1906, pp. 517-36.*

would call 'the humbler poet', and he made a plea for our honouring those who have written well the first pages of our literature.

And this the more, because nothing can be a more potent factor in the building up of a nation beneath southern skies than a healthy Australian sentiment, sprung from and nourished by a sound national literature.

He goes on to castigate the positive dislike some evince for Kendall, Gordon and Lawson; Australian literature has in fact made the progress that could be reasonably expected, for people have no time to be poets until they have settled into some more or less fixed groove of existence. (This makes good sense and he might have added that our word 'school' and the words that come from it derive from the Greek word for leisure. Over the centuries philosophy and literature flourished when the wars died down.)

Looking at the characteristics of Australian literature, he sees a sad note running through it, not unexpected, when we think of the convict beginnings of Australia. As he says, 'The clank of the chains of the convict gangs drowned the sounds of revelry'. Moreover, the weird melancholy aspect of the Australian bush naturally brought sad thoughts to the mind of the early settler transplanted from green fields and cosy hamlets. The miles and miles of waving tree tops, sombre hues unrelieved by any bright colours, spelt nothing but mystery and loneliness.

Further, every locality had its dismal story of how someone was killed or lost—how many Mounts Hopeless there are, how many Deadman's Creeks. All this helped on Kendall's melancholy nature to write weird verse reminiscent of Edgar Allan Poe. Indeed Kendall, Gordon and Marcus Clarke would have written in a melancholy strain wherever they were.

'Ogilvie, Paterson and others have presented the life of the Australian from a brighter and truer point of view,' said 'John O'Brien', and we might add that he himself was to set out to correct the gloomy pictures of the early writers; 'The Libel', 'Come, Sing Australian Songs to Me!', and 'St Patrick's Day' are examples of this.

Another characteristic of Australian literature is that it is about the present and the future—Australia has not the 'weed and mantled towers' to inspire writing. While other nations were 'signing in the book of Eternal Fate their stormy histories', Australia slumbered. The shock of arms and the booming of the cannon did not break upon her peace. Around her shores the long-backed rollers of the Pacific crooned a cradle song.

In looking to the future, Australian writers must see that those days are dying that saw the few fatten and the millions starve. For even here in Australia there is poverty, and when the writer hears beneath his window the patter of the little bare feet of the gutter children who are growing up in an unwholesome environment, it is natural that he 'sorrows for the faces in the street'.

Another aspect of Australian literature is that it has dealt generally with country life. Gordon, Paterson, Ogilvie and others are noteworthy for this, but pride of place must be given to Henry Lawson. He carried his swag, that is his worldly possessions wrapped in a blanket, with a water bag and billycan in which to make tea; a rough exterior beneath which was hidden a philosopher with views often sounder than those of many politicians.

Victor Daley was wider in his scope, as were the writers contributing to **A Southern Garland.** E.J. Brady and Roderick Quinn and others also provide veritable gems.

He pleads for the recognition of Australian writers:

We must recognise our literature, in order that we may recognise our own land. We have a good country here, despite the hard things that homesick exiles are continually saying about it. If it does not become great it is because we are half-hearted patriots mouthing empty nothings on every platform about a rising nation and a glorious destiny while at the same time we are pining after old world customs and old world traditions, and in our heart of hearts we wish we were not Australians.

He is the Cosmopolite that loves his native country best . . . but I believe that throughout the land a national spirit is arising.

He went on to point out that Australian writers have their work to do in fostering this Australian sentiment. When the war comes, the same courage which enabled them to face the trials of the backblocks will nerve them for the conflict. Love of country will unite the 'boys from the western creeks' and the city-bred and 'they'll fight for right or a grand mistake as men never fought before'.

If war never comes, he goes on, we are nevertheless building up a nation, and we must put our hearts and souls into the work.

We are waiting for the national poet who shall pulse a thrill from heart to heart throughout the land. When he comes, when we have a Bobby Burns to show the poetry in the common things around us, when we have a Charles Dickens to show the heroism of humble lives, when the works of Henry Lawson are read and appreciated, we

61

shall join our hands across the country's vast expanse in the strength of a grand Australian Brotherhood.

Another event in Father Hartigan's busy literary year of 1906 was the simultaneous publication in the **Bulletin** and the Albury **Daily News** of his poem: 'When the Circus Came to Town'. Both papers ran it on 9 August, the Albury version noting that it was in the **Bulletin.** In each case he used the **nom-de-plume** Mary Ann.

One of Father Hartigan's great interests was horses and he would talk at length on the history of the Australian horse. Nor was his interest purely academic—in those years in Albury he owned Swagman, a beautiful, well-groomed black animal, all of sixteen hands. It was an imposing sight to see the young curate mounted on this handsome steed, perfect in his equipment of gloves, cap and leggings. Once a week he rode out to the Common, a distance of about ten kilometres, for a gallop and jumping exercise. The handmaiden Truth—invoked earlier in this story by Father Hartigan—bids us relate that on one occasion Swagman shied at a Chinaman's cart with its unusual trappings and deposited his priestly pilot at the main doorway of one of the principal stores.

From horses he graduated to a motor bike. Fred Blacklock was a local agent for these machines. Looking round for likely targets for a sale, he picked on the curate, and his success story is told in 'My Curate's Motor-Bike'. (The illustrations are by 'John O'Brien' himself.)

My Curate's Motor-Bike

Before the lad invested we had comfort here indeed;
Our lives were as an open book, and he who ran might read;
But now we live in other worlds, for since the motor came
My yoke-mate ne'er confides in me, or treats me quite the same.

He used to be a candid man,—I liked him very well,—
But lately I must pick the truth from what he does not tell;
The news he gives is watered too, so when there's been defeat
I get one version here from him,—another down the street,

The madness got him bit by bit,—I marked its sure advance,—
An angashore upon a bike would land him in a trance;
He'd leave me talking to myself and watch it forge ahead,
And then he'd slowly stir himself, and ask 'What's that you said?'

Next, like a plague, loquacious men of marked civility
Swooped down, from Heaven alone knows where, upon the Presbyt'ry;
Each bird of prey a cushat dove in downy meekness dressed,
And each a fine philanthropist to save him from the rest.

And then typed letters came in sheaves, and pamphlets too galore,
The table there was strewn with them; I counted ten and more;
And morning, noon, and night he'd sit absorbing their contents,
The two heels round the bishop stuck with grave irreverence.

I've never seen a homing soul so doubt-tossed, I must say,
He'd spurn the faith to-morrow, that was in him strong to-day:
For 'someone told him something,' and unto that he'd cling;
'Twas this mysterious 'chap I met' who tells him everything.

The latest always was the best—the very thing he sought,
Much better than 'the rubbish' which my neighbour's curate bought;
'Twas fitted up with this and that; it was in short immense,
'Twould do sick-calls around the earth like falling off a fence.

He talked and talked like one possessed as on the madness ran;
Such folly surely never gripped the mind of any man:
'Ignition this,' 'combustion that,' I never heard the likes,
You'd think the world was spinning round on works of motor-bikes.

I took a stand as rectors should, and fussed and fumed and that,
And lavished pointed rhetoric and wisdom—on the cat;
But on he went from bad to worse: Bedad it shocked me much
To hear him speak of dignitaries as cylinders and such;

The horse-power of the clergy, too, I heard him dwell upon,
And I'm 'a last year's model' faith, 'with no kick-starter on,'
Still he laughs best who laughs the last, when all is said and done.
For when the smelly thing arrived, 'twas then we had the fun.

He donned the goggles and the coat, the cap, the gloves, the scarf,
And pushed it to the stable-yard, supported by the staff;
He jacked the wheel and kicked with fine spectacular disdain,
It gave a sort of wheezy cough, and so he kicked again.

Still no result: then undismayed he played the second card,
He pushed it off the stand, he did, and wheeled it round the yard:
He wheeled it up, he wheeled it down, until he near expired,
He forced the groom to take a turn, but faith, he soon got tired,

The small lads gave him useful hints, he told them to be gone,
And when he chased them off the fence he turned the petrol on:
Then, Man, he gave a thumping kick and swung into the seat;
And here my hero motor-man goes shooting down the street.

Along the king's high-way he sped on what he calls 'his top';
Upon his top; How are you! Heth, he found he couldn't stop:
His tank was full of 'juice' it seems, and in his misery
He worked it out the wicked thing would wheel him to the sea.

But through it all the mind was clear, he dodged the straying stock,
If tour he must, 'twere wise, he thought, to tour around the block:
So round and round and round he went, the eyes fixed straight ahead,
And every time at Mrs Flynn's the congregation spread;

And every time he passed the house which Granny Heafy leased,
That pious person jerked the knee, respectful to the priest:
So round and round and round he went with bump and swerve and skid:
Of course he never told me this, but fifty people did.

Now trouble's soon forgot, it seems, by all these motor-men,
I hoped he'd sell the wretched thing, but on he came again:
The front verandah corner there is like a tinker's shop;
Bad cess to it! I don't know where the thing is going to stop.

He's made this house a meeting-place for faddists and the likes,
And clerical mechanics come debating motor-bikes;
They talk a man unconscious with their cranks and gears and springs,
And bore and stroke, and this and that, and sparkling-plugs and things.

Now God be with the good old times for ever dead and gone,
When in this cheery room of mine I led the banter on;
For though we spoke of grave affairs, or touched the lighter side,
No man need sit and twirl his thumbs, because disqualified.

Well, youth must have its fling, I ween, and face the future, still
The old grey horse and I shall jog together down the hill:
We've come a long, hard, weary way, nor shirked the bonded load,
We'll carry on and see it through, Old Comrade of the road.

No, not for us the whirring wheel that greets the Morning's call,
We only have 'one speed,' my boy, and that's no speed at all:
The evening finds us laid aside, and dreaming in the sun,—
Two 'last year's models' right enough, with engines nearly done:—

But tell them this: Ere roads were made, by bridle-track we went,
And won the Bush with church and school across a continent:
The journey's o'er; the chapter's writ; and take it how we like,
The big things now are waiting for the young man's motor-bike.

Father Hartigan submitted this poem to the **Catholic Press.** The editor, Tighe Ryan, wrote:

I love the treatment but I'm nervous about the subject. The laity may not understand ... I'm afraid to use it. The reverence for the priesthood in the Irish is so sensitive that it is not safe to make a joke at their expense. Please don't stop writing and take lay subjects, and don't think too unkindly of a poor editor, who in steering his ship is always in danger of running into a mine or a sub-marine. [10]

The poem was published in the **Manly** of 1922 with the author's illustrations and in the **The Parish of St Mel's.**

A notable part of Father Hartigan's work in Albury was with the young men and the Catholic Young Men's Society he had founded and made a great success. Right from those early days he preached tolerance, and when he was being farewelled by the C.Y.M.S. he said:

Though they were loyal Catholics, there was never a hostile reference in their gatherings to the religion of another [applause].

Father Hartigan was taken aback by the applause and said:

I did not expect a clap for that and I hope the time will come when no man will be applauded for decrying sectarianism. There should be no such thing in a fine free land like Australia. [11]

His altar boy John Byrne graduated to the C.Y.M.S. and later became famous as a reciter of the poems of 'John O'Brien'. Father Hartigan wrote this introduction which was used on the programs for his recitals:

I Introduce the Joker

Many years ago, when I was a self-confident young curate in the first parish to which I was appointed, there was a little boy at the convent school who used to be brought out to sing and recite for the

10. *Dated 9 Feb 1915 and among Father Hartigan's papers.*
11. Daily News, *Albury, 13 July 1910.*

entertainment of visitors. He rose to something like fame among his small contemporaries who called him 'The Joker', and predicted a big career for him. It was then that I came into the picture. I 'trained' him for the local Eisteddfod. Machinely crammed with ten verses or so of a hard-luck story, he faced the adjudicator, and lost hopelessly, but fairly. Unknown to me, and uncoached by me, he had entered himself for other sections at the same competitions, all of which he won. I bore him no malice, and he proved very useful to me later on, in certain activities in which I was engaged. I was always assured of hearty applause whenever I introduced 'The Joker'.

Many things have happened since then, and Mr Byrne has become well known on concert platforms throughout the southern part of the State. He is sui generis *and harassed committees of St Patrick's Night Concerts have felt their worries fall away when they were fortunate enough to be able to place his name on their programmes. I have been among his delighted audiences, and have been much relieved to find that he has quite lived down the effects of his early training.*

To me it was a great pleasure to know that he will feature verses from 'Around the Boree Log'. He brings to the interpretation of these a sentiment—both Australian and Irish—which renders him singularly suitable for the work. I have heard him 'do' them many times, and must confess that he makes them appear new and fresh—even to me, their perpetrator.

'Joker' went to great trouble to get his rendering just right. On one occasion he confessed, that somehow his 'Said Hanrahan' did not click. Next time he met Father Hartigan, he was beaming. He had come across a 'cove' some miles out of town who was just the prototype he wanted. He proceeded to recite the piece, but stopped half-way. It still wasn't right. Off he went again to the old fellow and next time his rendition satisfied him—he had learnt to bend his leg at just the right angle.

Father Hartigan always remained in close touch with 'Joker' Byrne and wrote poems for his recitations. As a patient at Lewisham Hospital he composed this one for Joker's recitation in the Brisbane parish of Annerley (better known as Ipswich Road) then in the charge of his friend Father (later Monsignor) Jim Kelly.

Father Hartigan with John Byrne, 'The Joker', who became famous for his recitations of 'John O'Brien's' poems.

Good-Bye And God Be Wid Ye

I'll be off along the road now, so a fond good night I'll bid ye
Too long I've kep ye talkin and the fire is burning low:-
Good-bye now; good-bye now and the grace of God be wid ye;
May the blessed angels keep you safe wherever ye may go.
Och, 'twas good to have ye round me while we lived the old days over,
Though 'twas only for a little time it made me young again;
And I thank ye; Yes I thank ye; and to-night you'll hear the rover
With his friese coat wrapped around him mebbe, singing in the rain.

Good-bye now and God bless ye for the stout hearts in ye swelling
The grass is just as green, me boys, as when the world was young,
There are stories just as stirring, only waiting for the telling;
There are just as hearty songs to sing as ever yet were sung.
Good-bye, and God be wid ye where'er your paths may lie now
What way they lead, if rough or smooth no mortal man can know,
May the holy angels keep you safe; good bye now, good bye now
And the grace of God be wid ye wherever you may go.

He appended this note to the poem:

> *Dear Joker, How does above suit you? If I had flu for a month I'd give you*
> *enough stuff for six programs. Have the other finished and will send it to*
> *Ipswich Road. My love to Father Kelly.*[12]

During the thirties 'Joker' Byrne was at his peak, giving numerous recitals of the poems in New South Wales, Queensland and Victoria. In 1932 he gave a recital at St Columba's College, Springwood, and I can still remember the tremendous success it was. One of the students, Mick Henry of Toowoomba, wrote his impressions of 'Joker' in the **Manly** of 1933:

> *Before Joker began, we knew and loved, 'Around the Boree Log' but*
> *when he finished, we exulted in the possession of a newly*
> *discovered treasure.*
>   *Mr Byrne is too well known to need the feeble tribute of our*
> *praise, but we venture to say that as a humorist, a reciter, and an*
> *entertainer his equal will not easily be found.*
>   *Father Hartigan has placed before us a picture of early pioneers,*
> *living, moving, full of vivid colour and intense feeling. He is the*
> *faithful chronicler of our country's past, the poet-laureate of the*

---

12. *From a scrap-book among Father Hartigan's papers.*

*Irish-Australian people, singing their sorrows and hardships, their
glories, joys and triumphs. We see the noble, white-haired Father Pat
among his flock. We hear the hoof beats of Currajong, the little Irish
Mother says the 'trimmins', the old Mass Shandrydan rattles and
bumps along, the careful, solemn Josephine, the Pillar of the
Church, the Caseys, the Careys, become familiar to us, and when
we close the book we remember them as if they had been our life-
long associates.*

*And so they are. 'John O'Brien' has copied directly from nature,
from life. He knows the same Australian bush that we know. The
Irish-Australian generation that he has painted is not so remote that
we do not know it also. Every parish can show the characters which
he has drawn, the Pillar of the Church, Josephine, the Sugarloaf
O'Briens and 'Father Pat'.*

*Our poet is a master of the art of telling a short tale in verse. The
liveliness of the narrative, the swinging rhythm and the long line of
Australian ballad poetry, engage the attention at once, delight the
ear, and win the affection. The humour, the sentiment, the homely
phrase, and deep feeling, and above all the characters, remind us of
the ballad poetry of old Ireland. It is indeed Ireland transplanted to
Australia. The piety, the simple faith, the humour are Irish but the
flowers, the trees, the birds, the bush, the whole surroundings are
Australian and from the happy blending of the power and energy of
the youthful Australian spirit with that of the ancient traditions,
customs and religion of Ireland, we have the Irish-Australian, a type
distinct among the peoples of the earth.*

*We can appreciate the poet's meaning by a perusal of the book,
but all grew intensely real when Mr Byrne became by turn each of
the prominent characters. At times we were close to tears, at others
we could not control our laughter, but we were all sorry when the
recital was over, and we were brought back to earth again.*

*That spirit of optimism and generosity which pervades the pages
of 'Around the Boree Log' seems to be passing away with the years.
Just in time our poet caught it.*[13]

In Father Hartigan's last months in Albury he was engaged in
controversy in the columns of the **Catholic Press.** It came about in this
way; King Edward VII died on 7 May 1910 and next day Father Hartigan
made reference to him in his Sunday sermon:

13. Manly 4, 2, 1933, pp. 188—9.

While the flags of the world are half-mast high, and a whole nation is mourning his loss, our sorrow for the good man gone is as deep as that of any of his subjects. He was not a Catholic; but he belonged to the ampler church of those who believe their lives are right. He was the outstanding figure in the mission of peace and toleration. There was a time when the title King stood for aggression, and petty authority inhumanely maintained. Our King was greater in that he knew that a man is most manly and a King most Kingly when he understands that others have rights as sacred as his own; and in this he has placed a shining jewel in England's crown. While other nations are simmering with strife and intoleration, peaceful England stands with a finger raised in warning. When that ceases to be, we will understand what Edward VII meant to the world. But now that he has gone to be judged like the meanest of his subjects, we hope that the part he played, apparently so well, has found favour in the eyes of Him to whom we are all but players in life's drama. He discriminates not, we know, between him who plays the King and him who plays the peasant. All he asks is that the work he gave us to do has been faithfully done. We trust our Sovereign's part has pleased Him well, and that now—

Beyond the loom of the last lone star, through open darkness hurled,
Further than rebel comet dared or hiving star-swarm swirled,
Sits he with those that praise our God for that they served His World.[14]

A reporter of a Sydney paper happened to be at Mass at Albury and on his return home wrote an account of the sermon for his paper. The **Catholic Press** of 2 June 1910 contained the following letter:

Sir—Kindly allow me to draw attention to what the morning paper called a 'noteworthy' utterance of the Rev. Father Hartigan of Albury. Speaking of the king's death, Father Hartigan is reported to have said that the king was not a Catholic but belonged 'to the ampler Church of those who believe their lives are right'.
I would like to know.
(a) Is there any Church more 'ample' than the Catholic Church to which the King did not belong?
(b) Do those who believe their lives are right constitute a Church?
(c) Taking into account the Catholic teaching on the 'soul' of the Church,

14. Daily News *Albury, 9 May 1910.*

is the above 'noteworthy' utterance one that recommends itself to the Catholic instinct?

> *Yours, etc,*
> *AN OLD PRIEST*

Father Hartigan replied in the next issue:

> *Sir—If I can be forgiven for asking you to waste more space on the trifling troubles of 'An Old Priest', I would say:*
> *(a) Is there any Church more ample than the Catholic Church to which the King did not belong? Yes, the Catholic Church to which the King did belong.*
> *(b) Do those who believe their lives are right constitute a Church? Who said they do? They who do not belong to the 'body' of the Church, but who believe their lives are right belong to the 'soul' of the Church, which is thereby 'ampler' than the 'body' of the Church to which they do not belong.*
> *(c) Taking into account the Catholic teaching on the 'soul' of the Church, is the above noteworthy utterance one that recommends itself to the Catholic instinct?*
> *   If the notion of the 'soul' of the Church is sound Catholic teaching, it should not be offensive to the genuine Catholic instinct.*
> > *Yours etc,*
> > *P.J. HARTIGAN*
> *St Patrick's Albury.*

The issue of 16 June contained a reply from 'An Old Priest' which is too long to give here. The last paragraph is worth recording:

> *Your esteemed correspondent is welcome to his little joke in twitting me on my 'trifling' troubles. An old man, I suppose, takes sometimes too strong a view of the eccentricities in speech and manners of those who are young and inexperienced. But I confess that if Father Hartigan's ideas of Catholicism were prevalent amongst our young clergy, I should fear very much for the honour of the flag that we old fellows are handing on to them. His utterance was subversive of Catholic teaching, and it owed its notoriety to the fact that it rang false, that it swerved from the 'sound form of words'.*
> > *AN OLD PRIEST*

Then into the fray, for one foray only, came 'A Voice from the Bush'. He comments on Father Hartigan's statement that they who believe their lives are right belong to the 'soul' of the Church:

> What varied and wild interpretations are daily put upon such and similar inaccurate statements. How many thousands, whose souls are festering with mortal sin, shelter themselves under assertions like the above, from the person who rejects God and hell, to the individual who believes 'to do no harm to nobody' a sufficient passport to heaven.

The following issue had Father Hartigan's reply, and 'An Old Priest' came back again in the issue of 30 June. Both of these letters, unfortunately, were of a length to preclude their reproduction here, but we can gather their tone from the opening paragraph of the last letter:

> Sir—Father Hartigan's last letter generates more heat than light. He prances through two and a half columns of your journal, wasting energy on irrelevant matters, and not once does he seriously undertake to justify his 'ampler Church' reference. Let me say here, for clearness' sake, that I am solely concerned with the propriety of his public utterances. What his real mind was when he spoke, is no concern of mine. I presume that he meant well. But the innocence of the heart is not always accompanied by prudence of the lips and my point is that his words as reported are unjustified, and cannot be reconciled with Catholic dogma.[15]

Who was 'An Old Priest'? It was rumoured at the time it was Father Patrick Sheehy of the staff of St Patrick's College, Manly.

Father Thomas Hayden, watching the controversy from the sidelines, was reported as saying: 'The boy's right'.

---

15. The above summary account of this controversy has already appeared in Australasian Catholic Record LI, 1, 1974, pp. 65-7, and is reproduced here with permission.

4 Inspector of Schools

In 1910 Bishop Gallagher wrote this letter[1] to Father Hartigan:

> West Wyalong
> Sunday
> March 13, 1910
>
> Dear Father Hartigan,
>   I saw Father O'Riordan on last Friday—on my return from Lismore—at Lewisham Hospital. He is very much better and has the assurance of being restored to perfect health. But the Doctors tell him and his own opinion seems to coincide with that of the Doctors that he should not continue his present occupation of 'Inspector of Schools'. Hence in pursuance of the conversation I had with you in Albury, I feel certain that we must call upon you to take up the position as soon as we can get someone to fill your place in Albury—probably not before the 1st August. This would, however, give you ample time to get into a certain mastery of details, by visiting infant and parochial schools in Albury, by a review of Father O'Riordan's books and method of doing work so as to preserve a certain continuity, by perhaps receiving (if not entering) quarterly returns etc. At present I can do nothing from want of Priests. But the interval might enable you to get into line and touch with the Inspectoral work so as to pay a visit to most of the schools between August and December. I am not without hope of seeing you personally soon after Easter and considering further details. Meantime, I am, Dear Father Hartigan, with best wishes of the Holy Easter season.
>
> Yours sincerely,
> † John Gallagher
>
> Rev. P. Hartigan
> Albury.

The appointment took place in July and it meant that Father Hartigan was to leave the Albury presbytery and make his base at the orphanage of the Sisters of Mercy at Thurgoona (known also as Newtown) on the outskirts of Albury and say Sunday Mass for the residents of the locality.

It was the accepted practice that the inspector of schools would live in a small house there which had been built for Father Patrick Dunne. He

---

1. *Amongst Father Hartigan's papers.*

was, as we have already noted, first president of St Patrick's College, Goulburn, and had earlier been a pioneer initiator of Catholic schools in Victoria and of Irish immigration in Queensland. In his retirement he continued to wield the pen in newspaper controversies on many subjects of moment.

As Father Hartigan was about to leave the parish of Albury, the mayor, Alderman Daniel, presided at a meeting to arrange a farewell for him:

> It was generally agreed that Father Hartigan's work in Albury warranted public recognition, high tributes being paid to his sterling personal qualities and his unostentatious parish labours. It was especially emphasised that he had earned the respect and admiration of all denominations in the town. The Mayor had a letter from Father Hartigan saying he did not desire anything whatsoever, but he had also received letters from prominent townspeople of various denominations expressing a wish to show their appreciation of this reverend gentleman.[2]

Meanwhile on the following evening 120 members and supporters of the Catholic Young Men's Society gathered with the bishop and several priests to farewell Father Hartigan. The bishop was most complimentary, telling how it was his wish that the places of the pioneer priests should be filled by the 'sons of the soil'. He pointed out that as he spoke he was flanked by two such, Fathers Joe Dwyer and Hartigan, and it was a proud moment for him:

> Father Hartigan was the first priest to be born in the diocese, educated almost entirely in the diocese and ordained a priest to minister in the diocese.

He expressed the hope that in his onerous duties in his new post Father Hartigan would achieve such results as they were so proud of that night.[3]

The farewell social given by the townspeople took place in the Mechanics' Hall on 28 July. Canon Bevan:

> had never heard a more beautiful speech than their guest had given on the occasion of the Empire Day gathering when he was called on to propose the toast of "The Ladies". The beautiful sentiments he had given expression to profoundly impressed all on that occasion.[4]

2. Daily News, *Albury, 12 July 1910.*
3. Daily News, *13 July 1910.*
4. Daily News, *29 July 1910.*

Mr V. Flood Nagle, secretary of the committee, read an address in which he said:

> *as men and women representing all denominations, we are only too glad on behalf of all in this town who have the pleasure of your acquaintance, or have noted your influence for the good on this community . . . by no people can you be held in higher respect or warmer affection than by your old fellow citizens—men, women and children in Albury.*

Father Hartigan was given a purse of seventy sovereigns, a travelling bag and a writing desk. In his speech of thanks he made feeling reference to Father Dwyer, his pastor:

> *who knew him as a boy and to whom he owed obligations too sacred to be mentioned, and with whom the happy relations that always existed would, he hoped, long continue.[5]*

Father Hartigan left Albury by train on the Saturday evening, 30 June, and went to Goulburn to begin his work inspecting schools.

A report was issued at the end of each inspection, and this one is at the Convent of Mercy, Yass:

> *St Augustine's Boys' School, Yass. Examined 13th-15th June 1911.*
> *The marking shows that the school is keeping well up to the high standard of last year. Further care, however, might be bestowed with profit on the arithmetic of all classes; written and mental work should be arranged with a view to make the pupils ready and accurate.*
> *Too much praise cannot be given to the healthy tone of the school and the splendid discipline of the boys, and it is to be hoped that they will be taught in the future, as they have been, to be confident and enthusiastic without being disrespectful.*
> *P.J. Hartigan.*

Sister M. Annette Herbert of the Sisters of Our Lady of the Sacred Heart, forty years a missioner in Papua New Guinea, wrote a beautiful letter to Father Hartigan during his final illness in Lewisham Hospital in which she told him how much his kindness had helped her when he was

---

5. *Ibid.*

inspector of schools. Her letter gave Father Hartigan great joy. I wrote later to tell her this and asked her to jot down her impressions of him as an inspector.

The year may have been 1914 and I was in 3rd Grade of St Patrick's Primary School at Boorowa. Sister Bernard Shine was my beloved teacher. There were times when she put the fear of God into me, but she planted the seed of the love of God in my young heart. Sister was preparing us for a visit of the School Inspector, Rev. Father Hartigan. We had met him the previous year, so his visit did not hold any fears for the young scamps of our vintage. We loved him, and counted the days until the date of his visit.

We were lectured the day before the visit of the Mighty Inspector to wear our best uniforms; make sure we had groomed finger nails etc; 'GREEN BOWS' on our respective heads of hair, and 'mind ye manners above all'. My dad was not Irish, anything but—my Mum was a daughter of Johanna McInerney from County Clare. I was on Dad's side of the fence.

'I'm dashed if I will wear a green bow, I'll wear a yellow one'. My mother's voice prevailed as it always did when Ireland versus England was the subject of debate in my childhood home. We children all turned up wearing all that we were told, even to the green bow on hair. We marched into class as the tall, smiling Father Hartigan stood and watched us. Sister Bernard's eye, from over his shoulder keeping a dark and meaning glance on us. We didn't murder 'Swanee River', but we sang 'God save Ireland' as we tramped around the floor.[6]

Soon Father went to work on each class from 1st to 5th, giving each class an essay to write, nobody was to copy, or the 'goblins'll get yer' so Father said, matching his threat with a fearful frown, but not being able to hide from a group of smart little pairs of eyes, that heavenly smile that played around the corners of his mouth, even if he had his pipe in his mouth. We didn't copy for various reasons, although five different classes were hard at it, pens scratching across paper as we wrote our essays on whatever the given subject was. I loved writing essays. Some of the kids hated them. One of the supervisors went round and collected the various finished articles

6. *This is an example of the way in which in Father Hartigan's early years as a priest, the faith and Ireland were always linked together. 'No people', he once said, 'had Irish Patriotism so foisted on them as did the first generations of the Australian Catholics, and no people reacted to strongly against it'. Father Hartigan's own respect for Ireland and her traditions was a spontaneous growth and owed little to this outside pressure.*

from each class; while Rev. Father was giving Maths., etc., to other classes. He had a way with him, he never wasted time, he could keep five grades at work all simultaneously, without much effort.

The Inspector approached 3rd standard for maths. One heart began to skip a few beats, MATHS, ye gods!!! My sworn enemy!! What scoldings etc. were drawn down on my poor head over those maths. I was often called a dunce, a numskull etc., over the answers which would not just tally with what the class usually 'got'. Ah well!! We can't be good at all subjects, but our Inspector didn't say so. He was a real toughie on maths. Either you could do 'ye sums' or you couldn't and if you couldn't, I mean to say!!! Firstly it was oral arithmetic, fast and hard, then written sums. Not a correct answer did I give to either oral or written, and the hot tears were being squeezed back by little knuckles when Father wasn't looking. I knew I was 'done for', I nearly lost hope in the world, in my world anyhow.

Examinations were over, then there was a little impromptu concert. Every child in our class had to give an item. I plucked up all the courage I could muster and when it came my turn I jumped from my seat, held my head high, I had Irish blood coursing in my veins from the McInerneys of County Clare. I'd show 'em! I looked at Father, and the glorious smile of fatherly kindness and encouragement did the trick as I met his gentle gaze. It brought all the 'bit o'Irish' that was in me, to the surface. I started off the song, and well off the note at that:

> *Ireland, I love you, Acushla Machree*
> *And though your shores I may never more see,*
> *Always will you be remembered by me,*
> *Ireland, I love you—Acushla Machree.*

I finished two verses, getting more out of tune with each note. I looked up at Father Hartigan, he beckoned me to him, and stood me between his knees. He took my trembling little hands in his big, mighty fatherly hands, as gentle as a mother, and he said, 'You are a very good little girl, tell Sister Bernard you may be "Put Up"'.

Oh Thank you Father!!! I whispered breathlessly, and raced off to find the said Sister Bernard. 'Sister!!! Sister!!! Father said you can put me up.' Sister smiled knowingly and said in her dear Irish brogue:—'Sure and we will put ye up the chimney'.

We had a week's holiday, and I returned to school breathlessly approaching Sister Bernard who said, 'You are not in my class anymore, didn't Father Hartigan put ye up'. My day was made!

His travelling around the diocese of Goulburn was done largely by train—cold and uncomfortable often enough and waiting for him in the presbytery was the 'spare bed'—which was at times a rough affair! True, he was given a warm welcome by the parish priest—the inspector of schools was thought to be an invaluable means of picking up news in one part of the diocese and cross-pollinating another part. He told the story of the old parish priest who greeted him: 'Wait till I fill my pipe so that I can enjoy the scandal'. It was during his time as inspector that he took up smoking. He felt it put his host at his ease. At first he used a pipe, then later cigarettes. He rolled his own with a little gadget that almost became part of him.

Some of his poems were composed as he made his train journeys. One such was 'Imelda May', the story of an orphan girl befriended by the pastor, then going off to the city and marrying without any reference to him. Many were curious to know who she was. So often, however, a poet is started off on a train of thought by an incident or a person. The resultant poem may be only tenuously linked with the original starting point.

Thus on one occasion at the Bishop's House at Goulburn as Father Hartigan was about to set out on an examining tour he happened to answer the door to a girl seeking the help of a priest. She was engaged to a doctor in Sydney and was worried about a rumour concerning him. It so happened that Father Hartigan was able to reassure her—the doctor had first done some years in the Manly seminary with him and he knew him as a sterling character. The girl thanked him and a happy and lasting marriage ensued.

Father Hartigan caught the train to Junee and before he got there he had finished 'Imelda May'. From the incident of the girl who had sought advice he composed his poem about the orphaned girl who did not come back to consult the priest:

> *I thought you'd come ere the die was cast,*
> *But your voice was dumb and the days went past;*
> *I thought you'd come with your troubling doubt*
> *From your garish world whence they shut me out.*
> *For they made a jest in the social glee*
> *At the old man back at the presbytery:*
> *He was out of date and his thoughts were odd,*
> *And dull and damp were the paths he trod;*
> *Still I thought you'd come that the word I gave*
> *Would not charge me false from your mother's grave.*

Father Hartigan with Father Tom King in the Renault he bought in 1911.
'She never had no side-doors, and she never had no screen, Such things
were not invented when they built that old machine.'

> *But there it is in the news today,*
> *God grant you did right, Imelda May.* [7]

A short experience of fitting into inconvenient train timetables was enough to convince Father Hartigan that there must be better means of doing his travelling. He had already ventured into the motor world with his bike from Fred Blacklock. Early in 1911 he went to Sydney and at Davies & Fehon's, Hunter Street, he put a deposit on a second-hand 8 hp Renault. Next day when he came to pick it up there was an auction sale in progress and through somebody's mistake they were about to offer his Renault. He paid what was necessary to get possession and took it away.

He was terrified at driving it in the city with his previous experience confined to a motor bike in Albury; he tried to honk everything out of his way, even the trams.

In those days there was a garage at Goulburn and one at Albury—in many places the pioneer motorist went to the blacksmith to see what he could do. There were no bowsers, petrol was carried in 18 litre tins. The Renault had no windscreen and no side doors, which latter fact, on one occasion, was a blessing; a snake on the road was thrown up the sloping bonnet and landed at Father Hartigan's feet. Quick smart he put both feet up on the dashboard, and the snake went out one of the side openings. According to the maker's instructions, the Renault would do 45 kilometres an hour—if really pushed hard, 48, but this speed was 'not recommended'.

Father Hartigan used to claim he was the second priest in New South Wales to own a car, having been preceded by Father Patsy Kenny of Pambula. Father Hartigan enjoyed the fact that for many people in outback places his was the first car they had seen, so that the 'Ten-Twelve Shebang' was really autobiographical:

> *She never had no side-doors, and she never had no screen,*
> *Such things were not invented when they built that old machine...*
>
> *The first car in the district, lad; You should have seen the fuss*
> *The evening Charlie hit the town a-driving that there bus!*
> *You should have seen the mob go mad! You should have heard the noise:*
> *The tootin horn, the wild delight of all the dogs and boys ...*
>
> *The first car in the district, yes, and still left in the hunt,*
> *Three figures on her number-plate and bucket seats in front.* [8]

---

7. The Parish of St Mel's, *Angus & Robertson, Sydney, 1954, p.9.*
8. *Ibid.,* pp. 58-63. This poem was published first in the Bulletin *8 December 1923 and reprinted in its centenary issue, 29 January 1980.*

Frank Clune and Miles Franklin with Father Hartigan during a visit to Narrandera in 1936.

During these years as inspector he was writing verse and sending it to various papers. In December 1914 he sent to the Sydney **Catholic Press:** 'In Memoriam: Josephine—the Priest's Housekeeper', and signed it 'A Country Priest'. The following month saw 'The Little Irish Mother' in the same paper and both received enthusiastic welcomes.

He had now abandoned the pen-name Mary Ann[9] and he told us himself how he came to take 'John O'Brien':

By this time, I had changed my pen-name to 'John O'Brien'. It came about this way. I was in a town, the name of which I won't mention, when I saw going by a milk-cart owned by a man with a reputation for selling adulterated milk. The name on the cart was John O'Brien. Adulterated milk, I thought, that's me! So 'John O'Brien' it was from that time forward.[10]

The editor of the **Catholic Press** wrote enthusiastically:

At dinner we gave Father O'Reilly he spoke of the new poet 'John O'Brien' whose 'Josephine' was talked about in the Irish presbyteries and Father Whyte in his speech said O'B. was better than 'Banjo' Patterson [sic].[11]

'The Little Irish Mother' was followed a couple of months later by this poem:

9. *Miles Franklin, according to her biographer Marjorie Barnard, used the pen-name Mary Anne in writing to the Bulletin in the first years of the century.*
   When the series of novels under the name 'Brent of Bin Bin' began to appear from 1928 onwards there were all kinds of guesses at the identity of the author. Father Hartigan told me that they had even been attributed to him—but he denied categorically any link with them. It is now agreed that they were the work of Miles Franklin. Did the similarity of early pen-names play any part in the attribution of authorship to 'John O'Brien', the erstwhile 'Mary Ann'?
   Frank Clune in his Journey to Canberra, published in 1960 by Angus & Robertson, had a photo (opposite p.226) of Miles and 'John O'Brien' taken with himself on the verandah of the Narrandera presbytery, and on p.240 he told of his wife and himself taking Miles on trips with them and says: 'Wherever we went, we called on people who knew of her, Fr Hartigan ("John O'Brien") at Narrandera'.
10. *From Jim Kelleher's interview with Father Hartigan published in* The Catholic Weekly, *22 May 1952, p.10.*
11. *Letter of 11 October 1915 among Father Hartigan's papers. Father Maurice O'Reilly had just been brought back from Ireland to become Rector of St John's College, University of Sydney; Father James Whyte was Inspector of Schools of the Archdiocese of Sydney, and was later to be Bishop of Dunedin, New Zealand.*

The Angel at the Gate

I can see them from the hill-top where I've builded my retreat
Where I've come world-tried and beaten with the stone-bruise on my feet
Whence I gaze along the pathways of the sun-lit vale below
To the gateway in the distance where the teaming millions go.
And I see above the arches Sorrow's Stalwart Angel stand
Regretful, yet relentless, with a sword clasped in his hand,
And he guards that iron portal where the world's wide ways converge
And the blood is on the pebbles where the wildered pilgrims surge.
They are thronging up the valley—from a hundred ways they throng
And they know nought of tomorrow, I can hear their laugh and song.
Yet they smile and are glad-hearted, but for them the sword-stabs wait
And they step into the shadows when they blunder through the gate.
Thence they go with white-drawn faces stagg'ring on beneath the load
Strangers to the songs of boyhood that were theirs along the road;
Bearing in their arms the corpses, touched by Death's chill hand too soon
Of golden hopes of morning turned to ashen gray at noon
Feeling in their breasts a numbness where a live heart used to beat
I can see them from the hill-top where I've builded my retreat.
I can see them coming, coming with no shade upon the brow
With a dance and a lilting chorus, o'er the nodding daisies now.
I can see them going, going, I can hear the stifled cry
Like a wailing wind at midnight blowing sobs across the sky.
Saddened lives athirst for sunshine and the best that earth can give
That have gathered at the gateway to be martyred and to live
Till the stony way is ended and another gate appears
And a kind, blackhooded angel leads them from the vale of tears.[12]

He was active on the local literary scene also. A 'Shilling Fund' had been started in the **Daily News** to buy comforts for the soldiers. On 8 July Father Hartigan wrote commending this and donating five guineas, and on 10 July he contributed this piece:

A Soldier's Mother—Half-a-Crown
Written for the 'Daily News'

And there came a certain poor widow and she cast in two mites, a farthing,
And calling his disciples together, He said to them: Amen I say to you, this
poor widow hath cast in more than all who have cast into the treasury.
For they all did cast in of their abundance, but she, of her want
cast in all she had, even her whole living.

---

12. Catholic Press, 12 March 1915.

Her face was seamed with lines of care
  That maiden smile and blush destroy,
But all unconscious lingered there
  The pride of him—her soldier boy.
A thin grey tress once burnished gold
  Stole out beneath her bonnet's rim,
And tired eyes the story told
  Of tears and sleepless nights for him.
A-weary were the days, and long—
  And every hour she counted o'er—
Since last she harked his homing song
  And heard his footsteps round her door
And by her lonely lamp she read
  Each night the list that grew and grew,
And pondered o'er the 'Hurt and dead',
  To find the name of one she knew.
And thankful that she found it not,
  Sweet pity clutched her kindly heart,
That pain and want should be the lot
  Of those who played the soldier's part.
Who stood in grim red battle there,
  And of their best so nobly gave,
That no Australian mother e'er
  Should rock the cradle of a slave.
She plodded through the rain and mist,
  That clung about her faded gown,
To place upon 'the shilling list'
  Her little savings—half-a-crown.
She halted at the office-door,
  And shyly faltered, half in dread,
'I wish that I could make it more,
  But times are pretty bad', she said,
'Much harder since he went away
  His earnings kept the house, you know,
I'm dragging on as best I may:—
  Of course, 'twas right for him to go.
Yes, God has kept him safe so far,
  He breaketh not the bruised stem,
Though he's not hurt there's some that are,
  Just put this trifle down for them'.
'The giver's name'? a smile astray
  Illumed that sad face lined and brown,
'Oh, names don't matter much. Just say:
  'A Soldier's Mother—Half-a-crown'.
Outside the sumptuous motor sped
  And Dives nestled carelessly,
No son of his his blood has shed
  For Hearth and Home and Liberty.
He gives 'donations' here and there,
  And in the giving seeks renown,

But how shall his few pounds compare
With that much-needed half-a-crown?
Of old stood One beside the door
And read the deeds of men aright
He marked no rich man there, but saw
The helpless widow give her mite.
And He who blessed the kindliness
That cast the farthings in that day
Stood somewhere by the door to bless
The Soldier's mother on her way.
She sought her lonely home again,
To fret for him—her boy—apart;
But somehow felt, despite the pain,
A something singing in her heart.
And Dives' 'generous' deed is told
At crowded meetings up the town;
But angels' hands have writ in gold
'A Soldier's Mother—Half-a-crown'.

In the same period he wrote another war piece for the **Daily News:** 'Ownerless' appeared on 28 October 1915; with a couple of verses rewritten it was included in **Around the Boree Log;** others of that time, 'The Unsung Heroes' and 'The Boy That's at the War', remain among his papers. Of the same vintage is 'Walking Home', a reverie after farewelling a son off to the war. It appeared in **Around the Boree Log** as 'Making Home', after a daughter's marriage.

During these years he had a close association with the Mangans who ran the **Daily News,** as this letter of James Mangan indicates:

'Daily News' Office, Albury
March 14, 1916

My Dear Father Hartigan,

I was forcibly reminded of you this afternoon—by two incidents—(1) I unearthed 'To Mystery' while cleaning up some scraps under my blotting pad and (2) by reading of the death of Stephen Phillips, the poet-playwright in an English Clarion just to hand. Do you remember bringing under my notice 'Marpessa'? It is quite a number of years ago now. We were yarning on the tennis court at the back of the church when you 'came to light' with The Insane farewell repeated o'er and o'er, . . etc. I never forgot it, as between ourselves I know something of the 'Insanity' of the business!

Poor Stephen Phillips, I have read, died in penury just as Mozart did. Have you read 'Paolo and Francesca'? In his latter days the author of that and of 'Marpessa' was hawking poems round London at five shillings a piece! 'The hard lines of Phillip's life warped his genius', says one writer, 'and finally at the age of 51, after beating the spiritual life out of him they beat the actual life out of him'. They! *'Who are these poeticides'? asks a* Clarion *writer.* They *means, we hard, callous, rotten world, which gives Jack Johnson £29,000 to fight Jess Willard—I saw the fight on cinema last night, by the way—and permits the wolf to howl round the death-bed of a great poet. It* hurts, when you think of it. *If Phillips had sold oil, or soap, or even 'plate mender', or put sand in sugar he would probably have had a motor car and died in luxury, but he was only a Poet—only a genius who could make others feel that life was worthwhile—and precious England let him die a pauper. 'They' beat the actual life out of him—who could write words like these*

> *What is the love of men that women seek it?*
> *In its beginnings pale with cruelty,*
> *But having sipped of beauty, negligent,*
> *And full of languor and distaste; for they,*
> *Seeking that perfect face beyond the world,*
> *Approach in vision earthly*
> *And touch, and at the shadows flee away.* [13]

The company of such people was stimulating to him in his writing. His years as a curate were not greatly occupied with social activities—in his library the number of books with an Albury bookseller's mark suggests one who devoted a great deal of time to literary pursuits. His view was that for writing one needs to be close to stimulating folk, to be able to go to them when the mood dictates, and just as easily to be able to retire again to write. He made valuable friendships while in the parish of Albury and renewed these during his time as inspector when he had Thurgoona as his base.

It was during these years that he wrote a novel, **Australian Born.** He showed it to his brother Frank who replied with a two-page letter, damning it with faint praise. He later turned to historical writing and there his fine delineation of character, his ability to make the past live again, his humour and his sympathy were all revealed in talented prose.

In a class of its own is his beautiful story of his drive to the Australian Alps to minister to Riley, 'The Man from Snowy River'. Though it appeared later, it belongs to his time as inspector. It contains what we might call a 'position paper' on his views on Australian poetry. He had moved somewhat from his stand in his 1906 article when he made a plea for the recognition of Australian literature. Now he is more openly critical of the Australian writers who slavishly imitated English models and he comes down very heavily in favour of Paterson and Lawson. And

---

13. *Letter among Father Hartigan's papers.*

that was to be his firm view thenceforward, and it comes through very clearly in an interview which, in his last years, he gave **The Catholic Weekly.**[14]

The Man from Snowy River

It is now many years since I first followed him on that wonderful ride 'Through the stringy barks and saplings', and I haven't forgotten how he thrilled me.

When I was a lad at old St Patrick's Goulburn, one of the masters varied the monotonous round by reading to us selections from Banjo's book, which had just been published. Nothing in literature had ever affected me more; I had committed my only successful burglary. Creeping up to that good master's room when the coast was clear, and the lights were low, I 'pinched' the book to reward him for his kindness. I read and re-read it from cover to cover—surreptitiously in the study hall, and with open delight during the recreation hour—I dreamt of it, and without effort committed the whole of it to memory;[15] and then—to put the facts fairly—I replaced the volume where I had found it.

Though fond of verse as a child, I love my country more than poetry; and up to that time I had come across nothing worth while in the matter of Australian Colour. How I yearned for it! At the point of the bayonet I had been driven through 'Sweet Auburn, loveliest village of the plain', and revelled in it; still there was something which jarred.

'And parting summer's lingering bloom delayed'. I could not understand why 'parting summer' should be regretted. Its 'bloom' did not 'linger' as far as I knew. Then again portions of Gray's wonderful Elegy might have been done better:

'The lowing herd winds slowly o'er the lea'.

It is not sufficiently clear if these were the milkers feeding home,

14. *8 May and 22 May 1952. The 15 May issue repeats this story of his visit to Riley on the Australian Alps.*

15. *Father Hartigan often quoted Alexander Pope's description of himself as a youngster: 'I lisped in numbers and the numbers came'. 'John O'Brien' also found 'numbers' easy, verse came to him effortlessly. Moreover, he had to hear a poem only once and he could repeat it. Pixie O'Harris, the talented artist of the walls of the children's wards of our hospitals, once met him in Vaucluse and at his request recited one of her poems. He rang up next day and repeated it to her.*

or a draft of Jimmie Kidman's being overlanded to Homebush.
Similarly many another good thing was found wanting because of its
lack of local colour:—

> 'I come from haunts of coot and hern,
>   I make a sudden sally,
> And sparkle out among the fern,
>   To bicker down a valley'.

I had no first-hand knowledge of this kind of thing, and had to
take the word of someone else for the truth of it. Certainly there
were some 'coots' among my acquaintances, but they were not fit
subjects for poetry. The nearest I had got to the real thing so far was
a volume of verses entitled Musings in Maoriland, the treasured
property of a New Zealand student at Manly, since promoted to the
Episcopacy. 'Dunedin from The Bay' was fine; 'Old Bendigo' was
great; but after all I knew nothing of Dunedin, and did not care to
concede too much in those prejudiced days. Nevertheless for want of
a better idol, I secretly placed Thomas Bracken in the vacant niche
in the Temple of the Beautiful.[16]
Even the Australian writers, whom I had met, just missed the
intangible something which I was seeking. There were some
volumes of Kendall in the library. Very sweet, I thought them, but—

> 'The soft white feet of afternoon
> Are on the shining meads,
> The breeze is as a pleasant tune
> Amongst the happy reeds'.

To me that was a bit of quiet English scenery such as I had seen in
pictures. It reminded me of nothing with which I was familiar.
Kendall seldom saw with Australian eyes. He would have written
better poetry had he been born in the old world. Every Australian
worthy of the name quoted Gordon in those days, but here again was
the same old trouble—

---

16. In the interview published in The Catholic Weekly, 8 May 1952, 'John O'Brien' has this interesting
note about Thomas Bracken: 'He is probably best known for his poem "Not Understood" but few
people today know the story of how that poem came to be written. Bracken was the outstanding
literary figure in New Zealand and was strongly favoured for the editorship of the New Zealand
Tablet, published in Dunedin by the Catholic bishop, Dr Moran. But rumours were circulated
that Bracken was a Freemason, which if true, would put him out of the running for the editorship
of a Catholic paper. At a meeting called to consider the position, the bishop asked Bracken
straightout if the rumours were true. Bracken was so offended by the question that he refused to
answer and, of course, lost the job he dearly wanted. In a bitter reflective mood he wrote: "Not
Understood"!.'

'A gentleman rider—well, I'm an outsider,
But if he's a gent who the mischief's a jock!'

That was foreign. 'The Sick Stockrider', however, came nearly up to standard—

'Ah! those days and nights we squandered at the Logans' in the glen'

I had never known anyone who lived in a 'glen', still I was prepared to give 'The Logans' a certificate. The last verse was right—

'Let me slumber in the hollow where the wattle blossoms wave'

And the whole piece was 'highly commended'.
   There was at Manly at the time I speak of, a student who had literary leanings, and a memory second only to that of Macaulay. This disciple would sit on the old Tarpeian Rock, and inspired by the ocean, would recite with a loving lilt—

'It was when we held our races, hurdles, sprints, steeple-chases
Up at Gundaroo'

This epic left nothing wanting as far as local colour went, and some of its noble lines, notably 'Buck in Gundaroo' have passed into the language. From another poem in his vast repertoire—a pastoral—let me cull this gem—

'And he spent the time, he told me, earning tucker, bed and booze
Up at Tumba-blanky-rumba shooting kanga-blanky-roos'.

If there were any fault here it was that the local colour was laid on too thick. That pioneer in the field of Australian literature is now an honoured priest in the Archdiocese of Sydney, living in a district which must always be associated with the beginnings of what has grown to be the biggest and most scientific sheep-breeding industry in the world. In his maturer and more dignified years he loudly disclaims all knowledge of his early activities; but the handmaiden Truth bids me set it down with a fearless pen, even to his confusion.
   It was in this state of mind-hunger that I met The Man From Snowy River and Other Verses. Therein was what I had been waiting for. It intoxicated me. Much of this was due to the fact that I knew intimately the scenes and some of the persons of whom Banjo wrote. Banjo's father was manager of Bendenine, not far from the sleepy

town where I was reared. The Patersons' home was afterwards the first convent in Binalong. I had gone to school with scions of the Kileys and the Conroys. I had passed the bushranger's grave, where 'There's never a stone at the sleeper's head'.

There is a rough stone there now, but that is away from the point. I had heard the story of Gilbert and Johnnie Dunn from the lips of people who had known them; and my native town owned with something of a swagger that it was the birth-place of the latter. Also I had been on Kiley's run; and had heard the old hands tell, in their own weird way, the tragedy of Conroy's Gap: How Kate Conroy, a kindly young woman, moved by charity, had given the swagman work on the place; and how that swagman—Tommy Mundy—had a quarrel with Jack Conroy, and coolly sharpened his axe at the grindstone during the whole of one afternoon, and that night slaughtered the family, his benefactress included, the only one who escaped being the man whom he set out to kill. But apart from all this, here for the first time were the sweet eyes of my country smiling at me from the printed page. I too, had seen 'the vision splendid of the sunlit plains extended', and many a time, in a vague, non-committal way, I had longed 'to take a turn at droving where the seasons come and go'. I knew well the mentality of the old man who feared the country towns might send his letter wrong; but

'. . . five and twenty thousand head can scarcely go astray
You write to "Care of Conroy's sheep along the Castlereagh".'

Round it all was the true atmosphere of the Bush:

'The roving breezes come and go, the reed beds sweep and sway,
The sleepy river murmurs low, and loiters on its way,
It is the land o' lots of time along the Castlereagh'

Who would compare for Australian colour 'The soft white feet of afternoon are on the shining meads' with that, or with this—

'And far away one dimly sees
Beyond the stretch of forest trees—
Beyond the foothills dusk and dun—
The ranges sleeping in the sun
. . . On Kiley's Run'

And then

'The Man from Snowy River never shifted in his seat,
It was grand to see that mountain horseman ride'

No doubt it was. It was also grand to read about it. I had never been
on 'the hills' nevertheless I got the picture right: it could not be
mistaken—

'And down by Kosciusko, where the pine-clad ridges raise
    Their torn and rugged battlements on high,
Where the air is clear as crystal, and the white stars fairly blaze
    At midnight in the cold and frosty sky'.

Long years afterwards when the things of which I write were only
a memory, and Banjo's verses but an echo, I saw those 'torn and
rugged battlements' standing between me and what I had to do.
Word had come through to Albury that an old man named Riley was
dying at Bringenbrong, on the Upper Murray, and was calling for a
priest. I was not then attached to the parish, but had a motor car on
the premises, and the Adm. was a white man.
    'Go along with you' he said coaxingly, 'it would take one of us a
fortnight to get there and back with a horse; and it would cost a
fortune to hire a car'.
    The distance was well over the century mark, and so was the
temperature. Cars were by no means numerous at the time, nor
were they noted for reliability. Mine was a little twin-cylinder
Renault of eight horse power or thereabouts, a diminutive thing
'with a touch of Timor pony', but as 'hard and tough and wiry' as
that other pony which ran in the wild mob single-handed. For a
companion I picked the joker of the parish. The Joker would be
useful in many ways. As a gate-opener he proved to be as good as
any one else; as a mechanic in time of engine trouble he was an
annoyance; but as an entertainer he was inimitable. On the journey
up he was ballast merely, for I carried The Viaticum.
    We arrived at Jingellic—sixty miles on the way—at dusk. After tea
I prepared to go on, and deeming it prudent to disregard The Joker in
favour of someone more familiar with the road and with bushcraft, I
approached several of the young men in a manner known as
'wording' them. 'You won't get through tonight' was the
discomfiting assurance given by each. Selecting one of them as my
victim, I put the matter bluntly,
    'Will you come with me?'
    'Yes, I'll go; but you won't get through', he drawled.
    'I have good lights', I rejoined.

He smiled.

'Have you ever been there?' I asked:

'Yes, two or three times, but there's no road after you go up a bit, and if you miss the track you'll fall for a week'. This was not reassuring.

'Do you know a man at Bringenbrong named Riley?' I asked by way of varying the attack.

'Yes, there is a cove of that name up in those parts' he answered.

'Well, he's dying, and I must see him tonight', I said crushingly.

'You'll see him all the sooner, if you wait till daylight', he replied with annoying coolness. 'Mind, I'll go with you if you like, but you won't get through', he added with fine Australian indifference.

Now, when a bushman tells you that you won't get through, the position is serious. If you have to cross a swollen creek wherein the current will sweep your wardrobe out of the sulky, he will tell you that 'it's not too bad'; if he knows that the water will be over your horse's back, he will warn you that 'it's not too good'; if you have a mountain before you which will necessitate your tying a tree on to the back of your trap to keep it from dashing headlong, he will admit that 'it's a bit rough'; but when he tells you without any qualification that 'you won't get through'; believe him.

The situation was a worrying one. Here was a sick man who might not last till morning, and furthermore I had with me the Blessed Sacrament and how could I keep the King of Kings in a pub for the night! I knew what the rubric and the theologies had to say on the point, and once again I yearned for Australian colour. The theologians knew nothing of it. I made an act of adoration, and reverently hung my waistcoat on a nail behind the door. When I thought it out I had no compunction; for after all, what is a sanctuary lamp? What are gold and silk? What is ornate cathedral shrine: What is the greatest honour man can show in return for 'The living Throne, the sapphire-blaze, where Angels tremble while they gaze'. It is a big step down from Heaven to the best this earth can give; from the earth's best to its meanest is not far in the eyes of Him Whom I carried. He was born in a stable 'because there was no room for them in the inn'. The inn at Bethlehem: the pub at Jingellic. It seems almost blasphemy to mention them together: the one so tender and inviting, the other so rough and sordid. Still perhaps the difference is only in the local colour.

At daybreak we were ready for another start. 'On the table a meal for sleepy men' after which The Joker and I set out along the road which winds around the hills, and between the hills, and over the

*hills to The Upper Murray. Sometimes we were on the river's level,
at other times we saw it a tiny thread of silver hundreds of feet
below. Here was the setting of the famous ride, here were the
'stringy barks and saplings' and 'the gorges deep and black', and 'the
cliffs and crags that beetled overhead'. Up the steep gradients the
little eight-nine struggled all out on low gear; down the almost
perpendicular descents she felt her way, still in low gear and with
the grease frying on her red-hot brakes. Past Ournie; past Tooma;
past Towong; out upon the Bringenbrong flats at last covered with
tender trefoil and clover such as plains know in early spring. Mobs
of fine cattle being topped for the market stared in stupid wonder at
the extraordinary vehicle which swung into their solitude.*

*'All good colours' remarked The Joker, though he knew not what
he said. A splendid lot of young thoroughbreds raced after us and
circled round us. Real gentlemen are these Upper Murray horses,
perhaps the only surviving representatives of what we used to call
the 'Australian stockhorse' in the old days. Sons of Snowden and
Panic blood; 'the sort that could race and stay with their mighty
limbs and their length of rein'. They flourished throughout the land
once upon a time; they live still in song and story of daring deeds
and long, long rides through the night when such as 'Johnson
brought the doctor to his wife at Talbragar'.*

*On we sped as fast as the little bus could pace it, and soon the
roofs of Bringenbrong came in sight. This was the head of the
Murray. Two streams—The Indi and The Swamp Plain Creek or The
Tom Groggin—meet just below the homestead and thence they call
it The Murray. What a pity they did not leave it as the blacks had it,
or name it The Hume.*

*I enquired at the station for the dying man Riley, but they had
never heard of him. However, they informed us that if we went
along to a man who lived 'on a bit' we might get some information.*

'How far on?' was the question.

'About five miles', the answer.

*The man 'on a bit' had heard that someone was sick 'up the road'
but he did not get any 'particulars'. Anyway, they would surely
know at Khancoban.*

'How far is that?'

'They call it twelve miles.'

*H'm—five and twelve are seventeen. Twice seventeen thirty-four.
Thirty-four added miles, there and back—rough, steep, stony
miles—in the mountains. Still there was nothing else to do but face
them.*

'Now could you put me on the road?'
'Well, there you have me,' he replied with a suitable gesture of
perplexity. 'There's no road, that is to say not what you'd call a
road, but you'll pick up the tracks of the station dray if you keep a
sharp look-out'.
At Khancoban they had never heard of Riley, but at a house
further on etc.,
'How far is this house?'
'A matter of six miles'.
Six and six—another twelve. Has anyone here seen Riley? Well,
no; they couldn't say 'as they had'; but there is a sick man up at
Hickeys', and that might be 'him'—an old man, so they had heard.
'And how far is Hickeys?'
'A matter' of eight miles this time. As I wound up the little car
hoping to find at last the man I sought, my informant remarked:
'If he's not at Hickeys' youse can come back.'
'Of course, we can; but why do you say so?'
'Because you won't go no further.'
'But I shall go further', I replied. 'I shall go on till I find the dying
man who sent for me'.
'Well, you won't go no further up that way', he assured me.
'Hickeys' is the last house on the track; he's only a mile and a half
from the Gehi Wall'.
'But supposing I cross the Gehi Wall, what then?' I queried. He
smiled indulgently at my poor humour or my great ignorance, as the
case might be.
'Did you ever hear tell of Jack Cox of Mangoplah?' he asked.
I had.
'Well, he sent some sheep up here in the drought. They had a
sulky with provisions, and coming down the Gehi Wall, it started to
push the horse before it in spite of everything; so a big "pommy"
they had with them reckoned he could hold it. They took the horse
out, and the big bloke tried to wheel the trap like a wheelbarrow. It
got away from him, and they haven't found it since'. 'Do me',
murmured The Joker with conviction.
It was evident we were coming to the end of the track. The hills
before us rose boldly and more boldly still, and range seemed piled
on range. One peak was pointed out to us as 'Kossy'. Fourteen miles
away as the crow flies, but it would take two days to reach it with
pack and saddle. Kosciusko can be approached readily enough from
Monaro, but on the Victorian side it is extremely rough, and can be
reached only by long and hazardous detours. Parties of tourists make

the ascent from time to time, and their starting point is the house which we were nearing.

We found Riley at Hickeys'—a little old man who had battled out his life in 'the hills'. He was a guide on the mountains, and had not left it for two score years. His hut was at The Tom Groggin, and his mates had carried him on a pack-horse for forty miles through that almost impassable country, so that he might be within reach of the priest and the doctor. The busy world was outside his orbit altogether. He had never been in a train, had never seen a motor-car and knew very little of his religion. 'It's not much in my line', he informed me.

At least he had the Faith, and wanted to see the priest before he went over the mountain for the last time. He was so reverent about it all, and so anxious to do 'the right thing', that it was a privilege to have been chosen to gather in that sheep which had missed the mustering so long.

It being too late in the afternoon to begin the long, rough journey homewards, I was glad to accept the invitation and the advice 'to stop the night and get away first thing in the morning'. It was kindly meant. Although midsummer, the cold was intense. They lit a fire and what appeared to be a tree was set as a back log in a fireplace as deep and as wide as a room. Big, awkward, intelligent fellows gathered in as they do in the Bush when sickness comes. How often have I seen it! They loiter round and sit on the fence or circle about the fire in the kitchen, where they talk of all things but of what brought them there. They can do no good, they know, still they wait on 'so's to be handy if anything turns up'. Give me the bushmen and their ways. They have no conventions; they have only traditions. Around the kitchen fire anything is the right thing to do provided it is decent; and even under the shadow of trouble and sickness every topic of conversation is legitimate provided it is not 'a bit over the odds'. That night we had a rare meeting. For a time the 'evening' did not go. The priest was the trouble, but here I played The Joker. He sang, recited, and told funny stories and soon we were Australians All. Then we talked of their lives, and of 'the mountain' of which they spoke with awe—of the dangers of it, of the lure of it, of the mists that rise without warning to blanket out the world, and a lost man camps for the night on the brink of Eternity. We spoke of the wild horses. Yes, there were still some on The Pilot. Good sorts too; wasn't Snowden loose for a time on 'the hills!' Too right he was. Didn't Morgan the bushranger 'lift' him from the Bowlers, and when hard pressed let him go with the clean-skins.

It was time for another 'item' and I had something up my sleeve that would stagger them. My elocution was not the best, but it would surely pass in that company, the local colour at least would win through. So, uninvited and self-announced I rose and 'gave them' 'The Man From Snowy River'.

They bore it with patience, and when I had finished there was neither applause nor disapproval. Each man smoked in silence, and 'spat across the cat'. Sportsman-like The Joker commended his rival. The gloom was heavy and disquieting, and to dispel it—also to elicit some opinion on the merits (if any) of the effort, I remarked:

'It was somewhere up here that The Man From Snowy River did that ride, wasn't it?'
'That's him inside', said one of the company.
'Who? Where?'
'The old cove you came up to see.'
'What, Riley?'
'Yes, he ran in that colt, and up till he got sick the other day, no one could hold him down the mountain. Go in and have a yarn with him.'

Before leaving in the morning, I had 'a yarn' with the Man from Snowy River, and was astonished to find that he was by no means pleased with Banjo's version of the story.

'We often had to do that sort of thing, and had tougher "goes" than that', he said deprecatingly. 'I was taking a party up to Kossy, and was telling them about it, and one of them put it in a book; and he brings in the names of a lot of men who weren't there at all. There was nobody named Clancy; there was me and So-and-so and So-and-so.'

I have forgotten the names, but would have written them down, had I thought then of writing up the incident. I had confirmation of the facts when Riley died. Paragraphs appeared in most of the papers stating his identity. And Marie E.J. Pitt wrote some verses to a Sydney journal entitled 'When the Man From Snowy River Went Away'.

That was a few years after my visit. The old man recovered from the illness which brought me to his bedside and went back to 'the mountain'. The trouble recurring, his mates put him on the pack-horse and started on the long, rough track of forty miles once more.

103

*What men these bushmen are! Prepared to undertake a two-days'
journey like that, holding a sick man in the saddle, 'through the
stringy barks and saplings on the rough and broken ground';
undeterred by the tortuous climb and the more dangerous descent;
undismayed by their helplessness and their nothingness in the sight
of the awful, heartless tyranny of 'the mountain'.*

*He died on the track, and there, beaten at last where he once rode
to fame, The Man From Snowy River Went Away.*[17]

Jack Riley was born in 1834 at Castlebar, County Mayo, Ireland, and
migrated to Sydney in 1851. He went to Omeo, a Victorian goldfield
town, and set up a tailoring business to support his widowed sister. He
gave up his business to join the stockmen and hunt wild horses
(brumbies) in the Australian Alps. He returned to the tailoring business
from time to time but when his sister remarried in 1860 he closed his
shop for ever. By 1880 he ranked high among the best brumby hunters.

In 1890 Andrew Barton (Banjo) Paterson camped at Riley's hut and
drew from him the story of the epic ride. Paterson was enthralled and on
26 April 1892 'The Man from Snowy River' appeared in the **Bulletin.**
Allowing for poetic licence, it was Riley's yarn.

Father Hartigan's trip to give the last Sacraments to Riley took place in
1911. The old man recovered and went back to the mountains. Three
years later an Alpine guide, Bill Findley, heard that Riley again was
dangerously ill and he went with Alick and Jack McInnes and Bob Butler
to help the old man.

*The party reached the hut on July 12, but teeming rain held them
there till 9.30 am on the 14th. As Riley was too ill to ride, they put
him on a crude stretcher of saplings and blankets and carried him
down the rough track to Mt Hermit. Now facing a 2,000 foot climb
up the rough Hermit track, Findley knew that Riley would have to
ride. Butler slid back behind his saddle, then the others heaved the
sick man up in front of him. With Butler's arms around Riley, the
McInnes brothers took post on either side of the horse to steady the
patient in the rough, jolting ride. Half way up a near blizzard hit
them but somehow they kept going until they reached the summit
which was deep in snow and battered by a howling gale. There they
floundered across the ridge, then slithered down the far slope to the
shelter of the Murray Valley. When they lifted Riley from the horse*

to put him on the stretcher, he groaned a protest, for he wanted to die, if he must, in the saddle. Having pacified him, the party trudged on to a deserted hut at the Surveyor's Creek outfall. They had travelled only 12 miles and the worst of the journey through the long, tortuous steep-sided Indi Gorge lay ahead of them. Using saddles, the rescuers propped Riley up on a bank, then began yarning about Jack Riley and his famous ride. When the pannikins had been drained and the fire stirred, Riley's head lolled sideways. An era had quietly ended. Many years later the local shire council erected a headstone over his grave in the Corryong cemetery with the inscription: 'In Memory of The Man from Snowy River, Jack Riley, Buried Here 16th July, 1914'.[18]

Turning back now to Father Hartigan, the years brought him their share of family joys and griefs. In his early time at Albury it became evident that his eldest sister, Jane (Sister M. Michael), was a victim of tuberculosis, a common scourge of those times. It was his sad task to assist at her brave death in 1911.

His parents had moved to Summer Hill, Sydney. They were not well off financially and Father Hartigan gave what help he could. Moreover, deafness was an increasing affliction for them.

His brother Frank was ordained in Goulburn on 20 July 1913 and the Albury **Daily News** had this report:

Father P. Hartigan preached an eloquent sermon on the priesthood which greatly impressed and affected the immense congregation.[19]

In October 1913 Father Frank celebrated his first marriage, that of his beloved sister Annie to Dick Mecham of Lewisham, and Father Pat assisted him at the Nuptial Mass in St Thomas' Church there.

In September 1914 Father Pat was in Lewisham Hospital with pneumonia. In the following January he had a short holiday in Tasmania, possibly suggested to restore his health. It is worth mentioning that, through the years, he did not go away for holidays on a regular basis. He had priest friends in every part of Australia and New Zealand who had shared his student days at Manly. They often asked him to come and spend some time with them. He was, however, a shy man and unless

18. The details about Jack Riley's origins are taken with permission from an anonymous historical article in the Sydney Daily Mirror 19 June 1967, and the above account of his last illness comes verbatim from that same source.
19. 21 July 1913. Father Arthur Percy was ordained with Father Frank and years afterwards recalled that sermon. See p. 195.

definite arrangements were made, he would never write and suggest that he take up their invitation.

Nor did Father Hartigan have a regular day off each week. He never took up golf as did some of his contemporaries among the clergy, and he was not a regular card player. His exercise in his middle and later years was gardening, and he always had a beautiful display of flowers in the grounds around St Mel's Church, Narrandera.

5 Parish Priest of Berrigan

Father Hartigan's name was among the clerical changes at the beginning of 1916. He was appointed to Berrigan, a parochial district which had been in existence for twenty years. It covered a strip of territory along the Murray west of Corowa, and it included Tocumwal, at that time the township farthest west in the diocese of Goulburn, almost five hundred kilometres from the cathedral city. The **Daily News** made mention of the transfer and paid this tribute:

Apart from his great natural gifts and intellectual attainments, Father Hartigan is a keen educationalist with no stereotyped views regarding the training of the young, and the effects of his labours are likely to be felt for years to come.

The duties of the position of Inspector of Schools are strenuous, yet Father Hartigan was able to find time for a good deal of literary work of a very high standard. Some of his poems published in the press during the past year or so rank among the best inspired by the various aspects of the Great War.[1]

He took up his new post in March 1916. It is understandable that after almost six years of the work of inspector of schools he was anxious to settle down in a place of his own to do pastoral work for which he was ordained. However it was not easy for him to make the transition from the larger centres and the variety of his previous work to the quiet of Berrigan. For a while each time he came out of his presbytery he was dismayed to see just how tiny the town really was. Ever afterwards he was sympathetic to young priests who were senior curates with responsible work in centres like Goulburn, Albury or Wagga and then suddenly found themselves in charge of their first parish, a handful of people miles from anywhere.

In Father Hartigan's case, writing—to a lesser extent, sketching also—occupied him and part of **Around the Boree Log** had its origin in Berrigan. Not many of the poems can be tied to a definite event, but he readily acknowledged the inspiration of 'The Old Mass Shandrydan'.

---

1. Daily News, *Albury, 17 February 1916.*

The parish records at Berrigan show that Rev P. Moloney M.S.C. did a baptism there on 3 October 1916 and it is noted alongside the entry in the baptismal register that he was conducting a mission in the parish. His sermon on the Mass began with a vivid story of the family preparations for Mass Sunday, then the dawn rise, the long drive, the rivalry among the neighbours, the reverence for the priest. Father Hartigan was captivated by the tale and back in the presbytery afterwards he told the missioner: 'Thanks, Paddy, for the story. I would have given a ''tenner'' for it, and now I have it free'.

'The Old Mass Shandrydan' appeared first in the **Catholic Press** and among the early letters of appreciation was one from Father Arthur Vaughan of the parish of Kensington in the Melbourne archdiocese:

My Dear Pat,

I write to congratulate you on, and to thank you for 'The Old Mass Shandrydan'. The tears came from my eyes when I read it just now for about the fifth time. It brought back to me very vividly the Sunday mornings of the now long ago, when a Little Irish Mother bustled round in getting all the young Vaughans ready for Mass. Yes, Pat, the stage has changed—the world is . . . less enchanting, but I feel that your heart, like my own, I hope, has still the same deep, reverent feeling for our Irish parents, to whom we owe so much, as when you viewed the world 'O'er the tailboard of the old Mass Shandry-dan'.

By gum, you pictured the old man great—getting into a stiff white shirt and

'like a Bolshevik, athirst for human blood,
All a-tearing and ''a-wrastlin' '' with a fractious collar-stud'[2]

And I was right up alongside him on the driver's seat of the old bus on the way to Mass, enjoying to my heart's content the old man blocking them all. And every now and then I could see him lifting his hat to some old bachelor who was riding—per saddle—to Mass and thus could pass him—lifting his hat, just because he had his Sunday togs on. A tilt of the old head would do any other day.

Write us some more soon, Pat. 'Josephine', 'The Trimmings on the Rosary'—all you've given us are good . . .

I think an epic could be written on the annual Catholic Sports Meeting —the reunion of friends, the shy lads and lasses in their best 'rigouts'—the

---

2. Fr Vaughan is quoting this line from the version published in the Catholic Press, 22 August 1918. It was changed slightly when published in Around the Boree Log.

old pots getting their nags ready for the 'Farmers buggy race', the alarm clocks and scented soap to be won by the cane rings, the preparatory slaughter of turkeys, geese etc by the women for their refreshment booth etc etc. Why man, Virgil had nothing better. Get to it!

Bring out a book, Pat. Put me down for a dozen copies.

Your old friend and admirer,

Arthur Vaughan

P.S. I gave out the Shandry-dan etc at a big gathering of priests the other day—a tremendous reception 'Who is John O'Brien?' etc.[3]

When **Around the Boree Log** was published in 1921 it contained 'The Old Mass Shandrydan'. Father Hartigan sent one of the first copies of the book to Paddy Moloney with the inscription on the flyleaf: 'To the Suggestator from the Perpetrator'.

Father Moloney was renowned down the years for his 'musical stick'—his invention of a stick with prongs for striking chords as an aid to learning the piano—and also for his recitations of 'John O'Brien's' poems. His version of 'The Old Mass Shandrydan' always told of a crowd of Moloneys (not O'Briens) being roused for Mass or hurled out of their seats when the hat came off for His Reverence. He stoutly maintained he had the author's permission for this change of text.

Father Hartigan got the word 'Shandrydan' from his father—he told the story to Jim Kelleher:

[My father] was a born story-teller and could recite old Irish poems by the hour. He had an Irishman's love of a good horse and was inordinately proud of the turn-out in which he drove his family around the district. Anything else he met—and passed—on the road he referred to contemptuously as 'a shandrydan'. He invariably pronounced it 'shan-dradhan', Webster's dictionary notwithstanding.[4]

Years afterwards when Father Hartigan used the word in his poem, he accepted Webster's spelling. He regretted later that he had given in on the point. Because of this, his father's version was used where the word occurs in 'The One-Ton Truck', one of the poems in the collection **The Parish of St Mel's.**

Berrigan is remembered particularly as the locale for another of the poems, 'The Parting Rosary'. In the August of the year that Father

3. *Letter among Father Hartigan's papers.*
4. *Interview published in* The Catholic Weekly, *8 May 1952.*

Hartigan spent in Berrigan news came through of the death of Edward Powell on active service in France. It may well have been Father Hartigan's sad task on this occasion, as certainly it was on others, to break the news to the family. He would have heard from Mrs Powell the details of the lad's leaving for overseas not long before, and of the party the townsfolk gave. This was described by Sister Bernadette Watson, P.B.V.M.:

I like to remember that I was at the little home that night, excited to be part of the music-making, proud of being at a grown-up function, but too young to sense the sadness, the unspoken loneliness, that underlay the laughter and the goodwill speeches.

At last the good-byes were said, and the house was quiet again. Kneeling in the tiny parlour, with reminders of the party all around them, old Mrs Powell and her soldier son said one last rosary together—a 'parting rosary' in every sense, for Ted never came back. One more young life cut short—one more heart-broken mother.

The poignant lines of the poem still have the power to move us today, who live in a world ever at war.[5]

Sister Bernadette has a lovely tribute to Father Pat. Speaking of an American religious, Sister Madeleva, an authoress who formed lasting friendships with poets and writers, she had this to say:

Madeleva knew too many poets [to be able to acknowledge her indebtedness to them all] but did she ever have a poet for her parish priest? I think not. I did, though, long years ago in Berrigan. He was Father Pat Hartigan, a tall, handsome priest with an artist's gift of words.

I remember my mother's delight in his weekly sermons, the simple talks that were part of evening Benediction, with Sister Patrick, earnest and anxious at the organ and old Mrs Powell, round and rubicund, often conductor and choir in one ...

Father Hartigan would have remembered Sister Patrick as he remembered old Mrs Powell, for when 'The Boree Log' was published it was clear that he had not forgotten the little town that had once been his parish.[6]

During his time in Berrigan 'Joker' Byrne visited him from Albury. In

5. Embrace the Past with Remembrance, *Summit Press, Canberra, 1975, p.118.*
6. *Ibid., p.117. Mrs Powell was, of course, the mother in 'The Parting Rosary'.*

the course of conversation 'Joker' quoted a few lines of verse. 'Those are not bad, Joker,' said Father Hartigan, 'where did you get them?' Joker then reminded him of an evening in the presbytery at Albury when Father Hartigan had read out some verses he had written that afternoon, then crumpled them up and threw them into the fire. Joker quickly reclaimed them with the request that he might keep them. Though submitted to Angus & Robertson for inclusion in **Around the Boree Log,** they were among those omitted by the publisher. When in later years **The Parish of St Mel's** was being planned, Father Hartigan chose not to include these verses.

Keep Pushing Your Own Little Barrow

In the journey of life, midst the din and the strife
When the roadway is crooked and narrow
Each man in the throng that is jostling along
Is pushing his own little barrow.

The people you meet as you're walking the street
May stop just to wish you 'Good morrow',
But onward they go—be they high, be they low—
A-pushing their own little barrow.

The learned K.C. and the stylist M.P.
Profess to be 'straight as an arrow'
With talk they beguile and they meet you and smile
A-pushing their own little barrow.

The philanthropist too and the socialist who
Discovers the evils that harrow,
But feather their nest; the same as the rest,
They're pushing their own little barrow.

And the moral is plain: all waiting in vain
Your own little field you must harrow
Do all you can and be always a man
Keep pushing your own little barrow.

Put doubt on the shelf and depend on yourself:
(In that lie the pith and the marrow)
And come, yes you will, to the top of the hill
By pushing your own little barrow.[7]

7. *From a written copy in Father Hartigan's handwriting.*

111

Father Hartigan's last Sunday in Berrigan was 25 February 1917. In the following few days he did his packing, and then set out on the Thursday for Narrandera, where there was a reception that evening to welcome him. He now had his second car, a T-model Ford, known familiarly as a Tin Lizzie.

The Renault had served him well and eventually he had sold it to Father William Cahill, for many years administrator of the Goulburn Cathedral.[8] Father Cahill was an immense man and **Smith's Weekly** at the time facetiously remarked that Goulburn would win fame for having 'the biggest priest driving the smallest car in the world'.[9] When the Renault's useful life was finished at last, its remains lay for many years in a corner of the cathedral presbytery yard.

Reflecting that Father Hartigan spent only one year at Berrigan we may wonder what influenced him to move on so soon. In fact, about the same time he was interested in the parish of Gunning, which was eventually given to Father Frank Carson. Gunning, close to Goulburn and Yass and no great distance from his aging parents in Sydney, would obviously have been more attractive than the distant parishes of the Riverina.

It is understandable that Father Hartigan settled better at Narrandera than at Berrigan. Naturally it required time to make the adjustment from the variety and movement of his life as inspector of schools to the less eventful existence in a parish. When he got to Narrandera he was ready to settle.

Furthermore, Narrandera was his own choice—he was parish priest there with the stability afforded by that position. In Berrigan he was priest-in-charge, appointed there by the bishop. He had probably indicated to the bishop that he would like to be relieved of the position of inspector of schools. He may have been influenced in this by the attack of pneumonia he had suffered earlier and his consciousness of the difficulty of avoiding colds when travelling so much. Once he had made his request, it was the decision of the bishop as to when and where he would go.

In Berrigan he followed his younger brother Frank, curate there for nearly two years. Part of Frank's work in Berrigan parish was looking after Tocumwal. The convent school there presented him with a beautiful illuminated address:

---

8. *He it was who said once to Mollie Sullivan of Gundagai, a cousin of Father Hartigan and a boarder at O.L.M.C., 'Mollie, you're Irish!' 'No,' said she, 'I'm Australian'. 'Would you be a horse if you were born in a stable!' was Father Bill's rejoinder.*

   Mollie remembers Father Hartigan's deep love of Australia and it is epitomised for her in the story he told how once he went to a pharmacist for tooth paste. The man was apologetic because it wasn't British-made. 'It's not much good,' he said, 'it's Australian'. 'I'll take it', said Father Hartigan, 'even though it rots my teeth'.
9. *Quoted in J. Kelleher's article on 'John O'Brien',* The Catholic Weekly, *8 May 1952.*

*We feel sure that much as you will be missed by the grown-up
people of Tocumwal, none will feel your departure more keenly than
your little friends at the Convent School to whom you have endeared
yourself so much since you came to the Parish. You not only
interested yourself in our spiritual, but also our temporal welfare, as
shown by the many hours you spent in the School, and the lively
interest you always took in our advancement. We shall indeed miss
your visits to which we always looked forward with pleasure, and
we shall long and gratefully remember the many thoughtful acts of
kindness, by which you so often contributed to our happiness.*[10]

All reports indicate that there was tremendous love for Frank
everywhere in the parish of Berrigan. Did Pat find it difficult to live up to
the expectations he found there? Interested in books, writing and
educational matters, did he take some time to adjust to parochial life?
The natural warmth of Frank was apparent from the beginnings of his
work as a priest. The tremendous respect and love that lives on still for
Father Pat in Narrandera may well have been of slower growth.

The year 1916 was a momentous one in the modern history of Ireland
and it had its repercussions in Australia.[11] The Irish-Australians had
expected a peaceful granting of Home Rule for Ireland. When instead
Irishmen, aided by Germany, staged the Easter rebellion of April 1916,
the first reaction of Irish sympathisers in Australia was one of
condemnation.

However, the mood here quickly changed when the English executed
the rebels, imposed martial law and carried out mass arrests. All this
brutality contrasted starkly with the lenient treatment given the Ulster
Unionists who also were known to have used German aid. Many Irish-
Australians then began to see loyalty to Ireland, or loyalty to the Empire,
as a choice that had to be made.

In mid-July the government closed Lutheran schools, and Dr Daniel
Mannix, then Coadjutor Archbishop of Melbourne, warned that a similar
fate might overtake Catholic schools on the plea that they were disloyal.
In July 1916 the Orange Lodge called for Dr Mannix's deportation.

On 30 August 1916 Prime Minister William Hughes announced a
referendum on conscription. Dr Mannix came out strongly in opposition.
Its defeat occasioned a second referendum twelve months later which
was even more decisively rejected.

---

10. *Among Father Hartigan's papers.*
11. *See Patrick O'Farrell*, The Catholic Church and Community in Australia, *Nelson, Sydney, 1977
pp. 321-9.*

Father Hartigan had friends among ardent Irish priests such as Dr Maurice O'Reilly and Dr Patrick Tuomey. The latter was an early member of the Irish National Association who was quite prepared to defend it against his archbishop, Dr Michael Kelly. Banished from Sydney to the bush of Mittagong-Bowral, Tuomey was undeterred in his fight and as late as December 1918 was fined for encouraging disloyalty to the British Empire.

However, despite such friendships, Father Hartigan did not come out on the conscription issue. It was as if he stood on the sidelines in a detached sort of way, aware of the arguments of both sides. He was deeply concerned that Australia be saved and he spoke and wrote for this end. He left to others to work at the means necessary. Pondering his allegiance to Ireland and Australia, he began his reflections with the Irish:

Never yet were men more loyal to the holy ties that bind them,
And the love they gave their country made me conscious of my own.

He went on to develop his thoughts as an Australian:

An Australian, ay, Australian—oh, the word is music to me,
And the craven who'd deny her would I spurn beneath my feet.
Thrills the thought that, did the traitor stretch a tainted hand to foil her,
Did I see her flag of silver stars a tattered thing and torn,
Did I see her trampled, breathless, neath the shod heel of the spoiler,
And her bleeding wounds a byword, and her name a thing of scorn.
There would flash the living bayonets in the strong hands of my brothers,
And the blood that coursed for nationhood through all the years of pain,
In the veins of patriot fathers and of Little Irish Mothers
Would be hot as hissing lava streams to thrill the world again. [12]

Few have struck a better balance between love of Australia and respect for the Irish heritage: perhaps few were better able to ride out those stormy times with their struggles between the conscriptionists—among whom were numbered the Irish-born archbishops of Perth and Hobart—and the anti-conscriptionists led by the colourful Dr Mannix who succeeded to the see of Melbourne in 1917. After the war the Archbishop travelled through America to a hero's welcome from the Irish and, refused permission to land in Ireland, was taken off his ship outside Cork, brought to Penzance on a British destroyer and forbidden to speak at the main centres of Irish population in England.

12. 'St Patrick's Day', in Around the Boree Log, Angus & Robertson, Sydney, 1921.

6 Early Years at Narrandera

In 1829 Charles Sturt's successful journey down the Murrumbidgee River and his favourable report on the country he saw caused pastoralists to move west from stations around Gundagai. The first to come was Edward Flood who arrived in 1848 and took up 310 square kilometres which he named Narrandera Station. Early there was a punt across the Murrumbidgee at this spot and settlers from the Lachlan and Macquarie districts recognised this as an important crossing.

After the passing of Sir John Robertson's Land Act of 1861 selectors were attracted to the district and many took up conditional purchases. In later years, when some of the lands of the station holders reverted to the Crown and were made available for settlement, and also when some of the stations were subdivided, settlers from Victoria and South Australia and from other parts of New South Wales were attracted to the district.

In 1859 Surveyor Edward Twynam completed a survey for the village in the vicinity of the punt, and the town and the suburban lands were proclaimed on 28 April 1863, East Street being farthest east in the survey. Since that time the town has developed northwards and eastwards from the original area.[1]

In those early years the Catholics around Narrandera were cared for by Father Patrick Bermingham, parish priest of Wagga from 1874. He said Mass regularly at Gillenbah on the south side of the river and the people on the Narrandera side came over on a punt.[2]

Father Hartigan in **The Men of '38** tells us of another stage, the building of the first church in Narrandera:

Father Bermingham had secured a site[3] which was afterwards very valuable. [He began the building of St Brigid's] and was well ahead with the funds collected, but exercised no supervision over the tradesman to whom the building was entrusted. When the walls, for which progress payment had been duly made, were finished, the

---

1. *These facts have been gathered from the* Narrandera Centenary Publication, *1963. The double-letter spelling of the name of the town was not always used, e.g. in the early years the present local paper was the* Narandera Argus.
2. *Mr Peter Sullivan, speaking at the welcome to Father Hartigan in 1917, recalled the time when Mass was said every three months in a public house and a billiard room.* Narandera Argus, *2 March 1917.*
3. *Near the present post office.*

*whole outfit was discovered to be unsound and had to be pulled
down. The builder decamped by moonlight, and as no security had
been asked of him, the money was gone. By the end of 1882 the
episcopal patience, of which Dr Lanigan had no superabundant store,
was exhausted . . . In December Dr Bermingham was removed from
Wagga and sent to Corowa.*[4]

In 1884 Narrandera was made into a separate parish and to it was
attached the town of Jerilderie. The incumbent was Father Michael
Slattery who had already pioneered the parishes of Crookwell (1876),
Corowa (1878) and Temora (1881). His was the responsibility of
restarting the star-crossed St Brigid's Church.

Father Michael Slattery and John Gallagher (afterwards the bishop)
were the first to volunteer for the diocese of Goulburn after Dr Lanigan
had been appointed to it in 1867, and they were the first two priests
ordained for the diocese, the ordination being done at Maynooth by Dr
Lanigan in 1869.

It was during Father Slattery's time at Corowa that the Kelly gang
stuck up the bank at Jerilderie, a town at the time looked after by the
priests at Corowa. It was in February 1879 and Father Hartigan tells the
story:

*When the Kelly gang dashed across the Victorian border and stuck
up Jerilderie, they arrived on Saturday, 9 February, and the next day
was Mass Sunday. As a preliminary to the big business to be
transacted on the following Monday, they made things safe for
themselves by locking up the two local police, Sergeant Devine and
Constable Richards, in the cells, imprisoning the household in the
residence, donning uniforms, and allaying suspicion by posing as
special officers sent up on investigations connected with the
bushrangers.*

*Mass was said at Jerilderie in those days in the Court House—St
Joseph's Church, the foundation of which had been laid on 13
October 1878, was unfinished. Mrs Devine used to prepare the altar,
etc., and among her many protests against being locked up in her
own house, she complained that there was no one else to make the
preparations for the coming of the priest. 'What priest is coming?'
asked Ned Kelly, and on being told that it would be Fr Kiely, he sent
brother Dan along to help with the pious work and, of course, to*

4. The Men of '38 and other Pioneer Priests, *Lowden Publishing, Kilmore, Vic., 1975, pp. 222-3.*

escort the good woman back safely. The bushranger worked with a will; he swept the room, arranged the forms, and pushed into position the contraption which served for an altar, but Mrs Devine was forced to leave a note untruthfully informing Father Kiely that the family would be out of town on the Sunday, and would he be good enough to go up to the Royal Hotel for his breakfast. The blinds on the windows of the police station were kept down during the Sabbath, the doors were locked, giving the place a deserted appearance, while the congregation heard Mass not fifty yards away, and afterwards stood around and yarned about the new police who were sent up on a wild-goose chase after the Kellys, who they were certain were no nearer than Beechworth.

On the following morning the strange police took possession of the Royal and made prisoners of everyone who happened in for the Monday morning reviver. Others likely to be dangerous were gathered in and guarded, and then business was transacted at the Bank. £2400 was taken, also a thoroughbred mare from the stables of the Hotel. Joe Byrne was sent ahead with the booty while the rest of the gang galloped up and down the main street, shooting with their revolvers the insulators off the telegraph poles, thereby interrupting the service and treating the natives to a most nerve-racking display of fireworks. Then the Kellys left for the hills.

The point in the enquiry made by Ned Kelly as to what priest was coming on that Sunday was this. Jerilderie was attended from Corowa, which had been made a separate Mission only the year before and the priest in charge—to whom Fr Kiely was assistant— was Fr Michael Slattery, who was known far and wide as the greatest talker of his time. In fact, it was general knowledge that he talked right round the clock; and when Slattery talked anything might happen; for when he talked he rambled along in a non-stop run and touched on every subject under the sun; but when Slattery talked, that is when he really talked, there was nothing for it but to slip the mind into neutral and await the coming of a merciful unconsciousness—and still Slattery talked. Dan Kelly explained to Mrs Devine while cleaning out the Court House that had it been Fr Slattery who was coming on that Sunday he would have had to be put in with the rest for his own protection and every-body's well-being . . .

Fr Dick Kiely, though his discreetness appealed to the Kellys, came in for his share of bother through indiscretion. He was a noted mimic, and like many another so gifted among the clergy, debased his talent by what is known as 'taking off' the bishop—which *indeed, if well done, is a turn with a high entertainment value, and is always sure of a good reception by the Inferior Clergy. Your wide-awake artist, however, is always meticulously careful of the time and place for the show. Fr Kiely erred in this, and Dr Lanigan, who was the easiest man in the world to mimic, but didn't think so, paid an unconscious tribute to the excellence of the performance by promoting the playboy to the Backblocks. Kiely had a brother in an influential position in the Church at Salt Lake City, and thither he transferred himself. But that was in 1886, when the bushrangers were sleeping in unhonoured graves and their daring deeds only a memory.*[5]

To return to Father Slattery and his new parish, the Catholic Directory for 1886,[6] which would be recording the situation in 1885, tells of a parochial school at Narrandera with 107 pupils and one at Jerilderie of 43 children. The Sisters of St Joseph of Goulburn took over the school at Narrandera in 1890 and, until their convent was opened in 1898, lived successively in cottages belonging to the Ferriers and the Elworthys.

Father Slattery became parish priest of Wagga in 1890 and at Narrandera was succeeded by Father Carroll, a Tipperary man ordained from All Hallows in 1878. He had been in Albury, Tumut, Goulburn (as administrator) and Wilcannia before coming to Narrandera as parish priest in November 1890.

In 1895 Father Carroll went to Wagga and was succeeded at Narrandera by Father Tom Gray who hailed from County Longford and was educated for the priesthood at St Patrick's College, Carlow. He was ordained on 20 October 1880, sent on loan to the diocese of Bathurst and stationed at Orange for a couple of years. He was appointed to the staff of Goulburn Cathedral, was at Grenfell in 1885, then Tumut, and came to Narrandera in 1895 as its third parish priest.

When Father Gray came to Narrandera he found St Brigid's Church near the present post office. He built the convent and school where they are today in Audley Street and eventually put up a new church alongside them, at the same time changing the parish titular saint to Mel. The cathedral in Longford is St Mel's and wherever in Australia one finds a St Mel's church, there too was once a Longford man. Father Gray was responsible for building the Grong Grong Church also; it was burnt down

---

5. *Ibid., pp. 185 ff.*
6. *Copy among Father Hartigan's papers; it belonged to Father Gray who was at Grenfell that year and has noted all the homesteads he visited, Grants', Newells', Martins', Byrnes', Molloys', Cullinanes', Williams', Mardens' etc. He ministered regularly at Gooloogong and Young and got as far as Condobolin.*

three months after his death. There was a plague of mice at the time and Bishop Gallagher suggested that the fire may have been caused by the mice nibbling wax matches.[7] The presbytery was also Father Gray's work, as were the extensions which were finished a bare three months before his death from a heart attack on 1 January 1917.

Biship Gallagher made this note in his diary:

Father Gray was an excellent priest and did excellent work, both spiritual and material, in every parish in which he worked but especially in Grenfell and Narrandera. Non erit similis illi qui conservaret legem excelsi.[8]

The Month's Mind was held at Narrandera on 7 February and with it on the same day the **Concursus**, i.e. the assessing of those nominating for the parish. Father Hartigan was announced as the new parish priest and the local paper reported his arrival on 1 March. At the welcome the curate, Father Aeneas Hennessy, spoke of him as a personal friend and told of his appreciation of the new pastor's educational achievements and intellectual ability, well evidenced in his work as inspector of schools. Father Reidy of Leeton added that Father Hartigan stood on a pedestal among the priests and foretold that the people would soon learn to love and appreciate him. He was most worthy to fill the post of their late lamented parish priest.

Father Hartigan in reply reminisced on his ordination in Goulburn in 1903. He remembered himself then (to quote 'The Sentimental Bloke' of C.J. Dennis) as 'a long lingering streak of misery'—he had put on 19 kilograms in the intervening years. He continued in a humorous vein and concluded by noting that some of the happiest days of his life had been spent among children.[9]

He was early in correspondence with the Bishop about parish boundaries and the church to be built at Grong Grong.

The Bishop replied:

Bishop's House Goulburn
April 6 1917

Dear Father Hartigan,
  Many thanks for letter safe to hand enclosing cheque for £15.10.6, viz. £13.0.0 as Mission Fund Collection for 1917 and £2.10.0 as Marriage fees.

7. Bishop Gallagher's diary, Book C, p. 29 in the Archdiocesan Archives, Canberra, made available through the kindness of the late Archbishop Thomas Cahill.
8. Ibid., p. 21.
9. Narandera Argus, 2 March 1917.

*As to the boundary line between Narrandera and Ganmain for so far, I
merely wished Father Clarke and yourself to meet and reach an
understanding as to whether the Shire Boundary might not be, as alleged,
the best parochial boundary also. It could, of course, be more easily
ascertained. But as the old axiom: salus populi suprema lex is the
principle on which I act, I have no desire to interfere with the
conveniences and legitimate wishes of the people. Hence you can put the
matter fairly before them; and if they—or as many of them as
wish—prefer to remain in Grong Grong as the district with which they
are most familiar, and are prepared to aid in the rebuilding of the Church,
you can retain them by all means.*

*You may probably, at no distant date, lay the foundation stone of a
new church—especially if it is to be of brick—I will cheerfully give you a
Sunday for that purpose. Meantime you can ascertain the wishes and
convenience of the people. When I am in Grong Grong I can easily fix the
line—by naming the farm or owner, if necessary—who has selected Grong
Grong—and on the other hand the settler who casts in his lot with
Matong. I can scarcely think of any fairer plan.*

*With best wishes of the Holy Easter Season
I am, Dear Father Hartigan, yours sincerely,*

✝ *John Gallagher*

*Rev. P. Hartigan, P.P.
Narrandera*

*P.S. To settle the matter for once and all. Leave the boundaries between
Narrandera and Ganmain remain for the present as they were in Father
Gray's time. This however, will leave the further question still free viz. If
a large portion of the people on the boundary prefer (or rather insist on)
belonging to Matong, then both Matong and Grong Grong may be attached
to Ganmain, a second priest sent to Ganmain and Narrandera left with one
priest for the present.*

J.G.[10]

There was no mass exodus of parishioners to Ganmain and Narrandera
retained its curate. Father Hennessy was there until the beginning of
1919 and was replaced by Father Arthur (usually known as Bill) Percy
whom, as we have seen, Father Hartigan helped to get to Manly. It was a
happy relationship, Father Bill calling him 'Boss' and doing a good share
of the work while Father Hartigan was busy writing. Poetry was 'in'
around the presbytery, and the curate was tempted to send in a

---

10. *Letter among Father Hartigan's papers.*

composition of his own to the **Bulletin.** He got a letter back advising him to consult his parish priest!

Within twelve months of Father Hartigan's going to Narrandera, the diocese of Goulburn was divided, the south-western portion becoming the diocese of Wagga Wagga with Joseph Dwyer its bishop. He was nominated in March and consecrated in Wagga on 17 October 1918. The consecrating prelate was Apostolic Delegate, Dr B. Cattaneo, and Bishop Gallagher and Vince Dwyer of Maitland, brother of the bishop elect, were the co-consecrators. The Apostolic Mandate was read by Father Hartigan and the sermon was preached by Father Thomas Slattery, his successor as inspector of schools. The cathedral was crowded and there were ten of the hierarchy present including Archbishop Redwood of Wellington, New Zealand.

The rescript setting up the diocese laid down as usual that those priests who at the time were stationed within the area allotted to the new diocese were members of that diocese. Both Father Pat and Father Frank Hartigan, then curate at Junee, were in the new diocese. Father Pat certainly regretted severing his ties with old associations of Goulburn, the Bishop, Dr Gallagher—a hero to him since the days he was his school-master at St Patrick's College, Goulburn—and the priests with whom he had worked now for fifteen years and had such regular contact during the years he visited their parishes as inspector of schools. By the division of the diocese two thirds of those cherished friends were to remain in the old diocese of Goulburn.

One of the first[11] acts of the new Bishop was to appoint Father Hartigan as one of the diocesan consultors, the small group of priests meeting regularly with the Bishop for consultation on the important affairs of the diocese.

The new Bishop and Father Hartigan had been friends since Father Pat's schooldays at Goulburn when Father Dwyer was on the teaching staff. They were together again, as we have seen, at Albury and for many years they were, with Father Tom Ryan, the only Australian priests in the diocese (excepting, of course, the erratic Dr Dick Daly who spent much of his time in Europe).

They remained close friends for many years. Father Pat admired the Bishop's common sense, his lack of fuss, and enjoyed him as an Australian, militantly so when abroad. Father Pat delighted to tell the story of how he was waiting for Joe—as he always referred to the Bishop—in the Four Courts Hotel, Dublin. There were two Irish parish priests there who took themselves very seriously. Joe came in and Father

11. *The Latin document among Father Hartigan's papers is dated 13 October 1918.*

Bishop Joseph Dwyer, a man with a great dislike of pomp in any circumstance. While the usual elaborate ceremonies were being carried out at his funeral, Father Hartigan remarked: 'This is the best proof that Joe is dead. Alive, he would never have allowed such things.' (Photo courtesy of Father Bill Kennedy)

Pat introduced him as Bishop Dwyer. The parish priests went to kiss his ring but it was in his hip pocket. He then took out from the same pocket a plug of the foulest smelling tobacco, produced a shearer's knife (with 'castrator' written on the blade!) and proceeded to excise great hunks of this for his cherry-wood pipe. All the time he kept up a running commentary on a 'cow' he had bumped into down the street, and a 'cove' that had failed to turn up. Joe enjoyed deflating them and on his departure, wide-eyed they asked Father Pat: 'Did you say he is a bishop in your country?'

When Joe died they had the usual elaborate ceremonies customary at the funeral of a bishop. They carried the body around the cathedral and did many similar rituals. 'The best proof', said Father Pat, 'that Joe is dead. Alive, he would never have allowed such things'.

Father Pat had great admiration for Joe's wide knowledge of botany, but not always were his botanical forays successful. He and Father Pat set out from the Narrandera presbytery to find a boree tree. Some hours later they arrived back hot, tired and boree-less, only to find there was one of the species in the paddock alongside the presbytery.

With the passing of the years the two friends did not see so much of each other. In his later years Joe had a great deal of illness and spent considerable time in hospital. They met at consultors' meetings in Wagga, but at these it was mostly business that was discussed. In later years, there was a difference of view between them. The Bishop, looking at the numbers in the parish and the possibility of more frequent Masses at the outside churches, wanted a curate at Narrandera; Father Pat preferred to be on his own and felt there were other places that had greater need of a curate. So the easy friendship of earlier years was not maintained.

However, when 'The Little Irish Mother' passed to her reward in 1934 it was Bishop Dwyer who sang the Pontifical High Mass at Haberfield, Sydney. When in 1940 Patrick Hartigan senior went to his Maker, Bishop Dwyer had already rendered his account some eighteen months earlier.

Within a few weeks of Bishop Dwyer's consecration the Great War came to an end. At 7.55 pm on 11 November a telegram arrived at Narrandera Post Office from Reuter, Vancouver: 'Official Armistice has been signed'. The Mayor rang the fire bell, the great bell of St Mel's Church, rung by Father Hartigan himself, took up the signal, hundreds gathered at the monument and the people danced in the streets until well into Tuesday morning.[12]

12. Narandera Argus, 15 November 1918.

An impressive display of squatters' cars outside the Narrandera garage.

In the early years of Father Hartigan's pastorate in Narrandera, a great stir was caused right round Australia by the 'Ligouri Case'. This concerned Brigid Partridge, who had come to Australia from Ireland in 1909 and entered the novitiate of the Presentation Sisters at Mount Erin, Wagga. After some time those in charge of her training became increasingly aware that Brigid, or Sister Ligouri as she was by this time, was temperamentally unsuited to religious life and completely lacking in the qualities necessary for the teaching profession.

Mother Stanislaus, in her position as Superior, decided that Sister should return to her parents in Ireland, but when she broached the matter, there was a painful scene. Sister Ligouri protested repeatedly that she wanted to remain in 'Mount Erin' as a religious. She begged for 'any small corner with any duties'.

The Sisters' Council that shared the responsibility of decision making unwisely recommended that Mother Stanislaus permit Sister to remain. She was professed and various efforts were made to find a teaching assignment she could handle.

As inspector of schools Father Hartigan came to Ganmain and found her in charge of a class. He examined it and found the standard much below what was acceptable. She was hovering around and as he left the class put the question: 'How did they go?' He gave a non-committal answer 'You'll be right, Sister'. He went to the Superior and insisted that Sister Ligouri be taken off teaching immediately. She was recalled to Mt Erin and given non-teaching tasks, looking after the boarders' lunches and so on.

She gave increasing cause for concern, as when she refused medicine, alleging it was poison. Finally, at 12.30 pm on 24 July 1920 she left the convent by the back way and went to Mrs Burgess' place which was nearby. Two of the sisters called for her there a few hours later and she went back with them to the convent. Dr Leahy was called and she was put to bed. She asked the sister looking after her for a hot-water bottle and while she was out of the room getting it Sister Ligouri left the convent in night attire. She went to Mrs Burgess' house, got some clothes from her, then went to Thompsons' place. Next day she left Thompsons' and went by car about 68 kilometres to Mrs Howell's home. She was ill there for several days and went into a private hospital at Adelong. Next she went with Mr Barton, Grand Master of the Orange Lodge, first to Cootamundra briefly, and then to Sydney where she stayed at Kogarah with Mr Touchell, a Congregational minister, and his wife.

During these journeyings the Sisters in Wagga, not knowing her whereabouts, were concerned for her safety. Bishop Dwyer was unable to get from the police any information as to where she was. He received from Dr Leahy, who had attended Sister for some time, a signed affidavit in which he gave it as his opinion that she was of unsound mind and should be placed in a hospital for the insane for treatment and observation.

Acting on this Bishop Dwyer obtained a warrant for her arrest. She was found by the police at the Touchells' on 7 August and taken to the Reception House. She was there for a week, went before a magistrate and was remanded for seven days and remained at the Reception House. Before the end of the week she was discharged and returned to the Touchells'. The Bishop called at the Reception House but he was not allowed to see her.

The next stage in the drama was a suit filed against the Bishop in which Brigid sought £5000 compensation for wrongful arrest. The case was heard in July 1921.

Father Hartigan, normally a most tolerant man, known widely for what now would be called an ecumenical spirit, was stung to anger by the evident bigotry behind the case. In the course of a long sermon at Narrandera one Sunday morning he explained how Sister Ligouri could have been dispensed from her vows by the Bishop. He went on to say:

> There was no need at all to seek the help of a society or lodge, the one and only object of whose existence, as far as I can see, is to show hostility to the Catholics.

He made an impassioned defence of the religious sisters of the Catholic Church.

> There are in Australia at the present time 6600 nuns, and I open my Bible and I read these words: 'By their fruits you shall know them. A good tree cannot bring forth evil fruit and an evil tree cannot bring forth good fruit, wherefore by their fruits you shall know them'. What then are their fruits! Their schools are scattered far and wide throughout the length and breadth of a continent. If on every Sunday morning the Catholic churches are packed to the doors, it is because of a good seed planted in a child's heart by a gentle Sister's hand. Besides that they have 30 orphanages where they show a mother's care to thousands of little Australians above whose cradle misfortune has frowned her darkest frown, they have 16 hospitals, 10 refuges for unfortunate women whom they have rescued from the streets, 4 homes for the aged poor, 3 hospitals for poor little foundling babes besides industrial schools, schools for aboriginals and asylums for the blind, the insane, the deaf and dumb. All of which are open to

Catholic and Protestant alike. All of which are maintained solely by their own labours unaided by even one penny support from outside except the donations of generous Christians such as you. How many institutions of the kind can their slanderers boast of?

He concluded with these moving words:

One more word and I have done. I stand here this morning to cast no stone at the unfortunate cause of all this misrepresentation. I stand here as a Catholic to repudiate with all the vehemence that is in me all the calumny that is cast at our Sisters. I stand here and speak in just indignation as a man who watched four of his own sisters take the veil and one of them is sleeping beneath the currajongs in the little cemetery at the Orphanage at Albury, but in every white-souled Sister she lives to me and from the wounded heart of every nun she calls to me again. I stand here dressed in the vestments of the ancient church that has been persecuted from the beginning but has triumphed and shall again, in her nuns. I give my testimony that of all the institutions fostered by that Church throughout the two thousand years of her splendid history there is not one that does her more credit than the convents, and I ask God that founded her to bless them and with his own strong hand protect them in this hour of trial. It is necessary that scandals come, but may the Sisters keep their faces to the future—the Catholics are behind them to a man, and there is not one Catholic who does not feel that the honour of the Sisters is his honour as well.[13]

During the progress of the case, Pastor Touchell, at whose home Brigid remained, gave two public addresses in Narrandera and formed there a branch of the Protestant Federation with two hundred members. At the second of these meetings he was reported as saying:

He had heard that they had a good priest at Narrandera and he congratulated them on it.[14]

Father Hartigan felt very acutely for the sisters as they faced this trial. He realised that Sister Ligouri might have blown up his non-committal words to her at Ganmain into some kind of testimony of her suitability. He knew the sisters would be thinking back on their least statements,

---

13. *From a typescript among Father Hartigan's papers.*
14. Narandera Argus, *12 July 1921.*

even on their jokes, and wondering if these, magnified and distorted, were going to come out in evidence against them.

What actually happened is recounted in the book written to commemorate the centenary of the Presentation Sisters' arrival in Wagga:

> In the final analysis it was ex-Sister Ligouri herself who witnessed unconsciously, not for the prosecution, but for the defence. No cross-examination could force her to swerve from the truth.
>
> Mother Stanislaus, as superior, was cross-examined by both Counsel for Plaintiff and Defence. Her quiet and dignified demeanour in those alien surroundings, her sincerity, the clarity of her answers, made a tremendous impression on the Court. Persistent interrogation from opposing Counsel gradually opened to the world the minutest and most private details of conventual life. Confidence in truth gave Mother Stanislaus sincerity and composure. She feared nothing for herself and her community. 'Mount Erin' found the publicity distasteful, but did not fear it.
>
> The Bishop won the case and the sympathy of the Catholic world.
>
> In his summing up, Mr Justice Ferguson said (in part) '. . . but I cannot help thinking that it is very unfortunate for the plaintiff (Sister Ligouri) that, at the time she left the convent she did not meet somebody who would have shown a little common horse-sense . . .' Again, considering the evidence of alleged ill-treatment, his Honor said, 'Now Gentlemen . . . that is the whole evidence you have about unkindness shown to the plaintiff during the years she was in the convent to the day she left. Whatever your verdict may be, I am sure there is no fair-minded man in the community—no Protestant, however militant his Protestantism may be—who will not share with his Catholic fellow-citizens in a sense of gratification that these imputations, so far as the plaintiff is concerned, have been refuted—not by the contradictions of people interested—not by a balance of conflicting testimony—but by her own deliberate oath . . .' (Catholic Press, 21 July 1921)
>
> The poor deluded Sister Ligouri found herself still in the hands of Pastor Touchell and his wife. Though the Bishop won the case, he had to pay his own costs, since the Plaintiff declared she had no funds to cover them. Not only did more than sufficient money pour in to the Bishop from sympathisers, Catholics and non-Catholics, but it was unanimously decided, at the official welcome for the Bishop on his return to Wagga, 26 July 1921, to complete St Michael's Cathedral, as a magnificent monument to Bishop Dwyer's

'solid, manly, dignified defence of Catholic institutions and their rights'.

About 1940, ex-Sister Ligouri was admitted to a mental home for a time. A terror of Catholic reprisals should she ever wish to get in contact with her true friends, had obsessed her weak mind, but that she always remained warmly loyal to them is revealed in information supplied by an ex-student of Mt Erin.

Following the death of Mr Touchell, Brigid Partridge and Mrs Touchell continued to live in Sydney. Here the ex-student, Sheila Tearle, who as a child, had known the former Sister Ligouri well at St Mary's school in Wagga, met her frequently in the shopping centre of the suburb where they lived. Cut off from communications with the Sisters for so many years, Brigid Partridge longed for news of them. She spoke of different Sisters with affection, recalling the appearance of this one, the kindness of another, and always concluded by entreating 'Give them my love'.

The time came when Miss Partridge and Mrs Touchell could no longer care for themselves. They were admitted to the Rydalmere hospital, Mrs Touchell died within a short while after admission, and her poor companion was left alone. Mrs Tearle visited her frequently.

Brigid Partridge never recovered from her long illness. She died aged 76 years, 4 December 1966 in Rydalmere hospital, and she was buried in Rookwood cemetery.[15]

Sheila Tearle later added a few details:

Present at the funeral were the Congregational Minister and myself—whom the undertakers referred to as 'the mourner'. The Minister read some prayers and I joined in. The only flowers were some gardenias from our garden.[16]

---

15. B.T. Dowd and Sheila Tearle, Centenary, Sisters of the Presentation B.V.M., Wagga 1874-1974, Wagga, N.S.W., 1973, pp. 66-7. Alan Gill, in an article on Sister Ligouri in the Sydney Morning Herald of 19 July 1980, gave these additional details:

In 1939 Mr Touchell, who had vigorously opposed similar moves by the Roman Catholic Bishop of Wagga, himself had her committed to Parramatta Mental Hospital. Hospital records confirm the admission and state that she was suffering from paraphrenia (an old name for schizophrenia), delusions and hallucinations of persecution. After her release, apparently restored to health, Mary Partridge returned to live once more with the Touchells. [After Mr Touchell's death in 1954] a doctor visited Mrs Touchell and Mary Partridge in their house at Kogarah and was dismayed at what he saw. He submitted a gruesome report, which is still in hospital files, of finding decayed meat and vegetables, flies, filth and appalling squalor. Both women were admitted to Rydalmere Mental Hospital (now Rydalmere Hospital) on the same day, 14 November 1962.

16. Footprints (quarterly journal of Melbourne Historical Commission) 2, 12, 1977, p. 10.

The parish priest of Hurstville, Father Tom Dunlea, had tried to get her interred as a Catholic. He was unsuccessful, as provision for Brigid's burial had already been made in Mrs Touchell's will.

All during these years Father Hartigan was writing verse, sending it generally to the **Catholic Press.** One of his poems brought this lovely letter from Bishop Gallagher:

Temora, 18 Nov. 1918

Dear Father Hartigan,

I can't prevent myself from sitting down and sending you just a line to thank you from my heart for 'This Parting Rosary'. To me it is really beautiful and true to nature. You may look upon me as an 'old fool' fast drifting into second childhood. But I must admit I have now read it for the third time and I could not finish the third reading from the tears that somehow came unbidden and prevented me from seeing the letters.

It is amazing to me how you a 'native' can catch the Irish spirit and put those homely thoughts into words that touch the Irish heart so poignantly. For a moment or two it is just as if a sort of pain around the heart but oh! such a soothing pain for me.

God bless you and continue to give you 'a spark of nature's fire' to preserve the most tender associations of your grand old Irish faith in the warm loveable hearts of the good children of Australia.

The bringing back so many happy memories of childhood is the only excuse that can be given for writing thus by your old and grateful Master.

                                        † *John Gallagher*

Very Rev. P.J. Hartigan P.P.
Narrandera.[17]

Most of his poems of these years were published eventually in **Around the Boree Log** or the later collection, **The Parish of St Mel's.** One, however, that did not appear in either book is the successor to 'Josephine', the faithful old housekeeper.

The Thuckeen[18] at the Door

Now, there's that wretched bell again; it rings the whole day through;
Another blessed tramp, I s'pose, who wants 'a bob or two';

---

17. *Letter among Father Hartigan's papers.*
18. *'Thuckeen' is the diminutive of the Gaelic word for girl. It is sometimes used affectionately as is colleen, but here it has a derogatory sense, which is frequent.*

And there's the Thuckeen's little heels tick-tocking on the floor.
I've told that woman not to let the Thuckeen near the door.

For every tramp upon the road, and every loafer too,
  This presbytery for thirty years has been a rendezvous;
And be his colour what it may, his creed, his drink, his kin,
  Her Ladyship the Thuckeen will be sure to ask him in.

And then she trips along the hall, and calmly says to me,
  'A gentleman, please, Father, wants to see you privately'.
I fling the paper on the floor, and with a purpose grand,
  I go to meet my 'gentleman', prepared to take a stand.

But somehow, if I let him talk, the purpose won't endure;
  I think of sweet St Martin, and the beggar-man of Tours
I hand him out a 'trifle', and a sermon as a rule,
  And go back to my paper, and confess myself a fool.

The curate sometimes laughs at me; I meet it with a frown;
  He laughs his hearty laugh at what he terms 'being taken down'.
He says 'deserving cases' only one per thousand run.
  When I refuse, I'm troubled lest it be that very one.

They tell me sorry stories of this world of want and care;
  The job that's waiting somewhere, if they only had the fare;
The swag that has been stolen, with the 'billy-can and pup'—
  And give me confidential tips about the Melbourne Cup.

Last week, while reading Office in the shade behind the hedge,
  A battered party chanced along, and wished 'to sign the pledge'.
I pledged him (and I franked him), and advised him, too; and—well,
  He was drunk in twenty minutes down at Mrs Flynn's hotel.

Last Sunday's sermon they repeat—and, faith, to put it plain,
  I'd give them half a sovereign not to do the like again.
They've sold me back a turkey, which I found next day was mine;
  And stole the empty bottles that contained the altar wine.

'Twas Tuesday last, as here I sat upon this very seat,
  A dialogue was wafted from the corner of the street.
Said one, 'I'll go and "bite his ear", when no one is about';
  'The "Old Pot doesn't tumble", and you wait till I come out'.

Of course, it sounded Greek to me; I've always hated slang;
  And thought no more about the thing, until the door-bell rang;
'A gentleman to see you', said the Thuckeen from the door.
  A 'gentleman' in trouble met me on the parlour floor.

'A mirac'lus little medal' that he prized beyond all cost—
  A gift from Father So and So, that very day he'd lost;
And could I spare another? Well, the thought occurred to me,
  The miracles and medals must have missed him hopelessly.

Still, when I thought of how he thought of Father So and So,
  I gave him six or seven more; and as he turned to go,

He begged me to excuse him for the sentiment he showed,
  And borrowed something from me just 'to see him on the road'.

But while I pondered on the worth of rough and ready men,
  And felt I'd found the genuine 'one', the door-bell rang again;
'A gentleman to see you', said the Thuckeen as before;
  I found another 'gentleman' upon the parlour floor.

Connected well with Holy Church—he said he was, at least—
  His sister, Reverend Mother, and his brother, too, a priest.
The curate laughed his hearty laugh for half a day and more,
  And that's what comes of sending out that Thuckeen to the door.

Poor Josephine that's dead and gone was worth her weight in gold,
  I never realised it till we laid her in the mould;
For thirty years no Ishmaelite stood on that parlour floor,
  For Josephine herself would meet the caller at the door.

The tramp, the fraud, the agent, and the fellow selling books,
  She catalogued as 'loafers'. Faith, she gave them murd'rous looks;
Upon the well-dressed mystery she trained her heavy guns,
  And if she couldn't make him out, she'd send him to the nuns.

The lad who dared to ring the bell—she'd cut him like a knife,
  But if he ventured round the back, she'd chase him for his life;
She soundly scolded every one, then gave them quite a feast;
  But cleared her decks for action with 'the brother of a priest'.

Well, here's the Thuckeen's little heels tick-tocking like a clock;
  Now, what's the matter, Mary, in your shabby little frock!
'A gentleman to see me, and you asked him to wait!'
  A 'gentleman', how are you!—with his swag outside the gate.

Ah, well, perhaps, 'twill hoarded be where I shall need it more,
Poor Josephine, she'd never let that Thuckeen near the door.[19]

19. This copy of the poem (which originally appeared in the Catholic Press, 7 January 1915) was supplied
   by the late Father Joseph Cusack of Mosman, and was published in the Manly 1957 and is reproduced
   here with permission.

7 The Publishing of Around the Boree Log

The verses of 'John O'Brien' continued to appear spasmodically in the **Catholic Press** and were greeted with enthusiasm. To quote a reviewer in that paper: 'These gems were carefully cut out as they appeared and read again and again till the cutting fell into fragments and they were compelled to apply to the office for a reprint'.[1]

Some of the verses found their way to Ireland where they were reprinted as leaflets. As late as 1942 the **Pilot** of Boston published a version of 'The Trimmin's on the Rosary' which differed slightly from the one published in **Around the Boree Log** and may have come from one of the early Irish reprints. It is described as the story of the recitation of the rosary in an Irish home and no indication is given of its Australian origin; it is attributed to the Rev John O'Brien. The editorial in that issue of the paper was devoted to the poem and the lessons it conveyed.[2]

There was no more loyal supporter of 'John O'Brien' than Father Joe Cusack, the administrator of the parish of St Francis, Albion Street, Surry Hills (later parish priest of Mosman where he died in 1960). He had kept a scrap-book of the poems as they appeared in the **Bulletin** and elsewhere and had written in the **Manly**[3] and other publications urging Father Hartigan to publish. One evening in January 1921, the curate at St Francis, Father Eris O'Brien—then just two years ordained and eventually to be the archbishop of Canberra and Goulburn—arranged for George Robertson to visit him. He knew George because he was publishing with Angus & Robertson the first of his several books on the history of early Catholic Australia. Father Eris read out the poems from Father Joe Cusack's scrap-book. George Robertson was entranced. Next day he wrote to Father Hartigan:

1. Catholic Press, 15 December 1921.
2. Pilot, Boston, 7 March 1942.
3. Manly 1, 3, 1920, pp. 32-41.

ANGUS & ROBERTSON Ltd
   PUBLISHERS
Rev. Father Hartigan, P.P.,
   NARRANDERA.

                                                              89 Castlereagh Street
                                                                  SYDNEY 6/1/21

Dear Revd Sir,

At St Francis' Presbytery last night I had the pleasure of hearing a number of your poems read by the Rev. Eris O'Brien from Father Cusack's scrap-book. They are the best we have come across since the Sentimental Bloke happened along, and we want to publish them. If no other arrangements have been made for their publication, and if you will entrust us with it, we should be happy to bring out the volume on the same terms as those given to Mr Dennis. On receipt of a favourable reply, a copy of one of the Dennis agreements—the terms are the same in them all—shall be sent.

So much for the business point of view. Now I want to tell you that the tenderness and humour of the verses have made of me a friend for life, and if other arrangements for their publication have been entered into you may still count on every possible ounce of assistance we can give, as booksellers, to make the book go.

I was telling one of my partners about 'my find' this morning, and he said: 'Get him to immortalize Father Phelan, of St Mary's, (near Penrith). He used to steal his own fowls! and take them to the sick—Catholic or Protestant, it made no difference to him—with apologies for the feathers as his housekeeper "had no time to pluck them"'.

His Reverence's indifference to the loss of pair after pair (they always disappeared in pairs) made his housekeeper storm, and, finally, invoke the local policeman's aid. Alas, the officer was probably an accessory both before and after the fact, and nothing came of that, so 'Josephine' lay in wait herself. Picture to yourself poor Father Phelan caught in the act of removing, in the dead of night, a couple of slabs from the wall of his own hen house!

Now isn't that a beautiful story!—and it is true, too, for Mr Wymark says that a pair once came his way when he was a boy, and sick.

                                  Yours faithfully,
                                  George Robertson.[4]

True to his word, George Robertson did remain a friend for life and Father Hartigan cherished a warm regard for him and used to tell a story about him in connection with Henry Lawson's funeral. A newspaper

---

4. *Letter among Father Hartigan's papers.*

correspondent covering it saw a little man with a notebook scurrying around asking the names of those present. His dialogue with mourners went like this:

'Who is that in the tall hat?'
'That is the Premier.'
'I don't know him. And next to him?'
'That is the Chief Justice.'
'I don't know him. And the next one?'
'That is the Lord Mayor.'
'I don't know him either. Now who is the big man with the beard?'
'That is George Robertson.'
'Ah, yes', said the little man, 'I know him,' and he wrote George Robertson's name in his book alongside that of Henry Lawson. The newspaper correspondent turned to the little man and said:
'And who are you?' 'I am Fame,' he replied and drifted away among the mourners.[5]

Then there was the occasion when George Robertson said to Father Hartigan: 'One of my authors, a Catholic, is not practising his faith. Now that is no good to any man. If he gets sick and I hear of it, will you come down from Narrandera to attend to him? I feel sure that with your common interests you could do more with him than another priest.' In fact the author was reconciled to the Church later and Father Hartigan's promised trip was not necessary.

George Robertson's first letter to Father Hartigan was followed that same month by one from C.J. Dennis, the author of **The Sentimental Bloke**. He spoke of the excellent treatment he had had from Angus & Robertson and urged Father Hartigan to publish with the same firm.[6]

The contract bore the date 10 February 1921. The book was to be published under a title to be agreed upon by the parties. The royalty payment was 10 per cent.

At the time Father Hartigan had written only half a dozen pieces but that didn't worry George Robertson. 'Get busy with the others', he said, and within a month he had all that he required.

One of the conditions in the contract was that Father Hartigan should read all the proofs. Imagine his horror to find in the proofs all kinds of

5. *Story published by Jim Kelleher as a result of his interview with Father Hartigan,* The Catholic Weekly, *22 May 1952.*
6. *Letter among Father Hartigan's papers.*

changes made by Angus & Robertson's reader. Because, it was stated, of public feeling at the time, 'The Little Irish Mother' had been changed to 'The Little British Mother'. The author made a quick trip to Sydney and said to George Robertson: 'Listen, we've been very good friends since we met and let's part that way. You tear up your contract and I'll tear up mine, and I'll reimburse you for half your costs up to date'.

George Robertson would not hear of such a thing. He recognised the stupidity of the changes and called in Arthur Jose, the historian and the firm's head reader. 'You and Jose spend the rest of the week together and iron out all the troubles,' he said. They did so, though he did not find Jose an easy man to work with. Once during a long argument about a particular line, Jose was called out of the room and his typist whispered to Father Hartigan: 'You're right. Keep the line as it is, don't give in to him.' The typist's encouragement was enough to tip the balance, Father Hartigan stuck to his guns and the line remained as he wanted it.

One of the compromises reached was that rather than 'The Little Irish Mother' the book should bear a neutral title. Shortly after his return from Sydney he was on visitation round his parish and commented on the beautiful log fire in the hearth. 'Give me a book and a boree log and I'm set for the evening,' was the reply of his hostess. She went on to expatiate on the merits of boree as fuel. 'It burns', she said, 'with great heat to a fine white ash'.

He went home and wrote 'Around the Boree Log' and sent it to George Robertson as the title poem they were seeking. The book went ahead and in October came the following letter:

ANGUS & ROBERTSON Ltd   *89 Castlereagh Street*
Publishers   *SYDNEY 6/10/21*
Rev. Father Hartigan,
   The Presbytery,
   NARRANDERA.
Dear Father Hartigan,

    By same mail you will receive two sets of your proof sheets—one to correct and return as soon as possible, the other to retain for reference (and, perhaps, further corrections) while the book is still in the making. I also send you a list of the pieces selected for inclusion, showing the order in which we think of printing them, and a list of the rejected pieces.

    You will see that our poetry editor has made verbal alterations where he thought them advisable, and although he is the deftest man in Australia it is just possible that a few of them may not have been absolutely necessary. Also, he is a Protestant, and some of the lines he has altered may have possessed a significance which, as a non-Catholic, he was unable to grasp. However, the final decision rests with you, and the original text shall be restored in every case in which you prefer it. And, if you think any of the pieces which have been omitted should be included, they shall go in; but in that case you must indicate which you wish us to leave out in their favour, for the volume as sent you is just of the right length.

You may wonder why I did not get a Catholic poet to read the proofs; but the fact is that ninety-five percent of our poets have neither the grit nor the experience for the work. Indeed, as it is, verses here and there which were exceptionally troublesome to alter have been cut out, to the hurt, I think, of some of the poems. I particularly wish you to tell me of any of these that you think should be restored.

All the volumes of verse published by us have been subject to revision of a similar kind—even (although to a less degree) those by 'cabinetmakers' like Brennan and Quinn.

I may tell you that, on closer acquaintance, I like your verses better than ever. Their humour and tenderness, their human appeal, make me feel sure of a large sale for them.

Yours faithfully,
George Robertson.[7]

Accompanying the letter was the order of contents, and the titles of six pieces that were to be omitted. The order is almost identical with the published book. There were three poems in the proofs that ultimately were dropped, 'The Also Started', 'The Kites That We Used to Fly' and 'The Boy That Cleared Away'. Among those omitted by Angus & Robertson were four more that did not make the book: 'Keep Pushing Your Own Little Barrow', 'The Things He Has Flung Behind Him', 'Imelda May' and 'Mystery'. But there were two others which the publishers planned to omit that were finally included, no doubt at Father Hartigan's insistence. These were 'Laughing Mary' and 'When Old Man Carey Died'.

Two of the seven omitted from **Around The Boree Log** were included later in **The Parish of St Mel's.** Of the other five 'Mystery' was mentioned earlier.[8] Father Maurice O'Reilly, rector of St John's College and the author of a book of verses,[9] the best known of which is 'God Bless Our Lovely Morning-Land', had this to say about it:

---

7. *Letter among Father Hartigan's papers.*
8. *See p. 92. Earlier it was 'To Mystery'.*
9. *Maurice O'Reilly,* Poems, *Sands & Co, London, n.d.*

St. John's College
University of Sydney
Dec. 16th., 1915

My Dear Hartigan,

You did those verses 'To Mystery' on your top. I really must write to say, as one less wise, that I read them with great pleasure. I had got to know how good you could be in a light vein, and yet to learn to what heights your Pegastic aero-plane was capable of soaring. Do please let us have more from where that came.

If I could do anything like as good work, you would hear from me.

By the way, we have a visitor's room here now, and I hope that, when you come to Sydney, you will look me up, and, if possible, come under my humble roof to stay.

Again thanking you for the pleasure given me by 'To Mystery'.

Believe me, my dear O'Brien,
Sincerely yours,
M.J. O'Reilly, C.M.

Rev. P. O'Brien-Hartigan,
Thurgoona
ALBURY.[10]

Mystery

A goddess art thou; aye, and wondrous fair,
    To those whose eyes, of tinsel tired, behold
The white stars tangled in thy braided hair,
    Thy brow with gems immortal aureoled.

No dimpling smile upon thy sweet face lies,
    Thou seemest ever gazing thoughtfully
From velvet depths of soft dream-lidded eyes
    On life's poor plotless little comedy.

Thou comest in the shoreward creeping wave,
    In dark tumultuous waters gurgling deep,
In midnight winds that croon around a grave,
    In moon-kissed trees that murmur in their sleep.

Thou speakest in the silence of a star
    High thought of God in burning letters writ,
The mist-crowned crests thy temple's columns are,
    In pinpoint worlds thy altar fires are lit.

10. Letter among Father Hartigan's papers.

Thy garments rustle softly when the night
  Neath drooping wings has gathered land and sea
And Nature's heart, wrapped nun-like in delight
  Too full for words, pulsates a hymn to thee.

The golden marvels of the folded years
  Thou holdest safe from secret babbling Time,
The songs of poets and the dreams of seers
  Are moulded in that beating heart of thine.

From thee have bright transcendent longings birth,
  And winged fancies on thy breast repose,
And inspiration yet to glad the earth,
  And in thy lap grand impulse comatose.

Still though thy way is round the world of man,
  Though oft thy wings brush past his upturned face,
How few there are thy sainted features scan!
  How very few thy holy feet embrace!

But him whose heart beats out its march alone,
  Whose soul no soul for sympathy can bless,
Him from the throng thou takest for thine own,
  And blesseth him because of loneliness.

The other pieces rejected, and not later published, had titles which ironically enough, fitted their fate. There is no trace in Father Hartigan's papers of 'The Things He Has Flung Behind Him'. 'The Also Started' did precisely that, and 'The Boy That Cleared Away' likewise is missing from the two collections of verse. 'Keep Pushing Your Own Little Barrow' remains out on its own, having failed to make the collections of verse.[11]

The Also Started

When the hard-fought race is over, and the uproar has subsided
  The ten thousand eyes are straining, as they bring the winner back
And the prize is his for keeping, and the glory undivided
  In a line, the beaten horses, follow slowly down the track.

They are wet with hard endeavour, and their foam-splashed flanks are
                                                              dripping
  And the sun no longer glances, from their glossy satin skin
And the blood is flowing freely from the long spur's cruel ripping
  In the eager, anxious striving, of a race they couldn't win.

11. *It is included above, p. 111.*

All the dash and fire have left them, and they stumble broken-hearted
    Through the crowd that greets the victor, in the pride of place displayed
Just the sporting paper mentions them among the 'also started'
    But proclaims no cheering Bravo for the gallant run they made.

So in life's contested scurry, where the hand of fate has waited
    With a harsh uneven measure. There the light weights make the pace;
And applause awaits their efforts, from a shouting crowd elated
    While the over-burdened triers are defeated for a place.

When we gather at the setting, we forget the broken-hearted
    While the winner in our blindness, in a brimming cup we toast.
But the best and bravest often are amongst the also started
    They are winners—though they never land the colours past the post.

The Boy That Cleared Away

There's somethin' whisp'rin', something bad, just what I don't know right,
    But that poor lonely wand'rin' lad is in my thoughts tonight;
And my old heart is sort of dead and numb from day to day
    All achin' with a sinkin' dread for him who cleared away.

He always was the driftin' kind, bit reckless too and wild
    A thousand darin' things I mind he did while quite a child
And when he grew to be a man so tall and handsome too,
    I marked, as only mothers can, that wildness growing too.

The life of picnic, dance or ball, so bright and full of fun,
    A bit too easy led, that's all, and fond of frolickin'
His brothers never broke my rest, but always, strange to say,
    I seemed to love the wild boy best, the one who cleared away.

Himself, he's too severe by far, and naggin's always wrong,
    And that poor lad he'd cross and jar—I've said it all along—
But still for all his scoldin' tongue and bitter words of blame
    'Tis me that knows, when he was young, he'd do the very same.

They both were stubborn-like and proud, pig-headed as they say,
    On something that was done they rowed, and then he cleared away
I watched him far as I could see with strainin' eyes and dim
    Oh if they'd left the lad to me I could have managed him.

Then if he drifted down the stream and drained no bitter cup
    His home would be a pleasant dream with no sad wakin' up.
I wonder what's his dreams tonight, where'er his poor head lay
    May God protect and keep him right—the boy that cleared away.

He sent no word, I thought he might and waited day by day,
    I s'pose he felt ashamed to write or perhaps it went astray.
I know he'll not forget myself, and all that we have been;
    That's him there on the mantelshelf, when he was seventeen.

And I have heard him calling me and started up in fright
  To find 'twas but a restless tree, a-whimp'rin' in the night.
Ah, what's the use, I'm only one whose hopes have gone astray.
  There's other mothers mourn a son who went and ran away.

Himself, he don't let on to me, pretendin' hurt, he do,
  But from the way he smokes I see that he is thinkin' too.
But when we kneel together there, a silent prayer we say
  That angels guard with tender care the boy that cleared away.

The **Boree Log** appeared in November. It was an immediate and resounding success as George Robertson knew it would be. On the day the first copies went on sale, the man who not so many years before had with Angus started the firm with £10 between them sent Father Hartigan a cheque for the royalties on the complete first edition of 5000 copies.

The dust-cover design by Percy Lindsay featured 'The Old Mass Shandrydan' arriving at 'The Church upon the Hill'. There are several claimants for the honour of being the church in the picture, amongst them Morundah outside Narrandera and Barooga in the Berrigan parish.

The reviews were flattering. C.J. Dennis wrote of the verses in the **Bulletin**:

They are Australian first—bush Australian; they are Irish-Australian of course, but they are pure Australian too: good mates, good workers, full of healthy humour and a capacity for enjoyment that most of the world just now seems to have lost ... The verse that makes us acquainted with these jovial fellows is the direct Lawson-Paterson line mainly—unaffected talk about Australians, much as they would naturally talk about themselves. Yet if the subject needs eloquence, the author can rise to it. But he is best at his simplest, in the pathos of 'Making Home' and 'Vale, Father Pat', the happy humour of 'The Old Bush School' and 'At Casey's After Church' [SIC], or in the sheer rollicking farce (true to life, all the same) of 'Said Hanrahan' and 'The Careys'. And the bush is there, enveloping its people with the bird-song and the flower-scent that the townsman Marcus Clarke could not discover. At times it is colourful, too.

> *I've seen the paddocks all ablaze*
>   *When spring in golden glory comes,*
> *The purple hills of summer days,*
>   *The autumn ochres through the gums.*

This verse of 'John O'Brien' may well be admired for what it

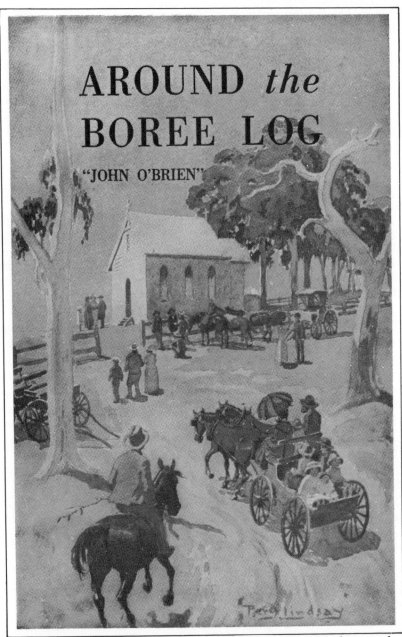

The jacket of the first edition of AROUND THE BOREE LOG, drawn and designed by Percy Lindsay.

*is—for its kindly humour, its gentle pathos, its honest pictures of
one phase of country life and its good Australian sentiment. The
book will find an army of readers all through Australia ...*

*As a book of healthy, happy verse moderately well constructed and
full of entertainment* Around the Boree Log *should be judged and
commended. As such it is a welcome addition to Australian
literature.*[12]

Dennis' remark that 'Said Hanrahan' and 'The Careys' were true to life
could with even more reason have been extended to another rollicking
farce, 'Tangmalangaloo'. The incident really happened to Bishop
Gallagher.[13] He had gone to a place called Tangmangaroo near Boorowa to
administer the Sacrament of Confirmation. Before he made the class
'strong and perfect Christians' he conducted the usual examination.

The 'overgrown two-storey lad' was actually there and he gave the
answer to the Bishop's question that has 'rocked' many an audience since
'John O'Brien' recorded it in his inimitable verse:

*And oh, how pleased His Lordship was, and how he smiled to say,
'That's good, my boy. Come, tell me now; and what is Christmas Day?'
The ready answer bared a fact no bishop ever knew—
'It's the day before the races out at Tangmalangaloo.'*

Bishop Gallagher loved that story and when he lay dying, he had it read to
him again and again.

The Catholic papers naturally gave the book an enthusiastic reception.
The **Catholic Press** announced that the first edition of 5000 was nearly
exhausted. It quoted a reviewer in the **Age** of Melbourne who was
guessing at the poet's identity:

*The writer is something more than a clever versifier. Many of the
pieces contain real poetry ... many phrases are strikingly apt and
beautiful, the treatment is always sympathetic and kindly. His
familiarity with the devotion of the Church suggests that the writer*

---

12. Bulletin, *29 December 1921.*
13. *In June 1952 Cyril Comins, originally from Yass, wrote to Father Hartigan from Tattersall's Club, Newcastle:*

    Bishop Gallagher's visit to Tangmangaroo and his questioning of the Confirmation Class will ever be remembered by us who knew that a race meeting was held there on Boxing Day every year ... I never see or hear your name without thinking of the time when the 'Dean' told you to 'Quench the lights' and you lit them up again.

    The 'Dean' was Dean O'Keefe—see Chapter 1, p. 14.

may well be one of its immediate servants. But whatever his identity, he has proved his title to a worthy place among Australian poets.

The **Catholic Press** itself had this to say:

The note of pessimism, which is so characteristic of Australian poetry, is entirely absent from 'John O'Brien'. As a matter of fact, pessimism is no essential of the Australian spirit; it is an evidence of paganism. It is strong in Poe and Swinburne. And when the Australian poets cut away from the sensuous word-stringing of the modern English verse spinners and draw their inspiration from the pure, free air of the bush, as 'John O'Brien' has done, we shall have the dinkum poetry which this sunny land deserves—as distinctively Australian as the 'Digger', the wattle and the wiree.[14]

The optimism of **Around the Boree Log** noted by the reviewer can be appreciated even more by comparing its version of 'When the Circus Came to Town' with the one published in the **Bulletin** and the Albury **Daily Mail** of 9 August 1906. The later one has obviously been polished so that when 'Out to the street with a shout we'd fly/ To look at the elephants marching by,' now in the later version it is out to the road we fly: 'To gape at the elephants trudging by', which fits better the youngsters and the elephants.

But over and above this polishing a note of optimism has been introduced, evident particularly in the new concluding verse. The earlier version ran:

> Now the circus comes to town,
> And it rattles along, and a barefoot throng
> Is cheering it up and down;
> And the elephants still are marching there,
> And the thud of the drums is in the air—
> But the hands of Time the mask will tear
> From many a painted clown;
> Clumsy, indeed, is the dancing bear
> And the wonderful band has a tinny blare
> When the circus comes to town.

This became in the 1921 version:

14. Catholic Press, *15 December 1921*.

> Now the circus comes to town,
> And it rattles along, and a bare-foot throng
>   Is pacing it up and down;
> And the elephants trudge as they trudged of yore,
> With the shabby shebangs, and the steeds galore;
> But the glee of the youngsters who shout and roar
>   At the tricks of the painted clown
> Is balm to my soul, and I call encore
> To the frowsy old jokes I've heard before,
>   When the circus came to town.

Favourable reviews flowed in from all over Australia and New Zealand and some from England, Ireland, Scotland and South Africa.[15]

The author was inundated with telegrams and letters of congratulations from all parts of the land. An early one came from Bishop Gallagher:

> *Bishop's House,*
> *Goulburn*
> *Nov. 28th 1921.*

Dear Father Hartigan,

How can I thank you sufficiently for your thoughtfulness in sending me almost the first copy of 'John O'Brien's' poems. I have today run through nearly every one of them (for the second time, of course)—and am more delighted than ever that they have been published. There is not the slightest doubt but some of them will be sung and recited a hundred years from now around the 'Boree Log'. They will be so reminiscent and so typical of the pioneer days—when the foundations of the faith were laid so deep and strong—in the Bush *Dioceses of N.S.W. Some of them, such as 'The Caseys', 'The Careys', 'The Old Mass Shandryn-Dan', 'The Rosary'—bring back to myself scenes and memories* quorum ego magna pars fui—*which will always be very dear to me.*

*God has given you a wonderful power of grasping homely themes—*cum callida junctura verborum—*which go to the very heart of our fine Catholic country folk. Blended as they nearly all are with thoughts or suggestions of religion, they will appeal to the business and bosom of our people and help to plant the faith more effectually than any book or sermons that could be written. Hence I would say: 'Don't allow such gifts to rust in idleness but to shine in use'.*

---

15. *Worthy of mention is a later review in* The Advocate *(Melbourne), 13 September 1928. P.1. O'Leary devoted his regular Literary and Critical Page to 'John O'Brien' whom he hailed as the Laureate of Catholic Australia. He emphasised his power of characterisation, his tenderness and his technical skill in winning lines which appear so artless.*

With renewed thanks for great kindness and wishing you every blessing
I am

Dear Fr Hartigan yours
sincerely,
† *John Gallagher.*[16]

The Bishop wrote again later enclosing a letter of appreciation from a classmate who entered Maynooth on the same day as he did himself in August 1863. This parish priest wrote from Castlederg, Northern Ireland: 'I have seldom read anything that has given me more pleasure than the book of poems you have sent me.'[17]

Father Eris O'Brien sent an enthusiastic letter. Bishop Dwyer wrote of the book in a humorous vein:

The only fault is that there is so little of it ... How is the Citroen?
Can you write a poem on it or does it produce lurid language?

Father Terry McGuire wrote five pages. While generally laudatory, he spent most of the letter suggesting ways of improving some of the poems. He wrote again a couple of weeks later: 'You were very gentle in your treatment of my unnecessary criticism but I have got past forty and feel that other blokes must be benefited by my opinions or perhaps don't feel that as much as the **cacoethes loquendi**.'

There were, of course, all kinds of guesses about the identity of the characters in the verses. We tend to forget that a poet is creative. So Father Hartigan declined to identify any particular person as the 'Little Irish Mother', though he sent off to his parents a copy inscribed: 'To Herself and Himself from P.J.'

Members of the family recalled small incidents: Michael remembered the 'Boxer Hats'—how, goaded to the limit, he put a fist through his. Annie used to tell of 'himself' cracking his fingers as he counted the Hail Marys.

'Laughing Mary' remains unidentified. Nor did he have a particular family in mind when he wrote 'At Casey's After Mass'; for this piece the only inspiration he could remember was a signpost near Tocumwal which read: 'To Casey's'. He compiled the poem as he drove, so it too,

---

16. *Letter among Father Hartigan's papers.*
17. *This letter of 1923 tells of the continuing saga of strife-torn Northern Ireland with its tragic loss of life. He goes on: 'For the last nine months we have been overrun by military of every description, soldiery, A Specials and B Specials. The A Specials live in barracks and we have had about 80 or 90 of them in this parish. The B Specials correspond to the old Yeomen—are armed and patrol at night. They are the local Orangemen.'*

along with 'The Old Mass Shandrydan' and 'The Parting Rosary' can be linked with his parish of Berrigan.

A strong local tradition makes John Shiel McEvoy (1850-1933) of Moombah, near Jindabyne, the original altar boy. He served Mass from sixteen until over eighty.

> *Now McEvoy was altar-boy*
> *As long as I remember;*
> *He was, bedad, a crabbed lad,*
> *And sixty come December.*

On one occasion at Wagga 'Joker' Byrne gave a recitation of the poems with Archbishop Mannix as the guest of honour. Present also was Father P. Hanrahan of Lockhart who was convinced that 'Said Hanrahan' was written at his expense. Nothing was further from the author's mind. Father Hanrahan went back-stage after the performance and accosted 'Joker'. 'Listen "Joker",' he said, 'next time you recite that drivel, instead of saying: "We'll all be rooned, said Hanrahan", say "We'll all be rooned, said Hartigan"—the two words have the same number of syllables.' The name in fact was chosen because of its sound—it is just right with 'rooned'.

The first edition was described in advertisements as 'handsomely bound in cloth gilt' and it cost 6s. It was repeatedly reprinted, some 75 000 copies in the first twenty-five years. A school edition, containing the more popular pieces, appeared early and the poems were used in English classes in Catholic schools.

One of the consequences of the success of the **Boree Log** was a request from Philip Walsh that he have the author's permission to make a six-reel moving picture from the book. The cost, including 100 guineas to the author for the copyright, was estimated at £1200. The story was to embrace the principal poems of the book and the scenario was to be submitted to Father Hartigan for his approval.

That permission was given. The hardest part of the project was the raising of the money—it was got from well-wishers with the promise that they would share in the profits. The life of the picture was estimated at one year and its profit was hopefully to be £2000.

Philip Walsh wrote to Father Hartigan from Goulburn[18] that he would begin to 'shoot' on Tuesday, 10 February. It is a long letter detailing the actors for each of the parts, such as Molly Donohoe for the grown-up

---

18. *4 February 1925.*

Laughing Mary. Most of them were from the Goulburn district, but Mary Renno, who had the leading female role, was a professional actress from Sydney.

The filming was done in the Goulburn district. The beautiful scenery won all the critics; it included such locally renowned spots as the Look Down and Governor's Hill. The Taralga race meeting figured in some of the scenes. The film was shown at the Crystal Palace Theatre in George Street, Sydney, and the **Catholic Press** was enthusiastic:

This beautiful picture drew vast crowds and the sign 'House Full' had to be displayed at both day and evening sessions. As, however, the season was limited to two weeks, it had to be withdrawn, but is now on exhibition at the SHELL THEATRE, opposite the Criterion in Pitt Street. The picture is making a strong appeal to our country people, vast crowds having witnessed the showing in Bathurst and Goulburn during the week. [19]

The **Sydney Morning Herald** critic was far from enthusiastic:

'Around the Boree Log'

Anyone who has not read 'John O'Brien's' poetry need no longer plead ignorance after he has been to see 'Around the Boree Log' at the Crystal Palace Theatre. The picture teems with it. In fact, there is more text than action. Even the best of poetry always seems rather insipid when it is flashed upon the screen in a crowded theatre, where every-one is looking, not for words, but for action. And this volume is of unequal merit even when studied in solitude. In any case, a cloud of random reminiscences about old pioneering days makes an unsubstantial scenario. These verses of Father Hartigan's require considerable stiffening with narrative to make them into a screen play, and this the producer, Phil K. Walsh, has failed to provide. One is always loth to depreciate an Australian film. The industry is in its first stages here, and producers have many difficulties to face. But as long as they continue to put forth these plotless plays we shall not get very far. The actors in 'Around the Boree Log' are all anonymous. Mr Walsh has striven to achieve

19. Catholic Press, 14 October 1925. The picture began a season in Melbourne on Saturday 20 February 1926 at the Auditorium.

local colour by picking out representative bush types on the spot, and letting them pose self-consciously before the camera rather than by relying on trained actors. The result is a sort of travelogue. It will give some notion of Australian bush life to city dwellers and people overseas, but the notion will be a somewhat incoherent one. These bush people buy from hawkers' waggons that stop at their door; they drive about in buggies; they go to funny little schoolhouses. But they have no dramatic interest. The scenery is the most appealing feature about the picture. There are some specially beautiful views of mountain and gorge near the end. Truly, Australia is a land where the camera-man can walk forth and take shots almost at random to make an effective sequence. The Roman Catholic element is very strong throughout the film. First one sees a priest reading the book of verses in his study—possibly it is the author, Father Hartigan, himself, though no definite information is put forward on this point. Later, groups of people in the Irish settlement where the 'story' moves fall devoutly to their knees and cross themselves; a priest rescues a boy who has been thrown from a horse; and about a quarter of an hour is devoted to incidents attendant upon going to early mass.

The Minister of Education (Mr Mutch) introduced the picture on Friday evening.[20]

Father Hartigan was still overseas when the film was first screened. He returned to Narrandera on 10 October of that year and later on saw the film. He was not overly impressed and confessed to being sorry to have given permission for an effort which as he described it, 'was done on a shoe-string budget'.

Mrs Gertrude M. Harber of Kurnell, New South Wales, wrote to him:

Do you remember many, many years ago (I have forgotten the exact year) at the Randwick Theatre I was sitting with my teenage children in the dress-circle and a young priest came and sat down in front of us. There were very few people there at that moment and you turned round to me and said: 'I have written the story round this film and I am a bit nervy and anxious about it. Will you please give me your opinion about it!' It was really beautiful and I have spoken of it hundreds of times in conversation with my friends but never met anyone who had seen or heard same. The exquisite lyric

---

20. Sydney Morning Herald, *28 September 1925.*

and prose, sweetness and wit of it are memories that I can never forget.[21]

Pictures from this film were used to illustrate a special leather-bound edition of **Around the Boree Log** produced by Angus & Robertson at the time.

The years following the publication of his poems in book form saw no great change in Father Hartigan's life style. He was one of the speakers at the Triennial Reunion of Manly priests at Melbourne in May 1922. The **Manly** of that year contained two new poems, 'Imelda May'[22] and 'My Curate's Motor-Bike' and the prose piece 'The Man from Snowy River'.[23]

'My Curate's Motor-Bike' was, as we have seen, illustrated by himself with nine pen and ink drawings. They show real talent, the last one particularly. It features the old parish priest addressing his horse, and in the background, unmistakably, is the church of St Mel, Narrandera, with the presbytery alongside it.[24]

From his earliest days young Patrick Hartigan wanted to be an artist—we are reminded of G.K. Chesterton and his attendance at the Slade School of Art. Like Chesterton too, Father Hartigan made no claim to competence in music, but also like him he had a great feeling for sound in his verse. He was full of admiration for Chesterton's skill in this field: he often instanced 'Lepanto' as an example of it.

The end of 1923 saw the death of his former teacher and life-long friend, Bishop Gallagher of Goulburn.[25] There was of course, speculation as to who would succeed him. The **Bulletin** had this paragraph:

Good news for the Australian hierarchy comes from a hint that the P.P. of Narrandera, N.S.W., Patrick Hartigan, late inspector of diocesan schools and a scholar of the late Bishop Gallagher when he ran the Goulburn College, is likely to get the Goulburn See. Long ago Hartigan was known to Bulletin *readers as 'Mary Ann' and his* When the Circus Comes to Town *had great popularity. Of late years he has written under the pen-name of 'John O'Brien' and he published 'Round the Boree Log' under it. A set of verses will appear in the forthcoming Christmas* Bulletin. *Maoriland has already two*

---

21. *Letter dated 3 June 1952, among Father Hartigan's papers.*
22. *The background of this poem is given on pp. 85-86 and on pp. 63-71 'My Curate's Motor-Bike' is reproduced and its story told.*
23. *Reproduced above, pp. 94-104.*
24. *Father Tom Linane and myself, editing Father Hartigan's historical writings, used this sketch on the dust cover of the book:* The Men of '38, *Lowden Publishing Co., Kilmore, Victoria, 1975.*
25. *The text of his appreciation of the Bishop which he wrote for the* Freeman's Journal, *13 December 1923 is given above, pp. 33-37.*

Narrandera visitors in the early 1920s: Father Arthur McHugh, with whom Father Hartigan holidayed in Campbelltown, standing on the right of Father Frank Hartigan of Jerilderie. Seated on Father Pat Hartigan's left is Dr (afterwards Mgr) Pat Tuomey, banished to the bush of Mittagong-Bowral for his stand on the 1916 conscription issue.

bishops from the Cardinal's College; but Father Hartigan, if he lands the job, will be the first Australian to button the collar behind a purple background.[26]

I never heard Father Hartigan make any reference to this report. He did, however, tell me there had once been talk of his being made a bishop and he quoted for me the comment of his erstwhile mentor and great friend, Father 'Tommy' Hayden, then president of Manly: 'Fancy making a poet a bishop!'

In these years he became more in demand as an occasional speaker. Thus in 1924 Monsignor O'Connell of Junee was fifty years a priest, and Father Hartigan was the preacher:

Go ye into the whole world and preach the gospel to every creature. Mark XVI.15.

When Our Divine Lord commissioned His Apostles to go into the whole world and preach the gospel to every creature, He initiated a missionary movement which had been remarkable for its thoroughness in every age, and which has retained its vigour even to our own time. The history of that movement reads more strangely than all the stories of adventure whether told by history or fiction, and it enshrines in its pages the noblest heroism, the most unflinching devotion to duty, and the finest charity of which the world has knowledge. The Apostles and their disciples went to every part of the then known world, and when younger nations arose further north and further west there were never wanting other disciples to obey that last command of the Divine Master 'Go ye into the whole world and preach the gospel to every creature'. And thus as civilization began to spread over the surface of the earth and into its remotest corners, hot on the heels of the plunderer and the explorer came the missionaries of Christ.

Nay, they have been among the greatest of the explorers. They left the trade routes and penetrated the primeval forests—anywhere, everywhere where the Standard of Redemption had not yet been raised. They dared to drag the barbarian from his centuries-old superstitions; they dared to tell the pagan of his vices, even though

---

26. The Bulletin, 6 Dec 1923, p. 20. *The verses referred to were* The Ten-Twelve Shebang *which appeared in the issue of 8 December 1923. The two New Zealand Bishops were Matt Brodie and James Liston. The report should have said: 'the first Australian from Manly' as there had already been four Australians from overseas Colleges nominated as Bishops.*

The author wishes to record with gratitude the work of Father Joe Purcell (formerly parish priest of Lindfield) in researching the files of The Bulletin.

the wrack and the burning pyre were the reward of their
outspokenness. Onward they pressed in spite of hardship and torture,
and what was harder to bear, disappointment and temporary failure.
Onward to preach the gospel to every creature and with them to
every land and every nation went the symbol of Love on which Jesus
died. 'Greater Love than this no man hath'. It went with the Apostles
themselves on the track of the Roman, and Carthaginian and the
Greek. It went with Augustine to find those fair-haired captives who
captured their captors in the market-place of Rome. It went with
Patrick returning to the land he had learned to love even as a slave.
It went with Francis Xavier to face the unknown perils of the East. It
went with the Jesuit and the Franciscan into the new world which
Columbus had discovered in the West. It made the martyr rejoice to
think that his blood might help to water that grain of mustard seed
which was to grow into a mighty tree. In the more settled countries
of Europe; by the sweep of broad American rivers; in the tropical
jungle; 'beyond the smoke of Asian Capes' there was no part of the
world in which the Standard of Redemption had not been raised, and
the gospel of peace and love had not been preached.

But while all this was being done, there slumbered on one
continent, to the evangelizing of which I beg leave to draw your
attention for a few moments this morning. That Island continent has
taken no part in the fierce and tragic opening acts of the world's
early drama. Tucked away where the long backed rollers of the
Pacific croon their southern summer song she lay concealed:

> with ease that never hearkened
> The sounds without, the cries of strife and play
> Like some sweet child within a chamber darkened
> Left sleeping far into a troubled day.

Old geographers looking at that vast expanse of waters which
marked the maps of the day, hazarded a guess that some
undiscovered land was lying there. A Portuguese trader beating
South and East from The Cape, and blown out of his course might
have seen her western shores, but if he did, he did not report it. A
Spanish captain, sent by his king to discover the great Southern Land
of the Holy Ghost, saw the outline of her northern promontory, but
he thought it was merely another of the numerous small islands he
had encountered, and passed her by. Dutch sailors trading to Java
scattered the names of their ships along her western sea-board from
the Leuwin to Carpentaria, but they set no value upon their

discoveries. A British buccaneer landed and pronounced her barren. Many years afterwards an English captain conveying a party of scientific men returning from Tahiti touched her Eastern shores and found a land of Promise, and eighteen years later a British fleet with upwards of a thousand souls on board dropped anchor in the finest natural harbour in the world.

One might be pardoned for wishing to dwell upon the strangeness and the incongruity of the happenings on that Twenty-sixth of January One Hundred and Thirty-six years ago. Here were the small high-decked, heavily-rigged ships of the period riding peacefully on the waters of a bay beyond which lay a silent empty land, in point of fact, one of the continents of the world, and nearly as large as the whole of Europe. It was a land that knew nothing of the vices which have stained and stained again the annals of elder lands, and now at last white men come to change the face of things. In those ships floating double—ship and shadow—on the unruffled waters of Port Jackson were the first white inhabitants which this country knew, and they were convicts, our early and one only shame in which we had no part. Some of them were criminals of the worst type. Some of them were victims of stupid laws wherein the punishment was in no sense commensurate with the crime. Some of them were innocent; and perhaps it is not wide of the truth to say that considering the iniquitous system of which they were the victims all of them were more sinned against than sinning. At least they were all human beings with souls which had been redeemed by the Precious Blood which had been shed on Calvary.

Among them were some who belonged to the ancient faith, most of whom had come from the troubled land the pages of whose story for seven hundred years has been smudged with tears, and whose sons have been sentenced to death, imprisonment and banishment for the heinous crime of loving their native land, and yearning with all the fire of a patriot's heart to make her a nation once again. Hard was the lot of these men on the inhospitable shores of Botany Bay, and hardest of all because they were denied the opportunity of practising their religion. To a Catholic that is the highest craftsmanship of cruelty. To an Irish Catholic it is a torture of soul worse than any torture of the body could be, for be this said of them in fairness that no matter where his wandering steps may lead, no matter how far he may stray from the traditions of the land of the persecuted Faith, deep down in the heart of every Irish Catholic there are two undying sentiments which no circumstances can crush—two altars so to speak, which no sacrilegious hands may dare desecrate, the altar of his God, and the altar of his country. It is told of one of these unfortunate prisoners of the time that he fashioned for himself a wooden cross that he might have near him in his desolation at least a rough made emblem of his redemption.

No priest had celebrated the Divine Mysteries for them since their arrival. The French navigator La Perouse had landed and laid to rest the remains of his chaplain, Pere Receveur, but no priest had gathered together that exile congregation. There were among the convicts three priests who had been deported in consequence of the troublous times of Ninety-eight. These gave what religious consolation they could to their fellow prisoners, but it was necessarily stealthy and incomplete. Twenty years after the establishment of the settlement a zealous Cistercian, Father Flynn, arrived to minister to those scattered sheep of the flock, but as he had dared to come without Government Sanction, he was sent back by the first available ship. It is a matter of authentic history that as he was not permitted to return to the house where he had preserved the Blessed Sacrament, he was forced to leave his Divine Master in a wooden tabernacle in a cottage which stood on the site of the present St Patrick's Church, Sydney, and for two long years the pastorless faithful said their rosary and made their adoration there. When at the end of that time a priest opened the pyx he found the Sacred Species in a perfect state of preservation.

In Eighteen hundred and nineteen—one hundred and five years ago, licence was given to two Catholic chaplains to proceed to New South Wales, and there began to flow a stream of Irish Missionaries, which, thank God, still continues, and which will always be associated with the immortal names of Conolly and Therry. It is not to my purpose to enlarge upon the trials and heroism of these two apostles, alone of all their kind in an unexplored continent. Their splendid story is told in Cardinal Moran's history of the Catholic Church in Australia and Father Eris O'Brien's fine life of Father Therry, two books which should be in the hands of every Australian Catholic.

I want to pass on to a later stage in this country's development. Blaxland, Lawson, and Wentworth had found a way over the Blue Mountains; Oxley and Cunningham had made excursions into the interior; Hume and Hovell had journeyed overland to Port Phillip; Sturt had traced the Murrumbidgee from Jugiong to the Murray; the last convict ship had landed its undesirable freight; Macarthur had already laid the foundations of the greatest wool-producing flocks in the world; Hargraves had discovered gold; a new day had dawned for the colony. *The news spread through the world and men of every country felt the old fever in their blood as they hurried southwards 'When the beacon was Ballarat'. The fiddle-bows of the immigrant ship ploughed the Indian Ocean in the wake of the lumbering convict hulks, and to this country came those sturdy men and women who built the first bark huts in the mining towns, who pressed forward and cleared the forests and dotted the lands with farms, and began the path of this country as we know it today, and along which it will continue to advance.*

But these settlers, too, were without the consolation of religion because there were not sufficient priests to minister to them. The few who were here did their best and a 'splendid best' it was, but when their only means of travel was the saddle-horse how could they cover a country nearly as large as Europe? Once again the command echoed down the years 'Go ye into the whole world and preach the gospel to every creature', and once again there were apostles ready to obey. Those missionaries came, for the most part, from that northern island which had never wavered in the faith which Patrick taught at Tara, and which seems to have been predestined to play so great a role in the founding of the Catholic Church in Australia. Certainly the first Archbishop of Sydney, Dr Polding, was an Englishman, so was his successor, Dr Vaughan. True also the English Benedictines wrote their records in the Catholic life of this country in characters which we shall not forget, but with these and a few other exceptions, the mission to preach the gospel to the Catholics of Australia and the task of founding in the southern part of the world that church, was entrusted to the Irish secular clergy.

They were a splendid body of men, these secular priests of the early days. Physically strong, and mentally alert, they followed the track of the tilted carts and bullock drays 'where human foot had ne'er or rarely been'. From mining camps to mining camps; by bridle track across the ranges; by the dog-leg fences; through uncharted forests where the trail was an axe-mark on a tree 'or a rough calculation based on the blaze of a star'. There were no railways, no roads, no motor cars. They went their way on horse-back, their guide their instinct, their motor power the courage that was in them to bear all things in obedience to the Divine Command: 'Go ye into the whole world and preach the gospel to every creature'. They spent long, long days in the saddle, lonely nights in the open with their tired heads pillowed on their packs, their roof the blue dome of heaven whence unfamiliar stars looked down upon their insignificance, and around them a silent, irresponsive country, the land-marks of which have been named from disaster—Mount Hopeless, Mount Despair, Point Despair, in a long line back to the Dutch Sailor's KEER WEER or 'Turn again'. In spite of all this, unconquered and undaunted they pressed onwards and planted the cross, and taught the faith in every part of the land. If you seek their monuments, you have only to look around you in any town of the Commonwealth and you will see their epitaphs writ in brick and mortar, you will see their crowning glory in the generous, devoted, and loyal people who throng our churches, and whose fathers were strengthened in the faith by those grand old pioneer secular priests.

This morning we are gathered to celebrate the golden jubilee of one of that noble band. The Very Reverend Dean O'Connell has completed fifty years of his priesthood, and all of it was spent in Australia. Half a century ago he came here in a sailing ship, the Lincolnshire, and for half a century he has taken the rough with the smooth, in this, the country of his adoption. He belongs to what we might call the second generation of priests who have helped in the building up of the church in our midst. He is a link between its founders and the present time. When he came here Archbishop Polding, the first Archbishop of Sydney, was still alive, and Father Therry, the Apostle of Australia, had been dead only ten years.

His working radius embraced practically the whole of southern and south-western New South Wales from Goulburn to Broken Hill, from Cobar to Albury, and every place that he knew has been better for it. A man of iron constitution, a far seeing man of affairs, a gifted administrator, through it all he has been ever loyal to the priestly promises he made in Carlow Cathedral fifty years ago. It may be embarrassing to the jubilarian to sound his praises in his presence, and perhaps it smacks of fulsomeness, but some day these things will be said from this place when he shall not heed the speaker's voice. Let me say them now. Let me say them to you while he is still with us, happily strong in body and clear in mind, and with—so it please God—many useful years before him; and I trust he will understand that these words are spoken with deep sincerity by one who reveres him and owes him much.

Throughout his career he has been a faithful steward of his Divine Master. Higher praise than this I cannot give. He has been as straight as an arrow in all his dealings. He has never been afraid to speak the truth that was in his mind (no one who knows him will accuse him of timidity in this respect). His word has ever been his bond, and he has never failed to lend a helping hand to one who

*needed it. This, I think, is the outsanding characteristic of the man;
and it is this, as much as anything, that has endeared him to
thousands throughout the Riverina. Today his name is respected and
loved in the back country perhaps more than that of any other
priest. 'Old Father Tim' they call him, and I have seen hard eyes
grow soft at the recollection of many a kind act done by him in the
dark hour of trouble which comes sometimes, somewhere to every
man.*

*It has always appeared to me that the most picturesque figure in
the Catholic life of this country at least, is the old Irish Parish Priest
with the long experience behind him. No one knows better than he
how to do the good turn 'which blesseth him that gives and him
that takes', no one knows a straighter way to the hearts of his flock.
In dear Old Father Tim we have one who is typical of his class. Only
the recording angel knows the good that he has done—the big things
in the crisis of some poor life, and the daily little unremembered
acts of kindness which have been crowded into fifty golden years.*

*Fifty years, it is a long way he has travelled, and what a different
prospect meets his eyes today from that of half a century ago. When
he came here the railway from Sydney was built only as far as
Goulburn, and that from Melbourne to Wangaratta. Wagga was
merely a tiny village by the river. There was no Junee. The sites of
the numerous towns which stud the Riverina today were virgin
timber. What a change! The twenty thousand ton liner cleaves the
waves where his old sailing ship rode the darkened seas in seventy-
four. The fast express behind the big 'N N' goes roaring down the
grade beside the bridle-track where he came on horse-back with his
valise strapped on the pommel of his saddle. The motor car
annihilates distance on the long white roads outback where he
trundled along in his buggy or in the coaches of 'Cobb & Co'. Still
he did his work without complaint. In the burning heat of the
plains, 'with the everlasting fences stretching out across the land', in
the winter rains when the bleak black soil roads were a swamp he
battled along to say his Mass in the furthest hut on the track to the
Sunset, or to give the last Sacraments and the consolations of
religion to a dying man beyond the camel-pad, when ears with death
summons ringing in them have listened for his coming and anxious
eyes and bleeding hearts have watched for Cobb & Co.*

*You people of Junee have done well in celebrating his Golden
Jubilee as you have done. It is an event which is of more than local
importance; it is one to which the attention of the whole country
will be called. Other priests at a later date may celebrate the fiftieth*

158

anniversary of their ordination, and therein recall change and progress, but none will see again the violent transformation which has taken place during the last fifty years. You did well to celebrate it because in your jubilarian we have one of the few survivors of the early days of the Church in the Commonwealth. He is the only link that binds us to the past in this part of the country. Of the sixteen priests who were in the diocese of Goulburn on his arrival, not one is alive today. Of the six young missionaries who came with him in the Lincolnshire in Seventy-four, not one is left to congratulate their old shipmate. The modest tombstones scattered throughout the land, mural tablets in the churches they have built tell the world that they have gone to render account of their stewardship, but I feel that their spirits are hovering near this morning, and if the dead rejoice over mundane things, they rejoice today at the consummation of fifty fruitful years.

You did well to celebrate it because it gives us of a later day an opportunity to add our felicitations. It gives us an occasion to hark back from the point of progress we have reached to the heroic struggles which made that progress possible. When an army marches in review with the colours bravely flying, there is one little squad which ever arrests the attention, and which catches at the heart. It is the Old Guard. The veterans with their scars who have won the battles of the past. Here is our army of today strong in body and strong in mind, prepared for any emergency that may arise; and here is the Old Guard with the snows of many winters on his head, and the honours of long and faithful service thick upon him.

Our rejoicing is all the more complete because he is still as strong and vigorous as he was in his heyday. He has not reached that stage when the present ceases to matter and all the interests of life are lying where his hopes are buried. He is still as alert to plan and as courageous to dare as ever. He is an old man with a young heart yet, and it must gladden him to know that his long and useful life is rewarded in the confidence of his Bishop, the respect and esteem of his fellow priests, and the love of his faithful people. What he has done has gone before him to the throne of God. May what he has yet to do be the crowning of the splendid achievements of fifty years.[27]

---

27. *Sermon taken from an unidentified and undated newspaper cutting among Father Hartigan's papers. The date of the jubilee was 31 May 1924.*

8 Trip to Europe

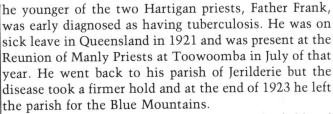

The younger of the two Hartigan priests, Father Frank, was early diagnosed as having tuberculosis. He was on sick leave in Queensland in 1921 and was present at the Reunion of Manly Priests at Toowoomba in July of that year. He went back to his parish of Jerilderie but the disease took a firmer hold and at the end of 1923 he left the parish for the Blue Mountains.

Later Annie took him to her home in Haberfield and had a trained nurse there to look after him. Then followed a sojourn in the Hospice at Darlinghurst until he expressed his wish to return to the mountains. One of the priests of the Sacred Heart parish travelled with him on the train as it was feared he might not survive the journey. He got back to Leura and died a few days later on 24 October 1924 at the age of thirty-four. He is buried at Wentworth Falls where the number of graves of young people of that era bears mute witness to the ravages of the disease which was then virtually a death sentence.

It was Pat who bore the main burden of worry about Frank. He was close enough to see him failing all the time, yet was unable to restrain his brother's generosity and selflessness that all the time was taking more and more toll. It was Pat also who made the arrangements for him at Leura, and spent a good deal of time on the mountains with him. He also had the sad task of collecting his belongings from Jerilderie including the T-model Ford he had driven.

Annie also felt Frank's death deeply and so Father Pat invited her and the five children to the presbytery for a holiday. We were there for Christmas and he played Santa Claus with much-appreciated gifts for us all. For me it was the first of a dozen holidays at the presbytery; as a student and young priest, most years I would spend a month at Narrandera.

After the worry and grief of Frank's illness and death, a trip to Europe for the Holy Year of 1925 had a strong appeal for Father Pat. He was able to get the Vincentian Fathers to look after his parish from April till October so the way lay open.

On Wednesday evening 18 February 1925 a function was held to honour the intending traveller, and the whole town and district took part—the local paper described it as the best attended and most representative ever held in Narrandera.[1] Priest friends came from towns as far apart as Tocumwal, Griffith, Balldale and Wagga (N.S.W.). Bishop Dwyer was prevented from being there by urgent business in Sydney. They were to meet later that year in Rome and Dublin.

The function must have been a marathon. There were a dozen musical items, several recitations and a dozen speakers before the guest of the night took the floor; after he had finished there were half a dozen toasts proposed and responses made. The time the function concluded is not recorded!

A purse of £600 was given to Father Hartigan and he confessed he was taken aback by this extraordinary presentation.[2] He went on to say:

> He was proud to hear the speakers say he was liberal-minded, for he hoped that he would never say anything that would wound the susceptibilities of anyone. He was born in the religion which he led in his small way, but he was prepared to think that other people were as sincere with regard to their denominations as he was with regard to his.
>
> He regarded every man as an Australian who worked for the good of this country, no matter where he was born. He hoped the hand of friendship would always be extended to men from overseas who came here to work for this glorious country. There was no room for bigotry here.
>
> He thanked his friends for making the night the proudest in his life.[3]

Father Hartigan sailed on an Italian ship, the SS **Remo.** He recalled that on one occasion his Mass was crowded with a tremendous number of the Italian crew and passengers. He was told that it was the anniversary of Garibaldi's march on Rome!

The first ever National Holy Year Pilgrimage, led by Archbishop Mannix, had left Melbourne on SS **Mongolia** on 14 April 1925. With it also were Bishops O'Farrell of Bathurst and Dwyer of Wagga and sixteen priests. The pilgrims arrived at Marseilles on 16 May, were at Lourdes next day and at Genoa, where Father Hartigan joined them, on 27 May.

Rome impressed him, but selectively. Gushing admiration for bas reliefs of horses brought his rejoinder: 'No horses ever had that motion'. He was at the audience given the Australian pilgrims by Pius XI. The

1. Narrandera Argus, 20 February 1925.
2. As a pointer to its value, at that time the P & O Shipping Line was advertising a five-week trip to England at prices ranging from £38 to £134.
3. Narrandera Argus, loc. cit.

Pope appointed Bishop Dwyer his interpreter. Father Hartigan recalled that the Bishop stood with hands folded, the picture of nonchalance. When the Pope had finished Bishop Dwyer gave out the translation with consummate ease and the Pope picked him up on only one word. 'The Pope', said Bishop Dwyer, 'asks you to take back his blessing to your country'. 'I said', Pope Pius objected, 'I command you. **Comando** was the word I used'.

Father Arthur Vaughan of Melbourne was chaplain to His Grace Archbishop Mannix and historian of this first Australian Catholic Pilgrimage to Rome. He wrote back to the Melbourne Catholic paper, the **Tribune,** the following account:

> *Nor did I in my wildest boyhood dreams ever imagine that I would do what I did a few days ago in front of St Peter's. There was need for an important announcement to be made to the assembled pilgrims. To make it more effectively, I mounted a marble balustrade, and there in the famous piazza that has re-echoed to the steps of countless millions; there in the shadow of the great St Peter's; there where Popes and Emperors and Kings and Tribunes and Senators and Dictators had addressed the multitudes, a denizen of an Australian country parish lifted his voice in an address to his fellow countrymen from the Antipodes. As I stood on that balustrade, I absurdly enough, thought of 'Rienzi, the last of the Tribunes'. Why, I cannot for the life of me explain! The humour of the situation struck and I sought and found in the crowd of faces before me the countenance of 'John O'Brien', the author of* Around the Boree Log. *We were schoolboys together, we knew each other well, and he accordingly smiled back to me in appreciation of the situation. Did you see the Careys! Which reminds me of the remark made by a hefty Australian after gazing for some time at the Basilica of St Mary Major, that triumph of architectural skill with its wealth of skilful detail—'a poem in marble' as someone has described it. 'It could do with a lick of paint', said the man from Tangmalangaloo.*[4]

Father Vaughan went touring in Europe after the pilgrimage. He died during his travels, at Wiesbaden, Germany, on 9 August 1925.

Father Hartigan had been writing to his parents at Haberfield from various ports. Then there was silence for some weeks and consternation in the home. Eventually this letter came:

4. Tribune, *6 August 1925.*

Rome
June 11th 1925

Dear Mother & Dad,

Here I am sending you a note from Rome. I had intended writing more frequently but it is not as easy as one imagines when you are knocking about. I found Dr Dwyer and the pilgrims from Australia at Genoa, and since have had a real good time. I met Mrs Woods and Kathleen Coen[5] among the first and have seen a lot of them since.

I had the bad luck to get a bit sick soon after coming here. Some gastric trouble so I went to the Blue Sisters for a few days, and they nursed me round. Some that used to be at Lewisham are here and they were delighted to see any one from Australia. Several of the Australians got a bit sick. My trouble I think was some thing I had eaten, but, Thank God, I am quite well again.

There are quite a number of people on the pilgrimage that I know and it made it very pleasant indeed. Father Moloney M.S.C. leads the show at all the spiritual exercises. We were at St Peter's at the canonization of St John Eudes and the Curé of Ars. It was a wonderful sight. There were about one hundred and fifty bishops, about twenty or thirty cardinals, and the procession took about an hour and a half to pass into the Church. There were pilgrims from all over the world for the occasion, between sixty and seventy thousand people were present in St Peter's. I will never forget the sight.

A couple of days later we had an audience with the Pope. They say he was more gracious to the Australians than to any other pilgrims. Anyway he gave everyone his ring to kiss and spoke for nearly half an hour. He gave a special blessing and told us it was for our people as well. I have a pair of Rosary beads which he blessed and which I will bring out to you. I don't think I will stay too long here. After seeing a little more of Italy I will go over to England and Ireland and I think leave for home about the end of August. That should get me home about the middle of October. There is no place like Australia. I am sure of that. I did not join up with the pilgrims, it is cheaper on your own, but I will meet them here and there.

Hope you and Dad are keeping well. Also that Annie, Dick and the youngsters are the same. Here is all my love. It won't be long till I see you again.

P.J.

P.S. Love to Lil, Bridge, Minnie and B. when you write.[6]

5. These were friends from Yass.
6. Letter among the papers of the Hartigan family.

Villa San Girolamo at Fiesole on the hills above Florence where Father Hartigan convalesced after his serious illness in Rome.

Contemporary reports suggest that Father Hartigan was really seriously ill in Rome. His friend, Mrs Bid Woods, found him very sick in his hotel and organised his admission to Calvary Hospital. The Sisters of the Little Company of Mary—the 'Blues' as he affectionately called them from the veil they wore—nursed him back to health. For his convalesence they transferred him to their beautiful Villa San Girolamo at Fiesole on the hills above Florence.

The ordinations of the students of Propaganda College took place that year on Easter Saturday and among those ordained was a young Doctor of Divinity, John Harper of Sydney, destined for the diocese of Wagga. Father Hartigan met him in Rome and later they had a memorable couple of weeks in Ireland. They were joined by Rev Dr Pat Tuomey of Sydney, replete with a T-model Ford. Father Hartigan's comment was: ' ''The Doc'' is a legend in Australia—you should see him on his native heath!'.

Together they visited Dr Mannix in his family home at Charleville, County Cork, and John Harper recalls vividly the magic of that occasion with three such conversationalists as the Archbishop, the 'Doc' and 'John O'Brien'. Dr Mannix had been cold-shouldered by the Irish hierarchy as one too political for them and he was devastating that day as he held forth on the Irish bishops.

It was also with Dr Tuomey, as we have seen, that Father Hartigan linked up with his mother's people in Lissycasey, County Clare. But apart from this family visit, he was content to go round Ireland as a sightseer.

He wrote these impressions to his friends the Rourkes of Narrandera.

> *The Muckross Hotel*
> *Lakes of Killarney*
> *August 8th, 1925*

Dear Bill,

So poor old Jack[7] has smoked his last pipeful of crook tobacco! I was real sorry to learn of his death from Joe's letter which I got in London. It must have been a shock to yourself and the Missus.

Well here I am by Killarney's lakes and fells. The lakes are all right, but everything in the old world has been told to us with a certain amount of exaggeration. There are many places in Australia as good as these. I went to the famous Dublin Horse Show and was disappointed again. The show was good in point of numbers. There were a great crowd of horses, but they were a rough-bred lot. Although I wasn't game to say that to

---

7. Old Jack, or Big Jack as the children called him, lived with the Rourkes and did odd jobs around the house. He died suddenly.

anyone. They think that it is the greatest show in the world.

I am enjoying Ireland. The people are just grand, so simple and friendly. I met a good number of priests from Australia since coming here, and that went a long way towards making things pleasant. It rains here every day which is the worst part of it. I hope to go on a motor trip through the country tomorrow, and then I shall get back to London, and after that to France and Genoa where I shall catch the boat for the good country at the end of the month. I'll keep all I have to say till one of those midnight chats which we will have again very soon, I trust.

Best wishes to yourself and the Missus.

P.J.H.[8]

Nowhere in his travels did he declare himself, though the Irish especially would have fêted him. Dr Harper recalls the time they went into a bookseller's in Dublin and asked for a copy of **Around the Boree Log.** The man behind the counter confessed that he hadn't read it, but he was told it was good. Dr Harper told him he was speaking with the author, and he felt quite sure the man did not believe him.

The same disbelief was evident in an Irish priest the pair met on a London bus. The Irishman was rejoicing in an attachment he had got for his push-bike; with it fitted to the front wheel he had a record of how far he had gone. He recommended that each of them get one to take back to Australia. When Dr Harper informed him that Father Hartigan was taking back a Super-Sports Alvis, incredulity was written all over his face.

On another occasion Father Hartigan was on his own on a London bus and an American priest sat down beside him. He made the observation that bus travel was a slow way of getting round and Father Hartigan told him of the Alvis he had at Coventry awaiting shipment and confessed that he did not relish driving it on unfamiliar roads. The American volunteered his services and they had an enjoyable couple of weeks touring England in the Alvis. When back home the American told his friends of his trip with Father Hartigan, he was informed that he had been in the company of 'John O'Brien'.

That same American priest was in Europe in 1950 for the next Holy Year and he happened to meet the present writer at La Maison du Bon Pasteur in Paris. When he found he was speaking with an Australian, he began to talk about his wonderful days with Father Hartigan. 'Do you know him?' he asked.

---

8. *Letter kindly provided by the Rourke family of Narrandera.*

Father Hartigan's story of getting the car was that he approached the Alvis people in Coventry. They assured him that the Super-Sports model would do 100 mph [160 km/h] and took him to Brooklands to demonstrate it. The needle went to eighty but would not go beyond it. Back at the pits the suggestion was to take off the mudguards and try again. 'I've had enough', said Father Hartigan, 'I'll take your word for it,' and the deal was made.

Late in August Dr Harper and Father Hartigan made their way back across Europe and arrived at Genoa to catch the **Rè d' Italia** for Australia. The shipping agents had been trying to contact them, as there was a maritime strike and the ship was held up indefinitely. They were told that the Orient liner **Orvieto** was due at Naples in a few days, so they travelled there and secured berths. Staff handled the baggage to get the ship away.

Father Hartigan enjoyed the voyage—the spacious decks of the English liner were very much to his taste. Dr Harper has some reminiscences of that voyage:

The Second Engineer was seated at our table and his cool politeness couldn't hide his dismay at the prospect of some weeks with two clerics as table companions. Even the wit and wisdom of P.J.H. failed to charm him until one night at dinner Paddy quite by chance quoted a few lines of his beloved Kipling. The Officer immediately raised his eyes and asked, 'Are you familiar with Kipling, Father?' 'I am indeed' said Hartigan and they launched into a kind of Kipling duet, capping one another's quotes. Dinner over, the Officer said, 'Would you care to come up for a drink, Fathers?' From then on our meal times became a feature of the voyage.

In the same voyage there was an old pastoralist from the Western District of Victoria. Alec was a somewhat grumpy character, his beloved merinos apparently his only interest in life. He spent most of his time alone stretched out on a deck chair until one day P.J.H. passed by and struck up a conversation. Within minutes the old man was delighted to find that this cleric had quite an extensive knowledge of sheep matters and so began a daily routine. After breakfast P.J.H. would stretch out beside Alec, get the pipe going and say something like: 'Well Alec, what about we drive down to the bottom paddock and take a look at those ewes? I think they could do with a bit of attention.' And so it went on for the rest of the voyage with a lonely old man made happy by an imaginative priest with knowledge of sheep almost equal to his own.

Like old Alec on the Orvieto, *people who met P.J.H. were constantly surprised at his many-sided interests. Literature in general, poetry, painting, cricket and many other human activities were ready subjects of his conversation. But on motor cars he was a real expert with a complete knowledge of the performance of any car then on the road. One of the first priests in Australia to own a motor car in the days when cars were 'serviced' at places like blacksmith shops, he became a first-class driver and finally graduated to perhaps the fastest road car then in Australia, the Super-Sports Alvis he brought back from this trip. The boat-shaped aluminium body of the Alvis became quite a sight in the Narrandera district. While his skill allowed him to drive this car really fast, he was always amused at the apocryphal local stories of his record-breaking trips, such as the fourteen miles [23 km] to Grong Grong in eight minutes.*

An amusing incident occurred one evening at Narrandera when P.J.H. dropped in to a Church Euchre Party and Dance. A stranger approached him, introduced himself with a certain name but added that P.J.H. would probably know him better under his car-racing name of Phil Garlick. P.J.H. was really delighted since at that time Phil Garlick was carrying all before him in car races in a Supercharged Super-Sports Alvis. P.J.H. immediately asked him a question regarding the performance of the Supercharged Alvis and from the answer knew at once that this couldn't possibly be Phil Garlick. One more technical question was enough to confuse the stranger, who quickly asked P.J.H. what sort of car he was driving. When told a Super-Sports Alvis he quickly excused himself and left the hall. Telling me of it a few days later, P.J.H. smilingly said, 'You know, I think that poor bloke really had bad luck. Fancy pretending to be an Alvis driver to a bush priest who was one of about six people in Australia owning a Super-Sports Alvis!'.[9]

Father Hartigan arrived back in Narrandera on 10 October 1925. He had enjoyed his trip to the Old World but he confessed to being very happy to be back in his own beloved Australia.[10]

9. *Reminiscences kindly supplied by Dr John Harper, formerly parish priest of Griffith, now residing at Clifton Gardens.*
10. Narandera Argus 13 October 1925.

9 'The Girls'

Soon after Father Hartigan returned from his trip abroad he got busy on the building of what was practically a new convent. In December 1926 Bishop Dwyer blessed the stone that was to mark the extensions. Part only of the original convent was demolished, additions were made and a second storey added. While the building was going on Father Hartigan gave up his presbytery to the sisters and he took a room in a hotel.

The newly constructed convent was opened in 1927 and accommodated the community of Sisters of St Joseph, in those days about eight, as well as girls from outlying country areas accepted as boarders. Father Hartigan had a lively interest in both the Sisters and boarders. His custom was to have afternoon tea very often with the Sisters and from them he got all the details of what was going on in the school and much of what was happening in the parish. He knew the boarders well and saw them often.

The hospital also was his constant care; he was there several times each week. He knew not only his own parishioners but everyone in the town, and anyone in the hospital got at least a greeting and a few words from him.

A moving story of those years is told by Mrs Mafe Sorrell who as Miss King was at that time a Salvation Army lass at Narrandera. She wrote:

Appointed to Narrandera in January 1925 to serve as Assistant Officer of the Salvation Army, myself twenty-five years of age, I very early became aware of the high regard in which the Priest of the local Catholic Church was held, although he was then away overseas.

On a bright sunny morning towards the end of 1925, my Commanding Officer and I emerged from the Post Office to observe the approach of a silver speeding car, the like of which had never before been seen in the district—it was of shiny aluminium, long and narrow, a sporting model. It stopped at the Post Office and out stepped, or should I say bounded, a tall, handsome Priest—hatless and smiling. Taking the steps of the Post Office two at a time in a hurry, he noticed the uniform of the two Salvation Army girls, came forward with outstretched hand and said 'Welcome to Narrandera'. He then introduced himself, wrote our names in his notebook and

Mafe Sorrell who as a young Salvation Army Officer at Narrandera experienced Father Hartigan's well-known generosity.

said 'It must be time for the annual visit of the Army for my cheque
for your Self-Denial Appeal. I never miss that if I can help it.' A date
for the call was there and then arranged. He collected his mail—then
turned to go down the steps—looking back with a decided twinkle in
his eyes he said 'Wear your Army bonnets when you come—I don't
like the hats'. That was Father Hartigan.

The appointment to collect the cheque in person was duly kept
and two Salvation Army lasses in full regulation uniform which
included bonnets and gloves presented themselves at the Presbytery;
escorted by the Housekeeper to the study to be received by a most
congenial Host, graciously and warmly. The cheque already written
prior to our arrival and our receipt exchanged and we were told to
relax over a cup of tea; the needs of the parish were discussed,
problems aired, solutions offered as though we were indeed 'one as
Jesus prayed his Disciples should be' and all this before we had heard
of the ecumenical movement and the uniting of the Churches.
Father Hartigan told of his visit Overseas and wound up by saying he
had had a good look at the World, including the little green Island
beloved of Catholics the world over, and had found nothing to
compare with the view from his own study window before us. After
a full hour's fellowship we left the study enriched spiritually,
financially, and remarking on feeling honoured by a Saint of God.

The next few months are best forgotten, memories of
unemployment—no jobs for willing workers—all classes
affected—shabbily dressed men (some highly educated) walking,
tramping, shuffling, some of them returned broken in body, mind
and spirit, from the Great War—all NEEDING something and Social
Workers like myself were broken hearted having to refuse so many.
My Captain had a nervous breakdown and had to go home. I was left
with full responsibility to serve as the Salvation Army Officer—
twenty-five years of age and a single woman—years before
Women's Liberation was popular. How I appreciated 'John O'Brien's'
reminder: 'The birds will sing again' and relied for guidance and
strength on 'A Great Big God' who never failed me.

One week-end in January 1926 there appeared at my door a young
couple well dressed and carrying almost new suit cases, asking to be
accommodated and given their fares to Sydney. They had lost their
job on a Station—had only been married twelve months, managed to
travel as far as Narrandera and couldn't go further without help.
Accommodation was out of the question—I booked both of them
into the Hotel for a couple of nights and supplied meals at my table
but my financial resources were so inadequate I could not afford the

£5 necessary for fares to Sydney. After trying every other likely source and failing I remembered seeing on the Marriage Lines the couple produced that they were married by Father Powers of Deniliquin. So I paid another visit to Father Hartigan to ask his help. This time I met the 'Priest on horse-back'—still the same genial reception and red-carpet treatment for me and the same sense of spiritual uplift—in a short space of time I was laughing over our financial problems with the £5 in my purse and Father Hartigan's assurance that we were doing the right thing. There was nothing to offer these people in Narrandera and the best thing to do was to help them to go to Sydney where they claimed relatives (whose address I had) and help. Father Hartigan didn't need a receipt—my word was good enough that as soon as the couple reached Sydney they would return the cash to me and I would pass it back to the Presbytery. I informed Father Hartigan of my impending departure—appointed to Sydney to office work—and he gave me his blessing.

Two weeks later, installed in my work at Headquarters, and back home to board with my family, I realised I was not going to receive the £5 refund from my Narrandera couple. I told my father the story and asked him to don his uniform and accompany me to the home of the relatives of the couple in another suburb. Well received, but no cash help—the couple had already exhausted the charity and good will of their relatives and they flatly refused to do anything about the matter. I had already received two weeks full salary for my maintenance and managed to make up £5 for a Money Order and sent it to Father Hartigan with a brief covering note of 'thanks', being careful to not mention it was my money. Back by return post came the £5 money order with a letter written by the great man himself; it said 'It was what you DIDN'T say I read from your letter and am returning the money asking you to allow me to share a little in this venture; you had the anxiety and work involved. I would like to pay the fares—after all they are really my responsibility'. Then he expressed the hope that the work I was engaged in would not rest too heavily on my overwilling shoulders; he concluded with his own autograph which for many years I treasured.[1]

While Father Hartigan was occupied with the many affairs of his parish, he was worrying about Annie's two eldest girls, Jean and Cecily. As noted earlier, his brother Father Frank, ill with tuberculosis, spent

1. *Letter written to the Australian Broadcasting Commission following the showing of the documentary* Behind the Boree Log, *and reproduced here with permission.*

The author's sisters, from left, Jean, Nance and Cecily, were all victims of Friedreich's ataxia. Father Hartigan showed great concern for them, giving his car for their use, and making them the beneficiaries of the royalties on AROUND THE BOREE LOG. Earlier, he had paid for Jean and Cecily to board at Narrandera's new convent school, in the hope that the climate and country surroundings might help them.

some time at Annie's home at Haberfield. With months in bed there, he had time to observe and he remarked that Jean was knock-kneed. At first with his sickness looming so largely in the family, little notice was taken of his observation. Only gradually did the realisation come that both Jean and Cecily were unsteady on their feet.

At the beginning of 1928 Father Pat Hartigan invited them to come as boarders to the new convent boarding school at Narrandera and he paid their fees, hoping that they might be strengthened by a change of climate and country surroundings.

They came home for midwinter holidays that year and I can still remember my parents' comment, 'they are no better but rather worse'. It was then quite clear that there was something seriously wrong. This was confirmed later that year. They had returned to Narrandera for the second half of the year and there Dr John Kieran, a local medico, remembered something he had done in his studies. He wrote to his erstwhile professor of medicine in Melbourne, describing the symptoms and giving his identification of the disease. The professor wrote back 'unfortunately you are right, it is Friedreich's ataxia. There is nothing that can be done. Tell the mother of those girls to spend no money on doctors but rather use it to make them as comfortable as she can'. The symptoms had been observed and classified by an Austrian, Dr Friedreich, the previous century. It is a degenerative disease of the nervous system ultimately affecting the muscles. The disease was given the name of its discoverer—ataxia means simply 'lack of control'. It is hereditary in the sense that it may attack more than one member of a family, but the exact laws of its transmission are unknown. There is no other record of it in either the Hartigan or Mecham family. It was Father Hartigan's heart-rending task to break this news to his beloved Annie.

A further blow was the verdict some years later that the youngest girl, Nance, was also a victim of the same disease. It did not attack her as soon, not until her early teens. One afternoon Father Pat came down to the convent for afternoon tea as was his wont. He began to cry and told the sisters he had just got the news that Nance too had the disease. Later on he had her also at the convent school and lavished kindness upon her.

Each of them in different ways were close to him. He called Jean 'a humorous dog' and she showed early an aptitude for poetry. She had a wonderful smile which was with her to the end. She was in Lewisham hospital when I visited her a few days before her death. She gave me a warm greeting and I said: 'That smile must be because you are my twin'. 'Don't be telling them my age' was her instant response.

No mother will accept easily the news that there is no cure for her children, and my mother was urged to take my sisters to this doctor or that as having been successful with some case 'just like your girls'. Eventually she took them to Dr Bickerton Blackburn, a renowned professor in the University of Sydney's medical school and also the chancellor of that university. Without knowing it he echoed the words of his Melbourne confrère 'take those girls home and make them as comfortable as you can and waste no money on doctors'.

Through sheer will-power my sisters were able to complete their secondary studies, though unable to do the exams because their writing was so slow. At first they went by tram to Domremy College at Five Dock, and afterwards my mother learnt to drive so that they could continue at school. The Presentation Sisters became life-long friends, particularly those who taught them and those who were their contemporaries at school. Nance travelled to Wagga by train for the reception into the convent of two of her classmates, Sisters Veronica Roberts and Mary Madden.

Cecily had a year as a boarder at Yass under the care of Mother Ignatius, the sister of Father Hartigan, and she retained always a great love for Mount Carmel College. Nance tried boarding at Yass with Cecily but lasted only a month—the attractions of home were too great for her.

My parents were helped in their care of their daughters by my brother Bernard who stayed at home until his marriage when he was in his thirties. He then lived close to them at Haberfield and afterwards he bought a home at Eastwood so that he and his wife Merle and their five daughters would be near St Catherine's Villa where my sisters were. The devotion of the families on both sides was a great help. Aunt Mary Mecham, with her daughter Mary and husband Dr Paul d'Arbon and family, uncle Michael Hartigan, his wife Irene and their daughter Pat Gilchrist and family, cousins Mary Howard and Mollie and Nance Sullivan —all these were particularly close and were supplemented by many loyal friends, with Rene Dickinson always to the fore.

The aunts in the convent were able to bring the great consolation that flows so perceptibly from dedicated religious and Mother Ignatius of Yass was especially a tower of strength. After her death in 1943, a cousin, Mother Imelda, and Sister Hugh, matron of the Sacred Heart Hospital,[2] Young, came to the rescue. They took my sisters to Young and gave them a wonderful holiday and my parents a rest. As the years went on and it was harder to get help in the home at Haberfield, the visits to Young and Cootamundra became more frequent. I had only to ring and say that I could not get nursing help in the home and three beds would be found

2. *Later known as Mercy Hospital.*

immediately in either the Young or Cootamundra hospitals of the Sisters of Mercy. As my mother got weaker, she was cared for at the Mercy Hospital, Albury.

Father Hartigan's love of my sisters took the practical turn of providing financial help whenever it was necessary. When he came to Sydney in 1944 to become chaplain of the Convent at Rose Bay he gave his car to my mother for the family use, knowing what joy it would give my sisters.

He expressed the intention of leaving them the royalties on **Around the Boree Log**. I objected that as they were invalid pensioners, whatever he willed to them would in practice be deducted from their pensions. 'What do I do then?' was his query. 'You leave the royalties to me', I replied, 'and I can spend them on things like a good car which they will enjoy'. As he got the lawyer to draw up the will his comment was: 'If Frank goes crook, we're sunk'.

With loving solicitude my mother took great pains with each of my sisters, as the disease made them unable to do the things other girls of their age were doing, to help them realise that this was God's plan for their sanctification. Never once did she question God's wisdom or goodness and her daughters likewise had a tremendous acceptance of God's will throughout their lives. She always said that when she was unable to care for them God would send someone to look after them. By 1956 the difficulties of caring for them had become formidable indeed. Father Hartigan was no longer there to be the support he had always been and my father had died around the same time. My brother, Bernie, had now married and moved out, though still close by in Haberfield. My sisters were at Cootamundra, my mother at Albury and the family home at Haberfield was closed.

It was then that I appealed to the Daughters of Charity. For some years they had been planning a 'home for incurables' at Eastwood but could not get the project off the ground. I asked them to think of sending two sisters to our home at Haberfield as a beginning of their work for incurables. To my joy they accepted, Cardinal Gilroy gave them permission for the Blessed Sacrament to be reserved in the room set aside for a chapel and I was able to say Mass there each week at an altar donated from St Joan of Arc's Church at Haberfield.

My mother was brought by plane from Albury—she would not have stood the car trip—and was delighted to be in her own home again. There she had Mass and Communion frequently and she knew there were those who would look after 'the girls' when she was gone. The Daughters of Charity were wonderful with her. In October 1956, a few months after they had come, she had a stroke and died peacefully soon afterwards.

Once the Haberfield venture had begun, the Daughters of Charity got a start with St Catherine's Villa at Eastwood. It was opened in March 1957 and the two Daughters of Charity who had been at Haberfield became part of the staff of St Catherine's Villa for Incurables, so that my sisters' transition from their own home to an institution was much easier than it might have been. The Daughters had the other patients in wards of four or six but they built a special room for my three sisters. Some of the furnishings from Haberfield went with them to Eastwood, the piano, the family clock which had come from Father Hartigan and other pieces. All this contributed greatly to their happiness in their new surroundings. The patients were just under thirty in number and it proved an ideal number—big enough to give variety and small enough to form a family atmosphere.

The Daughters of Charity by their dedication were able to attract around them a singularly dedicated staff and a voluntary auxiliary which provided outings and entertainments; also a committee that raised funds for further expansion.

My sisters were keen readers and always had library books and periodicals handy. Jean and Cecily wrote beautifully composed letters as long as they could and then Nance took over on her typewriter and did all the correspondence. For the last fifteen years when she no longer had the strength to use an ordinary typewriter she had an electric one. There was an immense number of friends with whom they kept in contact in this way. Also whenever a note of thanks was called for from the patients of St Catherine's Villa, it was Nance who composed and typed it.

My sisters enjoyed a constant flow of visitors. The Sisters of Mercy who had nursed them in their hospitals at Young, Cootamundra and Albury, travelled out to Eastwood whenever they visited Sydney. Friends came from Haberfield, the students from St Joseph's seminary opposite, Cardinal Gilroy on his return from Rome, the Mother General of the Little Company of Mary from the same city—all these came in a continual stream and they went off amazed and heartened to find such happiness despite years of immobility and increasing helplessness.

With everyone there was the same joy of friendship, the amusing anecdote, the interest in all that was going on. Whether it was presents for birthdays and feast days, or a gala night at the Opera House, they all equally claimed the attention and care of my sisters. To all they told of their genuine happiness with such words as: 'Hasn't God been good to us; the day is not long enough for what we want to do'. There was never any self-pity and they used to explain that they had no pain and in this were very blessed.

Not only did they enjoy the visits of their friends. They were able to get out by car, for many years in the one provided by Father Hartigan and afterwards in a succession of them made possible by his provision for them. They planned where they would take their friends, and always wanted a large car so that others could come with them. Corpus Christi processions at Manly College, football matches—St Columba's College, Springwood, versus St Patricks's College, Manly, at Springwood—these were their joy and doubly so if shared with others.

Nance particularly enjoyed very much seeing other places, whether it was a trip by plane or car as far as the north coast of New South Wales or the Queensland Gold Coast or, as more often happened, southwards to her beloved Sisters of Mercy at their hospitals at Young, Cootamundra and Albury. She got as far south as Melbourne where she stayed with the Daughters of Charity at Brighton. Always she returned to Sydney enriched by her experiences, yet always glad to be back again in her own city which can provide such a variety of beauty spots to one who must see them from a car.

Both Jean and Cecily died at just under fifty years of age, in 1965 and 1969. Nance expected her death at the same age and spoke about it freely to her friends. And so it was—she was fifty years of age when, one afternoon as she was typing, she got the cerebral haemorrhage which caused her death a couple of weeks later.

She died on 16 April 1974, as though she had chosen the day. It was the anniversary of my ordination to the priesthood. It had always been a great day for her. She would have a telegram despatched to me and we would have some small celebration together to mark the event.

She had arranged that she and I should share the one grave, and she prayed that she should be the first to occupy it. She asked not to live on, increasingly helpless and without the interest and the relief I could provide. She faced death with great faith and trust, confident that she 'had fought the good fight to the end'.

The large new church of St Anthony at Marsfield was filled for the Requiem Mass. Concelebrants included Archbishop Carroll, whom she had known and loved since her school-days, and Bishops Cullinane and Clancy and her friends among the priests. She and her sisters are buried close to Father Hartigan and other members of the family in the little Catholic cemetery of North Rocks, originally the burial ground of the Sisters of Mercy of Parramatta.

10   Later Years at Narrandera

Father Hartigan did not often leave his parish of Narrandera. However, reunions of Manly priests, held usually every three years, always attracted him, especially when they were held in Sydney where his parents were.

He had been present at the first reunion in 1914, when the New South Wales branch of the Manly Union was formed and he was elected the representative of the Goulburn diocese. During the 1919 reunion he was called on twice to speak: at the dinner in the city on Wednesday 8 August his theme was 'The Australian Sentiment', and he pointed out that there was a time when some of the senior priests had a lonely role to play promoting their own country; at this stage, however, he saw the Australian spirit as at last awakened, never to sleep again; at Manly next day he spoke on the theme of the Alma Mater, confessing his pride in Manly and expressing the hope that the Manly Union would be the instrument of many vocations to the priesthood. He was cheered at the words: 'Australia is meant for big things'.

It was not until 1929 that he got to a reunion again, the one held in Sydney in September of that year, and again he was in demand as a speaker. He proposed the Alma Mater at the dinner held at David Jones on Wednesday 25 September.

The sixth triennial reunion coincided with the opening of the Cardinal Ceretti Memorial Chapel in November 1935. Father Hartigan supported the toast of the Alma Mater at the dinner at Manly College. He set the mood with the words:

The Alma Mater has sent her sons, north and south, east and west. I was one of those who went west. And the further west I went, the more sure I was that the Wise Men came from the east.

Springwood was visited on the following Monday and there Father Pat proposed the toast to Father Bill Clark, organiser of the National Appeal for the Chapel.

Father Hartigan's last reunion was the one held in 1949 to mark the diamond jubilee of the college. (The golden jubilee celebrations had been cancelled because of World War II.) Father Pat preached at Vespers in St

Father Hartigan's few breaks from the Narrandera parish generally centred around the reunions of Manly priests held in Sydney. Here, next to the driver, he arrives at the 1935 reunion with, from left to right, Fathers Michael Tansey, Garratt Murphy and Tom Nolan.

Mary's Cathedral.[1] Two hundred Manly priests from all over Australia attended this reunion, and it was marked by the presence of the Cardinal and ten of the Australian hierarchy.

Loyalty to the Manly Union did not involve Father Hartigan in its struggle to obtain more Australian-born bishops. Nor was he ever on anything but the best of terms with the Irish-born clergy. Monsignor John Nevin (last Irish president of Manly) represented their view when he said at the time of Father Hartigan's death: 'Paddy was a prince'. The Manly Union's drive for bursary funds for candidates for the priesthood was fully backed by Father Hartigan and he was very generous to students, as I can testify personally.

One trip he made was to Townsville for the Episcopal Consecration of Monsignor Terry McGuire who had remained one of his closest friends since their first years together at Manly as youngsters. He travelled by ship with Father Bill Clark. The consecrating prelate was the Apostolic Delegate, Archbishop B. Cattaneo, and Rev Norman Gilroy D.D. was there as his secretary. The consecration took place on 25 May 1930 and at Pontifical Benediction Father Hartigan gave an 'eloquent sermon'—to quote the 1930 **Manly**—centred on the history of the feast of Our Lady, Help of Christians.[2]

Those years saw a steady flow of poems appearing generally in **Manly**.[3] Also in this period in **Manly** 1934, appeared his short story: 'Father Brendan's Christmas Day', well illustrating his power to convey in whimsical prose a convincing picture of the experiences of a 'Bush P.P.'

Father Brendan's Christmas Day

Father Brendan was quick-tempered, and the busybodies, the humbugs, and the tale-bearers of the parish knew it well. John Commins could tell you how, when he took occasion to point out how the place should be run, the good man 'went him'. Young Dolan also could tell you how he was 'roared on' for smoking outside the church when the sermon was going on; while Mrs Dacey

---

1. *This address is given in full in Chapter 13, pp. 304-311.*
2. *Extracts from this sermon were given in Chapter 2, pp. 49-51, when Bishop McGuire first entered into the story.*
3. *'When the "Sut" Drops Down' is in the 1929 issue; 'My Curate, Father Con' 1930; 'The Bush P.P.' 1935; 'The Old Home' 1936 (this poem was dedicated to 'Father J.K.', Father Jim Kelly of Ipswich Road, Annerley, Queensland, a Manly contemporary who was a close friend); 'The One-Ton Truck' 1939; 'Says She' 1942; 'Sittin' by the Wall' 1943; 'Old Sister Paul' 1944. These were all included in* The Parish of St Mel's, Angus & Robertson, Sydney, 1954.

still 'minds the time' when she went along to tell the priest some of the 'goings-on' in the parish, and he 'nearly took the two heels of her', so sharply did he close the door on her hurried exit.

Father Brendan was a correct man and a worker. Everyone knew that. Even those who had come under the lash admitted that he was 'a goer'. For ten years he had not taken a holiday. Day by day and year by year the dull grind had gone on in the groove of a bush parish and the rasping of it had found his nerves and sharpened his temper.

'Do you reckon he's getting pernicketty?' they would ask one another.

'Too right, he's getting pernicketty,' invariably was the reply.

Father Brendan was aware of this weakness, and was ever on the alert to keep his temper in check. So when Christmas morning came round he was afforded many opportunities to practise self-restraint. The parish was a scattered one and he had no assistant. He must say two Masses in the Church and as he made his way to the confessional before second Mass which was announced for eight o'clock, he noticed many people kneeling round the box who should have come along the evening before. Father Brendan would hear confessions at any time, but he had made it a rule that only those would be heard before Mass who could not come the previous afternoon or evening. He was strict on this matter and had referred to it time and time again in his instructions; but here on this hot busy morning were many who should have known better. A swift mental calculation assured him that he would be kept busy for at least a full half-hour after the time set down for the beginning of Mass. Father Brendan resented this want of consideration for himself and the rest of the congregation. Still it was Christmas Day so he went to his work and patiently remained till the last penitent was heard. Mass over and now more than thirty minutes late, he was hurrying to start on his journey for the third Mass, to be celebrated at Cowell's Creek—twenty-five miles away—when Joe Sexton from the Turn-back Jimmy sauntered into the sacristy, and with the beaming smile of one who has good news to give announced that 'the Missus has a little job for you'.

Father Brendan was on the point of asking Joseph in that sharp way of his which had made him feared, why himself and his Missus could not have picked on some time for the baptism other than on this morning when he was so busy and so late, but because it was Christmas morning he checked himself. 'Tell her to bring the child to the Baptistry quickly', he said calmly.

Father Brendan wondered at his own patience as he awaited her arrival. Thirty minutes late already, and Cowell's Creek twenty-five miles away, he wondered even more when she did come and in tardy obedience to his request to 'undo those things at the neck', laid the baby on her knee and began fumbling hopelessly at all manner of tapes and fastenings.

'Me fingers is all thumbs,' confessed Mrs Sexton. Father Brendan could have endorsed that observation gladly, but he kept his resolution and even went so far as to express a hope that the child would turn out as good a man as its father.

Jumping into his four-year-old car he drove that outfit towards Cowell's Creek so fast that it was one comprehensive rattle from the radiator to the tank. He knew that more than one hundred penitents would be waiting for him, so with a hasty 'Same to you' to the Christmas greetings from the 'Pillars of the Church', and the gossips round the door, he threw on his slip-soutane and went to the Confessional. They are excellent people, these parishioners of Cowell's Creek: kindly, generous, homely, still imbued with the simple faith which their forebears brought from Ireland and which is so good to see in these unbelieving days. Father Brendan could find but one fault with them. They were slow—slow to act, slow to speak, slow to think. Nobody had ever seen anyone from Cowell's Creek to hurry. No one from Cowell's Creek had ever been in a hurry, since Ben Miller 'seen' the Tantanoola Tiger the night they celebrated his brother Paddy's golden wedding; and Paddy Miller's dead goin' on this twenty year. This casualness was apparent also in their religious exercises. Not that they were lukewarm about them, but they were to a man exasperatingly deliberate. When going to confession they were like cricketers determined to play out time. They would saunter in and saunter out, and saunter up the church, and not till the footsteps of the retiring penitent had died away would the next one make a move. Father Brendan dreaded this, particularly on this hot, busy morning when the long fast had already brought the reeling head and the short temper. On the previous Sunday he had drawn attention to their slowness and had even asked them—had appealed to them—to come along quickly. He had pointed out that if there were one hundred penitents—as there would be—and each one were to waste one half minute, it would mean an unnecessary delay of fifty minutes; if each one were to waste even one quarter minute there would be a hold up of twenty-five minutes; but here they were dawdling worse than ever. It would have been a luxury to have stepped out and addressed a few pungent words to the stonewallers; but then he might say too much, and that would never do on Christmas morning; so he endured the torture till the last penitent was heard. The priest's step was a trifle unsteady as he made his way to the sacristy, and the weakness which he knew so well was making concentration difficult. While putting on the vestments a good bush knocking nearly stove in the door. It was the Rooneys—late as usual—'There's six or seven of us' said the spokesman with a hint of a challenge in his voice: 'farstin', he added by way of a knock-out. Again Father Brendan recalled that it was Christmas Day, and took off the alb and the amice without a word. On his way down the church he felt that no one had any consideration for him. They should know the physical strain this morning's work was imposing on him. That was self-pity: he put the thought away and went into the Confessional.

During the Mass, Cooney's baby beat a tattoo on the seat with its mother's rosary beads, and every stroke smote the weary priest who was trying so hard to keep his mind on the Sacred Mysteries. Mrs Cooney made no effort to quieten the child, but he bore with it. After the Communion he turned round to address a few words to the people—just a few words of greeting and good-will this Christmas Day—but Dolan's latest yelled so lustily and all the congregation stared so interestedly that Father Brendan found that he was talking to himself. He was on the point of saying that two things should be carried out on this occasion, viz. the Christmas resolutions he was sure they had all made, and—a crying baby. Remembering his own good Christmas resolution, he checked himself and let the baby have it. Still he felt a martyr to Mrs Dolan's want of consideration. Mass over he returned to the sacristy, removed the vestments and sank exhausted into the chair. His thirst was almost unbearable and never before had he felt so worn out. He would be better he knew, when he had the cup of tea and the piece of toast which Mrs Riordan—the good soul—prepared every Sunday morning for the priest. How he looked forward to that cup of tea; but Mrs Riordan had had an inspiration. All the families in the district, and far beyond it, associated with the name of Riordan, had announced their intention of having Christmas dinner with her and hers, and she had decided that it would be 'just lovely' to have the priest in their midst; so she bustled in to let him have the good news, and to tell him that she didn't 'bother' to make him the tea, 'so's not to spoil his dinner'. Heigho:-

'Christmas comes but once a year,
And when it comes it brings good cheer'.

Father Brendan rested in the chair for a while and held his throbbing head on his hand. It was no use, he must face Riordans' party. As he prepared to leave the church he was intercepted by Mrs Dolan with another 'little job' for him. It was, of course, the little 'job' that had howled him down in his address, and Mrs Dolan explained that she had 'kep' 'im' so that he might be christened on Christmas Day—the better the day the better the deed. Father Brendan could not see much point in the old saw at the moment.

'Who will hold the child?' he asked.

'Well one of the Mallon girls said she would, but she must 'ave forgotten'.

'Is there anyone at all outside who can do it?'

'No, they've all gone. 'Urryin' 'ome to git the Christmas dinner I s'pose.'

The last sentence was delivered in a mellow tone of voice calculated to excuse the whole congregation for their precipitous haste on the one occasion on which their slowness might have been of some service.

'Wait here,' said the tired priest; and he dragged himself down the hot, dusty road to appeal to Maggie Grady to come and hold the child.

And how that infant roared and kicked. In all his long experience his Reverence had never endured such a discordant, ear-splitting, head-racking, screeching; but he went through with it. It was Christmas Day.

'I'm terrible glad I kep' 'im till Christmas' said Mrs Dolan as she buttoned up the youngster. 'Was baptised meself on Christmas.'

'Just so', said Father Brendan.

And now for Mrs Riordan's Christmas dinner! He knew exactly what he would have to go through. Sitting round waiting with the men—crucified in his endeavour to be agreeable—while the women rushed about the kitchen, into the dining room, and into the kitchen again; the fly-screens on the doors banging every time. Banging doors and a reeling head! He dreaded the ordeal. Mrs Riordan might excuse him. He regretted that he had not been plain with her when she darted into the sacristy with the invitation; but then she had darted out again before he had collected an argument. She would be putting forward her very best effort today, and of course he was to be a sort of star guest. Mrs Riordan was a 'Showman'. She was out to let the other Riordans see how well the Cowell's Creek Riordans could do things—'And they had the priest out for Christmas', etc.—he really was not up to it. The dinner no doubt would be excellent for those who had appetites, but gastronomic murder for one who could only 'pick' at the best of times. Excellent beverage, two wines, ale, ginger beer, lemonade—for those who felt like it; but all he wanted was a bit of toast, a cup of tea, and—'forty winks'. Mrs Riordan shouldn't expect him to be on exhibition today. If he did go he would surely leave immediately the dinner was over and go home to have those 'forty winks'. But getting away would mean more trouble. The Riordans would be making a day of it and every attempt he would make to slip away would be ruled out. He felt he couldn't sit out the afternoon talking about the weather and such things, and trying to be affable. It was unreasonable this morning. He had a cup of tea down at Maggie Grady's, sent a word out to Mrs Riordan, and drove home over the pot-holes for the 'forty winks'. He threw himself on the couch a thoroughly weary man. An hour's rest would revive him, he knew, and after all, there was not much to be done this afternoon. Almost immediately the old-fashioned door-bell clanged. What a bell! The house-keeper will answer the door and establish a feasible alibi. 'Clang', went the bell. He'd stick it out. 'Clang, Clang, Clang', went the bell. 'Where's that wretched woman! Always away when she's wanted.' It was no use, he had to get up to satisfy the caller.

It was little Nellie Murphy whose mother 'kep' th' Boardin'-'ouse'. Nellie's mission was to tell the priest that there was a sick woman at the establishment who wanted to see him 'very particular'.

'Is she very bad!' he asked.

'She's not too good', answered Nellie.

'But what exactly does that mean!'

'She's not too clever.'

Hopeless. He had better go down and see the woman. He found the patient, who explained to him that she was a stranger to the town, and was feeling 'terrible lonely', so she sent for the priest, 'jist to have a bit of a yarn'.

On his way home Father Brendan felt that he was the most ill-used man in the world. No one had shown him the least consideration on this the busiest and the hardest day of the year. Still he had kept his resolution and was proud of himself.

He called into the Church to make a visit and to see if everything was in order. The sanctuary lamp had gone out. He attended to it. On his way out, he was met half-way down the aisle by a rough-looking individual who had his hat on his head, and his pipe in his mouth. This was too much for the sorely-tried patience of the jaded priest—the last straw, so to speak; and it broke him. He pitched into

186

*the intruder in his ablest manner for his want of respect in the
church: wearing his hat and smoking his pipe, no less! Didn't he
know that he was in the House of God?. What was the world coming
to? Why . . .? 'Don't be rough on me', said the stranger. 'I don't
belong to your mob. We only shifted into the house opposite a
couple of days ago, and me and the missus was reckonin' that you
was havin' a pretty stale Christmas, so she sent me along to ask you
to come and have a glass of wine and a bit of cake with us'.*[4]

During these years at Narrandera Father Hartigan suffered family
bereavements. The first of these was the death of his eldest sister, Lily
(Sister M. Gonzaga of Parramatta) who died on 30 May 1928; he
celebrated the Requiem Mass in the Convent Chapel and read the prayers
at the graveside in the North Rocks Catholic cemetery.

Then came the loss of 'The Little Irish Mother'. She died on 9
September 1934 after a short illness. It was at Annie's home and Father
Hartigan was at her bedside.

On Wednesday 19 April 1940 Patrick Joseph Hartigan died in
Lewisham Hospital whence he had been brought a few days before after
suffering a fall at home at Haberfield. He was ninety-eight years of age
and apart from deafness which had been an increasing affliction for the
last thirty years of his life, he enjoyed wonderful health and vigour.
Father Hartigan and his sisters in religion were at their father's side as he
died, together with Annie who cared for her parents in her home virtually
from the time of her marriage.

Father Hartigan was called on from time to time to preach the
panegyric at the Requiem of one of his fellow priests. Thus in March 1933
he gave the panegyric at the Requiem of that Father Patrick Hanrahan
whom we have seen earlier protesting that his name should have been
immortalised in the way it was in 'Said Hanrahan'. In the course of a long
sermon Father Hartigan had this to say of his deceased confrère:

*Your prayers are requested for the repose of the soul of the late
Father Hanrahan, for many years pastor of Lockhart, for whom this
Mass has been offered. While the Mass was being sung you joined
your prayers to the prayers of the Church that the soul of the
departed priest might find that rest for which his long life in the
sacred ministry was an earnest plea, and before you disperse this
morning and many times afterwards you will pray again that the*

---

4. Manly, *1934, pp. 34-8. Another short story, in a serious vein, had appeared in* Manly, *1919, pp. 63-9,
'His Little Irish Mother'.*

supreme blessing, beside which all other things are trifles, may in God's goodness be granted to him. His claim upon you for those prayers is the claim which every departed soul has upon a Catholic congregation. 'Your prayers are requested for the repose of the soul of Father Hanrahan' is no idle formula. There is a prison-house beyond the grave where souls are detained till the last farthing of atonement is paid. Your prayers are sincerely and earnestly asked that if there should be anything standing on the debit side of his account it may be remitted by the Omnipotent Mercy that the soul of the departed priest, if it has not already taken its place among the Blessed, may speedily find eternal Rest.

I will not weary you this morning with a recital of dates and biographical facts. These have been already given, and they are after all of little import. His biography may be read in the history of the parish of Lockhart, to which he was appointed over thirty years ago, and of which he was the first and only pastor. His achievement is that having consecrated his life to the service of his Master for five and forty years he has kept the standard flying. For five and forty years he has been a loyal soldier in the ranks, ever faithful to his trust . . .

How many good deeds are packed into that long term service which are known only to the Almighty God. Father Hanrahan was not the man to sound the trumpet that men might know what things he did. In his strength he did the work that lay around him and called it merely duty. There are some amongst us here today who remember him in the old days with a buoyant step and an active mind. He was a good and capable priest,—none better. We have seen him carrying the banner of his Master when his arm was strong and yielding to none in its defence, and we have lived to see him clinging pathetically to the standard when he had grown too feeble to defend it, and everything had faded from him but his faith. He belonged to a generation that has passed away, and is, unhappily, half-forgotten. Almost all those who were young with him have gone to render an account of their stewardship. One by one they left him. At Requiems such as this he took farewell of them all, then went forth companionless among men, strange faces—other minds—he had seen the black-robed messenger whom men call Death come in the morning and snap the thread of a bright young life; he had seen him come at noon-day and bid a fellow labourer leave his work unfinished. He had seen him come in the evening when weary steps and a tired heart were glad to be escorted away from the busy scene. For himself the summons was delayed till late in the day when the clouds had come to hide the setting sun. May he rest in peace. He sought no man's praise, he feared no man's blame. Satisfied to leave the assessment in the hands of the great just Judge he went his way a solitary figure on the highway of life, a lonely figure to the end. But this let me say, he kept his priesthood untarnished, and the hand that wrote 'Finis' to his story found no blot upon the page. Eternal Rest grant unto him O Lord and may perpetual light shine upon him.

Another panegyric he was asked to preach was that of his neighbouring parish priest, Patrick Reidy of Leeton, who died on 27 February 1938. He recalled the time thirty years before, when this Irish lad arrived at Goulburn:

No finer type had come into the priesthood. His enthusiasm was boundless and he had the strength to go with it. No dreamer was he—action was the breath of life to him. He was of the tradition of priests, one half of whom are now forgotten but whose epitaphs are the buildings that stand to their credit in every town throughout the country.

The ability of Father Reidy was early recognised and he was appointed Administrator of the Cathedral in Goulburn. This week after so many years, there were touching scenes in Goulburn when his death was announced.

Other parishes knew his worth but it was especially in Leeton that he gave proof of the undoubted mettle in him. There he was the first priest of a parish that now has three. He was a stranger to the comforts of these later days.

It is an axiom that it takes twenty years to establish an irrigation area. Trials and disappointments are plenty in the first years, prosperity only later. The sower does not always reap—many are not here today to see that their work was not in vain. Father Reidy was one of those—with sweat and tears he laid the foundations before the days of cars and all-weather roads; spending long hours in the open sulky on rough tracks, getting his meals when and where he could—such was his lot.

Then came the dire malady which dogged him from his middle thirties. Heroically he carried his cross behind him, struggling along on crutches; pain-racked as he was, no one ever heard him complain. Ten years ago he took to his bed to join the living dead.

Two things stood out in his suffering: his splendid resignation to the will of God and his great courage to the bitter end.

189

His parish has grown as he had dreamed it might but he was not to see it. The companions of his early years are nearly all gone—most of them went while he was awaiting the call. Of the priests gathered here today, only a few knew the late Father Reidy; chanting his requiem are voices he had never heard.

Suffering and self-sacrifice were the hallmarks of this admirable parish priest—his sterling qualities were tested in the furnace and were not found wanting. May he rest in peace.

In a lighter vein, Father Hartigan was the occasional speaker that same year at Father Arthur Percy's silver jubilee at Holbrook on 20 July.

And may the God of peace himself sanctify you in all things that your whole spirit and soul and body may be preserved blameless in the coming of Our Lord Jesus Christ. *Thess. 5:23-4.*

It is an old and a very happy custom to halt at certain periods of a man's life to offer our congratulations on the good that he has done, and urge him to further and still greater efforts. It is a very old custom, a survival from pre-Christian times, practised by the monks in their cloistered cells a thousand years ago, and handed on to us that we too may shake a valiant comrade by the hand and strengthen him by our appreciation. And so we are gathered here today, bishop, priests, and people to pay honour to a sterling priest who has completed twenty-five years in his sacred calling.

I have been asked to speak a few occasional words because among those I see around me, outside the members of his family I am Father Percy's oldest friend; and there is no one here—as shall be evident from what I have to say—who has more reason than I have to be proud of this sincere proof of admiration and regard which is being shown him this morning. Many years ago when that mysterious call came to him to devote his life to the service of the sanctuary, it was to me he came for guidance. A feeble reed was I to lean on—young in years and wanting in experience—I had one qualification only—I knew my limitations.

He was already set up in business and had a knowledge of the world which was far beyond mine. He was prepared to make every sacrifice, to sell his business, to burn his boats behind him so to speak, and place himself unreservedly in the hands of God. I knew that the potent seed-bed of a divine vocation was the good Catholic home, and there was none better than that from which Father Percy came. Honourable, upright parents by whom he was never shown the semblance of wrong—sisters and brothers all the soul of virtue—an environment where vice had never raised its ugly head, where every uplifting sentiment was cherished. All this was right.

His own life too had been all that it should have been, but in his particular case there would be difficulties and those difficulties would be very great indeed. It is not an easy thing for a man to lay aside the habits formed in five or six years of freedom and become a school-boy again. Then again it would be a very severe strain on the strongest constitution to abandon the activities of a man of business and embrace the sedentary life of a student, and I feared that the big sacrifices he was prepared to make might be made in vain. But there is something in the divine plan which passes human judgment. 'If thou wouldst be perfect', said the Divine Master to a hesitating young man of old, 'Sell that thou hast and come follow me'.

Everything connected with the call of a priest is so wonderful that no explanation can be found except the abundant influence and increasing operation of Divine Grace. The youth feels a strong wish to become a priest. No one knows why. He does not know himself. He may resist it or even try to fight it down. He may turn to secular pursuits and ignore it, but the still small voice keeps whispering 'You have not chosen Me, but I have chosen you'.

Why has this particular one been chosen? There are among his companions others just as good, others in whose path there would be no great difficulties. Then why has the choice fallen upon him who must sacrifice so much? I cannot answer why, but I do know that no one may assume to himself the office unless he be called as Aaron was.

St Peter was at his work mending his nets when he was called to leave these things and become a fisher of men. St Matthew was engaged in the unpopular task of gathering taxes when the summons came. St Paul was persecuting the Christians when he was struck blind. And a voice spoke to him: 'Arise and go into the city and there it shall be told thee what thou must do'. And so in a manner not to be slighted the summons comes. 'You have not chosen me, but I have chosen you.' 'Amen Amen I say unto you, He that entereth not by the door into the sheepfold, but climbeth up another way, the same is a thief and a robber. But he that entereth in by the door is the shepherd of the sheep.'

There is very little in the life of a priest to attract a young man in this independent, self-indulging age. It is at best a life of restraint. He must submit himself to a long and rigorous training. While his companions have already taken their place in life and are busily *hewing out for themselves a niche in the temple of the future, he finds himself a mere school-boy poring over his books. When the pulsing, maddened world is calling to his young vigorous heart in a hundred different ways, he must not go. And even when he is a priest, he must hold himself aloof. He is a sentinel moving round the wall with measured tread and watchful eye.*

And when the student course is over he is taken like Peter, James and John unto a high mountain apart. They clothe him in the long white alb of purity, across his bent shoulders lies the folded chasuble, a yoke that is sweet and a burden that is light only to those who have been called as Aaron was. In the hands of the Bishop he places his own hands, anointed and bound, as a sign of a strict obedience, and thus pledged and sworn they send him into the world again—to be in the world but not of it—a lonely ambassador to warn forgetful man that he has no lasting city here.

Father Percy obeyed the summons without hesitation and with a full faith that He who began the good work in him would also bring it to the fruiting, and looking back over the past twenty-five years at his never-failing devotion to duty, at his splendid child-like faith and ardent love for his Divine master, at his unremitting care to keep his priesthood unsullied at all times, one can only say 'The finger of God was there'. If any one is worthy, he is worthy. And when I touch upon those qualities, his earnestness in duty, his deep personal love for His Saviour, and his tireless effort to live up to the best ideals of his calling—I have mentioned the outstanding things which have rendered him an example and an inspiration to us all.

Submission to duty and God gives the highest energy. He who has done the greatest work on earth has said that He came down from Heaven not to do His own will, but the will of Him Who sent Him; and every priest who serves in that far-flung army of the Church is there under the self-same bond to do not his own will but the will of Him who sent Him; but unless he be keyed up by an undying love for his Master, the human daily round may become a weariness of spirit and searching for the limelight of great things which are remote, he may miss the things that lie at his feet and deem them small.

There are no small things in the work to which God has set His hand. The most insignificant of them reach beyond the ages into eternity and he who goes about them resolutely shall one day hear his foot-steps ring among the stars, though only faintly heard in the atmosphere of the world. Of the man whom we honour this morning let this be said: his full life's work has been to do the will of Him who sent him. He sought no mortal praise for what he did. He is not one of those who gives his best when the flags are flying and the drums are beating, but faithful, ever faithful, in the daily round for conscience' sake, for honour's sake because twenty-five years ago he put his hand to the appointed work and may not for a moment shirk the task.

I have spoken also of Father Percy's wonderful faith, and sincere charity. Simple faith is the most beautiful when found side by side with knowledge. An eminent scientist has said 'I envy no quality of the mind or intellect in others—not genius, power, wit or fancy—but if I could choose what would be the most delightful and the most useful to me, I would prefer simple faith to every other blessing'. That blessing above price has been bestowed on Father Percy. He never asked the why and wherefore of Divine Truth. With open arms he has embraced all things whatsoever have been commanded, with a Domine, non sum dignus upon his lips. All the scaffolding of the philosophers falls like a ruined edifice before that one word, Faith—let science deal with the things that are Caesar's, but in the things which are God's what has it to say? Gaze at the miracle of the Altar and confess your inability to answer. Kneel and thank your God for simple Faith, beside which Science is but a blind man's guess and history a nurse's tale.

Faith is the nail which fastens the soul to Christ. Love drives the nail to the hilt. Faith takes hold of Him and love helps us to keep the grip. Christ dwells in the heart by Faith and burns in the heart by Love like a fire melting the breast; and that great consuming love which is in Father Percy's soul, that intimate personal thing, explains why throughout the years of his ministry he had ever been the good and faithful servant—the trustworthy steward who has never been found wanting. It explains why too he has been so jealous of the good name of the priesthood. That high and holy office has suffered no stain because of him. Like the honest loyal soldier he has marched behind the Standard through many weary days, and no act of his, or any default has ever trailed the colours in the dust. But not only in a negative way has he shed lustre on his calling. Looking back over twenty five years at the various lines of offence and defence which had to be taken—the various methods which in their time seemed to carry on the work of the Church, Father Percy has entered into every one of them with that whole-hearted zeal which is characteristic of him. New occasions teach new duties, so today when we must all enter the arena—Bishop, priest and layman in the ranks of Catholic action in defence of the fundamental doctrines of Christianity, among the most eager for this combat is he in whose honour we are met this morning.

For these and for a hundred other things we wish him to know that he fills a unique place in our regard; we wish to assure him that his fine example and life of priestly work has not passed unnoticed, even here below. The secret consciousness of duty well performed, the public voice of praise that honours virtue and rewards—all these are his. And much more besides. I have touched in these remarks only on certain traits which seemed to me appropriate to this time and place, and if Father Percy in his humility should feel embarrassed that these intimate things which were intended only for the eyes of his Maker and his Judge should be laid bare, I can only say that in these things he has towered above us, and it is that the light be taken from beneath the bushel-measure so that weaker feet may the better see the way.

You will have other things to say of him when you meet him in a social way later on; the manly rugged character that never brooked deceit; the gentleness beneath it all to those in trouble, the loyal friendship—all these things are well known to you. They are known and remembered in every parish where he has been stationed and where he laboured better than he knew. And while you gather round him today to cheer his heart—you, the people of Holbrook, his faithful well-beloved flock, with the good Sisters of St Joseph, his loyal helpers so anxious to give him joy on this his jubilee day, with the little children whose vivid voices and all their faith and fairness will cheer him more than his ageing heart can tell, we, the Bishop and Priests assembled, will thank you for it, will bless you that you should pay honour to one of our own who has so richly deserved it.

And no one will watch it with a more grateful heart than I. I am, I think, the only priest here to-day who was present at Father Percy's ordination. On that morning in St Peter and Paul's Cathedral Goulburn two young men in their long white albs were presented to the ordaining Bishop, the other was my brother who was early called to render an account of his brief but, I trust, not unprofitable stewardship; so here after twenty-five years while Father Percy celebrates his silver jubilee alone, I take it that no one had a better right than I to the honour of being asked to be the preacher this morning.

It was Father Percy's wish that I should be here, and I thank him for remembering. I also thank Father Lacey, from whom the invitation came. The privilege is the greater in that after many years I should stand once more before the people of Holbrook in this dear old church hallowed for me by the memory of Father Campbell, and of many friends only a few of whom I see before me now. May God bless you and keep you in the holy bond of mutual affection and confidence between priest and people, which after the divine pronouncement has been the secret of the Catholic Church's unparalleled success.

And may the God of Peace himself sanctify you in all things, that your whole spirit and soul and body may be preserved blameless in the coming of Our Lord Jesus Christ Amen.[5]

Father Percy, in a letter written after Father Hartigan's death, had this to say:

He preached at my ordination (Goulburn 1913). And shall I ever forget that sermon at which a Bishop, John Gallagher, shed tears . . . He preached again at the twenty-five years' review of his first quaint find which was me, now an aging priest and again the tears would have rolled down this hard old face of mine had I not nearly bitten the ends off my fingers.

My last curacy was under him at Narrandera where he wrote most of his poems. For twelve months there together he asked me to attend to visitations as he wanted to do some writing. I say it myself but I did it very conscientiously and at the end I received his novel commendation: 'D—n sorry to lose you, Parish Priest,' proffering his hand.[6]

In 1933 twenty of the poems in **Around the Boree Log** were put to music by Dom S. Moreno O.S.B., a Spanish Benedictine from New Norcia, Western Australia.[7] The initiative for the project did not come from Father Hartigan but from Dom Moreno. The poems had been brought to his notice by some of the Irish members of the community of Sisters of St Joseph at New Norcia. The work was highly acclaimed. 'Calling to Me', for example, has frequently been rendered beautifully at convent school concerts.

Each year the priests of the diocese of Wagga travelled to the Redemptorist monastery at Galong, in the Goulburn diocese, for their annual retreat. At its conclusion the bishop held a meeting with his consultors and then the clerical changes for the year were announced.

There was excitement in the air at the end of the retreat of January 1935 when it was announced that Father Hartigan of Narrandera and

---

5. *From a typescript amongst Father Hartigan's papers.*
6. *Letter to Monsignor Tom Wallace, now amongst Father Hartigan's papers.*
7. Around the Boree Log, *A Collection of Twenty Songs with Piano Accompaniment, the Words by 'John O'Brien', the Music by Dom S. Moreno O.S.B., published by the Benedictine Community of New Norcia, W.A., 1933.*

Dom S. Moreno, OSB, a Spanish Benedictine who put twenty poems from AROUND THE BOREE LOG to music in 1933.

Father O'Reilly of Corowa were interchanging parishes.

For some years the bishop had been insisting to Father Hartigan that Narrandera needed a curate, and at different times one had been sent to him. Father Bert Gallagher, ordained at the end of 1929, was at Narrandera for his first eighteen months as a priest. Father Tom Desmond was appointed there in July 1933 and remained nine months. The parochial books show him as doing one baptism in that time and he does not appear at all in the register of marriages. Father Hartigan obviously continued to do most things himself. Then in the bishop's absence in Lewisham hospital in April 1934, the administrator of the Cathedral at Wagga needed a priest and asked Father Hartigan for the loan of his curate. The reply was: 'you can have him if you do not send him back'. The bishop on returning to Wagga was naturally not pleased to find that the curate he had appointed to Narrandera was now at the cathedral. He hit upon the idea of changing Father Hartigan to Corowa where at the time there was no curate.

A great stir was caused at Sunday Masses at Narrandera when the announcement was made. Quickly a number of men formed a deputation to go to Wagga to see the bishop. Tom Coughlan of Yarrabee station was one of its leaders, 'Scotty' Hepburn another. The bishop explained he wanted two priests at Narrandera; two Masses were necessary in the town; if there were only one Mass it would be uncomfortably crowded: Grong Grong and Morundah also had to be covered and with two priests both places could have Mass each Sunday. The bishop produced the parish returns to make his point and concluded by telling the deputation that he was willing to leave Father Hartigan at Narrandera provided he would accept a curate.

They went back wondering what kind of a reception they would get. They knew that Father Hartigan felt that acceptance of a curate meant somehow that he could not do the job, and at the time he was still vigorous and active. To their delight, Father Hartigan was in great form at the news and said he would willingly accept a curate. His words were: 'The bishop was bluffing and I was bluffing, and the bishop won the bluff'.[8]

Father Sylvester Bongiorno came there shortly afterwards and thenceforward there was always a curate at Narrandera and Father Hartigan grew to accept the fact. He remained always something of a

8. *This account of the incident comes mainly from Jack Coughlan who was interviewed on the ABC documentary* Behind the Boree Log.

recluse in that he loved books and writing and could get quite immersed in these things. Also, he had been on his own for many years and he tended to do a great number of things himself even when he had a curate to assist him. Moreover, the people of the parish, with no encouragement to do otherwise, naturally went to the priest they had known and loved for so long.

In 1934 a National Eucharistic Congress was held in Melbourne and Father Hartigan attended it. Over the years he made the occasional trip to Melbourne, driving there and usually spending a night on the way with one of the early Manly priests, often Jimmy Lawless of Rutherglen. In Melbourne, again it was with a contemporary from Manly that he stayed —Harry O'Grady of Preston being a favourite. Both in Sydney and Melbourne he often booked hotel accommodation lest he inconvenience anybody. Curates could be temporarily deprived of their quarters to make room for a visitor and he never wanted such to happen on his account. One trip he made to Melbourne was to give me my first look at that city, and again we went down together to select his last car, a 1940 Hudson Six Sedan. He had an eight-cylinder single-seater 1936 Hudson which was in excellent shape. He had, however, been caught at the end of World War I with a car that needed replacing, and replacement proved difficult and costly. He expected the same shortage to occur at the end of the Second World War and he wanted a car that would last over the immediate post-war years. He tried to get a Hudson Eight with overdrive, but there wasn't one in Australia. They had a Hudson Six Sedan on the water from America, so he paid a deposit on this, took delivery of it about a month later and paid it off in a year or so.

He had always been interested in cars, ever since the early Renault. When he came to Narrandera he had a T-model single-seater Ford. He bought a Citroen in 1921 which he kept for four years. Then it was a Vauxhall which he had for but a short time, disposing of it in early 1925 before he went to Europe. The Alvis he bought in England he kept until 1928 when he purchased a Buick roadster. He asked General Motors to make the differential ratio higher so that on the flat roads around Narrandera he would virtually have an overdrive. General Motors, however, refused to make this modification, and he sold the Buick a year later. He discovered that the engine and transmission were not properly aligned and he foresaw all kinds of uneven wear. It was then that a Packard representative, knowing his love of cars, showed him a demonstration model at a reduced price and this he bought.

In 1934 he obtained his first Hudson, an eight-cylinder roadster. He was very pleased with its performance but, later on, so that it would do even better, he had it fitted with light alloy pistons. But he was not

Father Hartigan's enthusiasm for cars was enormous. Here are just a few of the ones he owned: a 1921 Citroen; 1936 Hudson Roadster; 1925 Alvis Super-Sports.

satisfied with the change and replaced the 1934 model with a 1936 roadster. This was the one he had at the beginning of World War II.

He knew a tremendous amount about cars—there was a spare room in the presbytery chock-full of motor magazines. He was full of interesting tit-bits about the motor world; he knew the origin of every trade name in the business. To interest him, a car had to have ample horsepower and a long wheelbase, an interest not for our days of fuel shortage.

When extravagant claims were made about the performance of a car, he would know its engine revs, gearbox and differential ratios, and diameter of the driving wheels, and with quick mental arithmetic, he would produce a figure well below the alleged speed.

A fast driver, he was always a careful one; he drove on all kinds of roads for over thirty years without even a bumped fender. His mechanic was Fred Thompson, an excellent tradesman, and almost as particular about a car as he was himself. He had Fred service all the cars he bought during his twenty-seven years at Narrandera, and, of course, they became great friends. In the early years of their friendship he encouraged Fred in his courting of Eileen Behan, lending him the car for this purpose. He married them, baptised daughter Meg, and through the years always remained close to the family. About a year before his death he wrote to Fred as follows:

> Rose Bay
> December 5th 1951

Dear Friends,

Many thanks for those oranges, which arrived in tip-top condition. I did not need to see the name to know the sender. The packing was enough. It was very good of you to send them, and I appreciate the thought behind the gift very much.

I had the happiness of seeing Jack Jarman a few weeks ago, and his visit did me more good than a week's nursing. He gave me the latest about you all. I was glad to hear that you are keeping well. I had no doubt about business being brisk. How is Eileen, and Meg? I don't suppose the former is any more streamlined than she used to be. They tell me Meg is quite a woman of the world.

I am just fair missing on a couple of cylinders. It's hard to get spare parts for old models.

Again thanking you, dear Fred, may God bless all of you.

> Sincerely,
> P.J. Hartigan[9]

---

9. Letter kindly supplied by Fred Thompson.

Fred Thompson, second from right, in front of the garage at Narrandera where he serviced all Father Hartigan's cars for twenty-seven years.

In Father Hartigan's later years at Narrandera Bishop Dwyer did not enjoy good health and in 1937 the announcement was made by the Apostolic Delegate that Father Francis Henschke, parish priest of Jamestown in the diocese of Port Augusta (now Port Pirie) in South Australia, had been named an Auxiliary Bishop to Bishop Dwyer of Wagga. The consecration took place in Peterborough on 15 August 1937 and Father Hartigan, along with Father John Harper, travelled there and was one of the speakers. It was a revelation to the visitors from the Riverina to see just how tiny the churches and schools were in the scattered diocese of Port Augusta.

These later years of Father Hartigan's time at Narrandera saw him well established as a speaker of renown. He was called on to preach at the opening of the Chapel of Our Lady of Dolours, North Goulburn. For him it was a special occasion, for it was the chapel of the mother house of the congregation of the Sisters of St Joseph who staffed his parochial school at Narrandera. Over the years a great bond developed between these Sisters and Father Hartigan. He had the gift of being able to sense the problems of individual Sisters and the understanding and support he gave made them loyal friends for life.

Thus saith the Lord of Hosts. Heaven is My Throne and the earth My footstool; what then is this house that you will build to Me? What is the place of My rest? Isaiah.

The Charter of the Religious Life was given by Jesus Christ when He said to a certain rich young man: 'If thou will be perfect, sell what thou hast and give to the poor, and come follow Me'.

To enter at all into Eternal Life one must at least keep the commandments; but if one aims at perfection, something more is necessary. We are warned that the obstacles to this perfection arise from a too great attachment to worldly things, and from the cares brought about by their possession. So striking were the lessons of Christianity when first propounded that it is not to be wondered at that the first Christians embraced them in their entirety. The early converts of Jerusalem did put into practice the counsel of Perfection which the rich man found so difficult. They disposed of their goods and cut everything adrift that could hamper them. But God meant the world to go on. The early Church recognised that men of substance who used, but not abused their wealth, were necessary for its development; that Christian marriages were the chief means of increasing the number of adherents;—in fine, that the perfect state

was not for everybody, nor was everybody suited to it, and so the
Religious Life was confined to those rare souls to whom it was said:
'You have not chosen Me, but I have chosen you'.

Like Paul of Thebes and Anthony they went into places remote
from men; they built themselves crude cells somewhere, or selected
a cave with a hard plank for a bed, and the uneven floor their
kneeling-stool. Then came such as St Pachomius to gather these
scattered hermits under one roof, and the hills re-echoed the convent
bell and the chanting of the psalms of David. Then came the law-
givers—the rule-makers—the Basils, the Augustines, the
Columbanuses, the Benedicts, and cloistered life became a thing of
order which secular institutions still find it useful to study, and in
many cases to copy. Every warring passion was laid, every craving
except that of the thirsting heart for the Living Water was brought
into submission. Every call except that which said: 'Come, follow
Me' was ignored.

The invitation was no passport to a fruitless life. They ate no idle
bread—these holy ones who accepted it. It was, so to speak, a
background to that vast army of men and women which the
Catholic Church has been able to draw upon in her unending battle
with the powers of evil; and happy is the cause that can find
devotion, self-effacement, obedience and discipline such as theirs.
Wherever the fighting front may be, whether at her very door, or far
afield; whether the foe be Principalities and Powers, or the false
Prophet who in the clothing of one of the flock insinuates himself
into the fold; or the inimigus homo who sows the cockle among
the growing wheat; whether the battle-ground be the far-flung
outpost where forgotten ones crouch before their idols in darkness
and the shadow of death, or here at home where, in a land of plenty,
the lambs look up and are not fed; she has always been able to call
upon her divisions, battalions or single companies to go forth armed
with complete and perfect Charity to establish the Kingdom of
Christ in the hearts of men.

And so we see St Dominic and his band setting out to preach a
crusade against subversive doctrines. We see the tonsured sandalled
followers of such as the little poor man of Assisi combating the
inordinate love of riches and the soul-sapping effects of luxurious
living. We see the missionaries going forth to sacrifice and to
martyrdom that the Cross of Christ might be planted in every part of
the world. Whatever the circumstances, whatever the necessity
arose; be it to ransom the captive, to tend the wounded on the
battlefield, to take the orphan from the stricken home, or the

foundling from the doorstep, the Catholic Church has always been able to find a company trained and eager for the work.

So it was to be expected that in that field which she had always sedulously and jealously cultivated—the training of youth—she should call upon her Religious, those unencumbered followers of Him Who taught her that of such is the Kingdom of Heaven, to spend themselves even to exhaustion in the care of the little ones of the flock.

I have said that it is a field that she has always jealously cultivated. Philosophers before her had always been convinced that 'the fate of empires depends on the education of youth'. To her there is more involved than the material fate of empires. There is that eternal destiny, for which this life, however endowed, is but a probation; and there is—standing out above all things—the priceless value of every human soul. While bearing the torch of learning through the ages she has never lost sight of that. The headline which she has written on every page has been 'Seek ye first the Kingdom of God and His Justice'.

With that always in view her monasteries gathered the neighbouring children around her when the world was Catholic; her Catholic schools, her chantry schools, her guild schools, all bear testimony to her activities in the distant past, but the confiscation of the monasteries, the suppression of the benefices on which the chantries were founded, the removal of the Guilds from the control of ecclesiastical authority, the sequestration of the Church's possession wrote 'finis' to a brilliant chapter.

But as is usual in her long and eventful history, when a brilliant chapter closed, another and even more brilliant one was to open. There began to take possession of men's minds a belated principle that education, up to a certain point at least, is the birth-right of every man. No one welcomed the awakening more than the Catholic Church. She laid down that very principle in the decrees of her Councils and in the instruction of her Bishops a thousand years before. 'New times demand new methods and new men.' She adapted herself to the new methods as she has done in every age to the amazement of students and of critics. Her workers went forth with modern equipment but animated by the old, old spirit which sent the Apostles on their mission. Her policy had not changed. Learning without the guidance of religion is at the worst a dangerous thing, at the least a mere vanity. Religion is the goal to which all things tend: apart from which man is a shadow, his very existence a riddle, and the stupendous scenes of nature which surround him as unmeaning as the leaves which the sybil scattered in the wind.

And thus in every country, as circumstances showed the need to be urgent, she called into being the teaching orders, the teaching congregations, whose members, following the same invitation which drew the hermit to his lonely cell, lay aside all earthly ambitions, break asunder every earthly tie, even become anonymous and without scrip or purse or staff, go forth to fulfil the first and greatest commandment of the law, and the second which is like unto it.

As circumstances showed the need, St John the Baptist de la Salle founded the Brothers of the Christian Schools, Father Champagnat the Marists in France, Edmund Ignatius Rice the Irish Christian Brothers, Nano Nagle the Presentation Sisters, Mary Aikenhead the Sisters of Charity, Catherine McAuley the Sisters of Mercy in Ireland, Archbishop Polding the Sisters of the Good Samaritan in Australia—and then came Tenison Woods. Something of a genius, something of a mystic, his biographer says of him: 'As he ministered to his scattered flock one difficulty, one haunting care constantly troubled and saddened the mind of Father Woods. It was the problem of the children. What of their Catholic education! In the smaller centres there were no schools at all; in the larger, schools were very often unsatisfactory from a religious point of view.

'Then memory could recall to him certain places and persons in the rural districts of France. For the lowliest hamlet there were the Sisters of some teaching congregation, by whom no little one was rejected, no one neglected. Absorbed in the training of the young to be good Christians and good citizens, they sought no earthly rewards, avoided all ostentation, and never left their assigned posts for the sake of more showy or more lucrative positions. With such teachers the Catholic Church has been acquainted from the beginning, but they were as yet almost undreamt of in this vast Australia. How could they be raised from the soil? That, through solitary rides through the bush and solitary vigils at the Presbytery, was the chief occupation of the busy young pastor of Penola.'[10]

Just over fifty years ago Tenison Woods bowed his lonely exit from the stage whereon in his time he played many parts. His name is remembered because of many noteworthy achievements for the land he came to as an exile; but his greatest title to fame, the noblest and most enduring, is wrapped up with the vision and zeal which sent the Sisters of St Joseph upon their unobtrusive way.

10. *Father Hartigan did not identify the biographer he was quoting.*

If the dream he cherished in that unpretentious presbytery at Penola endowed every hamlet with the teaching Sisters by whom no little one was rejected, no one neglected, who, absorbed in the training of the young to be good Christians and good citizens, sought no earthly reward, avoided all ostentation and never left their assigned posts for the sake of more showy or more lucrative positions; never did the ideal translate itself into reality more faithfully than here. Making no bargain, laying down no conditions, they go where their work is waiting. Theirs the spirit of saint and hero, which spurns easy living lest it weaken the arm that should be stout, lest it soften the will that should be strong. 'Give me neither beggary nor riches. Give me only the necessaries of life, lest, being filled, I should be tempted to deny and say: "Who is the Lord?".' Undaunted by inconvenience or by extreme of climate, they take their country as they find it. In draughty weatherboard school-houses on the snow-line; in little pill-box convents on the scorching plains, 'out where the heat waves dance forever', in serge and wimple they carry on the tread-mill work for the welfare of the little ones, in the name of Him and for the sake of Him Who likened the Kingdom of God to a child.

No words of mine, and I believe, no words of any speaker, can assess the debt the Church owes to its teaching congregations. Angel hands have recorded it in letters that shall not be effaced. In every country where they have put their hands to the work, Religion has flourished; where they have not been encouraged, there has been no advance, and here in the land we know the best, who will write the epic of the planting and the tilling which have come so handsomely to the fruiting! We speak with pride, but I trust without boasting, of the burdens we bear for Christian education; let us not forget whose shoulders have taken the weight. If the seed the Sower scattered is bringing forth fruit a hundredfold or even thirtyfold, it is because their hands have tended the growing plant. If today the fields are white with the harvest, it is because their teams were on the virgin land, their cultivators on the fallow.

It is an epic of selfless devotion to a cause for which the world outside can find no parallel, and which it cannot understand. Well may it ask what is the sustaining force behind it all. What is it that maintains the fervour of the religious life through disenchantment, the disillusionment, the disappointment which send the mere idealist down from the mountain-top defeated! What can it be that keeps it through the fatigue of the daily grind, through the monotony, and through the ageing of the heart that comes to see nothing but delusion in the enthusiasm of youth?

Here is the only answer. In every cloistered home there is a simple oratory or a stately chapel where a ruby lamp burns night and day since King Alfred lit the candles at the shrine. That burning light proclaims the most stupendous mystery or Love that man has ever known. No human mind conceived it. No poet's frenzied numbers ever hymned the like. To the world because of the tremendous act of Faith involved it is still a 'hard saying'. To those who believe without doubting, the love which consecrates the Tabernacle is the Love which did not spurn the Manger, and did not shirk the Cross. 'Just Father, the world hath not known Thee, but I have known Thee, and these have known that Thou has sent Me. And I have made known Thy Name to them, and will make it known that the Love wherewith Thou lovest Me may be in them and I in them.' That ardent personal Love radiating from the Altar is the secret of the constancy of the Religious Life. 'Fear not, I am thy protector and thy reward exceeding great. Even to your old age I am the same, and to your grey hairs I will carry you. I have made you and will bear you, I will carry and will save.'

That is the reason why every religious house has its oratory, or its chapel, and the reason too, why they have striven to make it something worthy of the Word made Flesh that dwells among them. 'Thus saith the Lord of Hosts; Heaven is My Throne and the earth My Footstool. What then is this house that you will build to Me? What is the place of My rest?' They know only too well that no habitation made by human hands is worthy of the Guest Divine. 'If Heaven and the Heaven of Heavens do not contain Thee how much less the house which they have built.' Yet if the gift be not worthy, surely the love that offers it can be so.

Yesterday we assisted at the Blessing of this chapel erected to God's Glory by a little congregation of teaching Sisters—one of the last companies to receive the colours in the vast army of the Church. This house which they have built is beautiful by all human standards, and it is rendered acceptable, can you doubt, by the love that planned and the Faith that made it possible. As has been recognised by everyone, it has been a sleeping and a waking dream through many years of sacrifice. On sacrifice such as theirs the angels throw incense and here it stands today to the greater Glory of God, a memorial to their Father Founder, under the patronage of that sweet Queen whom the early sword of Sorrow made the first and surest comforter to the vast brotherhood of pain.

To us the completion of this chapel is just one more triumph for the Church: to the Sisters it is everything; the centre, the core of their whole religious life. Here they will take up their burden—if burden it be,—here they shall lay it down. Here they will come when the day is long and the road is stony; here they shall receive their consolation. At morning Mass they will kneel and on the snowy Altar-cloth Calvary will be repeated in this regard. Two by two they will come for the Supersubstantial Bread lest fasting they faint on the way. One by one as occasion offers through the day, they will spend a sweet moment here drawn by the Love that worketh ever. 'Show me whom my soul loveth where thou feedest, where thou liest in the mid-day.' Here will come the postulant with the freshness of morning on her cheeks and in her heart, asking for the holy habit of Religion that she may lay her gifts upon the Altar-steps. Here she will kneel—a novice; 'her eyes bright homes of silent prayer' as she gazes on her God. Here she will come again— professed, trained, leaving her school to search her soul in the annual retreat, to find out if devotion to her class and enthusiasm for her work may have rifled something in that heart of hers which should be the Bridegroom's very own.

Has her heart grown cold? Oh, rekindle there the fire of Thy Divine Love. Fove quod est frigidum. Does she bend to the yoke as on that bright morning years ago when she vowed to leave all things and follow Him? Flecte quod est rigidum. Oh, bend it gently, firmly, lest it be as the curse on the chosen of old to be broken in disaster but never bent again. And, what of the wedding garment? Is there any blur upon its whiteness? Lava quod est sordidum. Wash every stain away, be it grime from the strife or dust from the road. And here again she will come when her working day is over, when it's twilight in the empty school-room and twilight in her lonely heart. Here, where as one of a band of happy novices she went forth to meet the Bridegroom so eagerly, to that same Lover she will come behind the novices of another day with feeble step and genuflect in pain. 'Even in your old age I am the same, and to your grey hairs I will carry you.'

From here too, in the fulness of time, shall move that last procession . . . The children marching. The loitering motors purring low . . . away from the house that ye built for Me. Away . . . but not forgotten there. From here will rise to heaven the Requiem chant, the anniversary Mass, the Sisters' prayers for a Sister gone . . . Go write it large across her vacant stall 'Blessed are the dead who die in the Lord'. 'Amen, I say to you that you who have left all things and followed Me shall receive a hundredfold, and shall possess Life Everlasting.'

No wonder that the Sisters love their chapel. There is something extremely touching in their enthusiasm, and I do assure them that that enthusiasm is not confined to the members of their order. If I know His Lordship of Goulburn, and I think I do, his delight at this achievement is scarcely less than their own. His Lordship of Bathurst has come a long way to pay them the honour of his presence. Priests have assembled in their numbers to show their appreciation of the work they are doing so nobly and withal so humbly; while their ever loyal friends among the laity paid them a tribute yesterday afternoon that will not readily be forgotten. No one, I take it, will think it presumption in me, therefore, to crown these few remarks of mine by offering the combined congratulations of all assembled to the Sisters, both those who are present, and those who are at their tasks this morning in their convents scattered through the two dioceses.

And to her, that gracious humble lady, who guides the destinies of this Congregation of nuns, the heart of everyone goes out at this time. To her more than to anyone under God is due the success that has come to it. She has watched it grow from undistinguished girlhood to useful, confident womanhood; and if that womanhood is comely before God and man it is owing in the largest measure to her guidance and to her splendid example as an ever-faithful religious. I know that to continue in this strain would be trying to her in her humility, and it may not be the right thing to give due credit to a nun in her life-time, but if I have been in error in doing so, I am confident that my bad taste is being applauded warmly in the heart of every one of her Sisters.

Furthermore, all this, and much besides, will be said in this place some day when she shall not hear the speaker's voice—nor will she greatly care. Better the tribute now while her grateful heart is chanting a Te Deum *in the joy of a dream come true at last. 'Here is the house you have built to me. Here is the place of My rest.' She has watched every brick go into its place, and she had taken all the disappointments—and they were many—with the same resignation with which she has taken the setbacks of fifty years. All for the greater Glory of God, and the spiritual well-being of her community. That double objective achieved, she has all unconsciously erected her own monument and written her own epitaph.*

Need I express a hope that great graces and many blessings will flow? It would be superfluous. That is one thing certain in a world of uncertainty. When the Sisters pray the Angels hover in their flight to hearken. May I rather hope that when they pray for those who need it sorely in a sin-stained age, you and I shall be remembered here.

Mother M. Benedict, standing, the subject of warm praise from Father Hartigan during his address at the opening of the Chapel of Our Lady of Dolours, North Goulburn, in 1941.

'*That Thou mayest harken to the supplication of Thy servant and
of Thy people Israel, whatsoever they shall pray for in this place, and
hear them in the place of Thy dwelling in Heaven, and when Thou
hearest, show them mercy.*'[11]

The following year it was to be at Bombala, on the far south coast of
New South Wales, several hundred miles from Narrandera, that he was
invited to preach on the occasion of the blessing and opening of the new
church of Our Lady of the Blessed Sacrament.[12]

**And trembling he said: 'How awe-inspiring is this place! This is no
other but the House of God, and the gate of Heaven'.** Gen. 28:17

*One's first impulse on standing here this morning is to give thanks
to God that so fine a church as this has been built for the worship of
His Name. Wherever a church is built, whether it be in the crowded
city or in some outpost, it is a matter for congratulation, not only to
those who are immediately concerned, but to the whole Catholic
community. Even more, it is a matter for rejoicing in the heart of
every patriot, whatever his creed, that another fortress has been
erected on the long battle line against the forces of evil which
threaten the whole world today.*

*One's second impulse is to express one's admiration at the
elegance and solidity of the building, and to compliment Father
Griffin and you, his devoted congregation, on the zeal and courage
which have made this splendid dream a reality.*

*In building as you have done, you have but followed an impulse
which has moved the human heart in every age and every country.
Stirred by the holy influence of religion, man has ever striven to
raise to the Divinity a house worthy of His Name—worthy I say in a
human sense, for no work of mortal hands can be worthy of God.
Still, acknowledging this limitation, man has ever endeavoured to
express in elaborate design and construction, his belief in the
supremacy of the Lord-ship of the Eternal One.*

*And so we find that even in primitive times the first houses built
for prayer, though of little distinction judged by our standards, were,
nevertheless, prominent among the surrounding dwellings—the one
building of stone among the meaner huts of wattle and daub.*

11. Our Cathedral Chimes *(periodical of the parish of Goulburn)*, 7 December 1941, pp. 4-6.
12. *His Lordship, Most Rev T.B. McGuire D.D., Bishop of Goulburn, performed the ceremony on
17 May 1942.*

Gradually the temple made by hands became more dignified, more in accord with its purpose. Labour was never spared or expense considered. The House of God must be everything that human effort could make it. The temple built by King Solomon, though long ago overturned, is still remembered for its magnificence. Antiquarians still enthuse over the highly ornamented wood supplied by the neighbouring King of Tyre, of the cunningly wrought figures on the walls and on the columns, of the gold which was lavished upon it, 'And the house before the Oracle he overlaid with pure gold, and overlaid with nails of gold'.

Even the pagans who worshipped gods of their own imaginings—poor mental phantasmata prone to human weakness and degraded by human vices—even these raised glorious though shallow tributes which are magnificent even in their ruins. The Mohammedans built to their Prophet mosques exquisite in design and adornment. The Buddhists have squandered the wealth and splendour of the Orient on a deity which has neither sense or power to hear or help them. But if that impulse to erect to Divinity a worthy fane was prominent in the Jew and the Pagan, it remained for Christianity to bring it to the highest and most perfect fulfilment.

Undoubtedly the most striking structures in the old world are the churches and the cathedrals. It took centuries to build some of them, and their value in money could not be estimated today. Stone by stone they were raised, as funds permitted; the rich man gave of his abundance, the poor man gave his shillings, the widow gave her mite, the labourer who had nothing else to offer gave his toil. Genius gave its services that the best that could be done should be done, and eager faith was ever watchful lest good intent might wane or enthusiasm might lose its purpose.

Those were indeed the ages of Faith; and mark well, there was nothing hazy about that Faith. It was not a sort of vague belief in the refining influence of Christianity or in the uplifting value of the Sermon on the Mount. It was the unconditional acceptance of the Deposit of Revealed Truth committed to the Apostles and their successors. Therefore they built their churches on such an elaborate plan because they believed in the Real Presence of the living God upon the Christian altar. Therefore did they build them lofty and magnificent realising that in building for God 'Too low they build who build beneath the stars' to be the worthy dwelling on earth of the Word made Flesh Who consented to live amongst them.

Since those far off times the world has seen many changes. The running pen of history has filled many, many pages—some with the record of splendid achievements, some with a sad narrative written in blood and human tears which scalded ere they dried. If a workman who helped to raise the stones of the great cathedrals were permitted to visit this earth today, he would be bewildered at the altered state of a world he used to know. In his own craft he would see little with which he was familiar—new methods, new materials, new equipment. But one thing he would recognise in his confusion, and that is that the same belief in the Real Presence which has built cathedrals in every age including his own, is still building churches to the same great Faith, which if not as elaborate, are even more numerous and in God's gracious ways equally as effective.

You will see them scattered everywhere throughout the world—in the poorer streets of cities, in the villages—clinging as it were to the sides of mountains, hidden in the valleys, conspicuous on the plains. Minor churches, little churches if you will—unpretentious little churches some of them, but sharing the significance of the great Gothic classics in this that they too are Shrines of the Blessed Sacrament.

It was said of old 'From the rising of the sun even to the going down, My Name is great among the Gentiles, and in every place there is Sacrifice, and there is offered to My Name a clean oblation; for My Name is great among the Gentiles, saith the Lord of Hosts'. I wonder did the inspired one see stretching round the world a line of little churches each playing its part in bringing his prophecy to such an extraordinarily complete fulfilment—from the rising of the sun to the going down. When the sun has disappeared below the western rim in northern lands, it rises so to speak, and floods with light the southern world, and so this country of ours comes into that revolving, never-ending picture envisaged by the prophet.

And thanks be to God we have not been idle, for dotted over this the last discovered continent, wherever there is settlement you will find the little churches where is offered that 'clean oblation' which was the burden of the word of the Lord by the hand of Malachias. Some of them like your own are indeed beautiful, by every standard; some of them are simple, even primitive things built from the wood of neighbouring forest. Each is at least a gift from generous hearts, the best that circumstances would allow, and to each of them, even to the humblest of them, can be addressed those solemn words of the inspired poet who penned, 'And I heard a great voice from the Throne saying: Behold the Tabernacle of God with men, and He will dwell with them. And they shall be His people: and God Himself with them shall be their God'.

There is no room for wonder then that they continue in a spiritual sense those acts of mercy which the Man God performed so plentifully when He was on earth. In the administration of the Sacraments of the living and of the dead they are as those hallowed places where Jesus worked His miracles. That street in a certain city where a kneeling leper saw the scales fall from him. The pool called Probatica, which in Hebrew is named Bethsaida, where the sick were cured of their infirmities at the moving of the waters. That spot along the way where a blind man touched the hem of His Saviour's garment, and received his sight. They are as that ladder which the banished Patriarch saw in his troubled sleep, 'a ladder upon the earth and the top thereof touching Heaven; the angels also of God ascending and descending by it, and the Lord leaning upon the ladder'. Do you doubt it? Listen to this.

'Tis evening and the little church is wrapped in a solemn hush at Confession time. In the half light there looms a tribunal which has come down to us from one of the most solemn moments in history, 'And when it was late the same day, the first of the week, and the doors were shut, where the disciples were gathered for fear of the Jews,—Jesus came, and stood in the midst, and said to them: Peace be to you. Then He breathed on them: and He said to them: Receive ye the Holy Ghost: whose sins you shall forgive, they are forgiven them: and whose sins you shall retain, they are retained,' in that tribunal there sits a judge—a human judge—who would not dare to take upon himself that awe-inspiring office if the divine seal had not been stamped upon his commission: 'As the living Father has sent Me, I also send you'. Around that tribunal they wait with their sorrows, their infirmities, as they waited long ago by the wayside when they knew that Jesus would be passing by.

In the silence, broken only by the closing and the opening of the slide of the confessional, or the click of a Rosary beads on the wooden bench, a strong man with his face bowed in his hands, turns over the leaves of that book which is his conscience, on every page of which default is written by an accusing finger. But 'the lame man shall leap as a hare, for waters are broken out in the desert and streams in the wilderness'. In that silence, too, a woman's nervous fingers tremble on her Rosary. 'Strengthen ye the feeble hands.' The penitents go in and penitents come out; all the while the angels ascending and descending and the Lord is leaning on the ladder. But what is it that breaks so harshly on the ears of the priest as he hears them one by one? It is the voice of a girl—a child telling him something which jars him to the soul: something which the world outside makes light of; but the priest sees two pictures. He sees a young thoughtless lass dancing down the primrose path which leads to a cliff which frowns above an angry sea—a sea that shall calm its fury only when it yields its dead.

The other picture which the priest sees is a happy home where an unsuspecting father is doting upon the daughter whom he loves more than life itself, and dreaming maybe 'that when the snow show in his hair, a household angel in her teens will flit about his chair, to comfort him as he grows old, but now that hope is dim; Ah, Baby girl you don't know how you'll break the heart in him'. And the priest knows full well that to no one else in the whole world would that guilty secret be told. Daddy would never hear it: Mummy would never hear it: the Sisters in the school must never know of it: the priest himself outside would be the last she would tell.

But here in confession—oh woman great is thy faith—here in confession the gathering sore is exposed for the surgeon's knife. And the priest sitting there as physician as well as judge, realises that only he and the grace of God which his ministration will bring, stand between that life and ruin, between that soul and damnation. And as a father as well as a doctor and a judge he takes that soul in hand, and gently but firmly warns her, and entreats her by all that she holds dear. He reminds her of that ominous forecast of the Apostle, 'Whatsoever a man shall sow that also shall he reap', and the harvest of sin is a bitter crop. He touches even on a higher motive. He turns her to her crucifix, 'Whose pallid Burden with pain watches the world with weary eyes, and weeps for every soul that dies, and weeps for every soul in pain'.

Oh, the strength of little churches, 'And a lion cried out: I am upon the watch-tower of the Lord, standing continually by day, and I am upon my ward standing whole nights. The burden of Duma calleth to me out of Seir, Watchman what of the night? Watchman what of the night?'. Where in the whole world is there a power for good like this? They may build their Courts of Justice, their reformatories, their refuges, but what is their record compared to that of little churches in the hearts that have been healed, the homes that have been saved from ruin, and the lives of little children plucked like brands from the burning. They may make clean the outside of the platter or the cup, but can they scour the rapine and the uncleanness from within? They may bruise or even break the heart, but can they make it contrite? 'And how else, but through a contrite heart may Lord Christ enter in?'

In the little church when the rest have gone a penitent girl lingers

on to pray in the stillness. Humbled in repentance she gazes at the
tabernacle, her eyes bright with the sparkle of an unshed tear.
Fortified in faith she sees her thorn-crowned Saviour on His throne
of mercy, and hears Him say, 'Neither will I condemn thee'. Full of
grateful sorrow she vows that no act of hers will ever drive another
thorn into that aching brow. And strong in her purpose of
amendment she promises to avoid that evil thing which caused her
lapse, aye, 'to tear it from her bosom though her heart be at the
root'. Oh, the power of little churches! 'And he saw a ladder
standing upon the earth, and the top thereof touching Heaven: the
angels also of God ascending and descending by it, and the Lord
leaning upon the ladder—and trembling he said, How terrible is this
place! this is no other but the House of God and the gate of Heaven.'

What glory there is in all this, but there is a greater glory still, the
crowning glory when on their unpretentious altars the very Sacrifice
that was Calvary is perpetuated for just the same purpose for which
the eternal order of Heaven was disturbed so that the Second Person
of the Triune God should come down to earth and offer Himself a
victim for the redemption of mankind. Long before that stupendous
event took place, it was foretold by the most eloquent and the most
sublime of all the prophets whose hallowed lips were touched with a
coal of fire which an angel brought with a tongs from the altar. He is
called by the Holy Ghost the great prophet from the greatness of his
prophetic spirit by which he foretold so long before and in so clear a
manner the coming of Christ and the mysteries of the Redemption,
that he seems to have been an evangelist rather than a prophet. 'The
things that were first', said he, 'behold they are come, and new
things do I declare: before they spring forth, I will make you hear
them. Sing ye to the Lord a new song: his praise is from the ends of
the earth'.

I wonder did he hear in that new song of praise, the bells of little
churches joining in the universal benediction as they call the people
to Mass in the Sabbath stillness! The old order has passed away; the
old sacrifices have been supplanted, the clean oblation is being
offered in every place from the rising of the sun to its going down,
and the bells of little churches ring out the glad tidings. The Lamb
without stain is sacrificed for us. Not far away in some secluded
place but here in this place. 'Sursum corda', 'lift up your hearts'
ring the bells of little churches, 'For great is He Who is in the midst
of you the Holy One of God'. The Mass is Heaven's triumph upon
earth, and because of it the little churches stand on the same level
as the most inspiring cathedral in the world. For just as a lowly

stable in Bethlehem was elevated above the palaces of kings because of the Divine Presence nineteen hundred years ago; just as a plain supper-room in Jerusalem was rendered more sumptuous than regal banquet halls because of the changing of Bread and Wine into the Body and Blood of Christ; just as a barren hill outside the city assumed a majesty beyond that of the loftiest mountain, so it is the True Real Presence of Jesus Christ in the Eucharist—sacrament and sacrifice—which gives even to the poorest little church a sanctity and a significance which is only equalled round the throne of God.

And so I take it that each of you is very proud of the part he has played in the erection of this very beautiful church. You have reason to be proud of it, and it will become very dear to you as the graces it must surely bring become apparent. The Shrine of Our Lady of the Blessed Sacrament you have called it. Its very title is imposing; and I noticed on the invitation which was graciously sent to me by your widely known pastor—my esteemed friend—that under the picture of the church was displayed the words: Ad Jesum per Mariam, 'To Jesus through Mary'. What a beautiful thought. It sums up the whole meaning of the dedication; and sums up too, the whole reason for our great devotion to the Blessed Virgin. 'To Jesus through Mary.' There is no surer way. She was the first tabernacle. She was the first Monstrance, when with Virgin arms enfolding Him she showed Him to the Kings from the East and to the world at the Epiphany.

'Through Mary to Jesus.' Treasure that thought and teach it to your children. And when tomorrow morning as you dress them in their frocks and suits on their First Communion Day, when they will be tiny temples of the Real Presence, tell them the old, old story of the sweet and tender Mother who will guide them to Jesus when the mortal remains of their earthly mother is co-mingling with clay. Teach their unsoiled lips to pray tomorrow that they and you and all of us, holding Mary's hand in life and death, may be safely led to the Feet of Jesus.[13]

13. Our Cathedral Chimes, 7 June 1942, pp. 1-3.

11 Switch to Historical Writing

ather Hartigan's earlier writing in prose and verse had always had an Australian background. When Bishop Henschke asked him to preach at the silver jubilee of the diocese of Wagga in March 1942, he turned his gifts towards making that background come alive.

In the **Manly** of that year he had an article dealing with the early history of the Catholic Church in the south-west of the state. Entitled **'In Diebus Illis**[1] or As It Was In the Beginning'**, it is a valuable prologue to his jubilee sermon:

The history of the development of the South West of New South Wales and the growth of the Church therein begins with the history of the district and the Parish of Yass. The area in mind is sometimes referred to as the Murrumbidgee District and part of it as the Riverina: both inexact terms. The country I refer to extends from the Fish River, thirty miles [48 km] below Goulburn to the Victorian border, and from the Yarrangobilly ranges to the Lachlan. The name Riverina was originally applied to the land between that river and the Murrumbidgee. Wagga, the recognised capital, is outside those boundaries. Loosely speaking, the Riverina embraces all that territory which begins at the Slopes from the Tablelands and is watered by the Murrumbidgee and the Lachlan with the Murray as a definite termination on the South.

In good years it is a garden with lawns of trefoil and barley grass stretching away to the sunset. It is a colourful land with mauves and the ochres in the gums and the purple of the ranges in the background. Colourful in its flowers, gold and pink and blue and every shade between. Acres of them. It is colourful in its birds—vivid green and gamboge yellow; pale green and rich canary shot with scarlet; iridescent blue; gray lavender and salmon pink; barrabands, rosellas, ring-necks, galahs. Ornithologists had to resort to superlatives or near superlatives to describe them—superb,

---

1. *Literally 'in those days'.*

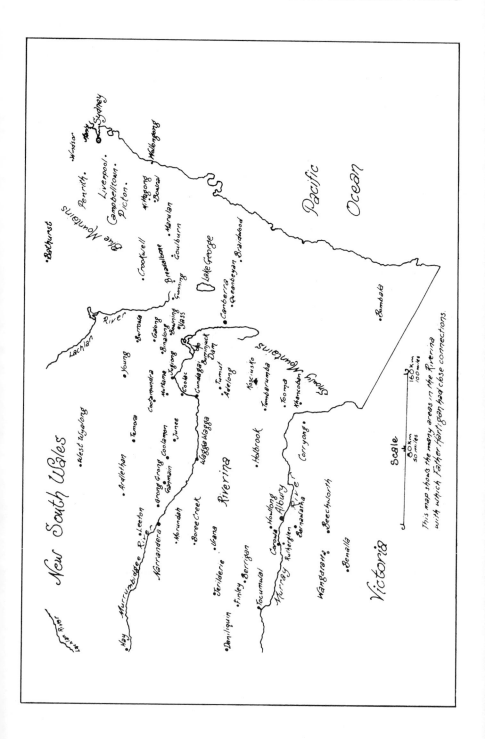

This map shows the many areas in the Riverina with which Father Hartigan had close connections.

Pulcherrimus, Eximius, Splendidus. It is a tuneful land when the magpies carol in the morning and the wirees and the thrushes 'in the gullies swap the old sweet melodies' and the kookaburra with his laughter signals knock-off time. A bounteous land where the wheat tops the fences and the glutted sheep meander towards the camp, and the fat cattle laze in the afternoon. In the afternoon when the sun is before you—the time the wily commission-agent picks to show a prospect over—it is as green as any country in the world. In the drought the inhabitants will tell you that it is so bare that you might flog a flea before you from Hay to Wagga. They take it all with a Mona Lisa smile and meet the green months and the brown months as they come. The diocese of Wagga is the centre of this Happy Valley.

It is not known who was the first white man to see the Murrumbidgee. In 1820 word went through to Sydney that some settlers had discovered a considerable stream in the South West which the natives called 'Morrumbidgee'. In 1923 Captain Currie, Major Ovens and a noted bushman, Joseph Wild, reached the river, which was in flood. Searching for a crossing place they went upstream and discovered open country which the blacks called 'Maneroo' from the number of conical breast-shaped hills with which the area is studded. This is now known as the Monaro.

In 1829 Sturt's party went down the river and opened up the Murrumbidgee district. George Macleay—the second in command—took up Toganmain near Hay. He was son of Alexander Macleay, who, as Colonial Secretary, dealt with the correspondence in the stirring days of Father Therry and who was afterwards Speaker in the first Parliament to meet in Sydney, 1 August 1843. His cousin, William, the benefactor of the Linnean Society, had the neighbouring station, Kerarbery.

In 1821 Hamilton Hume, while searching for grass to feed his sheep, which were in a sorry way on his station at Gunning, just ravaged by a bush fire, came on a stretch of open country which he called Yass Plains. He camped in a picturesque bend of the tiny Yass River, which has since been made more picturesque by willows brought from Napoleon's grave at St Helena. He made the same spot a halting place in 1824 on his trip with Hovell to Port Phillip. Shortly after his return from this last expedition the settlers came to Yass—Henry O'Brien to Douro, the Davises to Gounion, Dr John Harris (one of the many medico landowners of the early days) who was one of the witnesses chosen to given evidence in England against Governor Bligh, had a station near Binalong. The suburb

Harris Park, near Parramatta, was called after him.

Below Yass, the Murrumbidgee flows through very rough country between two precipitous cliffs or hills which are called Baron Jack and Black Andrew from two characters, one eccentric, the other notorious, who lived there. Running a wall between the two mountains the N.S.W. Government made the reservoir which feeds the Murrumbidgee Irrigation Area one hundred and fifty miles [241 km] away. To give an aboriginal touch to the name they wrote it Burrenjuck. One wonders what sort of a twist they would have given Black Andrew.

Sturt's original idea was to begin his expedition down the river from Good Hope, near Yass, where his friend and trusted advisor[2] in previous explorations had crossed it on his way to Melbourne. Had he adhered to this plan, he would have found it extremely difficult if not impossible, to pilot his drays through the gorge between Baron Jack and Black Andrew. It was Henry O'Brien, of Douro, who warned him and sent a black boy to direct him along a track round Bowning Hill to an out-station, Red Bank, which O'Brien had taken up on the lower river at Jugiong—Thugiong to the natives. It was from there Sturt started on a trip which, though beset with the gravest difficulty, was eminently successful.

Hamilton Hume, native-born at Parramatta, was the most skilful in bush-craft of all the explorers. In return for his services he was given a grant of 1280 acres [518 ha] by Governor Darling. The place he chose was the bend in Yass River where he had twice made his camp on his journeys, and there he lived till his death in 1873. His old home, 'Cooma Cottage', may still be seen near the Canberra turn-off beside the Highway which bears his name. He was a man of honour, and as a footnote to his differences with Hovell and the long-drawn-out controversy as to who is deserving of the credit in the Port Phillip expedition, it is to be noted that the old-timers to a man stood behind Hume and spoke his name with something like reverence. He is buried in the Church of England cemetery at Yass. A fitting epitaph might have been found in a sentence from the Vindication which he wrote thirty years after his dispute with Hovell: 'For the sake of those who bear my name, I should wish it to be held in remembrance as that of one, who, with small opportunities and limited resources, did what he could for his native land.'

---

2. *Hamilton Hume.*

When Hume decided to take out his grant on the Yass River,
Henry O'Brien, of the neighbouring Douro, was running stock there.
In those days there were, of course, no such things as surveys and
the squatter regarded the skyline as his boundary. The Squire of
Douro tried to keep Hume out, but his brother Cornelius—the
nominal occupier—let him have it. This led to an estrangement
between the brothers which was never removed.

Henry O'Brien was what is known as a hard man. He was
particularly hard on the ticket-of-leavers who called him Black Harry
and sang a parody which enumerated the residents of the corner in
the Hot Hereafter for which they were confident he was heading. He
was, however, kind to the Aborigines and maintained that if justly
treated they would give no trouble. Like many another who had
done well for himself in pastoral pursuits, he, at the same time, did
something for his country. In the early forties, when the price of
sheep fell to a shilling a head, he saved the sheepmen by
demonstrating that, in boiling down for tallow and saving the pelt,
the value of a sheep could be raised to twelve or thirteen shillings.
This tided the industry over one of the worst crises in its history.
The first boiling-down plant in Australia was Douro.

Henry was a friend and admirer of Father Therry. When, after the
arrival of Dr Polding, Father Therry was transferred to Hobart Town,
O'Brien, thinking that there was a catch in it somewhere (and from
the number of raw deals Father Therry had been subjected to, it was
natural) was about to organise a meeting of protest at Yass when
John O'Sullivan, the manager of the Commercial Bank at Goulburn,
cleared the air. The window behind the high altar in St Augustine's,
Yass, was placed there to the memory of Henry O'Brien by his
widow.

His brother Cornelius was of a more tractable type, a more
generous supporter of the Church, and generally a better citizen.
After the falling out he transferred to Bendenine near Galong, where,
in a later day, he was a fine support to that great church builder, Dr
McAlroy. When, later still, Bendenine came into the possession of
the Friend brothers its manager was Andrew Boyle Paterson, the
father of the writer of the best galloping rhymes in the language—
high-brows notwithstanding.

The 'Banjo' got many of his subjects, place names, etc., from the
surrounding district: Kiley's Run, How Gilbert Died, Conroy's Gap,
The Shadow of Death Hotel, Pardon, the Son of Reprieve. Reprieve,
should anyone be interested now, won the whole card at Wagga on
one occasion: he also did something nearly as brilliant at Randwick.

Conroy's Gap, on the Hume Highway, about ten miles [16 km] on the Gundagai side of Bowning, is called after a family that figures prominently in the subscription lists in connection with the original Sts Peter and Paul's Church, Binalong.[3]

The first priest to visit Yass was Father Therry in 1833. Naturally his visits to districts so far out were infrequent; the wonder is that he got as far as he did. Settlement beyond the coast was only beginning to be noticeable when Dr Polding came to Sydney in 1835. Two years afterwards the Bishop commissioned Dr Ullathorne to secure priests for the Australian Mission. Ullathorne may have been Monsignor Ego Solus, *as Cardinal Vaughan dubbed him later on, but he delivered the goods on this occasion. He got them from Ireland. Altogether fourteen priests and fourteen students resulted from the drive. There are illustrious names among them. Four of them became bishops and the others were at least the organisers of the oldest parishes in Australia outside Sydney. Two of them—Father Michael Brennan and Father John Fitzpatrick—were sent to Yass and Goulburn in 1838. Their jurisdiction covered practically all the southern part of New South Wales, the whole of Victoria, and as far into South Australia as they cared to go. There was no town or village between Yass and Melbourne.*

Albury, then known as the Crossing Place (by the Aborigines, Yarra-wuddah) had one building somewhere near where Hume struck the river in 1824. The first house appeared at Wagga in 1833—nine years later. Although towns had not yet risen there were settlers scattered over the vast area. The country along the Murrumbidgee as far as Hay has been taken up within three or four years after Sturt went down in 1829. In 1835 Ebden occupied land where Albury is today. The Huons were next at Wodonga, the Mitchells at Mungabareena. There were settlers, too, along the Tumut River. Even away from the main streams squatters had their boundless runs with their overseers, boundary riders and shepherds. Father Therry was one of these with one hundred and twenty thousand acres [485 km²] at the Billabong taken up in 1838.[4]

In the settlement of Victoria, which had a big influence in the development of Southern and South Western New South Wales, two factors combined. In 1836 Major Thomas Livingstone Mitchell

---

3. *We have already read in these pages the story of the cold-blooded murder of five members of this family. See p. 97.*

4. *See Rev Eris O'Brien,* Life and Letters of Archpriest John Joseph Therry, *Angus & Robertson, Sydney, 1922, pp. 277 ff.*

discovered the Western Districts of what is now the Southern State, and aptly named it Australia Felix. In his report he rose to something like rhetoric to describe the wonders he had seen: 'Fit to become eventually one of the great nations of the earth'; 'The sublime solitude of these verdant plains'; 'Of this Eden it seemed I was the only Adam' were some of the flights of phrasing. Mitchell dropped the purple stuff on his way back to Sydney.

Crossing the Murray at Oolong (since corrupted into Howlong—the native name means a crossing place) and running short of provisions, the party made its way through Livingstone Gully, near Wagga, towards the Murrumbidgee where they expected to find settlement and supplies. They had prepared their last meal at a spot which they called 'Cook and dine', now known as Cookardinia. They came upon some cattle at the river but were too exhausted to catch any of them. Driven to desperation, they slaughtered one of their own emaciated bullocks and journeyed on to the junction of Hillas' Creek where, at a newly formed station, they were given a supply of flour and beef. Mitchell was knighted by the young Queen Victoria. He was one of the most far-seeing of the explorers and one of the most accurate in his maps and surveys. He was a man of many interests and wrote pamphlets and articles on a variety of subjects. The screw-propellor for ships stands to his credit. It was tried out on the Queen's yacht and on H.M.S. Conflict. He evolved it from the boomerang of the Australian Aborigines.

At the time of the appearance of Mitchell's florid report of the discovery of the Western Districts of Victoria, the Southern parts of New South Wales suffered from one of the worst droughts in our history. In '37, '38 and '39 both the Murray and Murrumbidgee ceased to flow and were but a chain of water-holes for hundreds of miles. Around Camden, Liverpool and Picton water for domestic use had to be carted seven miles [11 km] on old-fashioned slides drawn by two bullocks. At Shane Park near Penrith, they were endeavouring, but not succeeding, to save the starving stock by digging up the roots of couch grass. Bread was selling at two and six the loaf in Sydney, at four and six at Goulburn. People were living on 'Valparaiso flour', which was a mixture of bad flour, ground rice and corn meal sent over from South America, mostly as ships' ballast. Those who were able to do so sent their stock to the Australia Felix of Major Mitchell.

In 1838 the first herds of cattle were swum across the Murrumbidgee at Gundagai on their way to stations taken up south of the Murray. Taafe from Muttama, David Reid from Illawarra, Faithfulls from Goulburn Plains were the first of the overlanders. Difficulties abounded, not the least being the hostility of the natives. Faithfulls' party was attacked at the Broken River, now Benalla, and nine out of fourteen drovers were speared.

Victoria was really opened up by settlers from Appin, Campbelltown and Illawarra, Goulburn and Yass. Later on, in the nineties there was a swing back. Many parts of New South Wales, notably the hay-growing and wheat-growing areas of the South West, were brought to their best by Victorian farmers who came over looking for cheaper land.

The first priests at Yass had a multi-sided flock to look after, and the spiritual aspect was worse than the material. Because of the difficulty of securing the services of a clergyman, many couples were living together unmarried. Children had no religious instruction whatever; many of them were not baptised. Shepherds and rural workers had not seen even the outside of a church. Through starvation in spiritual things a considerable number had developed a philosophy of their own in which religion had no part at all. In one place, so says a writer of the time, the people had lost their reckoning of the days of the week and were spending Sunday on Friday, for how long they didn't know. When a man died he was buried on the side of a hill facing the hut he had lived in and that was all there was to it. Ticket-of-leave men—and there was a great number of them employed on the stations, some of them becoming landholders themselves—were worse than careless, they were hostile. The cruelty they had been subjected to in the penal settlements in the routine and soulless compulsory attendance at Divine Worship had made them hate it. One such remarked to Father Therry on a visit to the McAlisters at the Gap near Goulburn about this time: 'I'm not going to trouble church again if I can help it. When I was in the iron gang at Windsor and Parramatta we had a bellyful of it. Old Sammy Marsden used to preach at us a hurricane one day and the next would get us fifty lashes for coughing while he was talking'.

Furthermore, hard drinking was a fine art. Fermented firewater was the chloroform under which the toiler, miles and miles away from everything that mattered, forgot both his troubles and the man he might have been. 'Mad from loneliness or drink, no matter which', says Henry Lawson. Hawkers used to cart the brew round under all manner of disguises, and lethal stuff it was. Sly grog

*distilleries were as numerous as the gumtrees. Lieutenant Irving,[5]
who lived at Mummel outside Goulburn in 1838, has recorded that
at that time Goulburn consisted of forty-four houses, eleven of
which were shanties; the population was made up of those who sold
grog and those who drank it. The magistrates had delicensed the
only two hotels in the town and left the clients to the mercy of
those who traded in the stuff manufactured on the sly. Melbourne
was half the size of Goulburn and twice as inebriate.*

*There was, of course, another side to the picture, and it was a
consoling one. Under the wise and careful rule of Governor Bourke,
good families were encouraged to emigrate. In previous years what
immigration there was had been haphazard and the supervision
slack. Bourke tightened it up. He set aside some of the money got
from the disposal of land to assist immigration, but it must be of the
right sort. There must be no more 'Red Rovers'[6] whether bond or
free.*

*Applicants for passages had to establish their fitness before they
were accepted; families were given preference, single women must
have a guardian, children under the age of one year were not taken.
As a consequence, from England, Ireland and Scotland, there came
many families who have been the stalwart builders of the Australian
race as we know it today. The Irish were mostly victims of
landlordism—*felix culpa *as far as we are concerned.*

*Among the immigrant ships of the period which brought valuable
foundation stock to the country may be mentioned two which are
referred to by the late Hon. James Gormly in his informative book:*
Explorations and Settlement in Australia. *The Gormlys—father,
mother, three sisters and two brothers—came out in* The Crusader *in
1839. On the ship were three to four hundred passengers all in
families with the exception of a few unmarried girls who were under
the care of relatives on board. The whole band—mostly from
Roscommon, a few from the North—had been carefully selected by a
board in Ireland. As suitable land was not available near the coast,
most of the company went inland towards the Riverina, where they
fought the fire, the drought, the flood with courage that has
characterised the pioneers. Sometimes the battle went against them.
The Gormly family, with the exception of the two boys, were
drowned in the Gundagai flood of '52, which accounted for more*

---

5. Irving joined Sir John Franklin's ill-starred expedition to the Arctic seven years later. His body was found near Cape Victoria thirty years afterwards. It was identified by a medal.
6. Notorious female immigrants of the early days.

than eighty. The Hon. James lived to a great age and was a pillar of Church and Parliament in the land of his selection. Fellow passengers of his on The Crusader were the grandparents of the late Sir Thomas Hughes, of Sydney, whose son, the Wing-Commander, is an ornament to his profession and his Faith.

The Lady McNaughton brought out the Downey, Keane and Cox families whose names are well-known and honoured throughout the Riverina. The original W.H. Downey built the first bridge over the Macquarie at Bathurst, the first bridge at Queanbeyan, and the first bridge at Yass. The last named bridge was washed away in '60, its successor went in the '70 flood. They made no mistake about the third one—it was built twenty-five feet [7.6 m] higher. The late Senator Charles Hardy, who was killed some months ago in a plane crash while on war work for his country, was a descendant of W.H. Downey.

John Keane was a direct victim of landlordism. He openly took sides with O'Connell in an election and lost his Irish farm. He was most successful in Australia, owning at different times Keane's Flat, Lake George; Tomorromo, near Tumut; Pullitop, Wagga. There were eleven children in the family, all of them subsequently land-owners. One of them married Luke Crowe, then of Muttama, and from that union there has come more than one who entered the sanctuary. A daughter was a nun in the Presentation Convent, Wagga.

The branches of the Cox family have spread over the Riverina, and both Church and country have benefited. It was John Cox, of Mangoplah, who came out on the Lady McNaughton as a child, that made it possible for Dr Bermingham in 1875 to erect the elaborate convent which is known far and wide as Mount Erin. John Cox and John Donnelly each gave £1500 to the building fund.

This much has been set out at some length to show the type of families which settled in the old Parish of Yass, and which, though balanced against the other element, left it a headache to the two young priests just out from Ireland in 1836. Distance and bad roads, or rather no roads at all, was the trouble. How could a man cover that vast area on horseback? They made a great attempt to do so. Father Kavanagh in the next decade used to average four thousand miles [6400 km] a year in Goulburn, Queanbeyan and Braidwood districts. Still, how could they find their way through that trackless expanse when there was not even a windmill or a boundary fence to guide them? Bushmen, for nearly twenty years after the time I speak of, travelled that same country by dead reckoning based on a compass and their instinct; but then the bushman's instinct is a

*mighty thing. Father Brennan and Father Fitzpatrick were not
bushmen then—that came later on. Another feature which added to
their troubles was the lack of means of communication. There was
no way of letting a man know that you were going to call on him
except to go and call on him.*

*The mail service through that area was begun at this very time.
John Bourke left Melbourne on horseback on 1 January 1838, to
carry the first mail to Yass, to be sent thence to Sydney by coach.
He was given a fortnight to do the trip. The 'boys' cheered him out
but shook their heads after him, for there was no definite route. The
unsympathetic aborigines speared his horse at the Ovens, but he
nursed it on the Hume (Murray) where it got drowned at Oolong
(Howlong), the Crossing Place. With the grit of Kelly and Shea as
well as his own, he swam the river with the mail. Arriving on the
other side very much as the Almighty made him, he sought to reach
a hut which he saw in the distance. The inexperienced dogs sent
him up a tree and the owner came across to shoot him. He explained
all about himself from the branches and was made respectable and
loaned another horse; and although he discovered at Albury that a
homing fat bullock escaped from the yards at Melbourne had made
better time to the border than he, John Bourke delivered the mail at
Yass on time. The gray horse he rode from Howlong lived for
another twenty-seven years and probably deserved to. The man
himself survived the horse and died in harness twenty years later
still.*

*Incidentally, it cost 13d to send a letter from Melbourne to Yass.
You paid your money over the counter before they took delivery.
Later, stamped covers were sold at one and three per dozen. That
was many years before Rowland Hill introduced the adhesive postage
stamp in England. The mail did not help the priest in getting in
touch with his people. The service was a through one and deliveries
at intermediate places depended on the temper of the mailman.
There were no branch lines and the telegraph was twenty years
away. However, the settlers who had the Faith, and some of them
would put modern times to shame, overcame the difficulty, to some
extent, in the way that Mahomet overcame the problem of the
Mountain. Yass, where the priest lived when he was at home, was
the only place where supplies could be got. There was no store
between it and Melbourne, so when in town on business the faithful
took the opportunity to 'see the Soggarth'. The only conveyance was
the bullock dray, the handy two-wheeler which solved the transport
question in Australia for many years.*

With twenty bullocks or more attached it was the ship of the Outback, with half that number and 'flying light' it was a handy runabout for going places. They engineered it through the big timber and the scrub, with a tree tied on behind they steadied it down the mountain track, they cajoled it up the hills with picturesque phrase; they anathematised it through the boggy flats; with a barrel at the tip of the pole and a couple more beneath the axle they floated it across creeks and rivers. It performed wonders in every capacity. It brought wool from Toganmain, near Hay, five hundred miles [800 km] to Campbell's wharf at Sydney Cove: it brought children from Albury to be baptised at Yass, couples from Wagga to be married there. All this is on record. It is recorded too, that in the Tumut district there was an imposing funeral where seventy bullock drays moved mournfully along behind the hearse, which was a bullock dray. At least no one could accuse it of indecent haste in the last sad rites.

The motor car today tries to take its place in the long, slow procession, but lacks its sincerity. The first person to use a motor so was the late Bishop of Wagga. Thirty years ago, as Father Dwyer, Parish Priest of Temora, he had a Renault car, twin-cylindered, of eight alleged horsepower, with three figures on the number plate, and thus mounted he chugged along before the hearse to the amazement of everybody but the corpse. All the newspapers of the day gave him mention. Such is fashion. The wonder of today is the accepted thing tomorrow.

Notwithstanding all the difficulties which confronted them, the two young priests were busy, Father Fitzpatrick at Goulburn and Father Brennan at the Yass end, as far as Burrowa and down the Murrumbidgee past its meeting with the Tumut—the Domot of the aborigines—to where the town of Gundagai stands today. A correspondent of a Sydney paper in 1839, contrasting the Roman Catholic activity against that of his own denomination, writes that in King's County, which at that time embraced all the country south of Goulburn, while the latter had only small congregations gathered in wretched hovels, the Catholics were erecting three chapels—one at Yass, one at the Domot, and one at Limestone Plains.[7] Furthermore, they were about to provide respectable quarters for their clergymen.

In 1838 a fund was begun for the building of St Augustine's Yass,

7. Queanbeyan.

*but progress was hampered by the drought—mentioned
before—which lasted from '37 to '43. St Augustine's is still the
parish church at Yass.[8] Towards the end of 1840 the two pioneers of
the South West were transferred to other spheres—Father Brennan to
Parramatta and Father Fitzpatrick to Penrith—and their late parish
was handed over to the watchful care of the capable and saintly
Father Lovat, who came to Yass in 1841.*

*Father Michael Brennan was born in the City of Limerick in 1810.
He studied at Carlow under the Rev. Dr Slattery, afterwards Bishop
of Cashel. Ordained in 1838 by Dr Murray, he was one of the
number of distinguished priests selected by Dr Ullathorne, arriving
in Sydney in July of that year. His companions of the voyage and
fellow-workers in a part of the Vineyard up to that time hardly
touched were Fathers Lynch, who did the spade work in what is now
the Diocese of Maitland, Mahoney, his co-worker in the task,
Murphy, afterwards the first Bishop of Adelaide, Slattery of Hartley,
and later of Warrnambool, O'Reilly, the founder of Bathurst, Rigney,
the well-known figure of Wollongong and Sydney, Fitzpatrick the
clarum et venerabile nomen of Melbourne.*

*From Parramatta Father Brennan went to Goulburn in '43, back to
Parramatta in '47, to Penrith in '52 where he laid the burden down
in 1864.*

*He was a man 'of courteous bearing, refined tastes and priestly
life'. So said his panegyrist. All that and much more was attested by
those who knew him and after he had gone 'the scent of the roses'
lingered long round the broken vase of life. Though of a gentle and
saintly disposition, he was ever ready to champion the cause that
needed the protection of the sword in the strong right hand. He was
prominent in the anti-transportation movement of the time:
prominent too, in defending the rights of the little primitive
Catholic schools. An address delivered by him at a meeting at St
Mary's in 1844 'to consider the proposals of the Government to do
away with denominational education' was long regarded as the final
word on the subject. He opened the first parochial school at
Goulburn. A church builder, too, he was instrumental in erecting
the first place of Catholic worship in the same town. Another
erected at Parramatta under his care did duty till it was replaced by
the present one built in 1854. He was ever on the move among his
people, and though he had nine districts to attend as well as
Parramatta he knew his flock, and his flock knew him.*

8. The old Yass Church was still the parish church when the author was writing. Later, in Archbishop
Young's time, a new church was built, the old becoming the Convent Chapel.

When leaving Goulburn in '47 he was given a send-off at which every one from the highest to the lowest took part. Captain Rossi was in the chair. Dr Waugh, the concocter of 'Dr Waugh's Baking Powder', read the address. The Anglican Dean Sowerby, with whom he had clashed over the school question, called for 'three hearty cheers'. Besides the cheers he was presented with a purse of one hundred and fifteen sovereigns, which they knew would not be in his possession long. He had a big generous heart which kept his pockets empty. He 'lent the quid and paid the fine', and when he died a miserable grab-all to whom he owed a few pounds put the bailiff in to seize his few sticks of furniture and his library. A couple of labouring-men working nearby recognised the ritual, and what they said and what they did would not be good for the pious eyes of those who may read these lines.

Returning to his home from a business call to Dr Polding who was ill at Wollongong, he was seized at Parramatta with paralysis—a stroke, I take it—while in the act of writing a letter to Dr John Forrest, the Rector of St John's. All night he lay embracing the crucifix. They took him to Penrith and laid him down beside his old shipmate Dean Mahoney.[9] The monument that was placed over his resting place was subscribed by Protestants as well as by his own—even non-Catholic children 'with moistened eyes and faltering speech' went round collecting shillings to erect a tribute to one who was the friend of all. The inscription reads:

Quae sunt mortalia hic reponuntur
Rev. Michaelis Brennan, hujusce
Ecclesiae per XII annos Presbyter
Missionarius eximius. Obit die XXIV Octobris
Anno Salutis MDCCCLXIV Aetate LIV
Cujus Anima Propitietur Deus

Father John Fitzpatrick, his fellow-worker at Goulburn and Yass in '38, needs no biographical notice here. He was for many years Monsignor and Vicar-General of what he saw grow to be the great Archdiocese of Melbourne. There his magnificent work was done, and as long as the graceful spires of St Patrick's point to heaven, his name shall be revered. He was its builder and there he lies. He died 21 January 1890.[10]

---

9. *Father Hartigan was in error on this point: Dean Mahoney, who came out on the barque* Cecilia *in 1838 with Father Brennan, is not buried in Penrith but Maitland. See* The Men of '38, *pp. 78 and 79.*
10. *Manly 6, 4, 1942, pp. 25–34.*

The story of the diocese of Wagga was vividly presented by Father Hartigan at the cathedral on Jubilee Day, Sunday 1 March 1942. Before the Mass he dismayed the bishop by telling him the sermon would go for an hour. It did too, but in that time he held his audience spell-bound as he ranged from early Australian explorers to Cobb & Co, from the pioneer priests to the horses they rode:

My Lords, Very Reverend and Reverend Fathers and dear Brethren, I propose this morning, while we are here to celebrate the silver jubilee of the Diocese of Wagga, to tell the story of the early days, to glance at the great achievements of the past, and to recall some splendid names now seldom spoken of by a forgetful generation. The history of the Diocese of Wagga reads very much the same as that of every country diocese in Australia. Change but the names and what is told of one might be told of all. In practically every case you will find a handful of Irish Priests belonging to no religious order ministering to exiles of their race scattered throughout a sparsely settled continent. I am not unmindful of what the Benedictines did in this matter; still with these and a few other exceptions the building up of the Catholic Church in Australia has been the work of the Irish secular clergy. And what a fine body of men they were—all more or less of the same type. Physically powerful, mentally alert, of good masculine faith. Of real vision, they stood out among the leaders of the day as men with an unbounded confidence in the future of this country. They carried out their work under what seems to us insuperable difficulties. They never knew the meaning of the word 'defeat'; and if you would seek their monuments, you will find them on a hill in every town throughout the country, where church and school and convent testify to the farsightedness and generosity of priests and people of the early days. So now to my story. In 1829 Charles Sturt started out from Jugiong to trace the course of the Murrumbidgee. On the 7th or 8th of December he passed by where the town of Wagga stands today. He does not mention it, but so much can be inferred from his diary. In 1832, that is about three years afterwards, Robert Holt Best took up the first land round here and called his property 'Wagga Wagga Station'. Other areas were quickly taken up down the river, and this locality became a meeting place for people from the neighbouring settlements.

Fourteen years later there were about a half dozen houses of a kind, and it was proclaimed a Town by notice in the Government Gazette in 1846.

At this time Wagga was in the Parish of Yass, which, by the way, once included Melbourne. The Parish of Yass had begun in 1838, extending from five miles [8 km] on the Goulburn side of Gunning to the junction of the Lachlan and Murrumbidgee Rivers. It embraced parts of the present Diocese of Goulburn, part of the present Diocese of Wilcannia-Forbes and the whole of what is now the Diocese of Wagga. The pastoral charge of this immense area was in 1857 entrusted to two priests whose name will ever be associated with the advancement of the Church, and its glories in this part of the country. They were Father Michael McAlroy, afterwards known as Dr McAlroy, 'The Apostle of the South', and his scarcely less distinguished assistant, Father Patrick Bermingham, afterwards known as Dr Bermingham. There were at that time about five thousand Catholics scattered through that region where today sixty thousand would be a conservative estimate. The task set these two priests was to find out and minister to those five thousand people in the mining camps, in the tiny hamlets, on the big runs further down, in the little holdings tucked away in the dense timbered hills. How they accomplished it I leave to your imagination to explain. There were no motor-cars, no railways, no roads, no bridges. They went their way on horse-back with their Mass-kit packed on the pommel of the saddle—past the dog-leg fences, past the chock and block till they picked up the bridle track which led to the slab dwelling where Irish eyes grew misted at their coming. Their highway at best was the wheel marks of the tilted cart or bullock dray; their signposts an axe mark on a tree or a 'rough calculation based on the blaze of a star'.

Almost immediately they set out to follow the settlement down the river. Always down the River went the seekers of good land; Jugiong, Gundagai, Mundarlo, Wagga Wagga, Buckingbong, Bundidjarrie, where Rolf Boldrewood was at that time raising sheep before he took up the pen which gave us Robbery Under Arms, Narrandera, where in the old station cemetery is buried Dr Trollope,[11] the son of the English novelist, and so on to Cogeldrie, Hay and Balranald.

One year after his arrival at Yass, 27 September 1858, Father McAlroy blessed the foundations of the first Catholic Church in

11. The preacher is astray here. F.J.A. Trollope, the son of the novelist, lived for a time in Hay and died early this century. William Trollope, who was buried in the old Narrandera cemetery, died in 1878 and there is no evidence that he had the title Doctor or was linked with the novelist. My thanks are due here to Sir Anthony Trollope of Roseville, a direct descendant of the novelist, and to Mr R.L. Goss, Shire Clerk, and Father R.O'Donovan, Parish Priest, Narrandera.

Wagga. Mass had been said on a few occasions previously in the village by Father Thomas O'Neill who afterwards founded the Parish of Boorowa in 1865. On 4 December 1859 the church was opened and dedicated to St Michael in the presence of 250 people, some of whom had come one hundred miles [160 km] to witness the ceremony. It was an unpretentious ceremony. Father McAlroy himself blessed the church and the curate preached the sermon. When we look around his morning and see so many bishops, so many priests, and this crowded congregation gathered for another opening it looks a small affair indeed; but listen to this:—'At that time Jesus spoke this parable. The kingdom of heaven is like to a grain of mustard seed which a man took and sowed in his field: which is the least indeed of all seeds; but when it is grown up, it is the greatest of all herbs and becometh a tree, so that the birds of the air come, and dwell in the branches thereof'. After more than three-quarters of a century of chance and change and progress old St Michael's is still standing with its little square tower and cupola. It served for many years as a Boys' school, and is now a technical school under the care of the Christian Brothers. Eighty-three years ago it was looked upon as a fine example of modern architecture. It has grown old-fashioned but it has watched Wagga grow to the fine city that it is. When it was built the site which is crowned today by a splendid cluster of buildings,—Cathedral, Bishop's House, Brothers' residence and spacious schools—was virgin bush. There was a blacksmith's shop hard by and not far away the local pound. Wagga was a mere village with a few primitive houses scattered along rambling streets between the river and the Wollundry Lagoon. There was a court-house walled with slabs and covered with shingles, a police-station roofed with bark, a post-office, but no telegraph office. The first telegram was taken at Wagga on 10 June 1861, nearly two years afterwards. The hospital was a slab hut. There were one or two shops, a few hotels to one of which was attached the principal store of the town—a long-headed arrangement, for the customer at the latter had his change handed out to him over the counter next door in the shape of fermented and spirituous liquors. Where the Town Hall now stands were the stables of Cobb and Co. The coaches crossed the river on a punt. The first bridge, which was known as the Company's Bridge, was not opened till four years later. Hampden Bridge was built in 1895.

*   The cost of old St Michael's was £1500 and they had in hand after the opening £1487. The population of Wagga must have been less than 600. The Australian Almanac of 1865, that is six years after it*

was blessed, gives the population of the township as 627.

It is not stated where they put all that money for safe keeping. The Commercial Bank which opened about that time closed its doors almost immediately through fear of bushrangers. A police sergeant was shot by Morgan, the most bloodthirsty of the whole of them, and Henry Bayliss, the first Police Magistrate, was wounded by the same outlaw. Captain Moonlight and Blue Cap were two other marauders who showed a liking for Wagga; but it is nowhere on record that the funds of the Catholic Church were ever used for their upkeep.

Soon after the opening of old St Michael's, Father Bermingham suffered a breakdown in health, and was ordered by his medical adviser, Dr Morgan O'Connor, to return to Ireland to recuperate. He was appointed a professor at Carlow College, later becoming Vice-Rector. He appears again in this story and the building of Mt Erin is associated with his name.

After his departure, Father McAlroy carried on his immense parish alone until help could be found for him. I wish that in a few words I could give you a pen-portrait of this truly remarkable man. He was big in every way; big in build and handsome. He was big in his pastoral care for every member of his flock, and knew every one of them as a father would know his children.

He was a great horseman. He is credited with having ridden many a time a hundred miles in a day on the same horse. Again if I were not preaching a sermon I would love to say a word on the Australian horse of the period. Known as the Murrumbidgee Waler, and mostly of Snowden or Panic blood, he was the hardiest horse in the world. The climate had given him a wonderful constitution and splendid feet. Some of these horses had never been groomed or stable-fed. Ridden hard from daylight till dark, then hobbled and turned out to forage for themselves, they were capable of doing two and three hundred miles a week without injury. One hundred miles in twenty-four hours was not beyond the endurance of the old Walers. They've passed with the men who rode them, but they come to the muster now and then when grey-heads dream again of far-off things and battles long ago. Father McAlroy tried them out to the very limit. He visited every part of his parish.

An extraordinary combination of the deeply spiritual man and the shrewd man of business, he was at the beck and call of every member of his flock in their eternal as well as their temporal difficulties. Even to many who were not of his faith, he was a counsellor. His vision was almost that of a prophet. He seems to

*have been able to sense the possibilities of every part of this vast,
unpredictable country. Wherever he erected buildings which seemed
too elaborate at the time, the subsequent advance of the locality has
justified him. He was constantly urging his people to take up the
land, and many who have comfortable holdings today can thank
their stars that their fathers took the advice of Dr McAlroy.*

*It was in his zeal for the Church of God that he was, I think I can
say, supreme. A list of churches and convents which he called into
being would stagger us out of our smug self-satisfaction today: The
Convent of Mercy Goulburn, the Bishop's House, Goulburn, both
still in use; a church at Breadalbane, another at Grabben Gullen, the
old church at Taralga, now a school-hall, a church at Gunning; he
enlarged St Augustine's Church at Yass which was begun by Dean
Lovat in 1839, and which has been the parish church at Yass for over
one hundred years. The quaint little church standing beside the road
at Jugiong was built by him, a church at Binalong, one at Gundagai,
another at Tumut, old St Michael's at Wagga as we have seen, the
present fine church at Albury, the Convent there, the old Star of the
Sea at Corowa, a church at Howlong, St John's at Thurgoona, still
the parish church attached to Newtown Orphanage, St Francis de
Sales', Bowna since submerged by the waters of the Hume Weir, St
John's, Wymah on the Upper Murray. What a record! He lit the
sanctuary lamps from Goulburn to the border. 'Behold a great
priest.'*

*What money he raised for all that I cannot say, but it is on record
that in four years from 1857 to 1861 he raised for church building in
the parish of Yass with its 5000 people the sum of £1400. 'There
were giants in the world in those days.' Besides that he sent to the
Donegal Relief Committee in Melbourne a handsome sum to provide
passage money for the Irish farmers evicted from their homes by the
unscrupulous John George Adair at Glenveigh in 1861. Another large
contribution went to the fund for establishing St John's College.
When the estates of Pius IX were attacked by the despoiler, he sent
along £472.*

*His working day was a comparatively brief span of twenty-three
years. He was taken in his prime: he was not more than fifty when
he died.*[12] *His valiant dust is sepulchred behind the high altar in the
fine church he built at Albury seventy-two years ago. His name is*

---

12. *Father Hartigan is in error here as Father Michael McAlroy was sixty when he died after a working
life of thirty-three years.*

inscribed on a mural tablet there. And of all the unsung heroes of our Land, who in their time and in their own sphere did splendid things for God and Country, and whose achievements are summarised in a line or two upon a stone, our short and simple records hold no greater name than that of Michael McAlroy.

About seven or eight years after the opening of old St Michael's Church a Bishop was appointed to Goulburn. Dr Lanigan took over the Diocese of Goulburn. He had five priests. In 1871 the Bishop, accompanied by a young arrival from Ireland who was then known as Father Gallagher, drove a pair of horses to Wagga in the good time of four days, and the Catholics petitioned His Lordship to appoint a resident priest to the district. Father William Bermingham was the first priest stationed at Wagga. The parish embraced Wyalong, Temora, Cootamundra, Junee, Coolamon, Ganmain, Narrandera, the Irrigation Area, Lockhart and Urana. The Railway had not then come to Wagga, and Cobb and Co's coaches reigned supreme.

If I were not preaching a sermon I would love to dilate upon the fascinating story that is woven round the magic name of Cobb and Co. It was the only link between the world and the vast outback—the only thread that connected up the wanderer's life with all he'd left behind. Many a time it carried the priest on his sacred errand bearing in his breast pocket the Eternal Remedy both of body and soul—Qui tollis peccata mundi—and rough, but friendly, passengers wondered why he was so strangely silent:—

> 'The roaring camps of Gulgong, and many a digger's rest;
> The diggers on the Lachlan, the huts of fartherest West;
> Some twenty thousand exiles, who sailed for weal and woe —
> The bravest hearts of many lands have watched for Cobb and Co.'

At their peak Cobb and Co were harnessing 6000 horses a day. Their coaches were travelling 28,000 miles per week, more than once round the earth. Their pay sheet was £100,000 per year; and they received in subsidies for the carriage of mail £95,000 a year. But this is a digression.

In 1874 there happened an event which perhaps more than anything else has achieved the solidity and the stability of the Catholic Faith in Wagga. Dr Bermingham came back to Australia bringing with him five Sisters of the Presentation Order of whom the late Mother Stanislaus of saintly memory was the last survivor. The old presbytery was turned into a Convent, the stables into a school, and Dr Bermingham, who replaced his brother Father William Bermingham in the charge of the parish, set about the beginning of that splendid pile of buildings which crowns the hill above the town, and which is known far and wide as Mt Erin.

Here is a coincidence which I think is noteworthy. When Dr Bermingham gave over the presbytery to the Sisters, he and his assistant found accommodation at one of the hotels for a time. Then a generous lady, Mrs Jackson of Boree Creek, who was not a Catholic, gave him the use, free of debt, of a dwelling called 'Foxborough Hall'. In the great flood of 1870—that is, four years previously—Foxborough Hall in a great act of charity and mercy had thrown its doors open to those who had been rendered destitute by the visitation. Fifty years afterwards the Wagga Church Committee under the late Bishop Dwyer secured 'Foxborough' as a hospital for the Little Company of Mary—The Lewisham Sisters—who are renowned and loved for acts of charity and mercy wherever the blue veil goes. The assistant priest who lived with Dr Bermingham at 'Foxborough Hall' was Father Tom Long who was afterwards Parish Priest of Lewisham, Sydney.

Mt Erin was opened in 1876 in the presence of Archbishop Vaughan of Sydney and the bishops of Goulburn, Maitland and Bathurst. The Archbishop, who is said to have been one of the greatest speakers the Church in this country has known, was the preacher. The building, or rather that part of it that was erected at the time, cost over £9262 and thanks to those generous people like the Coxs, the Donnellys, the Hallidays and many others whose names obviously it would take too long to enumerate, only £475 debt remained on the building.

To get a proper perspective of that achievement it is necessary to go back to the Wagga of 1876. The Railway was not built till 1878. Adelaide was Wagga's seaport; steamers were on the river—the Victoria, the Albury and the Wagga Wagga. You could hear their paddles 'chunkin' as they nosed it round the bend. Here is the final entry in the log of the last of them: 'Steamer Wagga Wagga, 40 tons, barge Wakool in tow: cargo, miscellaneous. Captain, Thomas Bynon. Wharf to wharf, four days.' The veteran captain is still alive at Narrandera; and at low river you can see what is left of the old Wagga Wagga hard and fast on a mudbank. There was a sugar mill in the locality those days. Wagga people have always been optimists. Wiser in his generation was Anthony Marshall who grew eight acres [3 ha] of wheat on lot 21, Tarcutta Street. Wagga was not then a Municipality. It was 'poorly lighted, ill-kept, and the streets were paved with broken bottles'. I quote the Advertiser of the time, and it must be true, for the Advertiser has never allowed anyone to hurl a stone at Wagga. The population of the town could not have been more than a thousand, the population of the whole police district was given as 3888. And it was in a place of these proportions that they were game enough to build a place like Mt Erin.

Dr Bermingham's name was for years a household word throughout the Riverina. He survived his fellow worker Dr McAlroy by three years. He died in London in 1883.

Another achievement which stands to the credit of the pioneer priests and people is this Cathedral. It was built as a parish church by old Father Dunne more than half a century ago. Father Dunne built the nave. It was completed as it is today—the Cathedral of the diocese—by Bishop Dwyer in 1925 in the presence of the Apostolic Delegate, seven archbishops, ten bishops, and a gathering of people estimated to be 10,000.

Father Patrick Dunne, parish priest from 1883, is another of the remarkable men associated with this parish . . .[13] Four years later he moved to Albury as Parish Priest and Vicar-General. I saw him once, a little old deaf man—as peppery as you would wish to see— spending the evening of an eventful life among the orphans at Thurgoona. He built a four-roomed cottage there which till recently was the residence of the Inspector of Schools. He is taking his last long sleep near the Convent cemetery hard by, where twenty-five plain wooden crosses mark the resting place of Spouses of Christ who, like himself, when the Bridegroom called we may be sure were found watching.

In 1887 Father Dunne was succeeded in Wagga by one who, in some respects at least, was the 'noblest Roman of them all', Very Reverend John Gallagher D.D., P.P. He was the first Parish Priest of Wagga, and the first Irremovable Rector appointed in the Southern World. At the First Plenary Synod held in Sydney in 1885, Cardinal Moran presiding, it was resolved to submit to Rome a recommendation that some of the senior clergy should have a title to share to some extent that permanency position which hitherto in Australia had been possessed only by Bishops. In this land of ours Wagga was the first parish so constituted.

Dr Gallagher came to this town with academic honours thick upon him. He had brought St Patrick's, Goulburn, to the front among the educational establishments of the country. He was its second and its greatest president;—and I say this not unmindful of

---

13. Father Hartigan then spoke about the earlier years of this pioneer priest, an interesting story which is given on pp. 252-255.

the many outstanding men among the Christian Brothers who have
directed its destinies since 1898. He was the finest classical scholar
of his time. Even to the end his very conversation suggested 'The
glory that was Greece and the grandeur that was Rome'. He was
among the leading educationalists of a period which was not lacking
in brilliant names . . .[14]

After he had spent eight happy years in Wagga, old St Patrick's fell
on evil days—the number on roll fell to twenty-eight—and the
bishop and his counsellors were about to decide to shut the College
doors. Then the old chief with lightning in his eyes and thunder in
his voice jumped to his feet and defied them to close his old school.
Much as he loved Wagga, and he did love it, he would go back and
save the place where half his heart was buried. In 1895 he resumed
the presidency and became a school-master once again. He carefully
selected his teachers, both clerical and lay; he expounded his well
loved classics once more. The palmy days of the College were about
to be reborn. The numbers had risen to over forty in the first term.
Then, in the middle of the same year, they made him Co-adjutor
Bishop of Goulburn. Even with all the duties his new position
brought with it, he continued the presidency and the teaching till
1898, when he was instrumental in having the institution handed
over to the Christian Brothers. This after his own brilliant services
was the greatest benefit he ever conferred on St Patrick's College.

As a bishop, though he did not inaugurate, he did intensify the era
of the Catholic school. Up to this the priests had been church
builders; he turned them into a generation of school builders. At the
time, because of necessity, in very many places one building had to
serve as church and school. This would not do. There must be a
school separate from the church in every parish.

While he was Parish Priest of Wagga he built St Joseph's, the
forerunner of the beautiful building which will be blessed this
afternoon. The population of Wagga was then around 4000. He also
extended Mt Erin.

As a master of Sacred Eloquence he was in a class by himself.
They called him 'silver-tongued'; and, by the way, no preacher ever
had his stuff so barefacedly stolen and served up without
acknowledgement by other men. But the Old Man did not care;
there was plenty more where that came from; and every man must
live.

14. Father Hartigan then referred to Dr Gallagher's nomination for Rectorship of St John's College,
   mentioned above, p. 35.

He was the humblest of men—a man of deep and simple piety.
Though his outlook was masculine, he had the faith of a child. He
was a hard worker; no-one ever saw him idle. 'Better wear out than
rust out' was a truism that was often on his lips. He never failed to
keep an appointment, even through indisposition. Never! Well only
once. When old age had overtaken him, and he was confined to his
bed through weakness, against the advice of nurse and doctor he
tried to rise to meet an engagement in a distant town. The effort was
too much. He fell back exhausted and disheartened with a quotation
from Shakespeare on his lips: 'Superfluous lags the veteran on the
stage'. He never left his room again till they placed him where he
lies beneath the sanctuary of St Peter and Paul's.

But if high attainments gladly used in humble service and devoted
unselfishly to the House of God; if great intellect keeping constant
company with simple-hearted holiness; if all that is meant by
'priestliness' inspire us still, that grave should be remembered. I pay
this tribute to his memory at some length because a tribute is
overdue; and I pay it here in Wagga to remind a forgetful generation
that on their honour scroll of celebrated names there is one that
sparkles with a brilliance of its own.

But I must hasten, for I have already kept you too long. Dr
Gallagher was succeeded by Father Slattery who was the Father
O'Flynn of the company. He was a man of infinite jest, but behind it
all was a great organiser and a parish-builder. Whenever a new parish
was to be formed, they always seemed to pick on Father
Slattery. . . [15] *The Presbytery here at Wagga was built during his*
regime at a cost of £2000. The population of the town at the time
was 5108, the Catholics being 1720.

Father Buckley, afterwards Monsignor, was the last of the parish
priests before the Diocese was formed in 1918. During his pastorate
the Convent Chapel and St Eugene's were built at Mt Erin. In
bringing the Christian Brothers to Wagga he conferred the greatest
service to education that had been done at any time since Dr
Bermingham brought the Presentation Sisters.

Dr Joseph Wilfred Dwyer was consecrated the first Bishop of
Wagga in 1918. He was in reality the third priest who had at one
time or other been stationed at Wagga to be raised to the episcopate:
Dr Dunne, first bishop of Wilcannia, was here with Father William
Bermingham in 1871, Dr Gallagher 1887-95, Dr Dwyer was curate in

---

15. *Father Hartigan then detailed Father Slattery's parishes, noted above, p. 116.*

*1898, and as is meet, the successors of all three are here for this
jubilee this morning . . .*[16]

*Besides what he did in this town, Bishop Dwyer had perforce to
disperse his attentions through the other parts of the Diocese. He
had to do what might be called the spade work, and he did it nobly.
He passed an extremely well equipped diocese into the capable hands
which wield the Shepherd's Staff today. The fine school which will
be blessed this afternoon will keep his memory green for many years
to come.*

*In 1918 the Diocese of Wagga had fourteen parishes, today there
are twenty-one. There were twenty priests where now we have
thirty-six. Teaching Brothers have increased from seven to twelve
and the nuns from 142 to 204. The children in the Catholic schools
have grown from 2000 to over 4000. The Catholic population of the
Diocese is much the same as it was in 1918, which makes one
thoughtful. There has been considerable growth in Wagga, in Albury
and in the Irrigation Area. Outside these districts some parishes have
merely maintained their old level, some have fallen below it. The
call of the city, the lure of the Neon lights, poor markets, bad times
and the lack of the pioneer grit to face them, the empty cradle—all
have contributed.*

*Of the twenty priests who began with Dr Dwyer in 1918, only ten
of us remain. Of the sixty to whom we bade farewell when leaving
the old Mother Church of Goulburn, only seventeen are there today.
Among the congregations we knew in those days, the Bearded Reaper
has been very, very busy. Such is the retrospect of five and twenty
years. And so I end my story.*[17]

In August of the same year 1942 there was held at Yass the Golden
Jubilee of Mother De Sales and Sister Brigid and the preacher was billed as
'Dean' Hartigan, a title he was reluctant to wear.[18] Moreover, he regarded

---

16. *The preacher then spoke of two other priests of the original diocese of Goulburn who became bishops, Dr Patrick Clune, late Archbishop of Perth, and Dr Patrick Phelan, late Bishop of Sale. In fact there was only one, Dr Clune. Father Hartigan confused Bishop Patrick Phelan with his brother Michael who was in Goulburn and later became a Jesuit. Patrick never worked in Goulburn diocese.*
17. *This sermon is from a typescript among Father Hartigan's papers. It was reported in full in the Daily Advertiser, Wagga, 2 and 6 March 1942.*
18. *The title had been conferred on him some years before and he hated it—possibly he had told too many stories with Deans as their butt, e.g. 'Why was Cardinal Moran like Brian Boru? Because he banished the Danes', referring to the fact that Dr Polding had frequently conferred the honour of Dean and Dr Moran did not confirm these titles (see The Men of '38, p. 80). In the course of this sermon at Yass Father Hartigan said: 'Father O'Keefe was not "Dean" then [1877]—that came about twelve years later and I was present when he explained to us with illustrations the true signification of that exalted title!'*

'Dean' as a poor substitute for 'Father'—a title he revered, as these lines from 'The Pastor of St Mel's' reveal:

They call me Father here around, and I have found it good;
The rich, the poor, the down and out all share that fatherhood;
A father to the thoughtless lad whose friends have been his foes,
The comely lass who cannot see beyond her powdered nose,
And in the dim-lit silent church each weekend over there
I'm Father to the erring ones who need a father's care.
And men of every creed and none they greet me with a will,
Except the perky bank-clerk who calls me Mister. Still,
I'm Father to the ninety-nine and I would have you know
I wouldn't swop that title, faith, for aught they could bestow.[19]

This Yass sermon, too, was a Herculean work, occupying four pages of **Our Cathedral Chimes**.[20] The first part covers much the same general history of Yass as does the **Manly** article presented above.[21] The latter part tells of the coming of the Sisters to Yass and much of this has already been given when dealing with Father Hartigan's youth in Yass.[22]

It was during these years that the American edition of **Around the Boree Log** was launched. In 1941 Father Hugh Donnelly of St Columban's, Essendon, communicated with Father Hartigan and sought the American copyright for the poems which were to be published first as single titles in the American edition of the Columban Fathers' monthly production, **The Far East,** and afterwards in book form. Father Hartigan co-operated gladly and arrangements were made with Angus & Robertson.

The April 1942 issue of **The Far East** (American edition) contained a biographical note about Father Hartigan, extracted from him with difficulty by Father Hugh Donnelly. Poems appeared in succeeding issues and in December came the first American edition, illustrated with line drawings. It was of 6000 copies and a second printing was necessary within twelve months. By 1950 it had reached the fifth printing bringing the total copies to 22 000. A great number of Americans wrote to 'John O'Brien' telling him how much they enjoyed his verses.

For many of them, it was a case of renewing earlier fleeting joys. Monsignor Fulton Sheen in his tremendously popular radio broadcasts had often quoted from 'John O'Brien', and those who were touched by the

---

19. *From* The Parish of St Mel's, *Angus & Robertson, Sydney, 1954, p. 116. This poem was republished in the illustrated edition of* Around the Boree Log, *Angus & Robertson, Sydney, 1978, p. 76.*
20. *Our Cathedral Chimes, 6 September 1942, pp. 1-4.*
21. *See pp. 218-231 above.*
22. *See Chapter 1, pp. 10sqq, 14-16 and 21sq.*

verses were anxious to get the book. Naturally enough many of these were Irish or of Irish descent and the story of the pioneer days in Australia stirred fond memories of their own past.

In 1942 **Manly** had a feature, 'Personalities', and Father Hartigan was numbered amongst them.[23] The pen-pictures are unsigned, but that depicting Father Hartigan may well have been by the highly esteemed Monsignor Gerry Bartlett, who was editing the **Manly** during the war years while the editor, Father Treacy Boland, was chaplain with the Australian Imperial Force.

No one of Manly's sons has been more acclaimed than Father Pat Hartigan. Few of them have deserved it more. Known far and wide as 'John O'Brien', poet-priest and whimsical troubadour of the Catholic pioneers, he has sung his way into the hearts of his countrymen, and the echo of his song has been caught and held in lands far from his own. Tall, clear-cut and humorous, and rated one of the best after-dinner speakers in the land, he is the direct antithesis of the popular conception of a poet. And yet there is some indefinable quality about his simple verse, some subtle suggestion of sunshine and shadow which gives it its peculiar charm and which may or may not be indicative of the man himself. Ordained in 1903, he has served with distinction in the Southern districts of New South Wales, pausing all too seldom to put pen to paper and give vent to his undoubted genius. That the years have not taken his enthusiasm and that yet once again he will strike the lyric full and free is the fervent wish of all Manlians wherever they may be.

Those first years of World War II touched Father Hartigan in various ways. An Air Force Station was established at Narrandera and he had many personal contacts with officers and men. It was proposed to make him chaplain to the Air Force base and a medical examination and a scrutiny were required. In a whimsical mood, Father Hartigan asked the serious presiding officer: 'Do I have to wear one of those Boy Scouts' uniforms?' He was 'scrubbed' on the spot, medically unfit to drive the four miles from his presbytery to the base. This at least was his story and, as can be imagined, it lost nothing in the telling.

At a deeper level, Father Hartigan was sorely distressed at the turn the war was taking. The loss of the battleship **Prince of Wales** and the battle-cruiser **Repulse,** followed by the fall of Singapore, spelt for him deepest

23. Manly, *pp. 37-9, at p. 38.*

disaster. He spoke with admiration of Britain's ships, but he did so as an Australian—which he was first and foremost. He thought of England chiefly as the ruler of the seas and the custodian of our safety. Though the bard of the Irish-Australians, he was never an Irishman in his politics. England as the long-term despoiler of Ireland was far in the background of his mind.

He welcomed the Americans who came to Australia's aid. In the Coral Sea battle they turned back the Japanese who were so close to our shores that the newly arrived American planes, from bases in North Queensland, could take part in the fray, and repulse the invaders.

His parish had its share of the missing, the wounded and the dead. At times he had to break the news to the families—and thus involved in their grief was quick to help the bereaved. As he put it so beautifully in an Anzac Day sermon:

Our pity is for those whom these leaf-brown heroes have left behind, the sister who has no brother now, the aged father left alone like a solitary stalk, the grey-haired mother who dreams and dreams and dreams of other days and other hopes. May God pity and comfort them.[24]

During these years of the war he had passed the milestone of his silver jubilee in the parish and the parishioners organised a function in July 1943. He was presented with a wallet containing £500 and there were speeches by Father T. Shanley (Leeton), Father N. Duck (Narrandera) and prominent parishioners expressing their esteem for Father Hartigan and gratitude for the work he had done amongst them.

Father Hartigan's response provides us with a bird's-eye view of what he had done to provide for the spiritual and temporal needs of the parish over the twenty-six years he had been their pastor. He had said Mass at the altar of St Mel's Church 8500 times, married 320 couples, baptised 1380 children and on 485 occasions led the slow procession to the last resting-place beyond the hill. On a similar number of occasions he had been called to the dying bed and never once had he failed to go. He admitted to failure or scant success at social functions but when the shadows of the wings of death were showing on the cottage roof he was always there. He felt that:

Those dear ones of ours whose salvation with God's grace has been

---

24. *Extract from his book of written sermons.*

achieved will be united in prayer for us. These are the things that bind us together.

Father Hartigan traced the story of the material progress of the parish, as we have followed it in earlier chapters. In the twenty-six years of his pastorate, £212 000 had been raised and he praised the goodness and the generosity of the people of the Narrandera parish, giving special mention to those of Grong Grong.

He felt he could not let pass the opportunity of paying tribute to the work of the Sisters of St Joseph and the co-operation he had received from them during his term of office—they had borne the burden of the parish.

The earlier speakers had expressed the wish that God would bless and preserve him so that he would be able to continue his holy office for many years. He however told them he had lately felt that he was getting stale; he had reached the stage where if priests retire he would have reached the retiring age.

The hill is getting steep and I've been forty years on the track and the swag as I grow older gets heavier. I would not like to stay here if I should be a burden; therefore this gift of yours is going to be very, very handy to me. I'm going to put it away for a rainy day, and may God bless and keep you all.[25]

In that same year, on 7 September, Father Hartigan gave a talk in Sydney to the Catholic Historical Society; it was entitled: 'Round Bowning Hill' and treated of early Catholic history in the Riverina. There was a large attendance and he was enthusiastically received.

One of the last tasks Father Hartigan undertook from Narrandera was to be guest of honour and deliver the address at the seventieth anniversary of his old school, St Patrick's College, Goulburn.

On the evening of Thursday 28 October 1943 the official party in the Assembly Hall contained Bishop Terence McGuire; Very Rev Father Blakeney, Adm; Hon. J.M. Tully, M.L.A.; the Mayor, Ald E.J. Darcy. There were musical items, a report by Brother Lynch and then Father Hartigan, as guest of honour, distributed the prizes. His talk was printed in full in **Calamus Scribae,** the term magazine of St Patrick's College:

It is nearly fifty years—half a century—since I passed through the gates of old St Pat's, and though I left no record behind me, except

25. Our Cathedral Chimes, *Goulburn,* 1 August 1943, p. 4.

246

perhaps a name carved upon a desk in terrible letters, it was a kindly act on the part of its President to invite me here to give the address this evening. After the family circle itself there is no place which has had more influence in a man's life, and no place which arouses more tender memories than the old school he attended when life was fresh and young and impressionable; and I do confess as I sat here listening to the programme and the school report, noting that some things have changed and some things are unchangeable, a hundred recollections came around me, some of which have been with me through the years, and some of which came to life again warmed by the emotions of an occasion like this.

Prominent among the emotions engendered tonight is a feeling of thankfulness which an ex-student must have at the success which has come to his old Alma Mater. The Latin phrase means kindly Mother—that is a beautiful term in which we refer to the school of our formative years. I knew her in the hard days—her days of struggle—when she gave a mother's care under the greatest difficulties, but never did she excite my pride more than now when she has achieved success greater than anything her founders ever dreamt of.

Her success is the more gratifying when we recall that her foundation was a valiant attempt to keep all forms of education, the higher as well as the primary, under the influence of religion. In no other activity has the Catholic Church been more careful than in this. For this she has elected to be misunderstood, to suffer; and nowhere in her mighty realm has her ideal been more stoutly upheld than in our own country. When settlement began to spread throughout this land of ours she took her stand from the beginning. Wherever a few settlers built their shelters of slab and sheeted bark, the early priests saw to it that the children were taught, and they were careful that even such education as those primitive times afforded should walk hand in hand with a knowledge of God and the observance of His Commandments.

When Father Brennan took charge of that immense area, which included Goulburn, just one hundred years ago, he found no school outside the town itself. In twelve months he had schools established in every place where a few families had gathered. To do this he contributed £20 out of his meagre government salary of £150 a year and induced the more wealthy of his flock to do the same.

Rough and ready were those old bush schools, and rough and ready were the teachers. Untrained in many cases, and short tempered in nearly every case, they drove their meagre lessons in by the order of

the stick, and sometimes even by the order of the boot; their
approach to the work depended often on the state of their liver, and
the 'hangover' from the bibulous entertainment of the night before.
'Full well the boding tremblers learnt to trace the day's disasters in
the morning face.' Frequently what they taught in thundering tones
was all they knew themselves. But this at least must be recorded to
their credit; those rough bush schools kept the candle burning until
the dawn broke fair with the Nuns and Brothers doing so easily and
so efficiently the good work which was carried on in spite of the
greatest obstacles by the old denominational teachers.

In the little college cemetery behind the hill there is a grave which
holds the mouldering remains of one of the last of them, old
Anthony McGaurin, who taught the school in Goulburn in 1872,
and in other places round the district before that year, and who
ended his days here with the good Christian Brothers caring for him
to the end.

In that God's acre, too, may be traced the various steps by which
we have come to the fine system with which we are blessed today.
Not far from the resting place of the old denominational school
teacher is the grave of the first priest ordained in Goulburn—Father
Coffey—who had studied in France, and had come hoping that our
better climate might restore his health. He was a brilliant young
man, and it was hoped that he would take his place on the staff of
the College, but it was not to be; he was called to his account while
the College was building. Near him is Father Patrick Lanigan, a
nephew of the founder of St Patrick's. There, too, is Father Denis
Walsh, who built the school at North Goulburn at a time when
Henry Parkes' Education Act of 1880, while sounding the death
knell of the denominational system, was ushering in the brighter day
of the convent schools. There also rest two lads, James Comans and
Thomas Treacy, students in the days when the light of St Patrick's
College was showing through the mist—a rush light, if you will, but
the herald of brighter things to come. There, too, rest the treasured
remains of three Christian Brothers—the torch-bearers for whom we
waited—the saintly young Brother McQuillen, Brother Dowd, from
whom such great things were expected, Brother Fitzgerald whose
name is amongst the most illustrious and the most cherished in the
whole history of St Patrick's.

But let me not anticipate. Long before the doom of the
denominational system was sealed by the Education Act of 1880,
those early priests—men of vision—both because they saw on the
horizon a cloud then no bigger than a man's hand, and because they

were anxious to secure the best teachers for their schools, whether those schools were destined to be private or State-supported, made efforts to get the teaching orders from Ireland to take up the work in Australia.

It was not easy to get them, for those teaching orders were then in their infancy. Our days of struggle were days of struggle to them as well. Many attempts were made to get the Christian Brothers. However, in 1859—that is, 84 years ago when the whole of N.S.W. was in the diocese of Sydney—that energetic worker in the Catholic Cause, Archdeacon McEncroe, at the instigation of Dean Richard Walsh (who must not be confounded with Father Denis Walsh, who built the North Goulburn School 20 odd years later), selected in Westport, Ireland, a band of teaching Sisters for Goulburn.

They were the first Sisters of Mercy to come to New South Wales, and the convent, which was being built by Dean Walsh to receive them, was the very first building designed and erected as a convent in the whole of Australia. Dean Walsh was not able to finish what he began because of want of funds. Furthermore, he was a sick man, and in 1861 he returned to Ireland, where he lived in an unpretentious little cottage at Ballybricken in his native Waterford, and died in 1869. While the walls of Our Lady of Mercy's Convent were standing unroofed there was at Yass a priest whose name in our history stands out as a church builder without a peer—the great Dr McAlroy, who has been called the Apostle of the South . . .[26] Dr Polding brought him here to Goulburn, and in less than a year the Sisters were in their convent.

Not only did he finish the convent at Goulburn, he established the Sisters of Mercy at Albury, he selected the nuns for Yass; he got the Presentation Nuns for Wagga, and induced his old friend Dr Bermingham to resign his vice-rectorship of Carlow College and accompany them to the Riverina so that not only every church, but every convent and school through the area I have indicated (excepting those under the care of the Sisters of St Joseph) is associated with the deathless name of Michael McAlroy; and this is the man who first conceived the idea of St Patrick's College, Goulburn.

In 1860—15 years before the nuns arrived in Yass—he had established there a boarding school for girls, and this he transferred to Goulburn in 1864, and so made the beginning of Our Lady of

26. Father Hartigan then went on to describe Father McAlroy's church building, a story given in his jubilee sermon at Wagga, pp. 232-242.

Mercy's College, which is known far and wide today. Having made provision for the higher education of girls, he set about making a like effort for the boys, and for that purpose bought from D. Thorn a portion of land known as South Hill in 1866. The following year a bishop was appointed to Goulburn, and it was not Dr McAlroy, although popular acclaim had him already securely seated on the new episcopal throne. In 1868 he went to Albury and served as a faithful Vicar General and loyal support of his superior till his death 12 years later. On 12 October, a year after he left Goulburn, the land was sold, but sixty years subsequently after it had passed through many hands, it was purchased by Bishop John Barry and others—the 'others' being the Sisters of Mercy, Goulburn—and it is now known as Marian Hill.

The actual founder of St Patrick's College was Dr Lanigan, of whom it must be said that he was one of the most active and most fearless advocates of Catholic education, and especially primary education, in our history; and bear in mind that he did his good work at a time when so much depended on laying the foundations deep and strong. He also saw the necessity for an institution where the higher studies would be pursued and thus he began this College.

A government grant was secured (two separate grants, I think—one for a Bishop's residence, and that was why the 'Villa' was built) and in February 1873 the foundation stone was laid by Archbishop Polding. Twelve months later, 1 February 1874, the building was blessed by the same pioneer prelate, who, on that occasion, paid his last visit to this part of N.S.W., which for thirty-six years he had tended with zealous pastoral care. I take it that it is one of the most cherished memories of the sons of St Patrick that their Alma Mater was blessed by that saintly old white-haired Archbishop, the first in Australia—for nothing but success could follow the benediction of such a one. He has been called the greatest missioner of modern times, but I would say that if the magnitude of his work—that of organising the Church throughout a whole continent—is taken into account, if the extent of his journeys and the hardships he endured be considered; if, in short, the classic example—perils by land, perils by sea; aye, and perils from false brethren, too, be the standard still, then the venerable name of Polding would not look out of place in a list of the greatest missionaries of all time.

At his side at the ceremony, and on his first visit here, was another Archbishop—the Most Reverend and Most Illustrious Roger Bede Vaughan, so soon to raise aloft the banner of Christian Education, and beside him stood three bishops, Drs William Lanigan

Bishop William Lanigan, the founder of St Patrick's College, Goulburn, Father Hartigan's old school. (Photo courtesy of Father Bill Kennedy)

(Goulburn), Matthew Quinn (Bathurst) and James Murray
(Maitland), whose names are indelibly written beside his own on
that flag which, though unfurled for seventy years, has never once
been trampled in the dust. There, too, was another great
educationist, Father William Kelly, one of the first Jesuits to come
to Australia, and perhaps the most eloquent of them all. He was the
preacher of the sermon. The priests of the diocese were there, too.
The College was opened on the closing day of the first retreat held at
St Patrick's. The priests numbered sixteen. Seven years before when
the diocese was formed, they were but six. There was one
absentee—Dr McAlroy, who was away in Ireland on that fruitful
tour in the cause of education which secured the Presentation Nuns
for Wagga and the Sisters of Mercy for Yass.

Thus was St Patrick's sent upon its way. It was a daring
undertaking at the time and in the circumstances. There were then
only three established boarding schools for boys in the whole of
Australia—St John's and Lyndhurst in Sydney, and St Stanislaus' at
Bathurst. (Perhaps I should mention a fourth at Sevenhill, South
Australia, where the Jesuits had a few students for a time.) Of these,
Lyndhurst has gone. St John's is in a different category, leaving as
the two oldest boarding schools for boys in the country St
Stanislaus' and St Patrick's. They are older than Riverview, older
than Hunter's Hill. This is, I think, an eloquent testimony to the
keenness which animated the pioneer bishop and priests of inland
Australia over seventy years ago.

The first President of this College was Father Patrick Dunne,
whose memory is revered—or rather I should say ought to be revered
—throughout three States—Victoria, Queensland and N.S.W. He was
ordained in 1846, and at the invitation of Dr Geoghegan—who was
later on appointed the first bishop of this diocese, but at the time
was Vicar General of Port Phillip—he came to Melbourne when
there were only four priests in the whole of Victoria. He made the
fifth. He was the first priest to say Mass on the Ballarat Goldfields—
the first priest to erect a church there, but it was only a tent.

Returning to Ireland in 1857, he was appointed President of St
Bridgid's Classical and Commercial Seminary at Tullamore. In 1860
and 1861 because of the American Civil War, the Irish farmers
evicted by Landlordism found themselves in dire straits. America
was closed to them, and they had nowhere to go. Father Dunne
brought before them the claims of Australia, and especially of
Queensland. He made arrangements with the agent of Queensland,
and went on a lecturing tour through Westmeath and King's County.

He met with plenty of opposition, even the clergy looking upon the whole thing as a hare-brained scheme of a hare-brained man who had faith in the future of Australia. Father Dunne persisted, and whenever he managed to get into a pulpit, taking his stand with the Epistles and Gospels in one hand the the Queensland Land Act in the other, he preached the goodness of God and the advantages of Queensland till he had enough volunteers to make a shipload.

With the help of the Queensland Government, and throwing into the venture every penny he could lay his hands on, he chartered a ship, called her Erin-go-Bragh—'*Ireland for ever'—and with between four and five hundred souls aboard, started for Australia. The* Erin-go-Bragh *was perhaps the worst ship on the seven seas. She rolled along, she plugged along, and made such poor time that her passengers called her the* Erin-go-Slow. *She sprang a leak near the Cape, and there was a hullabaloo on board when it was discovered that evil-minded persons at Liverpool had bored a hole in her timbers and uncovered the copper plates, and boasted that the old tub would never reach her destination. But that hullabaloo was nothing to the hullabaloo of futility which shook the ship when it was discovered just in time that some miscreant had put a junk of salt meat in the pea soup on a Friday; but in spite of these alarming experiences, the old* Erin-go-Bragh, *battered and torn, with the sea salt white and sparkling crusted on her waterways, made the Queensland Coast after a voyage of six months.*

There are several successful farmers living in the Riverina today whose parents came to Australia with Father Dunne in the Erin-go-Bragh. *The eldest member of one family—still alive and well at Young—was born on her, and of thirty children who first saw the light of day on the old ship, he was the only one to live and reach Australia.*

Father Dunne returned immediately to Ireland for another consignment of immigrants. Having had enough of the Erin-go-Bragh, *he chartered another boat, the* Fiery Cross,[27] *and she was not much better. He landed one shipload of immigrants, but on the way back for another, in order to pay expenses, he carried passengers returning to England. Somewhere in mid-ocean the* Fiery Cross, *true to its name, went ablaze from stem to stern. The passengers and the crew took to the life boats, but Father Dunne, the cook, and a couple of stalwart sailors, stuck to the ship. They were rescued by a*

27. It was the Fiery Star, *as Fr Denis Martin of Brisbane pointed out when this story appeared in* The Men of '38, p. 146.

passing barque the next day, while of those who went off in the boats not one was ever heard of.

Bishop Quinn, of Brisbane, continued the scheme inaugurated by Father Dunne, and altogether some 600 were brought out, most of whom settled on the Darling Downs, and if that rich area has been of the greatest service to Australia and the Catholic Church, our thanks are due to the first president to take charge of St Pat's. It was one of the best immigration schemes ever launched in this country. The right type of colonist was selected, and there was a place to put them when they arrived. It would have developed into a very big thing, but bigotry showed its head, sectarianmongers asserting that if Bishop Quinn's project was allowed to go on, the name of Queensland would have to be changed to 'Quinnsland'. Yielding to the uproar, the government withdrew its support and further activities were abandoned.

Father Dunne himself settled in the Northern State, then of course, a colony. While at Sandgate he had a plan ready to bring out the Redemptorists to Australia, and it seems that he intended to join that Order on its establishment here; but the disturbed state of the finances in the Diocese of Brisbane made the thing impossible. A year or so after Dr Lanigan was made Bishop of Goulburn, he came here and acted as Administrator of the Cathedral; then when St Pat's College was opened he was made the first president. He was a man of scholarship, but his strong points were his business ability, and his capacity as an organiser.

Having put the College on a sound basis both as to finances and general arrangements, he went to form the parish of Gundagai, which, at the time, embraced all the country to Cootamundra and beyond it. He succeeded Dr Bermingham in Wagga, and while there planned and built the nave of what is now St Michael's Cathedral. Wagga was then a township of not much more than a thousand people.

He went as P.P. to Albury in 1887, and when he felt that the shades were closing in he built the little cottage near the Newtown Orphanage, and there he waited for the summons, and I have no doubt that the greeting he met with from the Master whom he had served so faithfully for four and fifty years was: 'Well done, thou good and faithful servant'. He was a man of superlative courage and feared no foe, whether he came in shining armour against the principles of his Church, or in private capacity as an assailant against himself. On one occasion when he was nearing the three score and ten a burglar attempted to get through the window of his little presbytery at Newtown, but the old man sprang to it and what he did to that burglar was a tradition in the neighbourhood for many years.

He was just the man to preside over the College in the rough times of its initiation. Many of the boys who came at the beginning were really young men of settled habits. Some of them had whiskers; some of them smoked, all of them had arrived at the age of reason, though at times they didn't use that reason.

With Father Dunne as the first staff was a priest who was called at the time 'Little Father Gallagher'. He taught the classics. There was O'Ryan, a University man, and afterwards a barrister. Then there was Edmund Butler, who as Father Butler, was a well known name at St John's in the days of Archbishop Vaughan. Edmund Butler was a brother of the more famous Thomas Butler, Professor of Latin at the Sydney University, the favourite pupil of the celebrated Dr Badham, who was one of the world's greatest authorities on the classics. Tom Butler was Badham's biographer, and he is the source for the oft-quoted statement of Badham that little Father Gallagher, of Goulburn, was the finest classical scholar in Australia.

However, there is no doubt about the humble little priest's attainments in that field, and no doubt about his ability to coach his pupils. In the very first year of the College's existence he sent up six students for the examination conducted by the University, five of whom matriculated, one gaining the proxime accessit to the medal in Latin. Not one of those boys had opened a Latin or French grammar before they went to St Patrick's. It was the first occasion that a scholar from any Catholic school in the whole of Australia had sat for a public examination.

The following year, 1875, Father Gallagher was made President, which office he held for the next twelve years, and all the success which came to St Pat's—and it was considerable—is due to him. He stands out as one of the greatest headmasters of any school in the whole of our Australian history. It is not possible to put one's finger on the particular quality which made him so. He was a fine scholar, but then there have been others just as keen. There was in him just some spark of genius in this regard which is not given to many men. No boy ever questioned his ruling or even regarded as undeserved his strictures or the punishments he often dealt out. No one ever showed him disrespect even in his absence. Every one trusted him instinctively, and felt he couldn't be wrong even if he tried.

And years afterwards, when life had opened out to them other cares, other interests, other viewpoints, I have seen them gather

Bishop John Gallagher, regarded in his day as the finest pulpit orator in Australia, but remembered best as a brilliant headmaster of St Patrick's College. (Photo courtesy of Father Bill Kennedy)

round him—lawyers, doctors, legislators, businessmen, priests—with
the same love, the same veneration, the same child-like trust which
they showed in the old days of his presidency. Right to the end he
was their Old Master, and right to the end they were his boys. He
was afterwards a great bishop, and was regarded as the finest pulpit
orator in Australia, but it is as a headmaster he is remembered best.
As the Chief of Old St Pat's, he takes his place among the
immortals. So no matter what triumphs are yet in store for this
school, no matter what greatness as the years go by may be
connected with her—and there shall assuredly come to her more
brilliant sons and finer achievements than any that have gone
before—still no matter what great names may be emblazoned on her
honour roll, his shall ever sparkle there with a lustre of its own.

In 1887, through failing health, he relinquished his duties here
and went to Wagga, the first Irremovable Rector appointed in the
Southern World, and after his departure troubles thick as autumn
leaves descended on St Pat's. Through want of business
management, lack of interest and dissensions among the staff, the
next seven years saw it dying bit by bit, and in 1894, to spare those
who loved it the misery of watching its death agony, it was resolved
to close it down. But like the milk-white hind, though doomed to
death, it was destined not to die. When the question of winding it
up was being discussed the Old President left his parish of Wagga
and came back full of resolve to save the school, which was the core
of his heart. He would, no doubt, have brought back the glories of
the palmy days, but four months later they made him a bishop, and
with the many cares of a diocese falling mostly on his shoulders, he
could no longer give the College his undivided attention.

It was then that a decision was made which was the weightiest
and the most far-reaching in the history of the institution. It was
decided to bring a Teaching Order, and Old St Pat's came under the
control of the Christian Brothers. It had really come to a hopeless
state. Only the shades of a brilliant and useful past hovering round it
even in its decay redeemed it from the dishonour and the
degradation of an undertaking that had failed.

I remember the first day that Brother Treacy, the Superior of the
Christian Brothers, came to take over. He was a man of exceptional
business ability. He had a firm chin and a solemn expression, but
the chin seemed to grow firmer and the face more solemn as bit by
bit he discovered what he had. He reminded me of a man who had
bought a horse at a sale, but on getting him home found he was
blind in both eyes and lame in every leg. I can remember him as he
walked round with his hands behind his back and examined what

had come to him—the shabby ink-stained walls, the ceilings clustered with darts made out of pens and paper, the desks covered with names that didn't matter then and have not been heard of since, the windows broken where stones had come through—some of them by accident, some by well directed shots and malice aforethought—the spouts plugged up with discarded hats, and the couple of dozen nonedescript human beings inaccurately described in the catalogue as 'students', mooning around, doing time 'with the fruitless years behind them and the hopeless years before them'.

Yes, I can see that brave old Brother, with his knowledge of methods and ideals, viewing the wreck and shaking his head reflecting, 'These be thy gods, Oh Israel'. I remember, too, how, during the closing months of 1897, he and that fine old Brother, Vincent Hurley, laboured and slaved to get the wreck ready to take the sea again, putting up more accommodation, re-establishing the old, doing most of the work with their own hands getting the place ready for a new lease of life and a new era.

Tonight I look back on the part of that new era which has gone and marvel at what has been achieved. The old order was tried, and in spite of many splendid things to its credit, it failed, the new order with other methods and more capable men has raised St Patrick's from the ashes and has placed it again in the forefront of the educational establishments of the country. The second temple which they have built is far greater than the first, and the true history of St Patrick's is the history of its career under the Christian Brothers. It was under the old regime for about twenty-three years; it has been under their control for forty-seven. We love to dwell on the first period because it is picturesque as all the struggles for the Faith in the early times are picturesque, but the great work of St Patrick's College has been done since then in the daily routine of heavy toil in the class rooms and her achievements there are written in her annals for all the world to see.

But there are other achievements and greater achievements, too, which have not been recorded by any human hand. For it is not by examination results alone—no matter how successful they have been in this—that the Christian Brothers are making good the objects for which St Pat's was founded. There are other achievements which, though not recounted by any human hand, must always be in the aim of a college such as this. That aim is, while giving those so circumstanced all the advantages of the higher education, to safeguard their Faith as well; to so form the outlook of those who, because of the position that will come to them, will be leaders in social activities, that they will not scorn to be leaders in Church

258

movements also; to so ground them in the knowledge of their
religion that they will at all times be able and ready to give reasons
for the Faith that is in them, to stand up to the hostile, toe to toe to
meet the critic argument for argument.

There are times when a Catholic who becomes a professional man,
or for that matter a prominent man in any sphere, has to bear with
the scoffs of his fellows because he follows the simple practices of
his Church, and sometimes he may be tempted to forsake them just
to curry favour with the irreligious or gain the goodwill of the
sceptic. But it is not worth it. 'The Atheist's laugh is a poor return
for Deity offended.'

In the daily atmosphere of a school where God is always first, in
the constant contact with the brilliant teachers who might have
carved for themselves a road to any preferment had they a mind to
do so, and most of all by the example of these same men who had
sacrificed everything just to create in others a true perspective of the
things that matter, there is built up—there must be—that grit and
that fearlessness which make a man true to his principles, which
make him stick to his colours no matter what the cost. This is why
St Patrick's was founded, this is why it functions still.

Don't remind me that she has had her failures. She has had her
success, too, and I, from out the olden time, pay an earnest and
sincere tribute to the Christian Brothers who, for no earthly reward,
have worked on that ideal for nearly half a century. I pay my tribute,
too, to a long line of Presidents—gallant and sturdy captains who
have handled the old ship in many troubled waters and have brought
her safely through, always steering by a star; and in that long line,
Brother Director, your name though the last, is by no means the
least.

And to you, My Lord, may I say one word. Our acquaintance is of
longer standing than any other here tonight. We knew each other
before either of us knew St Pat's, and in those old days, even though
we knew that you were destined for greater things than the rest of
us, it never occurred to me that you would be graciously standing
aside in your own Diocese, as you are doing tonight, that I might
have this honour on the seventieth anniversary of my old school. No
one is more pleased with the success that has come to St Patrick's
than is Your Lordship. No one gives her a more kindly blessing for
the future. May the future be worthy of the past. May she ever serve
our God and our country.[28]

28. Calamus Scribae 6, 3, 1943, pp. 2-7.

12 Decision to Leave Narrandera

The Catholic Church in Australia had its beginnings with the three convict priests, Fathers James Harold, James Dixon and Harold O'Neill—transported after the Irish rebellion of 1798—whose work was confined to a very few years. Then came Father Jeremiah O'Flynn, unauthorised by the Government and not allowed to stay, and after him Fathers John Joseph Therry and Philip Conolly and their few associates. The first organised Church here was Benedictine; Dr William Ullathorne O.S.B. was Vicar-General for Bishop William Placid Morris O.S.B. of Mauritius and then Dr John Bede Polding O.S.B. was consecrated as the first bishop with the designation of Vicar Apostolic of New Holland and Van Diemen's Land. However, the work of the Benedictines was largely confined to Sydney. Dr Ullathorne and Dr Polding tried in vain to get further recruits from their English Benedictine confrères. They then turned to the Irish Church and a band of young priests and students came out from 1838 onwards. They went as missionaries wherever there were Catholics and it was largely due to them that the faith flourished in the outback.

The story of these priests of the bush had not been written and Father Hartigan set out to gather the details. He began a series of articles in the **Australasian Catholic Record** in the issue of January 1943. The instigator of his undertaking this project was Monsignor Edward O'Donnell, rector of St Columba's College Springwood. He had written Father Hartigan a letter[1] of congratulations on his sermons at Wagga and Yass. He urged strongly that they should be put in some permanent form, perhaps as Australian Catholic Truth Society pamphlets. Father Hartigan wrote back saying he was contemplating a larger work. A second letter[2] from Monsignor O'Donnell suggested the proposed work, In Diebus Illis, should be published by instalments in the **Australasian Catholic Record,** a theological quarterly of which he was editor. Father Hartigan readily agreed and the series was a great success with the demand for the journal outstripping the supply.

1. *8 September 1942, among Father Hartigan's papers.*
2. *19 September 1942, among Father Hartigan's papers.*

Most of the priests of the outback were Irish, but among them (and a special hero of Father Hartigan) was the Englishman Charles Lovat. Of this esteemed priest he wrote: 'They spoke of him as the gentle Father Lovat, the scholarly Father Lovat, the saintly Father Lovat'.[3]

'In Diebus Illis' was fascinating writing, with so often the grave and gay closely intertwined as in this story of Father James Hanly (Brisbane) and John Rigney (Singleton):

For nearly ten years [they] used to meet once a month under a certain tree which was reckoned to be half way between Singleton and Brisbane. It meant a journey of nearly two hundred miles [320 km] to each of them, and only once did they miss out. The defaulter was Hanly, the better bushman of the two; he got lost and was not heard of by the other for some weeks. He used to tell the story when in a reminiscent mood towards the evening of his life. After wandering about for two days without food he came upon a shepherd's hut apparently deserted. Searching the premises for the staff of life he found a stale damper and the lad that shouted 'eureka' had nothing on him. But here was the point to be decided; was the damper wholesome or was it made of poisoned flour and left as a bait for the aborigines as was so often done at the time! It would have been easier to decide what to do if he had had his interview with Rigney. But here it was, and as he used to tell with a twinkle in his humorous eye, he made the best act of contrition he was capable of, and took the chance.[4]

The work involved in writing these articles was constant and heavy. Father Hartigan, keenly alive to the sound of words, would type many versions before he was satisfied he had the expression he wanted. As he became absorbed in this work and experienced the need to be near such sources as the Mitchell Library, he began to think more and more of retiring to a chaplaincy in Sydney.

At the same time he felt his parish load getting harder to bear, as he had intimated publicly at the gathering in the previous July to honour his silver jubilee in the parish.[5] He reasoned that there was no parish in the diocese of Wagga to which he could go and carry out his duties satisfactorily. All of them, with the exception of Tumbarumba, were on the flat plain of the Riverina, scorching hot in the summer, cold in winter

3. Australasian Catholic Record XX, 3, 1943, p. 170. The articles were brought out in book form: The Men of '38, Lowden Publishing Co., Kilmore, Vic., 1975; this quotation is from p. 35.
4. Australasian Catholic Record XXI, 3, 1944, p. 140 (The Men of '38, p. 105).
5. See Chapter 11, p. 245sq.

and liable to rains which could bog a car for days on end. He reviewed every parish—they all had their Sunday travelling for Mass at an outback church, and he could not see himself able much longer to wrestle with a wheel which needed changing or dig himself out of the mud.

He contemplated at first getting extended leave from his parish to see if he would be able to settle in the city. The bishop, however, favoured his resignation so that the parish could receive a new pastor immediately, thus catering better for the needs of the people.

Archbishop Gilroy was approached and replied promptly:

> *St Mary's Cathedral,*
> *Sydney,*
> *8 January 1944*

> *Very Rev. P.J. Hartigan, P.P.,*
> *c/o Lewisham Hospital,*
> *WAGGA WAGGA.*

> *Dear Father Hartigan:*
> *I have received your letter of the 7th instant and sympathise with you for being stricken down. 'Flu, etc., do not seem to be much, but they can be terribly devastating.*
> *The proposition that I have to offer you is the Chaplaincy at the Convent of the Sacred Heart, Rose Bay. The Chaplain's quarters are in a cottage apart from the main building and overlooking the Harbour. There is no more charming spot in Sydney. It is what the Italians call* incantevole. *The duties consist of morning Mass for the Community and boarders, the Confessions of the boarders, a weekly instruction to the boarders, and a periodical conference to the Novices. Benedictions are no more than, I think, twice a week—Sunday and one other day. The usual Chaplain's stipend in the Archdiocese is £100 per annum.*
> *The sooner you would be prepared to begin the more would the Mother Superior and the Parish Priest of Rose Bay be pleased. The Mother Superior has expressed her delight at the proposition of your being their Chaplain and anxiously awaits confirmation of the proposal.*
> *Trusting that this will help you to make a complete recovery,*
> *I remain,*
> *Yours sincerely in Our Lord,*
> ✝ *N.T. Gilroy*
> *ARCHBISHOP OF SYDNEY*[6]

---

6. *Letter among Father Hartigan's papers.*

Father Hartigan replied accepting the offer. He was instructed to let Mother Superior know the date of his arrival. He received a warm letter of welcome from Mother McGuinness, Vicaress (i.e. Provincial) of the Religious of the Sacred Heart:

> *Convent of the Sacred Heart,*
> *Rose Bay,*
> *Sydney,*
> *23rd Jan 1944.*
>
> *Dear Father Hartigan,*
> *Since the Archbishop suggested the possibility of your being our Chaplain we have been thanking God for our good fortune. Only the fear that you may not wish to accept restrained me from writing. Now your letter has just come removing all doubts and fears. We are deeply grateful to you, dear Father, and we look forward to welcoming you on or about the 1st February. Whatever arrangements you make will be satisfactory for us.*
> *These last days at Narrandera will not be easy ones, there cannot but be much to sacrifice after twenty-seven years.*
> *Our thoughts and prayers will be with you.*
> *Again assuring you of our welcome and asking you to bless your flock at Rose Bay.*
>
> *I remain, dear Father,*
> *Yours gratefully and respectfully*
> *in Corde Jesu,*
> *D. McGuinness.*[7]

This was the beginning of a friendship between them based on deep mutual esteem. She was to say of him after his death: 'No matter who we had here at Rose Bay (and they had quite a few notables), Father Hartigan was always the most important person in the gathering'.

The move from Narrandera to Rose Bay meant a great deal of work. His curate, Father Norman Duck, and his housekeeper, Rosie Bourke, were helped by many friends. Books and pictures had to be packed; all that accumulates in a home during twenty-seven years had to be evaluated and decisions made as to what to keep; parochial records and procedures had to be set out clearly for the next man; then final good-byes, particularly to the old and the sick. His many friends were saddened by his impending departure but could see the good reasons behind his decision. The Sisters of St Joseph were particularly grieved and he too felt

---

7. *Letter among Father Hartigan's papers.*

the parting deeply. During his years at Narrandera he always found the school holidays a lonely time with the Sisters away.

There was no time to organise an official farewell before he left. It was decided that he should return to Narrandera for a function on Tuesday 28 March.

That night the Plaza Theatre was crowded for the farewell. It had been arranged by a committee appointed at a public meeting some weeks before, with the mayor as chairman and the town clerk as secretary. Fittingly enough, the treasurer was a bank manager. An excellent concert program was interspersed with the speeches.

The president of the Yanko Shire (Councillor E.J.V. Martin) commented on Father Hartigan's 'broad outlook on all matters which had made him many friends throughout the whole district . . . he trusted that in his new location he would have more time at his disposal to devote to his writings which were read throughout Australia'.

Mr J.J. Kennedy of Grong Grong related how many pairs of misty eyes there were on the Sunday at Grong Grong when Father Hartigan announced his intention of taking his departure. On a recent trip to New Zealand he found the name of 'John O'Brien' to be known throughout the dominion.

Councillor Tom Brennan of Urana Shire, representing the Morundah-Widgiewa part of the parish, had been at school with Father Hartigan at St Patrick's College, Goulburn, and fittingly he lauded the educational work done by Father Hartigan in the parish, well exemplified by the fine convent he had built and the high standards set in the school.

Emeritus Archdeacon Rawlings was the next speaker. He and Father Hartigan had been friends for years and the Archdeacon duly paid tribute to his colleague's great work in the town and district and spoke of the influence his poetry would continue to have in the years to come. Father Hartigan in his reply referred to the Archdeacon as 'the doyen of us all, one whom I admired greatly for his many qualities as a Christian gentleman and a broad-minded, cultured man.'

Mr R.H. Hankinson spoke on behalf of the citizens of the town, Mr Arthur Charles for the Presbyterian community, Mr J.J. Quirk as one of Father Hartigan's flock, while Mr O.O.H. Dangar said he represented 'the man in the street'.

The mayor presented a cheque for £415, at the same time recalling that their friendship began twenty years earlier when Father Hartigan invited him into the presbytery for a cool drink when he was working nearby on a hot day. He mentioned particularly Father Hartigan's work at the hospital where he had a word and a smile for people of every denomination. According to the **Daily Advertiser** (Wagga) 'thunderous applause' greeted Father Hartigan when he rose to respond in the following words:

I want to thank you from the bottom of my heart for coming here in such numbers and for your wonderful gift; and if while listening to those speeches so earnest and so flattering I sometimes felt uncomfortable and guilty, I felt very proud as well in the knowledge that all of the speakers had meant every word they had said—though I could not vouch for it all being true ... If the picture was overdrawn, then it was not the first time I have been embarrassed by the people of Narrandera.

When I was about to take my departure from the home which knew me so well, His Worship the Mayor waited on me to ask if I would accept a send-off, I replied that I didn't expect it. 'Why not?' he said 'You have been a good townsman'. I looked at Tommy Gordon and Tommy Gordon looked at me, and I examined his kindly eye to see if I could detect therein any glint of sarcasm, or any intention on his part to remind me of the man I might have been but wasn't. I knew in my heart that I hadn't been a good townsman. All my time had been given to my duties at St Mel's and I felt that civic movements could be safely left to men more experienced and more capable than I. But what I can claim—and this is perhaps what His Worship meant—that even if I was not an active worker for the material advancement of this good town, I was always an enthusiastic supporter—a barracker on the fence, so to speak—and like all such barrackers I was as one-eyed as any of them.

I am unrepentant for that sin of prejudice, and I feel certain, as I have always done, that it would be a good thing if we were all a bit more one-eyed about the old Spot. This is the only place I know where the citizens take a delight in belittling it. We tell everybody about the heat and the dust and the drought and you'd think no other inland town in Australia suffered from heat and dust and drought. We never seem to think that when there's a scorching hot day here, nobody in the towns round about us is wearing his overcoat. We magnify the heat and the dryness till we place the good old town on a pinnacle of bad repute something akin to the Hot Hereafter from whose bourne no traveller returns. One has to get away to other surroundings to get the picture right. Absence makes the heart grow fonder, and many a time since I've said Good-bye I have seen in memory a vista of tree-lined streets equal to anything in the Commonwealth. I have recalled the ample civic services, the

265

abundant water supply, its swimming pool which is unsurpassed in any country town.

Yes I've seen the bare paddocks and the sun-parched country. I've seen the heat waves shimmering on the plains, on the yellow grass, and the iron roofs. I've seen the drought, but I have also seen the mellow sunshine when the early autumn rains have come, the colours on the hills and in the gums and the barley grass billowing in the breeze as green as any country in the world. Yes, I have recalled a generous kindly community of people whose hearts come through their skin. Yes I have seen all that and it kept me here contented for twenty-seven years.

But I feel now that it is not enough to be a barracker only, one should take a hand in the game. Everyone should take his part in the duties of citizenship to make this town a better and brighter place every year. I have no excuses to offer for my neglect and there is not a great deal of consolation in reflecting that most of you who are listening to me are as bad as I am. We are being left behind in the race while other places with no more to offer than we have, but with an expanding faith in themselves, are forging ahead. I have this excuse to offer that might possibly get away with it. I have always thought that a clergyman's presence in a civic movement,— especially if he wants to have all the talk as the clergy sometimes do—is apt to give a sectional touch to an enterprise which should be general and therefore he may be better out of it.

And so I told the Mayor I didn't want a testimonial. I was very careful not to tell him that I didn't need it. There is a difference between wanting a thing and needing it. Some men want what they do not need, and some, but they are very few indeed, need things but do not want them. That class is composed mostly of philosophers and tramps. Anyway, I had to tell the Mayor that I couldn't think of another send-off because some very good friends of mine last year gave me a send-off when I had no intention of going. They celebrated a jubilee when the jubilee was two years passed, but I knew that their kind old hearts were bent on giving me something because they knew that I needed it, and I was very careful not to let them think that I didn't want it. Up to that time I was in an unique position. I had nothing, owed nothing, wanted nothing and expected nothing, but this generous gift altered my social status and made me an object of interest to the Income-tax Commissioner. 'But' said the Mayor 'that presentation was from the congregation of St Mel's and because of the conditions prevailing, what with war collections, extra taxation etc. they confined it pretty well to themselves. But you have many friends and well-wishers who do not assemble with you on the Hill'.

I was delighted to hear him say that. I knew it, but was glad to be assured of it. I could not help knowing it because there wasn't a man in the town who didn't give me a kindly nod as I passed, and there wasn't one to whom I could not return the compliment. If after twenty-seven years of service here, I had no friends outside those of my own Faith, I would regard myself as a narrow-minded man indeed, and a misfit in a big broad country like Australia. I could never understand why anyone would penalise a fellow-man because of his religious belief especially in a land like ours. Our fathers built this country up working side by side; they lived together in peace in nearby selections, shared the same tent on the diggings, boiled their billies together at the camp-fires of the fencers by the furthest panel west; were cronies in towns like these when they were but villages, visited one another as family neighbours, had their fun together, and I wouldn't be surprised to hear that they had been 'run in' together. And I, the son of a pioneer, while cherishing a sympathy for the Land that gave him birth, have absorbed the spirit and the ideals of this the Land he made his own. And so on the basis of our Australianism I met you, mixed with you, and appreciated you.

By that word Australian I don't confine the term to an accident of birth. Every one who has cast in his lot here, who is loyal to our aspirations and who is doing his bit to make this country the great country it ought to be, is an Australian to me. And being one hundred percent Australian it therefore is a source of the greatest pride that my countrymen are reckoned among the most efficient soldiers in the world and are fighting in defence of a great Empire of which we are, or should be, no insignificant part. And I am proud to know that boys who sat with me at St Mel's are standing shoulder to shoulder with their compatriots who have worshipped otherwise, in the defence of the principles of our common Christianity. You will find them side by side on every front where the Union Jack is floating as the symbol of Justice to be won, of liberty to be retrieved. By the olive groves of Italy; in the desert; in the jungle; aye and lying side by side in heroes' graves afar.

And their Australianism and their religion have made no difference to the splendour of their courage and the intensity of their sacrifice. No decent-minded Australian ever thought it would. 'Shall I ask the brave soldier who fights by my side in the cause of mankind if our creeds disagree? Shall I fly from the friend who is trusted and tried if he kneel not before the same altar with me!' That question was taken as answered by every Australian every time the Empire has been in danger and it is not even considered today when our own country is being threatened as never before. It was the closest thing, and only for the help which came from the old country and from our powerful Ally across the Atlantic, we would be in bondage today. But let us not underestimate the part played by our own. They gave their very best to keep their country free as it ever was: they gave their lives that no Australian mother should ever rock the cradle of a slave.

I confess that I have never been able to understand that inferiority complex which grips some of us when we talk of Australia or why we are always apologising for it. It is a good country and we never fully realised how good it is till we nearly lost it. We have followed the mistaken policy of looking overseas for help instead of making our own defences adequate. That help will be readily given where possible we know, but when the war clouds burst in a global eruption the lean gray ships of England, mighty as they surely are, cannot patrol the world. We nearly woke too late. After all, he is the true cosmopolite who loves his native country best.

But all this seems a strange note to introduce into this symphony of friendship, still the reflection of what we are going through is in our minds whether at work or play. But better times are coming. Victory is not yet but there is a bright splash of sunshine darting through a break in the clouds which twelve or fifteen months ago were very dark and grim. I remember in '18 the news came through that an armistice was signed which ended the last war, I remember how the whole population of this town flocked into the street and marched up and down hand in hand, old men and babes and loving friends and youths and maidens gay accompanied by the playing of the band and the ringing of the church bells and prominent among the latter were the sombre notes from the tower of St Mel's. I remember it because I rang it myself. I shall not be at my post in the belfry when the good news comes again, but when it does, and God grant that it be soon, I can promise that the iron tongue of St Mel's will not be silent in the chime of thanksgiving that our cause has been victorious, that what we stand for, you and I and all of us, has been upheld by the strong right arms of our countrymen and by a benignant Power mightier far than all armies of the earth.

And now my friends, getting back to earth again, if I had been prolix in what I have been trying to say you can put the blame on what Tommy Gordon said to me. In trying to overcome my very natural reluctance to any demonstration he said 'You are not the only one to be considered; you have occupied a public position and what would be thought of the people of this town if they were to allow one who held the post you held for twenty-seven years to go away without something in the nature of a farewell?' The public position was a new one on me. I was aware that I was something of a public institution to tramps and dead-beats because I had a Roman collar on, and because of my six feet odd that Roman collar was usually poking up above the heads of everybody else in the street. But beyond that I was not aware that I held a public position; still the Mayor said I did, and on reflection I felt he was referring to my pastorate at St Mel's.

For twenty-seven years I was the spiritual leader at least, and at times the adviser in lesser things, to 1200 souls in the Municipality or of roughly 1700 in the Parish, and that is a considerable number and I felt that it was to honour them as well that you wished to honour me; I take it as a token of the goodwill that has existed between all denominations in this town, which I trust will always continue. During all the years that I have been associated with the Catholics here I have never heard a bigoted thing said or known a bigoted thing to be done and I am very proud to be able to say so. But just as it takes two or more to make a row, the credit must be given to two or more when rows are avoided, and so I want to pay my acknowledgments to the ministers of the other denominations.

And to you, the people of Narrandera, I want to express my gratitude for much help as well as your unfailing toleration. In every work I undertook you gave assistance freely. In the £200,000 or so raised for Catholic church purposes during my time here, people of all denominations gave as our own. It gives me great pleasure to be able to acknowledge all this. It is a spirit which not only is creditable to all of us, but at the present time it is an omen of a solidarity which is going to be needed in the near future. If ever there was a time when it was necessary for the various denominations of the Christian Church to take their stand together on common ground, that time is surely now. There is no doubt that this war, when you get to the primary causes of it, is a show-down between Paganism and Christianity, between no God at all and the Christian God, and the battle won't be over when the last shot is fired.

What is more, the fight that is to come when the guns cease firing will be a bitter one. A House divided against itself will surely fall and it is therefore incumbent on us all to recognise one another as

*fellow christians and as such to hang together, because if we don't
hang together, we'll all hang separately. This is my reading of the
signs of the times, my interpretation of the Writing on the Wall.*

*Finally, My Friends, my thanks to you for this generous gift, and
much as I value it, I value more the goodwill behind it. You have
done more for me than I have ever done for you, even in other ways
than this, and I always felt that if ever I stood in need of aid,
financial or otherwise, you would come to my assistance gladly. The
financial help, Thank God, I never wanted, my needs were few and
the bread that returned on the running waters sufficed. Early in my
ministry I learned the hermit's philosophy:*

> *'Turn pilgrim, then thy cares forgo;
> all earthborn woes are wrong.
> Man needs but little here below,
> nor needs that little long.'*

*Your help in other matters was given when I asked it, and though
I did not often call upon you, I knew full well that it was there and
only waiting for the asking. My notion of Friendship is not that
which comes with ostentation and the loud and sometimes empty
greeting: my idea of a true friend is one that perhaps doesn't often
sit at your board because of circumstances, but who turns up with
his help and his cheery word when you are most in need of it.
'White when he's wanted' is the friend indeed, and that I think has
characterised the mutual bond between us.*

*And so I am more than grateful, I am humbly thankful for this
demonstration for it reassures me—if that were necessary—that I
take with me into my retirement the friendship of those I prize, that
a hundred golden memories await me in the sunset and the sky is
clear. In the sere and yellow leaf one values old associations the
more because one is not likely to establish new ones. And so Good-
bye and thanks again. In the days that still remain to me there will
come scenes in which you and I co-mingled, words that you and I
have spoken and, maybe, dreams that you and I have dreamt
together and over all with a white hand stretched out in benison will
stand the gracious angel of a cherished and enduring friendship.*

> *'There is all of pleasure and all of peace
> In a friend or two;
> And all our troubles will find release
> With a friend or two;
> It's in the grip of a clasping hand
> On native soil or in alien land;*

But the world is made, — Do you understand? —
Of a friend or two.

The brother soul and the brother heart
  Of a friend or two
Makes us drift on from the crowd apart
  With a friend or two;
For come days happy or come days sad,
  We count no hours but the ones made glad
In the hale good times that we've often had
  With a friend or two.[8]

The newspaper accounts speak of 'spontaneous applause' and tell of the choir and company singing 'Auld Lang Syne' and 'God Save the King'.[9]

The following day the pupils of St Joseph's Convent provided a musical program to farewell Father Hartigan. The presentation included two beautifully coloured photographs of St Mel's Church and St Joseph's Convent. Father Hartigan feelingly responded, thanking the children for their gift and complimenting them on the excellence of the entertainment and said their singing, playing and accent left nothing to be desired. The inevitable holiday granted for next day was greeted with the expected applause.

Most of the priests of the diocese were present next day at a farewell dinner at Wagga, hosted by Most Rev F. A. Henschke, D.D. A presentation was made and Father Hartigan replied in a humorous vein.

The Riverina was not to hear him publicly again. He had spent almost all of the forty-one years of his priesthood there, living at Albury, Berrigan and Narrandera. During his half dozen years as inspector of schools it was the base for his forays to every part of the original diocese of Goulburn. He returned to the Riverina on two occasions: in November 1947 for a celebration by the priests of the diocese to honour the new domestic prelates, of whom he was one; and for the Requiem and funeral of Monsignor William Slattery in Albury. Rather surprisingly, he was not called on to tell the story of the man he had known and loved since they were young curates there together from 1904 onwards.

At the time Father Hartigan was leaving Narrandera, Bishop Henschke was about to leave on his annual holidays. It was only when the Bishop returned that Father Hartigan sent to him from Rose Bay his formal letter

8. *The address by Father Hartigan is from a typescript among his papers.*
9. *Both the Wagga Daily Advertiser and the Narandera Argus of 31 March 1944 reported the proceedings in full. They both, however, omitted the couple of paragraphs where he treated the 'lean gray ships of England' and reminisced about Armistice Day, 1918.*

of resignation of the parish of Narrandera. He received from the Bishop two letters. The first was the formal acceptance of his resignation:

> Bishop's House
> Wagga Wagga N.S.W.
> 9 March 1944

> Dear Father Hartigan,
> I regret to learn from yours of the 7th inst. that you are finding it increasingly difficult to carry out your duties as Parish Priest at Narrandera, especially on Sundays with the necessity of binating,[10] and that you would like leave of absence. But I am pleased to know that you intend devoting your time to writing. Wagga as a Diocese and I as the Bishop can ill spare you but the Church in Australia will benefit. So regretfully I accept your resignation from the parish of Narrandera and grant you unlimited leave of absence. But I wish to assure you that you still remain one of the Diocesan clergy and will continue to do so no matter how long this leave may last. You retain all the privileges of the Diocese as e.g. your right to benefits of the Sick Priests' Fund and any time you may wish to return a place awaits you.
> Finally I wish to thank you for your loyalty to the Diocese and to my predecessor and to myself. I wish especially to thank you for the friendship you ever showed to me—coming as I did as a stranger amongst you, you have no idea what your companionship and sympathetic help meant to me.
> Trusting that your health will improve in the more congenial surroundings and with renewed thanks.

> Yours sincerely in Christo
> † F.A. Henschke
> Bishop of Wagga Wagga[11]

There was also a covering letter on a personal basis:

> Bishop's House
> Wagga Wagga N.S.W.
> 9 March '44

> Dear Father Hartigan,
> Enclosed is your formal leave of absence. I trust you consider it sufficiently protects your interest. I have kept a copy here so there should never be a question of your rights.

---

10. Saying two Masses on the same day. This often entailed a trip to another church. In Narrandera it meant a 64 kilometre return trip to Morundah, and 23 kilometres each way for Grong Grong.
11. Letter among Father Hartigan's papers.

Not being a Jesuit, nor yet one of the elite, I have never visited Rose Bay but now that you are there I may have courage enough to visit you in your eyrie. I spent only a few hours in Sydney when returning from my holiday—got there in the afternoon and left that evening. Next visit will be for the annual Bishops' meeting after Easter combined with the Silver Jubilee of the Delegate.

I suspected your move would cause speculation, and whilst thanking you for, and appreciating your endeavours to defend me, I am afraid human nature (even in priests) is such that they would hate to think there was not some bust-up. And naturally the Bishop is the 'nigger in the wood pile'. So let them have their fun.

Narrandera is still vacant—there will be a meeting of the Consultors next week—by the way, I forgot to accept your resignation as one of them but we can presume it.

Though I thanked you in that formal letter for your friendship and loyalty, I do not mean it as a mere form. I appreciated your long trip to my Consecration much more than you perhaps realised—I felt almost guilty in coming to Wagga—and you provided the highlight of that day—the old dad (God rest him) chuckled over that speech of yours till his dying day. And any time I felt I could drop in at Narrandera—be welcomed—and chat as friend to friend. So without being sickly sentimental—thanks—and, as you say, may our friendship continue down the years.

Every best wish from
Yours sincerely in Christ
† *F.A. Henschke.*[12]

That friendship continued for the remaining years of Father Hartigan's life. Whenever the Bishop called on him he enjoyed renewing their happy association in Wagga diocese. As a faithful priest he manifested always, alongside that friendship, a reverence for one who stood for him in the place of Christ, sharing the sacred powers that had been given first to the Apostles.

---

12. *Letter among Father Hartigan's papers.*

13 Years at Rose Bay

The Convent of the Sacred Heart, Rose Bay, was founded in 1882.[1] In that year five Sisters, Religious of the Sacred Heart, an order established in France in 1800 by St Madeleine Sophie Barat, arrived in Sydney from their convent at Roehampton in England. Their superior, Mother Vercruysse, was a Belgian. They were welcomed by Mr and Mrs John Hughes of Kincoppal, Elizabeth Bay, who were great friends and benefactors of the convent. The nuns spent their first weeks at the Convent of the Good Samaritan Sisters in Pitt Street—the convent that was later demolished to make way for Central Railway Station.

A lease was taken on a large two-storied house in Rose Bay, Claremont, standing in seven hectares of ground with breathtaking views of the harbour. It was covered with wistaria, had extensive lawns, an orange grove and a little winding path that led to the bathing house and jetty. There was a gardener's cottage, which is still standing, though divided from the convent by Vaucluse Road.

The nuns were charmed with their new home and two years later they bought it. Some of their friends thought it too remote, though an omnibus drawn by four grey horses went to the city three times a day, the trip taking an hour. There was a small ferry, the **Golden Rose,** which took rather longer.

All around was luxuriant bush, full of ferns, flowers and birds. There were few houses in the neighbourhood and the lovely bush was often dangerously alight in summer. On May evenings an exotic touch was added to the wilderness by the strange sounds of Aboriginal corroborees. These occurred when Aborigines made camp somewhere near the present Rose Bay shopping centre while they waited for the distribution, on Queen Victoria's birthday, of their yearly apportioned blankets—one per person!

Claremont had been built in 1852 by George Thorne, a merchant, on land acquired three years before from W.C. Wentworth who had got it in 1827. Wentworth is famous for his opposition to both Bligh and Darling, and W.C. Wentworth who retired recently from federal politics is of the same family.

---

1. *The author is indebted to the Sisters and Barbara Fisher for these details about the convent and its beginnings. See Inspection Leaflet No. 804 of the National Trust of Australia.*

The view from the Convent of the Sacred Heart, Rose Bay, when Father Hartigan was chaplain from 1944. Ships had fascinated him when he was a youngster at Manly, and from Rose Bay he was able to get to know them well.

A month after Claremont became a Convent of the Sacred Heart the school opened with five children. A temporary wooden chapel was built and two years later work began on the south wing and its turret tower from stone quarried at Pyrmont. The chapel was opened in 1900, its stone being quarried on the property. It is the masterpiece of John Horbury Hunt, one of the founders of the Institute of Architects of New South Wales. The chapel is English Gothic in style, and its high altar is of Carrara marble, carved in Sydney. It has a ribbed barrel-vaulted stone roof, probably unique in Australia. Beautiful oak stalls, confessional and pulpit came from the original mother house in Paris, the clock and organ from the convent in Bordeaux. The anti-clerical Government of Coombes in France (1904-08) abolished the schools of religious orders and forty-five Convents of the Sacred Heart were closed.

The parlour wing—now the library—was built in 1922 and the stone for this was also quarried on the property. It incorporates Hunt's ideas, though he died not long after the completion of the chapel. Later buildings have harmonised with the austere Gothic style of the original concept of Mother Vercruysse and her architect.

So it was then to a French tradition that Father Hartigan was introduced when he took up his duties as chaplain at Rose Bay early in 1944. It was an atmosphere very different from that of his upbringing and his priesthood amid an Irish-Australian people. He received a warm welcome from Mother McGuinness and from the local superior, Mother L. Kennedy, and he learnt to respect deeply the authentic spirituality of their French tradition.

He found the routine of his new life conducive to his work of research. The tram from Watson's Bay passed the door and took him to the Mitchell Library where he was a familiar figure and gets a mention in Patrick White's novel **The Solid Mandala.**[2] His afternoon walks were often to Watson's Bay and he never tired of the beauty of the harbour.

Ships had fascinated him as a youngster at Manly and now he had the chance to get to know them well. He bought books on their flags and with a pair of binoculars he got to know every ship that came into Sydney, its funnel markings, house flag and so on. So much was he attached to the harbour that he was amazed to find how much he missed it when he was away at Campbelltown for a few days, the guest of his long-time friend, Father Arthur McHugh.

His love of children and his years as inspector of schools enabled him to become the friend and the confidant of the youngsters at the school. His

---

2. *Patrick White*, The Solid Mandala, *Viking Press, New York, 1966, p. 163.*

special favourites were the country girls and above all those from his beloved Riverina. He found the youngsters delightful but he realised that they came from surroundings that could spoil them. It is hard to avoid becoming a snob if snobbery is the prevailing climate. He saw the danger of these young girls leaving the school with high spiritual ideals and yet failing to withstand the materialism of the milieu in which their lives would be lived. So he was ready always with the debunking remark, with the joke and kind smile to cut down to size the would-be snob.

It was no secret that he missed his parish very much, especially in his first years at Rose Bay. A parish priest gets very close to the families of his parish and Father Hartigan had known many of his people a long time and had their confidence in a special way. A parish priest, moreover, has the arranging of the affairs of the parish—and again, Father Hartigan had been making administrative decisions virtually all his life except for his years as a curate. It required some adjustment to fit into arrangements made by others, to get used to ideas that came from a different tradition.

His first two years at Rose Bay were occupied very much by his continuing articles in the **Australasian Catholic Record.** In his researching he made trips to Maitland, and to Mudgee where his host was Monsignor Edward Flanagan, originally a student at St Charles' Seminary, Bathurst, in the era before Manly College; he was to live on till 1957 to the age of ninety-four, seventy years a priest. This Mudgee trip included a stay with Monsignor O'Donnell at St Columba's College, Springwood.

In his first years at Rose Bay, Father Hartigan went back to Galong and rejoined the priests of his diocese in their annual retreat. Later on, he went with the Sydney priests to this yearly spiritual exercise at St Patrick's College, Manly.

One of his joys was to visit our home at Haberfield; he came regularly each week, usually on Wednesday, travelling out by tram. We would all gather there and Annie—Mart he teasingly called her from her second name—would have a meal she knew he liked.

Usually my brother Bernie would drive him back to Rose Bay in the Hudson he had left with the family. Bernie shared his love of cars and P.J., as we called him, was all admiration for his handling of the traffic. He no longer drove himself; he was put off by the speed of Sydney's cars—especially through intersections—and he did not know his way round. He was the first to admit that he had no 'bump' of location and even in the days of his country driving he could get lost easily.

From 1946 onwards when I had moved from the staff of Springwood to that of Manly, he came out to Haberfield for the midday meal on Sundays. In the afternoon we would drive to Rose Bay for Benediction of the Blessed Sacrament. Sometimes I would give the Benediction for him and stay on for the evening meal and a yarn afterwards.

The Jesuit Fathers were at that time at Campion Hall, Point Piper (now the Ave Maria Retreat House) conducting a preparatory school for Riverview College. They helped out regularly at the Convent of the Sacred Heart and the chaplain greatly enjoyed their company.

Right from his arrival in Sydney, Father Hartigan was in demand as a public speaker. The Christian Brothers secured him as the preacher at the cathedral for the Mass on 27 August 1944 to mark the centenary of the death of their founder Edmund Ignatius Rice. In his sermon he traced the role of the Church in education and the part Religious had played in that story, particularly in Australia. He followed generally the line of thought he had developed in his sermon at Goulburn a couple of years earlier.[3] He had this to say of the Brothers:

> The Christian Brothers are not claiming that only their feet have trod the furrow, but the work of the Christian Brothers has by no means been the least.
>
> They were the first Order of teaching men to come amongst us. In general seniority they are second only to the Sisters of Charity. They came to us at a time when Catholic education was carried on under the greatest difficulties. We had our penal days, when Catholics were driven by the lash to services in sheds, when the principles for which we have always stood were being put into the foundations associated with the names of Therry, McEncroe and Polding.
>
> Dr Polding brought the Christian Brothers here and schools were opened, one in Macquarie Street (somewhere near where Sydney Hospital now stands), another at St Benedict's, and another at the bottom of Kent Street.
>
> The good work they did is on record. Because of some local attempt to change their Rule, they were advised to go back, and the work of Catholic education in Australia was for a time brought to a standstill. They returned in 1868.
>
> Today the Christian Brothers have seventy houses in Australia, and three in New Zealand. They have control of 25,000 boys and their personnel is 650.
>
> In the celebrations we bear in mind that it is the work the Brothers have done, their wonderful attention to duty and their faithful observance of their Rule that is focusing the spotlight on their founder this morning.[4]

3. See Chapter 10, pp. 202-211.
4. From the typescript of the sermon among Father Hartigan's papers.

Also in that first year at Rose Bay Father Hartigan was asked to give the Advent sermons in the cathedral. The Archbishop was well pleased with them and sent this handwritten letter:

St Mary's Cathedral,
Sydney,
5 January, 1945.

Dear Father Hartigan,
Please accept the expression of my sincere thanks for preaching the Advent sermons in the Cathedral. Each one of them was admirable, so admirable that I am extremely sorry that they were not all printed in full.
We see too little of you at the Presbytery. At least occasionally when I am present, come and have dinner with us. Unless you do, I shall be wondering what I have done to displease you.

Best wishes for 1945,
Yours,
✝ N.T. Gilroy.[5]

Among his closest relatives were his Sullivan cousins at Coolac and Gundagai. In 1945 it was known that 'Dolly' Sullivan was seriously ill and we drove down to see her. She died in February 1945 and we went down and were present at her Requiem in the Coolac church and officiated at the graveside. Few people had been so close to Father Hartigan as 'Dolly' Sullivan, and indeed she shared many of his characteristics, his faith, kindness to the sick and his sense of humour. Her last trip in her car—known as the 'Coolac Ambulance'—was to convey a daughter to her dying father.

Father Hartigan had a wonderful gift of bringing comfort in times of bereavement. As with the Sullivans on that occasion, he would stay overnight and as he wove yarn after yarn, the past would live again—the time would fly and somehow the grief seemed tolerable, the pieces in the jig-saw of life seemed once again to be making a pattern. After holding us enraptured for hours, he would suddenly break the spell with the remark: 'Go to bed, you fools'—only he could bring the session to an end, it would have been sacrilegious of anyone else.

A constant stream of visitors came to see him at Rose Bay. There was a special welcome for Narranderites, for the clergy and for his family.

Cardinal Freeman, then a priest on the cathedral staff, called on him from time to time and would listen spellbound as Father Hartigan talked on books and recited poetry endlessly. A love of literature bound them

5. *Letter among Father Hartigan's papers.*

closely together; indeed, they shared a deep underlying love of men and women and an appreciation of the real values in life of which literature is the mirror.

Dr Joe Coen, originally from Yass, remained one of his closest friends. He lived not far away and called often at Father Hartigan's cottage in the convent grounds. It was he who looked after him medically, and occasionally had him admitted to Lewisham hospital with a bout of the 'flu or something similar.

There were often important visitors at the convent, from overseas and other parts of Australia and these he enjoyed immensely. Father Sydney McEwan and his Scottish mother stayed there and the singer and the poet got on famously. Father McEwan told him that despite the number of appearances he had made, he was always nervous until he got his first applause.

Not only did visitors keep him occupied. He had a stream of letters and he kept in touch with his friends, particularly in their times of sadness. Thus he wrote as follows on the occasion of Judge O'Mara's death:

> Rose Bay,
> 20th October, 1946

Dear Sister Vianney,

My heart went out to you all when I got the news of Tom's death. It was a shock to me as I had no idea that his useful life was to be such a short one and I think I know how empty it has left the world for those he has parted from. One could wander on speculating why so valuable a career should be cut off at its peak while so many who could be spared remain, but what's the use. The more I see of life and death the more I am convinced of the inscrutable ways of Providence and the only explanation is our Faith. It is at times like this that one should thank God for it and I know you have fallen back on that great support. I said Mass for him when I got the news and I added a prayer that the great God would pour some balm of consolation into the wounded hearts of his three sisters and his family. I have written Goulburn.

> May God bless and keep you,
> Sincerely,
> P.J. Hartigan[6]

To another of that family, Mother Magdalen, Mother General of the Goulburn Sisters of St Joseph, he wrote when he heard of her serious illness:

6. *This and the following letter were kindly supplied by Sister Vianney of the Sisters of St Joseph, North Goulburn.*

Dear Mother Magdalen,

You have been so much in my mind—so very much—lately that I just have to send this note. I get, of course, reports from time to time—the last was more re-assuring—but I do hope you are not suffering. I believe from what I hear that is an idle wish. I have heard of your wonderful courage. That is as I would expect it. You have been a splendid example in many ways to us of lesser worth. As I look back—the looking back covers some five and twenty years—to the time when I was struck by Mina O'Meara sitting in the back unassuming—yet the star pupil. As I look along the track I know of no one who measures up better than yourself. This is not mere gush, but as I said you have been in my mind so much that I had to pen an appreciation which may be of some value.

I have said Mass for you the other morning and I have put your name in every Mass I say, that God may bless you and keep you. That He will reward you, I have no doubt.

> *My dear Magdalen,*
> *Sincerely,*
> *P.J. Hartigan.*

My regards to Vianney, Dolores and all my friends. Do not bother answering this. P.J.H.

During 1945 Bishop Eris O'Brien gave a lecture on Cardinal Newman in the Great Hall of the University of Sydney. Father Hartigan was there and Monsignor Tom Veech tells the story:

The artist, E.M. Smith saw a head among the audience and made up his mind to paint it. There were quite a number of 'Heads' present that evening, but the artist discerned and predestined one. To get that head on canvas Mr Smith had first to paint his brilliantly modern study of the Bishop of Goulburn (now at Archbishop's House, Goulburn). His Grace was so pleased with it that he asked Monsignor Hartigan to sit. Here we have what many think is Mr Smith's best work. It has life and character; it is more than a photograph; it is 'John O'Brien'.

The Australian priest-poet most graciously gave this glorious canvas to the College, which rejoices in the possession of a painting of a distinguished son. It has been placed in the Professors' Common Room.[7]

---

7. Manly 1948, p. 55. Since the time that article was written the portrait has been moved to a place of honour in the main corridor of St Patrick's College, Manly.

The Manly student annalist, relating the events of 1947, tells us of the presentation:

> Bishop McGuire and Monsignor Hartigan were present at tea on the occasion of the Bishop's presentation to the College of Mr E.M. Smith's portrait of the Prelate-poet. The ready wit and ripe old flavour of the reminiscences of both the Bishop and the poet were a reminder of the richness of the heritage which their generation has bequeathed to us.[8]

In October of 1947 came the news that Father Hartigan had been made a domestic prelate with the title of Right Rev Monsignor. He had been approached by Bishop Henschke some months earlier and the rescript from Pius XII bore the date 20 June 1947 and the signature Jo Bapt. Montini (afterwards Paul VI). The letter from the Bishop was as follows:

> *Bishop's House,*
> *Wagga Wagga, N.S.W.*
> *20 October 1947.*

> *Rt Rev. Monsignor P.J. Hartigan,*
> *Convent of the Sacred Heart,*
> *ROSE BAY. N.S.W.*

> *Dear Monsignor,*
> *It is with very great pleasure that I convey to you the news that Our Holy Father, Pope Pius XII, has recognised your many years of service in this diocese and has considered also your great contribution to Catholic Australian Poetry and History, and has, accordingly, conferred upon you the rank of a Domestic Prelate.*
> *I trust that the years to come will be happy ones for you and fruitful in much work for souls, and that the years of service rendered to God in the past will be but an earnest of greater strivings in the years ahead and the pledge of a blissful eternity.*
> *I enclose herewith the Papal Brief of your appointment, together with a document setting out the obligations, rights and privileges of a Domestic Prelate.*
> *In forwarding me the notice of your appointment, His Excellency, the Apostolic Delegate, asked me to convey to you his personal congratulations on your appointment to the ranks of the Domestic Prelates to His Holiness*

8. *Ibid.*, p. 75.

Father Hartigan, as Heth of the BULLETIN saw him, around the time that Pope Pius XII appointed him a domestic prelate, with the title Right Reverend Monsignor. (Reproduced by courtesy of the BULLETIN)

and to these I wish to add my own good wishes and felicitations on this happy occasion.

You will be pleased to know that Monsignor Barry has been created a Prothonotary Apostolic by the Holy Father and that Monsignori W. Slattery and O. Clarke have been appointed Domestic Prelates.

Kindly drop a note of thanks to His Excellency, the Apostolic Delegate.

With every good wish,
Yours sincerely in Christo,
† *F.A. Henschke*
Bishop of Wagga Wagga.[9]

This letter was followed a few days later by a personal note from the Bishop in which he said:

My last letter was a coldly official one—dictated in fact as I was in a desperate hurry that day. So this is an informal one to say just how pleased I am that the Pope saw fit to honour the four of you—I don't know that these requests are always granted. I suppose I should have made this move years ago but, to be candid, I did not want to seem to be buying popularity. That the appointments are popular I have no doubt—not only to the recipients but to all the Diocese. And in asking for them I had the diocese in mind—Wagga has treated me well and loyally and it is up to me to recognise it.[10]

Literally hundreds of congratulations poured in to Father Hartigan, from the diocese and from the cardinal, bishops and priests, religious and laity all over Australia. It was as though so many who had enjoyed his verse and his historical writing—as well as many he had ministered to in the parish and elsewhere—took this chance of expressing a joy and thankfulness that had been welling up within them for years.

Father Hartigan got himself a set of monsignorial robes from Vanheems in London but they remained hanging in his wardrobe.

He had great love for the lay Sisters at Rose Bay. They looked after his needs, served his meals and so on. He was not happy with the idea of this division of communities—it is something that has now disappeared from religious congregations and he would say rightly so. He saw it as an unnecessary class distinction—to use his expressive phrase: 'the lay Sisters were not in the stud-book'.

When one of them died, he rang up his friend, Monsignor Tom

9. *Letter among Father Hartigan's papers.*
10. *Ibid.*

Wallace, who organised a number of prominent people to be present. Father Hartigan then for the first time donned his monsignorial robes and appeared as a stately figure among the other monsignori and dignitaries.

When afterwards the visitors were gathered for afternoon tea at the convent, one of the superiors, delighted with Father Hartigan's part in the function, said, 'I suppose we shall be seeing your robes often now, Monsignor'. 'It all depends who dies,' was his quick retort.

The early months of 1948 brought a grief to Father Hartigan. His brother Michael was diagnosed as having a malignant growth of the throat. He had to give up his position in the public service and for six months alternated between the hospital and his home in Mosman, dying there on 13 May.

The remaining members of the original Hartigan family, Minnie (Sister M. Peter) and Annie, assisted at the Requiem Mass celebrated by Father Pat at Clifton Gardens—Bridgie (Sister M. Ignatius) had died just before he left Narrandera. As always, his presence was a great consolation in sorrow and Michael's widow and son and daughter were deeply appreciative of the help he gave them in their grief.

He continued to be in demand as a speaker. The week after Michael's death he addressed the Holy Name Society in St Mary's Cathedral:

But about the eleventh hour he went out and found others standing, and He saith to them, Why stand you here all the day idle? They say to Him, Because no man hath hired us. He saith to them 'Go ye also into My Vineyard'. Matt. 20: 6-7.

It often occurs to one that the part laymen have played in the great work of making this world a better place, and of saving man from his own folly, has been overlooked, and the part he still can play is not sufficiently stressed. I mean by a layman one who is not a priest. The term is used in all the professions to denote anyone outside that particular profession. A doctor, for example, will call a layman anyone who is not a doctor, a lawyer one who is outside the legal circle and so on, but I am using it tonight in its original meaning as one of the laity from the Greek word Laos, *the people—as distinct from those who are in Holy Orders or have given their lives to Religion. I just mention this to avoid confusion, because in my remarks tonight I shall refer to doctors, lawyers, scientists and others who have done great things for their God and their Country both in their own sphere and beyond it.*

Everything that a man does for the true benefit of his fellow man is, if done with a clean intention, an Act of Religion. Emerson in a

285

*striking passage says: 'Every glance we give to the realities around us
with intent to learn, proceeds from a holy impulse and is really a
song of praise. What difference can it make whether it take the
shape of exhortation, or of passionate appeal, or of scientific
statement. These are forms merely. Through them we express at
least the fact that God has done thus and thus'. Through them I add
we acknowledge that God is truly great. When God made the world
with man as the dominant figure, He meant it to be a happy place. It
was man's disobedience to a divine command which sent that plan
astray; and the world could still be a happy place today if man would
only let it. His pride, his greed, his abandonment of self to sensuous
living—all of which amounts to a denial of God, or at least a wilful
disobedience to His laws that turns this other garden of Eden into a
wilderness of disorder and hate. Anyone who does anything however
small to make this world a place where man might live in such a
way that he can reach his eternal home is doing God's work most
surely, and must receive his reward.*

*And so the Church to which you belong while she has ever
counselled austerity and mortification has readily lent herself to
everything whether it be an advance in science or a lesson of
philosophy regulating the social order which would lighten the
burden a man has to bear on this earth, provided always that nothing
is done or taught to obscure his vision of Heaven. And in this she
has accepted the work of laymen as well as that of ecclesiastics. I
could quote for you a long and imposing list of Catholic laymen who
have done things in this regard which have made their names
remembered for all time.*

*But it is not my purpose tonight. You are not working in the more
or less exclusive world of Science but in a commonplace field if I
might use that word commonplace to denote what is after all the
most important business of life, viz. to prepare yourselves to attain
the purpose for which you were created which is to love, serve and
adore God in this life and to enjoy the Beatific Vision in the next
and at the same time by your example, your prayers, and your
charitable endeavours to help a fellow pilgrim whose feet are
stumbling on the stony road beside you. In other words, the
objective is first of all to make yourselves spiritually and morally fit
and then to go into the wheatfield and lend a hand to get the
Harvest in.*

*The field that lies before the layman in this regard is immense and
telling examples of what laymen have done in a quiet way could be
quoted. The St Vincent de Paul Society was established by a layman*

286

and is carried on by laymen, and if there is one organisation in the world today which does good without self advertisement, following out the old injunction of letting not the left hand know what the right hand is doing, heeding that same old insurance that even a cup of cold water given to the needy in the Holy Name is an act of Religion—if there is one band of men who are making things easier for the unfortunate and making Heaven clearer to pain-blinded eyes, it is the St Vincent de Paul Society. The Legion of Mary, too, was founded by a layman. Similarly Mat Talbot was a layman.

But if you want eloquent examples of what laymen can do come and have a look at our own country and our own times. Everyone must admit that the Catholic Church and the Catholic Faith are firmly established in Australia; you see the church and school and convent on a hill in every town throughout the Commonwealth, you see its institutions everywhere. We are not proud of these just because they impress the sightseer, nor are we proud of our progress just because we have grown numerically strong. She is the servant of God, and all these buildings—churches, schools, institutions and so forth erected under difficulty and trouble are necessary equipment to enable her to continue the work which was begun by the shelving shore of Galilee. You see the crowds streaming along the footpaths on the way to Mass, you see the numbers going to confession in the dim lit church on the Saturday evening, you see them coming row by row to Communion—all of which is proof she has been about her Father's business.

But what is her story? It is a wonderful story—'a leaf from a great-hearted tale of magnificent years of the past'. Never was a more unpromising grain of mustard seed planted anywhere in the church's history than that which was planted here in Sydney Cove. We began with a few hundred prisoners sent out in chains, some for crimes, some for political transgressions, some for minor offences which would be met today by a fine or detention till the Rising of the Court. These men and women were marched under threat of the lash to Religious Services which were not their own. There were three priests here at that time,—convicts—transported because of real or alleged complicity with the Irish Rebellion of '98, but, except on one or two occasions, they were not permitted to minister to their co-religionists or assemble them for instruction. Anyway they were sent back early in the piece.

Still when the next priest Father O'Flynn, came sixteen or seventeen years later he found a scrawny plant sprung from that grain of mustard seed struggling for survival. It was not dead and *forgotten. But who kept it alive? Some unremembered layman who risked the cat of nine tails to gather a little circle together somewhere and say a Rosary or read prayers from a tattered prayer book which he had managed to smuggle through from the convict ship. When Father O'Flynn was deported because his papers were not in order who was it kept the poor plant green till Father Therry came five years later? Father O'Flynn left the Blessed Sacrament in a chest in the home of William Davis where St Patrick's Church stands today, but it would have been forgotten and perhaps desecrated if some laymen had not rallied round to protect it.*

Their names should be written large across the page which tells the story. Davis himself, Michael Dwyer, a co-rebel of Robert Emmet in the troubled times which followed '98, Francis Kenny of Appin, afterwards one of the first settlers on what is now the Federal Capital Territory, James Dempsey of Kent Street, Lacy of Parramatta, Byrne of Campbelltown, Fitzpatrick and others whose names have not survived. These men formed an Adoration Society and gathered their fellows round that improvised tabernacle and said the Rosary in the evening or the Mass prayers on Sunday. The cottage was not big enough to accommodate them all so they knelt on the road unmindful of the sneers of the passers-by, a cheated people praying for the dawn of a better day.

When Father Therry came in 1821 he was surprised to find in the prison settlement which then was Sydney Town a small choir of currency lads and lasses who could sing the age-old hymns of the church—something at least to praise God and keep the Faith alive. Who trained that little choir? A layman and all that has come down to us concerning him was that his name was McGuire. That name assuredly should be added to the list of those who kept the grain of mustard seed from perishing.

For some years after Father Therry's arrival he was the only priest in Australia. In the next decade or so there were three. One hundred and ten years ago there were less than a dozen. The population had wandered over the boundaries set by Governor Darling and had straggled from Sydney Town to Moreton Bay, from Campbelltown to the Murray and across it, from the Blue Mountains through Bathurst to the Sunset. This handful of priests went after them riding sometimes a hundred miles a day, but what could they do unaided. Once in every three or four years was as often as they could visit the far-flung outposts.

Who was it kept the lamp glimmering in the meantime? The Catholic layman who yoked his bullocks to the dray and tramped

288

two hundred miles beside the dray to have his children and those of his neighbours baptised. The layman who read the Mass prayers to a be-draggled congregation. The mother who taught her bush kids that there was a God above them, who turned out her slab kitchen and made it a temporary chapel and summoned the neighbours from thirty miles around when the priest was coming. Were such as these not labourers in the Vineyard of God?

It is a glorious story, Men of the Holy Name, and I could go on and on, but listen to this, and I am taking it in substance from the Daily Mirror of 29 March of this year. Over one hundred years ago ships were coming to Sydney bringing immigrants to people the empty spaces of Australia. Among them were many unprotected girls from Ireland, England and Scotland. Single gentlemen in search of housekeepers, notorious bludgers, pimps and brothel keepers met the boats and combed the town picking up destitute immigrant girls—some of them as young as nine years old—who roamed the streets by day looking for work, and slept under the rocks in the Domain at night. No less than 600 of them prowled round Sydney in despair, while many more who had found employment were reduced to slavery by unscrupulous employers who took every advantage of the immigrants' destitution. Such was the state of things when Caroline Chisholm began her noble work.

Caroline Chisholm, who was called the Immigrants' Friend, was a Catholic married woman and a devout one. Years ago when I was a little boy at Yass, I used to see a Police Magistrate named Chisholm kneeling at Mass, and I remember how he impressed us all by the reverent way he assisted at the Holy Sacrifice. He was a son of Caroline Chisholm. But to get on with the story. When this Catholic lay-woman saw the wretched state of these immigrant girls she was, of course, amazed and shocked that nobody was doing anything about it. Her sympathy was whipped into resolution when she saw one Sunday morning a young Scotch lassie blind drunk with a bible in her hand and talking suicide. The good lady Samaritan who had no one to help her managed to find some sort of disused shed which she turned into a shelter, gathered immigrant girls into it and looked after them. At her own expense she enlarged these premises, ran up huts and so forth round about till she could accommodate all the strays.

Then she set about finding employment for the girls in respectable homes. She found decent husbands for them. When she couldn't get all she wanted in Sydney she went into the country and got in touch with families out back. She escorted her charges to their destination *herself, and it was no uncommon sight one hundred years ago to see her riding on horseback through the bush tracks piloting a team of tilted carts carrying the immigrants to safety and protection as far as Bathurst, Port Macquarie, through Goulburn and Yass on to Gundagai 250 miles [400 km] away. No wonder that in Australian History she is known by the beautiful title of the Immigrants' Friend. Altogether she placed 11,000 of these girls out of danger of misery in this life and damnation in the next. 11,000 saved from the burning to be the foundation of the Australian stock—the great-grandmothers of the Anzacs. Was not this going into the Vineyard?*

And so dear Men of the Holy Name when you see your church flourishing today with its orphanages, its foundling homes, its Magdalen shelters, its schools where nuns and brothers devote their whole lives to service, and over all the bells of handsome churches calling thousands to the Sunday Morning Muster, while giving due credit to Bishops, Priests and Religious who brought all this about, don't forget your meed of praise to the part played by the layman. In the background of the picture there is an earnest pale faced man perhaps in chains, but with an invisible halo of the Blessed already round his tousled head passing a prayer or a word of God to a mate for whom the gallows is waiting, a congregation kneeling in the street outside a cottage on St Patrick's Hill while a layman stumbles through the Mass prayers, laymen too helping Father Therry and the early missioners in their almost superhuman task. In that background too there is a Catholic woman on horseback escorting her drays—a Moses in bonnet and shawl leading her people from bondage to the Promised Land. And to fill in that shadowy background there's a tired priest on a tired horse ending up a hundred weary miles, the Mass-kit strapped to the pommel of the saddle; there's a settler's hut built of slabs where a bearded man is proudly waiting, there's his wife beside him who once was an immigrant girl, but with the bloom still upon her cheeks and the brogue upon the tongue, with the children at her knee, and the neighbours gathered in from thirty miles around. There's a room tidied up, the kitchen dresser for an altar, a spoon in a tumbler as the Sanctus Bell whose feeble tinkle is music in Heaven; and so on and on even to the present day.

Men of The Holy Name, that is the tradition that is behind you, that is the heritage you have walked into. What of yourselves? Every period has its problems, every period has its opportunities. How are you meeting those of today? Are you standing round all the day idle? Don't say to me: 'No man hath hired us'. The terms of your engagement were drawn up nearly 2000 years ago when it was said: 'he that gathereth not with Me, scattereth'. You belong to a Society which is world-wide and has been established 700 years, the object of which is to instil into its members reverence for the Holy Name and for everything that Holy Name stands for. Your first duty is your own sanctification which you will promote by strict observance of the rules of your Association. You will thus become the salt of the earth. Just as salt sprinkled on food keeps it wholesome, so you sprinkled, as it were, through the different grades of society should be a force to make the world a better place.

But remember if the salt should lose its savour, it is worse than useless. It is good for nothing anymore but to be cast out and trodden by the feet of men. You will find ample opportunities in the world you live in to exercise your influence for good, for the old enemy who first defied the ways of God is as active and as successful today as ever he was. I know it is old-fashioned to speak of the devil as the power of evil in this enlightened twentieth century. Men laugh at the idea and have placed him back among the myths that peopled their childhood. They have voted him out, but listen to this:

Call him what you will. Call him Demon, Satan, Thing of Evil, but don't call him the Spirit of the Age. It has been the same in every age, and our own is probably no worse than those which preceded it. There has always been the foul breath to wither the harvest if it is not gathered quickly. Here is where you can exercise an apostolate. Extend the influence of The Holy Name. No, no one wants you to turn your collar round and become a preaching nuisance. That would only defeat your object, but by your own solid example and by the timely word you can accomplish much.

There's a man of your acquaintance whom you know to be a Catholic but who has drifted. He is a friend of yours, you make a date with him to go to the football match or for a game of bridge, you could possibly make a date with him to go to Mass if you were game enough ... There's a boy living in your street who is a newcomer to the city. You used to see him at Mass and Holy Communion when he came first. He doesn't go now, he is drifting. If you don't gather him in some other body which is an enemy to everything you cherish assuredly will. Bring them round to the Holy Name Society and let the inspiration of a gathering such as this do its work. Men of The Holy Name, that is my message.[11]

11. Sermon among Father Hartigan's papers, slightly abridged.

Later that same year the Holy Name Men were addressed by Monsignor Fulton Sheen and they were almost hanging from the rafters to hear him. That was the occasion when at St Mary's Cathedral Father Hartigan was introduced to Fulton Sheen as 'John O'Brien'. The American embraced him warmly and said 'How are you, Father O'Brien. I have been wanting to meet you ever since I first read your poems. I have used them often in my radio work'.

In mid-September the Archbishop of Canberra and Goulburn was staying with Mgr Gerald Bartlett in his Sydney parish, and he sent this letter to Father Hartigan:

> Forest Lodge,
> 15 September 1948
>
> Dear Pat,
>
> On Sunday 26 September, the Delegate will invest me with the Pallium and the Auxiliary will Pontificate; also be welcomed at a garden party that afternoon, also the clergy all meet at dinner next day. Will you come up and preach a nice little sermon? 20 minutes will do as there will be a little formal talking by the Delegate and 2 words by myself. Now do come to comfort me.
>
> † T.M. McGuire,
> Archbishop of Canberra & Goulburn.[12]

The invitation was accepted and Father Hartigan spoke as follows:

> In this Cathedral of St Peter and Paul and in the earlier church of St Peter and Paul which this has superseded there have taken place during the last one hundred years many ceremonies, each in its way important as marking another forward step in the establishment of ecclesiastical authority and leadership in obedience to the Divine Command: 'Go, teach ye all nations'. Priests have been ordained here, bishops have been consecrated here, and today for the first time an Archbishop will receive from the Representative of the Holy Father the Pallium which typifies his participation in the supreme Pastoral Office which is exercised in its fullness by the Pope as the first Bishop of Christendom.
>
> The Pallium is a circular band stamped with black crosses worn around the neck and shoulders and having two pendants, one hanging down in front and one at the back. It is made from wool taken from two lambs presented annually as a tax to the Church of

---

12. *Letter among Father Hartigan's papers.*

St John Lateran in Rome. These lambs receive special attention. They are taken when quite small in a basket to be blessed after the Pontifical Mass in the Church of St Agnes on the feast of the Saint and offered to the Pope. They are then taken back to the Convent of St Agnes and cared for till the time that the wool can be removed. This is kept in a guarded place to be woven into the Pallium to be conferred on Archbishops throughout the world. The Pallium is something in the nature of a commission from the Vicar of Christ to an Archbishop. It is a personal thing. The Archbishop may not perform certain pontifical functions without it. He cannot will it to his successor or give it to another. If it is mislaid or destroyed he cannot borrow one from a neighbouring Archbishop but must immediately apply to Rome for another. This has been the practice very much as I state it for about fifteen hundred years.

The history of Goulburn as a Parish covers just a hundred and ten years, the Diocese is just eighty years in existence, and it is significant of the indestructibility of the Catholic Church as well as the advance it has made in this country in one century that this symbol of Archiepiscopal rank which was introduced long before William the Conqueror landed in Britain in 1066 A.D. should today be bestowed by a representative of the successor of the Pope who instituted it on the first Archbishop of the Federal Capital of a Continent which was all unknown when most of the world was old, and whose possibilities of Nationhood were never guessed by the storm-tossed mariners who first sighted its forbidding coast-line.

That is a thought which comes unbidden to the mind when one contemplates the conferring of this age-old symbol in the but recently constituted Archdiocese of Canberra and Goulburn. Besides emphasising the antiquity of the Ancient Church it pin-points the advance of eighty or one hundred years and announces that another step is taken and a new phase entered into in the fulfilment of the Mission which that Church received to teach all men.

It would seem that the many roles the Church under the guidance of the Bishops has assumed in every country are all of a pattern. The reason for the institution of the Church in the first place is to save souls in continuation of the work which brought the Son of God from Bethlehem to Calvary. State it how you like, it all comes back to this, that the Church's mission is to teach man that here he has no lasting city, that the worthwhile philosophy is to know, honour and serve God in this life so that he may be happy with him forever in the next. In doing this the steps which have had to be taken were more or less the same from the beginning.

First of all the Gospel which enshrines that philosophy had to be made known so the missionaries have gone forth to preach it even as they did from the cobbled streets of Jerusalem to the market places of Rome. It was the Bishops who led the preachers then through the countries lying north where the great nerve-centres quiver today and the pulses beat, through desert places, beyond the smoke of Asian Capes to announce the tidings far and wide.

Then came the church-builders, the organisers, to be met with strong opposition from enemies of whom it had been prophesied that they would persecute the servant as they had persecuted the Master. That opposition was twofold. There was physical violence when the purple as the symbol of episcopal rank was also the symbol of martyrdom, and the placing of the mitre on the brow singled it out for the axe of the executioner. They withstood all that and in time it died down or at least became dormant, but the other opposition has never ceased to dog their steps right till today. It is subtler opposition fought with the weapons of the mind with which misguided intellects have ever fought Religion and endeavoured to undermine its simple philosophy.

The Gospel which Jesus Christ preached on earth was presented by Him in the plainest terms, it was clothed in the simplest language, it was illustrated by the most beautiful parables. It was in fact the obvious which had been written on the human heart before the Divine finger traced on the tables of stone on Mt Sinai. Clothed in the simplest language, it was illustrated by figures taken from the daily lives of the congregations who heard it. The Wheat-field, the Sowing, the Harvest, the Fishing-net, the Lilies of the Field, the Birds of the Air were woven into poetry so telling and so convincing that the Truth was made clear to the understanding of everyone. It had to be accepted by all in its entirety, adding nothing and subtracting nothing. 'All things whatsoever I have commanded you.'

But simple and self-explanatory though it was, it was destined, in some cases, to be most grievously misunderstood and in others to be falsely and viciously interpreted. There is no truth so evident but some will deny it, no Sacrament so holy but some will spurn it, no language so plain but some will misunderstand it. There is no cause so mischievous but some will espouse it and even bless it with a text, and thus often and often we have seen the white form of Truth upon the scaffold and the hateful face of Wrong leering from the Throne, but that scaffold guards the future 'Behold I am with you all days even to the end of the world'.

The Gospel had to be guarded from all error, it had to be handed down in its purity, but there have been times when men of learning, men of great brains, giants in the world of thought have tried to scan with human eyes the Living Throne, the Sapphire Blaze where angels tremble while they gaze and have endeavoured in the pride of intellect to force upon the world an individual opinion or a dishonest selfish doctrine in place of the saving eternal doctrine that was preached by the shelving shore of Galilee. That and not fire and sword has been the great conflict in which the leaders of the Church have been engaged.

If today we have in our keeping just nothing more or less than what was entrusted to the Twelve;—if today we still have the handmaiden clad in the flowing robes of integrity instead of the spurious tinselled garb of the wanton, it is due to our leaders who have taught all nations, the sound of whose mighty blows still ring down the corridors of Time to defend, where defence is needed, the Successor of the Fisherman.

And referring back to the ceremony we are about to witness in this Cathedral today, when an Archbishop will receive from the Representative of Pope Pius XII the charter of his enrolment, it is interesting to note that Goulburn and its district have already gone through some of the stages I have enumerated, and as the Archdiocese of Canberra and Goulburn is to embark upon another.

You have had your missionaries preaching the same Gospel which the Apostles preached and carrying the standard far afield . . .[13]

Then eighty years ago in Goulburn a bishop was consecrated in the old Church and Dr Lanigan with six priests under his jurisdiction began the organising of parishes in the Diocese of Goulburn from Marulan to Deniliquin. Then came the school-builders. The bishops and priests of other days who, true to the traditions of the Catholic Church down the ages, saw to it that the children were taught. They brought the nuns and established them determining that where there could be assembled thirty pupils there should be a Convent School. They even dared to establish Our Lady of Mercy Boarding College and St Patrick's College when there were only 500 children enrolled in the whole diocese. Today there are according to the official directory 814 in the city of Goulburn and 7600 throughout the diocese.

Mighty things were done in the past, but today even a further step

---

13. At this point Father Hartigan told the story of Goulburn's early priests. See above, pp. 223-242 passim.

is taken. In the times I have been speaking of Australia was a far country lying beyond the world's ken somewhere in the Southern Seas. Things that were happening in troubled Europe touched her but remotely if at all. Wars began and ended before she was aware of it. Philosophies were enunciated and gained adherents by the thousand of which she only read in belated newspapers. And it was the hope of many men that it would be always so. 'For them a continent undreamed of, peerless, a realm for happier sons of theirs to be, One land preserved unspotted, bloodless, tearless, beyond the rim of an enchanted sea.'

But it could not be. The radio and the aeroplane broke down our isolation and brought us in among the peoples of the world. When the Crimean War ended it was months before this country knew it. A gun fired in Europe today reverberates among our hills before the smoke has cleared away. Today Australia takes her place at the Council tables of the world and her Federal Capital, Canberra, is one of the world's cities. It had to come also that an Archbishop should be appointed to such a capital to watch the interests of The Truth, to maintain advancement on world standards, to be on the alert for error enunciated in any part of the globe. That Archbishop would have to be a man of keen judgement, unafraid and outspoken, a man of zeal and piety. There was happily no need to look afield. That man was already here, the Bishop of Goulburn.

I remember how the dreamers in the past used forecast the advancement of fifty years. I remember one especially, a silver-tongued bishop who when he dipped into the future painted a picture that was all rose and gold, but I wonder did any of them foresee such a scene as we are witness of today. An Archbishop receiving the Pallium from the representative of The Holy Father, and that in his own Cathedral, supporting him a young auxiliary bishop who comes with the highest credentials for learning and judgement and piety who makes his bow to you today. We wish them length of years and God's blessing.[14]

Towards the end of the year he was back again in the pulpit of St Mary's Cathedral when on 24 November he addressed the Legion of Catholic Women:

About one hundred years ago there lived in Paris a harassed painter

---

14. *Sermon amongst Father Hartigan's papers.*

trying to keep his family by his art. He showed great promise but because of poverty had to paint not the pictures he wanted to paint, but those that would sell, and these were mostly suggestive figures in the nude which appealed then, as they do now, to prurient minds. He was just able to keep his family on the sales of these pictures, but one day he heard someone say: 'There goes a man who can make only nude drawings.' The remark stung him so deeply that he threw aside his models and devoted himself to something more ennobling. The world knows him today as Jean Francois Millet, one of the founders of a French School of Artists who painted things as they really are, not as certain adventurers would endeavour to have us see them. One of the first pictures exhibited by Millet in this mood was the world-famous 'The Sower', a work of epic grandeur which shows a farmer engaged in his common task of broadcasting the seed but which symbolises the Present preparing for the Future. The next picture was another masterpiece showing a cornfield being harvested. In the distance are the labourers building the stacks which stand white to the sun; and in the foreground are the figures of three earnest women whose sturdy forms are contrasted with the still beauty of the landscape as they bend to the task of picking up and saving the ears of corn which the reapers have missed. This painting is called 'The Gleaners' and a reproduction of it is included in every collection of great paintings.

Somehow the lesson of that picture kept recurring to me as I thought out what to say to you, The Legion of Catholic Women. The idea of comparing the world to a wheat field where the souls of men are the golden grain is as old as literature, and Jesus Christ in his sermons uses it often and always with telling effect. The Harvest indeed is great but the labourers are few. When the Great Sower said: 'Pray ye therefore the Lord of the Harvest that he send labourers into His Harvest', He was no doubt referring to priests and missionaries who equipped with positive instruments such as the Sacraments and the Holy Sacrifice of the Mass, are the real reapers of souls, but with all their zeal, and in spite of all their efforts, they will miss many a stalk which will be left on the ground to be trodden on and wasted. No harvest in any case is likely to yield one hundred per cent but with watchful and laborious picking up a great amount of what would otherwise be lost can be saved. This is how the Gleaners can prove themselves so valuable. I call you The Gleaners, not because what you are instrumental in garnering is just bits and pieces; on the contrary, it is of the greatest importance and substantially augments the total of the harvest.

Today you have assembled here at Mass as a wind-up of your official year's work and I am sure you feel in your hearts the sense of satisfaction that something you have attempted has been done; you will be careful to thank your God for the opportunity he has given you of doing your part in the great work which was the reason for Calvary and the Cross, and I am equally sure that, while your thanks go out to Him upon His Altar, His thanks come back to you for what you have done, or at least earnestly tried to do.

Your work is not always easy and sometimes it is made unpleasant by the criticism of some who should be working at your side. I must say that in a long experience I have been many times amazed at the grit and courage of Catholic women who give their best in working for causes such as you are interested in. They sometimes get more kicks than haporths. If they fail they are told about it prompt and often, if they succeed they seldom get that word of acknowledgment which means so much to every one of us, sometimes even they are treated as though they were doing pretty well for themselves out of the business. At best the good work entails much sacrifice—sacrifice of your time, your pleasures, your outings. Sometimes even the home has to suffer and I have often wondered what good husbands they must have to stand it. When you meet with success you come home elated with something singing in your heart, but there are times when having met with discouragement from without and, what is worse, perhaps with disunion among your own ranks, you come back feeling defeated, dragging aching feet and nursing a disappointed heart, and wondering if after all your efforts are worthwhile and if it wouldn't be just as well to pitch it and cut your losses.

What keeps you to the task is your christian wish to do something worthwhile as you pass through this life, which has been so aptly called A Valley of Tears. Your simple Faith reminds you that it was to save souls that one of the Divine Persons left his throne in Heaven to live as a labourer in the planting and the harvesting here below, and the greatest work that any mortal can be engaged on here is to lend a hand in whatever way he can in the work the Saviour came to do: 'And he must know that he who causeth a sinner to be converted from the error of his ways shall save his soul from death and cover a multitude of sins'. If men would but follow out the clear straight teaching of Christ they would arrive at their eternal home which is the purpose behind their creation; but some lives are cast in the thorn and the bramble and, through accident or misfortune or their own fault or what you will, drag on in privation and even misery.

We are told that suffering sanctifies, and so it can. It has made saints, but in the ordinary humdrum of life there are some who just can't take it. There are some eyes that cannot see God at all because of tears. Every act of mercy or social service that is done to make the lives of such as these brighter so that the eternal future may be clearer, is an act of religion, and if done with a clean intention will not pass unnoticed where even a cup of cold water given in His Name does not go unrewarded. Kipling in his untheological way wrote an In Memoriam poem to his brother which contains these lines:

> Beyond the loom of the last lone star
> Through outer darkness hurled
> Farther than ever comet dared
> Or hiving star swarm swirled
> Lives he with those who serve our God
> Because they served his world.

And I take it, Ladies of the Legion, that is just what you are doing: Serving God by serving His world. It is more than mere philanthropy. Philanthropy does its work solely because it loves the human kind, you do yours through Charity which means to love God above all things for His own sake and our neighbour as ourself for the love of God. And so there is a motive which raises your service above other human effort; you do it for the love of God and that is what makes it acceptable above. 'If I should give all my goods to feed the poor and did not do it for the love of God, it would not profit me anything in the hereafter.'

It is this underlying motive of Charity as Christians understand the word which places you in the tradition of the Catholic Church which throughout her long and eventful history has always regarded social service as a necessary auxiliary in the essential work of claiming souls for God. For that end she built the first hospital far back in the middle ages, mistakenly called the dark ages; she opened homes for the deaf and the blind and the dumb; she has taken the orphan from the stricken home and the foundling from the doorstep and placed them in the arms of her nuns and brothers animated with the spirit of Vincent de Paul; and on looking through a list of your welfare work modestly set out in the Legion Review, those are the lines on which you function. You have your patients. You are mindful of the blind and the deaf—those whose lives must be passed in darkness or in silence who have never seen the colours with which God has painted the canvas of the day, or ever heard the *sweet and sympathetic music which is the human voice. All these things must be pleasing.*

All these things, and your many other like activities which need not be mentioned in detail, must insure your own sanctification in the eyes of Him who while on earth turned aside many times to console the deaf and the blind and the sick and I can hear floating over the years His Divine assurance 'As long as you did it to one of these, you did it unto Me'. But continuing on down your list of good works, one comes to something more and notes that, still in the Catholic tradition, you have your Bethany, a guest-house for children whose mothers are temporarily indisposed. 'Suffer the little ones to come to me', and surely your work here knocks at the very door of that Divine Heart who likened the Kingdom of God to a child.

Then again you are interested in the welfare of the working girl and thereby save many from taking a path which leads to disaster. And again what you are unable to prevent, you endeavour to save, you visit the courts and lend your aid to rehabilitate those who have stumbled but who are given a chance to redeem themselves. Then one further notes that you are lending your help to the vital work of a training centre for delinquent girls. No words of mine can stress sufficiently the importance of these last-mentioned projects of yours. All one can say is, God bless you and the work.

The great problem of the Church is leakage. Do you know that of all those who are baptised, we lose nearly half? We can deal effectively with those who remain with us, but what becomes of the thousands we do not hold. They are daily swelling the ranks of those who would wreck all morality and uprightness in the world. If there is a dishonour and iniquity rampant today, it is because so many have drifted from the religion they were taught and ultimately abandon all christian principles while still calling themselves Christian. These are the young girls who are thrown upon their own protection to earn their living. If by your hostels, your court guilds and this training school for delinquents you can do something to stop their drifting away from their religion, you will accomplish a mighty work for your God and your country.

God and Country are linked very close together, and both will be served most usefully by attention to young girls who are coming to the time when they will have their own responsibilities in the home as the mothers and the first and most influential teachers of the citizens of tomorrow. If we are raising a band of women strong of character and firm of purpose whose ideal is goodness, whose breastplate is modesty, which after all is the same thing as decency, then all will be well, but if, on the contrary, we are producing a flippant generation who have thrown decorum and restraint to the winds, who regard it as old-fashioned to observe the common code of ethics, whose heart's desire is to have the so-called good time and pay the price in full for it, then

> *'the harlot's curse from street to street*
> *shall weave this nation's winding sheet'.*

It has happened before in the history of peoples and it can happen again. But I hasten to say that I am not pessimistic that it will happen again. Fully do I subscribe to the heartening words of a distinguished Spaniard: 'At the present day I swear to thee that there are women in the world of such excellence that I have more envy for the lives that they lead in secret than of all the sciences the ancients taught in public' and I do firmly believe that this big clean land of ours has daughters who still think it noble to be good, who are old-fashioned enough to be virtuous, and I am confident that our Catholic schools are turning out girls who have been taught that a woman's chief adornment is her self-respect, and I am confident also that they will ever be true to the splendid traditions of their religion, cherished by the nuns who trained them, back through a long line of valiant women, many of them martyrs in the noble cause, right back to the spotless Mother of God, the brightest of whose glories as sung by the Seraphim is that she was Immaculate.

> *'I think of Thee and what Thou art,*
> *Thy Majesty, Thy state,*
> *And I keep singing in my heart,*
> *Immaculate, Immaculate'.*

Would that the echo of the song the angels sing might ring in the heart of every Australian girl to remind her that virtue is a dowry greater than riches.

Unfortunately there is looseness in the lives of young women today which leads to irreligion and often to delinquency. And here I want to make it clear that I have no stone to throw at the modern girl. There is nothing wrong with modern ways except sin, and the abandonment of restraint which leads to sin, and that is as old as the world. The modern girl, in her new-found freedom and her open-air life, can be as innocent and as good as women ever were. We

301

complain that she spends too much time admiring the picture in the mirror. Well, did not they always do that? Anyway, twenty years will settle a lot of it. Again, she is too much a slave to the fashions. Well, why shouldn't she as long as she doesn't overstep the line? Fashion has always been the way of her sex. The expression of the female mind has always been by the way of adornment. New modes, new styles from season to season and who is to find fault if this universal striving for something new has evolved the smart, trim, clean set-up of the modern girl? You won't stop the march of fashion, and it is only wrong when it lays aside the common standards of decency; but you can direct it and that is where your sense of decorum, your good taste, and your example will come in.

But you tell me that she is so headstrong and so satisfied that the whole world belongs to young people and that older people should apologise for being in it at all. Twenty years is going to settle a lot of that, too. The younger set thinks that maturer women are fools and all maturer women know that the young ones are. Nevertheless, young women sometimes have their heroines and they are not always movie stars. Sometimes they admire very much some good woman whom they do not even known personally but whose good example of correct living is going to colour their lives, if not now, at least later on. But be careful how you walk. Prudishness never accomplished anything except creating opposition and prudes have been nagging young people from the beginning of time, pointing out that everything they do is wrong, and especially in the matter of the fashions. When girls first rode bicycles they threw up their hands in horror, also when they abandoned the unspeakable side-saddle and rode astride, the same when they started surfing. Nor did the way they dressed ever escape criticism. The first young things who tossed aside the crinoline were considered fast. Perhaps they were, for the bustle certainly gave no delusion of speed. Similarly every new style has been called daring right back to the old leg-of-mutton sleeves which Auntie wore to the picnic ... How futile and absurd it all was you can demonstrate for yourselves by taking out the family album and having a look at the museum pieces in the hats and the lace-up boots who were then accused of going too far.

All this is to the good in defence of the modern girl, but on the other hand it must be pointed out that her modern ways expose her to more dangers than beset her sisters in the past. For one thing, most of the salutary restraints have gone, and public opinion, which was a tremendous force in the prevention of wrong doing, has altogether changed. Things that one time would have put a person outside the pale for ever, pass unnoticed today. Then her reading and her entertainment are of a broader kind than those her mother knew. A book that would be banned as indecent a couple of generations ago would be a dull milk and water affair beside some of the accepted publications of today. Then her ambition to excel and become talked about are directed along lines which are not helpful. Beauty competitions are often nothing better than mere animal exhibitions, with never a reference to the intellectual ideal, let alone the spiritual or the religious. Then over all is that wretched fetish of a good time. Everything is measured by it and mostly it means breaking away from all restraint. Are we surprised if this leads to delinquency?

The female delinquent we have had always with us as well as her opposite number the male one, but we write him off, and keep harping upon the delinquent girl. We must admit that there are many things in our modern way of life which make her lot inevitable, and the pity of it is that many of these girls are not really bad;—silly, if you like, and blind certainly. Led astray for the most part, they are dancing down the primrose path of a good time which leads to a cliff that frowns above an angry sea which never gives up its dead. Some of them because of circumstances have to work for their living among strangers who look upon them as fair game. They are attractive. Yes, their simple doom is to be beautiful and with eyes blinded by the glare, they must take their chance removed from all parental care.

You with your guilds and your welfare auxiliaries may be the means of keeping away from the old folk at home by the fire a sorrow whose shadow once it falls is never lifted. You yourselves have never known the bitterness of shame, the foul thing has never breathed upon the fair name of the household angel in her teens who is the treasure of your life. It is one of the choicest gifts of God which has been given to you. Acknowledge it on your knees with a Domine, non sum dignus on your lips. Then, as a thanksgiving offering, throw yourselves right into the work you have in hand of helping others who have not been as protected as your own. If you can do anything worthwhile in this regard, future generations will arise and call you Blessed. If any hand can save them, that hand must surely be a woman's. There is the mother instinct behind what you do,—a woman's tenderness, a woman's understanding. Men acknowledge it but they cannot imitate it. So bend to the work like the Gleaners in the picture and happy will you be if through your instrumentality there should be saved even one solitary stalk forgotten by the reapers.[15]

15. Among Father Hartigan's papers.

On Sunday evening, 2 May 1949, Father Hartigan was the preacher at
Solemn Vespers in St Mary's Cathedral to mark the diamond jubilee of St
Patrick's College, Manly.

**God forbid that I should glory save in the Cross of Our Lord Jesus
Christ.** Gal. 6:14.

*The events we have been celebrating during the week when some
hundreds of priests have assembled to honour the Diamond Jubilee
of their Alma Mater, while focussing attention on the success which
has been achieved by St Patrick's College, Manly and its daughter
College, St Columba's, Springwood, brings naturally before us a
wider and more important thing—and that is the universality and
the longevity of the Priesthood of the Catholic Church. There are
about two hundred priests gathered at these celebrations; they have
come from every part of Australia, but their chief glory is not that
they are alumni of one particular College but that they are members
of the greatest force the world has known during the past nineteen
hundred years of its history. When we speak of a 'Priesthood' we
speak of a calling which in some shape or form is as old as man.
Whether as a separate institution or combined in the office of Elder,
Chief or Soothsayer, we find it prominently noted since History's
busy pen began to chronicle the splendid achievements and the
sordid mistakes of mankind; but of that wide conception, whether
devout or merely fanatic, whether fraudulent or sincere, it is no part
of my plan to speak tonight.*

*I want to bring your minds to the time when God's own Son made
man preached a gospel which had been foretold in figure and
prophecy long before His Virgin Mother wrapped the swaddling
clothes around Him, and which being above all material things, was
beyond all national aspirations. When His own time on earth was
drawing to a close, He instituted a Priesthood, and entrusted to it
the guardianship and the spreading of the most momentous Message
ever given to man, which like Himself was to stand for the
Redemption and the ruin of many, and for a sign that would be
violently contradicted. 'As the Living Father has sent Me, I also send
you' has been the marching orders given to every one of them, and it
would be a monumental work indeed were some historian to set out
in factual detail how they have performed the Mission that was so
solemnly entrusted to them.*

*That Magnum Opus would tell of obedient Apostles who
preached it, of Confessors who lived for it, of Martyrs who died for*

it, of missionaries who carried it to those who sat in darkness and the shadow of death. It would tell of a grim and heroic determination to hold the Truth and to teach it in spite of banishment, of torture and social ostracism greater than anything of its kind of which the world has records. It would show that the continuation and the vitality of civilization—which has never anywhere survived the abandonment of the Ten Commandments— has been maintained throughout the ages by the morality taught and practised by the Priests of the Catholic Church.

It would show that the survival and the spread of education through the world has been fostered by the Priesthood of the Catholic Church. That democratic Slogan: Education for All was first uttered by a Pope. The major Universities of Europe grew to what they are from schools taught by the monks, and even in their constitutions today you will find the clean clear legacy of the Catholic Priesthood glorying in nothing but the Cross of Christ by whom the world was so often crucified in them and they to the world.

It would show, too, that the cultivation of the beautiful by which the soul is drawn to the God of all Beauty because He is the God of Truth—the lifting of the mind by Art, Music and Literature was fostered by the Catholic Priesthood. Sometimes they were their only patrons. And if Art and Music and Literature have been sometimes profaned, it was never done by the Catholic Priesthood.

It would show that in all that stands for the relief of suffering and disease it has been prominent. It built the first hospital. The strides made in modern times in the alleviating the handicaps of deafness and blindness were suggested at least by the methods used by them to instruct those so afflicted in the rudiments of the Faith and in the preparation for the reception of the Sacraments. And so on and on.

But while considering these things as a means to a noble end, what shall be said of the priesthood as the Salt of the Earth since its institution? What shall be said of their prayer through the ages? The world has been saved by prayer more often than it dreams of. What shall be said of the Masses which have been offered that God might save what He created to adore and love Him but has turned time and time again to worship idols. This might be called the routine work of the Priesthood, and sublime is that Calling whose routine work is to perpetuate Calvary in a world that so often forgets the Crucifixion and the Redemption. 'Do this in commemoration of Me', 'from the rising of the sun to its setting', 'Whose sins you shall forgive they are forgiven them'. How sublime is that Calling whose daily routine *task is to work wonders such as this.*

That preamble sketch brings me to the first point I want to make. Though the Priesthood of the Catholic Church is above all nationality, every race and every colour has contributed to its glory. It had to be so or it would not have achieved its divine objective: 'Go teach ye all Nations' . . . But it was early recognised that the spiritual needs of a people are best served by a clergy that is race of the soil of the folk to whom they minister. This was a truism in missionary theories long before it induced Father Hand, the Founder of All Hallows College, Ireland, to send Irish priests to follow their countrymen scattered through America and Australia. Always when the missionary went to an alien land, after clearing the forest for the school and church, they trained the native lads to become new labourers in the universal vineyard—new apostles of the Truth. The church cannot be said to be virile in any country until the sons of the soil enter the Sanctuary.

When St Patrick went to Ireland he was quick to enrol the fervid and generous young men of the land in the great Christian army of self-immolation and devotion. He engrafted the indigenous piety and sacrifice on the parent stem and that was his great contribution to the world. The priesthood of the Catholic Church flourished with a luxuriance of its own in the land which the leader of his people had wrested from the druids. Her sons became prominent for scholarship and holiness on her own fruitful soil—Columba, the dove-like and Carthage, the wise—and have left behind them names which the followers of the Truth still cherish. Great priests like St Columbanus, St Gall and a hundred others carried the Faith revitalised by the warmth of Irish hearts on Irish soil, across the seas afar and brought it to a second spring where the crop had grown thin and spindly. In such numbers did they go on this holy service that the land that bore them became known, world-wide, as the Island of Saints and Scholars.

And this brings us to a point of major significance as we celebrate the diamond Jubilee of St Patrick's College, Manly. It was from that bud which Patrick engrafted on the parent stem unwithered after strenuous years of persecution and the penal days that the first green shoots of the Faith were planted in Australia. Father O'Flynn, Fathers Therry and Conolly, Father Power, Father Dowling, a Dominican, and Father McEncroe were the first to light here a fire akin to that which Patrick lit on Tara. This is a fact attested in our history. When the first Bishop of Australia, an English Benedictine, was seeking recruits to aid the few priests already working here, his agent Dr Ullathorne was not able to find volunteers anywhere but in Ireland. We were not wanted then, we were not popular. We were little more than a jail in a wide empty, forbidding, uninviting continent lying somewhere in poorly charted seas. But the Catholic Priests from Ireland took up the challenge, and in 1838 there appeared the first trickle of a stream which has not ceased to flow till the present day. Seeking no other glory than the Cross of Christ and the reward it brings hereafter, working at the beginning under an English Bishop, they have written a page of missionary history telling of endurance and devotion equal to anything the world has to show.

Then in due time came an Irish Archbishop, the first of his race to occupy this See of Sydney. Clad in the Roman Scarlet, a Prince of the Church, he was a man of vision and purpose. No one knew the history of missionary enterprise throughout the ages more thoroughly than Patrick Francis Cardinal Moran. No one knew the story of the planting and growth of the Catholic Church in our country better than he, its first major recorder. Though full of admiration for what had been done by his countrymen here, and was still being done, he realised as the Apostle of the Truth in his native land had realised fifteen hundred years before that the Church cannot be virile in any country till the sons of the soil take their place in the Sanctuary.

And so like St Patrick he set about enrolling the fervid and generous young men he saw around him in the great Christian army of self-immolation and devotion, engrafting thereby indigenous piety and sacrifice on the parent stem and linking the church he came to govern with the age-old and glorious traditions of the past. He founded St Patrick's College, Manly for the education of priests sixty years ago. In doing this, which was the greatest of many great services he rendered here, he rounded off the generous contribution to the universal Truth made by a long list of Irish missionaries headed by the immortal name of Father Therry.

It was not as easy a task as it might seem. He had to face the opposition of public opinion and its derision. Other attempts had been made but they had been only moderately successful, and it was stated openly by those who thought they knew that Australian boys—unlike their sisters who in numbers had entered convents— would never take kindly to the priestly vocation. The big white college which he erected at Manly was called a white elephant and was known as The Cardinal's Folly. But history has a happy way of debunking prophets of defeat. The number of Australian priests,

307

both Diocesan and Religious, serving at the Altar in their native land today is an answer and a refutation. Today the Cardinal's Folly in the tender role of a loved Alma Mater *welcomes to her Diamond Jubilee 200 priests of the Catholic Church drawn from every part of the Land of The Southern Cross representing 878 alive or dead who have passed through her halls, every one of whom is at her feet in spirit.*

And so on this her day of honour St Patrick's College looks back on the work of sixty years and proclaims that it is good. Great as was the progress made in the first sixty years of our Catholic history the progress in the last sixty has been greater. The signs of it are everywhere. Busy with their God-given task, churches, schools and convents are prominent in every city and landmarks on a hill in every town throughout the Commonwealth. The footpaths are black with people flocking to Mass, and the long white roads outback are vibrant with whirring wheels as the lovers of the old, old Faith hasten to the Tragedy of Calvary. The saving lessons taught by the shore of Galilee are living here in this Land of Promise.

For all this Manly College claims only her meed of credit. Just as her sons were not the first in the field, they have not been the only workers in the years just passed. There have been active in every sphere of Catholic work men and women of many lands and many obediences, all doing their share and glorying in nothing but the Cross of Jesus Christ, by whom the world is crucified to them and they to the world. Manly College, therefore, on this her day with her own sons gathered round her salutes with reverence her co-labourers in the wide and universal Vineyard. It is the work of God alone that matters.

She salutes with affection the many similar institutions of Ireland whose sons in the old days sowed in tears that she might reap in joy, and whose alumni are working still for the great Cause, shoulder to shoulder with her own. The renowned Colleges at Rome, also, and the other seats of theological and philosophical learning of Europe—to mention them all by name would seem like a page from the Litany, for there is scarcely a College in Western Europe to which we do not owe a debt.

She salutes with tenderness her younger sisters on Australian soil, Werribee, Banyo, St Francis Xavier's, Adelaide, St Charles, Perth; and across the Tasman she extends a hand to those of the sister Dominion with whom there are golden links in Dr Verdon, her first President and theirs, most Rev. Bishop Whyte a kindly professor here in her cradle days, Most Rev. Dr Liston, the second Manly

*student to be raised to the episcopate and the senior living, Most
Rev. Dr Lyons who at least began with her; Rgt Rev. Mons. Delaney,
her oldest living son in point of ordination; Rgt Rev. Mons.
Kennedy, Father Pat O'Neill, cherished names of the cradle days and
others who were with her for a time at least.*

*She salutes with no less accord the priests of the many Religious
Orders. Earnest men banded together in units under constitutions
drawn up by illustrious priests of the Catholic Church the world
over, they have won the admiration of the rest of us by their
devotion to the inner and holier way, by their spirit of prayer, their
zeal and their example calling us back to the fervour of our first
charity, stirring in us the grace that was given us all by the
imposition of hands and joined to us by the unbreakable bonds of
our common priesthood. She acclaims these twice-regimented men,
for the harvest is white and there is need of every reaper.*

*Then again looking back over the progress of sixty years, St
Patrick's College salutes with enthusiasm the Teaching Brothers. No
efforts however earnest in the building up of Religion and the
Church would have been availing if it had not been erected on the
broad foundation of the Catholic school. What manner of men are
these who dig the trench and mould the base? Endowed with every
gift of heart and brain and human strength they might have reached
the dizzy heights which men of the world so covet, instead of which
they have followed a beckoning star, obeying the same stern call
which led the hermit to the cell, they have laid aside all earthly
ambition, severed every human tie, have even become anonymous,
and without scrip or staff or purse have devoted their lives and their
talents to the fulfilment of the first and greatest commandment of
the Law and the second which is like unto it. The heart of the old
Alma Mater beats with a faster pulse as she salutes their self-
sacrifice and their devotion. Many a priest who has raised the
Consecrated Host and the Chalice on high in after years received his
first inspiration at a Brother's school, and many a humble old
teacher has magnified the Lord when the newly consecrated hands of
a lad he taught have been laid in affectionate blessing on his
silvering head. May the yoke be ever sweet and the burden light.*

*And what does St Patrick's say tonight as she salutes the
sisterhood. With an overflowing heart she sends them greetings. She
has seen them at their work in the orphanages, in the hospitals
ministering to the neighbour in need for the love of God, and the
second commandment of the Law which is so like unto the first is
sweetened by a woman's tenderness. She has seen them in their*

schools with Australian mothers of tomorrow around them, teaching them that above all things and in all things a woman's greatest adornment is her modesty, holding them in the glorious tradition of the Catholic Church back through a long line of virtuous daughters, some of them martyrs to maintain it—right back to the spotless Mother of God, the brightest of whose glories, as sung by the choirs of Heaven, is that she was the immaculate Mother of our Saviour. Consider the lilies how they grow. Consider how they grow in sinlessness and vestal whiteness, and I say to you that Solomon in all his glory was not arrayed as one of these.

And last but by no means least, Fellow Manly Priests,—you brothers of the mystic bond—the Alma Mater salutes you with a mother's love. It would be only mock modesty and quite dishonest to leave unexpressed the pride she has in you. You are bone of her bone and flesh of her flesh, you are her joy and her crown. If a mother's heart is big with joy when her successful children come back to her, then her heart is overfull tonight.

I wonder did her Eminent Founder when he dreamt his hopeful dreams of the fruit that would come from his enterprise ever picture a scene like this. I wonder did he dare to think that a successor in his See, but one removed, holding the same exalted rank as himself, would come from the College he founded. I wonder did he ever think that when the Archbishops and Bishops of Australia assembled to honour his memory on this the jubilee of the monument he erected that there would be so many of his own amongst them, and did he ever hope, my fellow Manly men, that 800 of you would in sixty years represent his legacy to the Church in Australia.

At such a time as this a mother's heart might be too overcharged to express the pride she feels. But if I might be her spokesman, I would pay you this compliment which stands unchallenged. You have shown yourselves true and worthy members of the Catholic Priesthood. Your traditions are the traditions that have been handed down. And you have been loyal, yes, always loyal. Loyal to him who sits in the Chair of The Fisherman, loyal to those who bear the Shepherd's Staff, loyal to the land that bore you, that and your solid Faith which is a wonder in an age when everything is questioned, when even eternal truth is debated. This is the Victory which overcometh the world, your Faith. All the scaffolding of the philosophers crumbles before that one word Faith; and thus equipped you have faithfully used your scholarship to expound the Truth in its entirety, adding nothing, changing nothing. And the tender mother is very proud of that. She gave you scholarship. In the waxen

*years she instilled into you that spirit of Prayer, your loyalty comes
to you in the blood of your forebears, but your Faith was given
mysteriously from Heaven.*

*It is your precious privilege to spend your gifts in your Native
Land among your own people—your ain folk, so to speak, and where
in the world are there hearts more kindly or warmer welcomes?
Where in the world is there better ground where the seed the sower
casts will bring forth such abundant fruit be it thirty, sixty or a
hundred-fold? Unprivileged perhaps but unfettered, unpersecuted,
you have an open field and the race will be to the swift and the
battle to the courageous. 'Go through the gates, go through the
gates, prepare the way for the people, make the road plain, pick up
the stones and lift up the standard', yes, bravely through the gates.
Your stars are shining now.*

*And a final word St Patrick's gives to you. Have no fear for the
future; When you lay down the torch and your day is done your
places will be taken by priests the counterpart of yourselves. Though
you have left forever the maternal roof for other scenes and duty,
though the waves around her feet still chant the immemorial
anthems, a band of young levites, eager for the work, are learning
the selfsame splendid things you conned beside the sea. St Patrick's
faces the coming years with confidence, God helping. Be it yours to
pray that that confidence will not turn to disappointment. Human
effort is nothing 'if God does not build the house they labour in vain
who build it'. Paul may plant and Apollo may water, but from God
alone can the increase come.* Non nobis, Domine, non nobis, *not to us,
O Lord, but to Thy Name be all the glory of Manly's work for God and
for Australia.*[16]

16. *Among Father Hartigan's papers.*

14   *Final Illness and Death*

The year 1951 marked for Father Hartigan the beginning of the illness that was to bring about his death. First there were unexplained bleedings and weakness—one morning he collapsed as he was at Mass in the chapel and Father Jeremiah Hogan S.J. who happened to be there that morning (he was a regular visitor as one of the confessors for the Sisters) was able to give him the Sacrament of the Sick. He was in Lewisham Hospital then for tests, again for a couple of months in the middle of 1951, and briefly once more at the end of the year and yet again for a couple of months early in 1952.

During this time, Monsignor George Crennan, a friend from his days in Wagga and the Federal Director of Catholic Immigration, came to Rose Bay to assist him in the chaplaincy work. It was a great help to have a friend in this capacity and the priest-poet was deeply appreciative.

Between his spells in hospital he was working on his final book on the history of Darlinghurst parish. He was aided and abetted—to put it mildly—by his friend Monsignor Tom Wallace, the parish priest of Darlinghurst, and he found the story of the parish an absorbing one. Monsignor Wallace in March 1952 provided him with thirty titles as possibilities. The ultimate choice was **On Darlinghurst Hill.** One of those rejected was **A Church was Built.** Later Father Hartigan thought they might well have used them both: **On Darlinghurst Hill a Church was Built.**

The book was published by Ure Smith and the first week sales came close to setting a record in Sydney; a week later it was announced that the first edition was already rapidly selling out. It was reprinted the following month, and again a few weeks later. The Red Page of the **Bulletin**[1] was most complimentary:

In its easy, light-hearted way the monograph is really a model of its kind, full of good stories and colourful personalities that would make it readable anywhere. It has been put together not by some desperately polite and nervous amateur, as are so many local histories, but by a writer who is, for all his apparent casualness, a born raconteur.

1. *28 May 1952*

312

To introduce this book, Monsignor Wallace arranged for the editor of **The Catholic Weekly**, Jim Kelleher, to interview Father Hartigan. He produced a centre spread of two full pages in the issue of 8 May 1952 and long instalments on the two succeeding weeks. Superbly written, these accounts of his six-hour interview tell a great deal about 'John O'Brien' and his writing.

Bishop Henschke was one of the many who wrote to thank him for his new book:

> Bishop's House,
> Wagga Wagga, N.S.W.
> 19 May 1952.

Dear Monsignor Hartigan,

Thanks for a copy of Darlinghurst Hill—I have read and enjoyed it which is a tribute to the author as I am not very concerned about Sydney parishes. But this is more than a history of Darlinghurst and so has a general interest.

I hope the health is better—it is a good sign that you can publish a book and give interesting interviews. It was a stroke of genius to begin your reminiscences on the day the price of the Weekly was put up.

All here with the exception of Tom Desmond are well and his trouble is his tonsils—or, to be more exact, the one on the Epistle side. Probably it is out by now—he went to Sydney over a week ago.

> Every best wish from
> Yours sincerely in Christo
> † F.A. Henschke.[2]

Another warm letter of congratulations came from a friend of his Manly days, Bishop James Liston of Auckland.

> Bishop's House,
> Ponsonby,
> Auckland W.1. New Zealand.
> 9 June, 1952

Dear Monsignor,

Let me thank you ex corde for the thoughtfulness of your gift and the pure delight the reading of Darlinghurst Hill has been; two readings already and others to come. Sydney is of course known to you, but how you have been able to walk right into the heart of men and places is another matter;

2. Letter among Father Hartigan's papers.

A portrait of Father Hartigan taken in 1951 at the time his book ON DARLINGHURST HILL was published. This history of the Darlinghurst parish came close to setting sales records during its first week of publication. (Photo courtesy of May Moore Studio)

our gain. Those guys who love him would have been glad to read a sketch
of the present pastor!
    I hope you have made or are making a good recovery from your illness.
A visit to New Zealand later in the year would be in order!

Every kind wish and greeting,
Yours sincerely,
  † *James M. Liston,*
  Bishop of Auckland.[3]

Monsignor Wallace also arranged a dinner at the Australia Hotel to
launch the book and he brought the author from Lewisham Hospital. He
got him to the May Moore Studio and had him photographed in his
monsignorial robes—quite an achievement.

At the dinner one of the guests Father Hartigan met was his friend of
many years, Monsignor James Freeman. His light-hearted quip was:
'Have you come for my resurrection, Jimmy?'

During those early months of 1952 Annie's husband, Dick Mecham,
was taken to Lewisham Hospital for an operation. A malignancy was
discovered and Dick did not recover from the operation, dying in April.
His death was a great grief to Father Hartigan as he was very close to all
the family and saw an even heavier burden on Annie's shoulders, and at a
time when the years and their sorrows had taken their toll of her and she
was far from well.

What was to be his final stay in Lewisham began at the end of July.
Visitors poured in to see him and he greeted them all with interest. There
was a special welcome, of course, for his own folk, Annie particularly,
and for his fellow priests and his friends from Narrandera days. Letters
came from everywhere, that from Mother McGuiness of Rose Bay had an
unusual provenance:

Aircraft, T.A.A.,
Macdouall Stuart,
about 8000 ft. above
Nullarbor Plain
15 August 1952.

Dear Monsignor,
    This is a greeting from the skies, since my attempt to contact you by
'phone last Wednesday was unsuccessful—Somehow I must secure your
blessing before leaving Australian waters—(I drop from the Perth sky about

3. *Ibid.*

9.30 this evening). When you read this, please raise your hand in blessing towards the west to speed Mother Lista Coen and me Romewards. We both have a special claim on you. Mother Coen was speaking of your Father and Mother. My claim is more recent, but is based on our joint-company to run Rose Bay Convent.

As the address tells you we are 'Westering', not Home—alas. The air trip has been of the smoothest. There was an hour and a half's delay at Melbourne because the aircraft chartered for our flight was bogged in Canberra's mud so the M.P.'s boarded another 'Skymaster'. Two are on this craft so the air-hostess tells us, but more interesting are five lads of 11 or 12 in full midshipmen's uniform. They look as if they are on the stage for 'Pinafore' but they are only school boys from the naval college somewhere near Canberra!

We enjoyed 24 hours at our Malvern convent. Mother Woodlock had not been well for some months, as she had severe attacks of Tic Douloureux; though better, she looks fragile. Unfortunately she has never learnt the art of taking care of herself.

And how are you Monsignor? It was a relief to hear a good report from Monsignor Crennan, though I hope you will wait your friend's return[4] before going home. I do not like the thought of your being in the Villa alone.

This feast of the Assumption had been a gala day at R.B., your friends Judy and Betty with two others making their vows. To us older people there is always something inspiring in the simple enthusiasm of these young girls making their offering. Crashaw's summary of today's dogma 'Heav'n must goe home', seems, in a distant way, true of them also.

With every good wish for a speedy recovery, and sincere gratitude, Monsignor,

I remain,
Yours respectfully,
Dorothy McGuinness.[5]

Almost at the same time he had a letter[6] from Papua from Sister Annette Herbert which also gave him great joy. She recalled his goodness to her when long ago he was inspector of schools.

During the weeks following the publication of **On Darlinghurst Hill, The Catholic Weekly** published some of the poems that were not in **Around the Boree Log,** such as 'Imelda May' and 'Cooney's Daughter'.

---

4. *Monsignor Crennan was away for a few weeks in Europe on migration work.*
5. *Letter among Father Hartigan's papers.*
6. *Dated 10 August 1952; this letter was referred to in Chapter 4 dealing with his years in the schools.*

There was one recent one amongst them, 'The Durkins', inspired by a family Dame Enid Lyons knew at Devonport, Tasmania. At Lewisham Father Hartigan received this letter:

> St Thomas More's School
> Newstead, Tasmania
> 25.8.'52

Dear Monsignor Hartigan,

I am one of the many 'Durkins' and on behalf of those Durkins I would like to express my appreciation of your recent poem entitled The Durkins.

Two years ago one of our Tasmanian students for the priesthood told me of an address given to the students at Manly by a priest, on your poems, during the course of which he mentioned the poem about 'The Durkins', on which you were then working.

A few weeks ago we had the pleasure of a visit from our former Archbishop, Dr Simonds of Melbourne. He told me all about the poem then and promised to send it to me immediately it was published.

This morning however my parish priest presented me with my first copy published in The Catholic Weekly. I think you might have some idea of how I felt. I read it and re-read it, picking out each individual as they suited.

I am hoping to be able to show it to my father this week. To him I think it will be a foretaste of the joy that is his to come. He has shouldered the many crosses of recent years in a spirit of great Faith. Mother died in 1943 and three years later our eldest sister, Agnes died leaving three baby children. We were eight in all, five boys and three girls. Our home was in Devonport. Catherine and I became Sisters of St Joseph.

I wonder did you ever know Fr John Durkin of Maclean, N.S.W.? He was Dad's brother. He died in 1947. He was a dear and I feel we owe a lot to his prayers.

I believe, dear Monsignor, that at present you do not enjoy the best of health. I am sorry to know that. I would like to assure you of a daily remembrance in my prayers, always. Especially will I remember you in my daily Mass and Communion. Never will I forget, I promise.

Please accept dear Monsignor, my thanks and I am sure the thanks of all 'The Durkins', for the time and energy you spent on your latest poem.

With many prayers and asking your priestly blessing.

> I remain,
> Yours gratefully,
> Sister Mary Alban
> (Anna M. Durkin)

May God Bless you.[7]

The poem also brought a letter from a young Durkin priest just ordained from the Victorian seminary at Werribee. Allan Fraser, the member for Eden Monaro in the Federal Parliament, likewise wrote, as his secretary was a Durkin. It was my privilege at that time to reply to these letters on Father Hartigan's behalf.

As the weeks went by at Lewisham and Father Hartigan got no better but grew thinner and weaker all the time, everyone, including the patient himself, realised he would not recover. The diagnosis was inoperable cancer of the intestine.

Cardinal James Freeman reminisced with John Yeomans of the **Herald** (Melbourne):

I was the first person to go into his bedroom after he had been told he was dying. It was then I realised most of all what a remarkable man Father Hartigan was. He said to me: 'This is going to be an interesting time, Jim—very interesting, indeed. And by a bit of luck I got a royalty cheque yesterday from some of my writings and that should pay for the funeral'.[8]

As he grew weaker he was moved to a more commodious room which was alongside a small chapel on the first floor. He made a joke of the changeover: 'It will be easier here to get my coffin out'. Really he rejoiced in the change and a remark to Bishop Muldoon, then a priest on the teaching staff of his beloved Manly, revealed the depth of faith beneath his apparent nonchalance. They were speaking of the fact that the head of his bed was against the wall where the tabernacle was in the room next door. Father Hartigan observed: 'Tom, I've got my head next to His head; and it's a good place to be'.

He was cared for wonderfully by his doctors and particularly by the Sisters of the Little Company of Mary whom he had known and loved for so long. The chaplain was Father Vince Kelly whom he knew well from his frequent stays in the hospital and they appreciated each other. Father Kelly visited him often and he was with him at the end.

I was called out of the confessional at Drummoyne on Saturday evening 27 December and told that the end was near. When I got to Lewisham it seemed as though he was waiting for me. 'All the best,

7. *Letter among Father Hartigan's papers.*
8. *The* Herald *(Melbourne), 13 June 1975, reprinted in the* Messenger of the Sacred Heart, *January-February 1976, p. 6.*

Frank' were his last words as I gave him the absolution he always requested.

On the following Tuesday Solemn Requiem Mass was celebrated at St Mary's Cathedral. Celebrant of the Mass was Rev Dr John Harper, parish priest of Junee (Wagga diocese), friend and admirer of Father Hartigan ever since as a newly ordained priest he met him in Rome; Very Rev Monsignor Tom Wallace, parish priest of Darlinghurst and a close associate was the deacon, myself the sub-deacon. Cardinal Gilroy was at the time legate to a Eucharistic Congress in India but there were in the sanctuary four archbishops: Dr Eris O'Brien, Auxiliary to His Eminence; Dr Justin Simonds, Coadjutor Archbishop of Melbourne; Dr Terence McGuire, Archbishop of Canberra and Goulburn; and the Apostolic Delegate, Archbishop Marella. Two bishops also were present, Dr Francis Henschke of Wagga and Dr John Toohey, Coadjutor Bishop of Maitland. More than a dozen monsignori and a large number of priests joined with a large crowd of religious and laity in paying their respects. It was reported[9] that every religious order in the archdiocese was represented, and amongst the laity were some who were associated with him in the literary world. His two sisters and a sister-in-law and four nieces and two nephews were the principal mourners in the congregation.

It was not the practice at the time in Sydney to have a panegyric at a Requiem Mass; its absence was symbolic of the stilling of a voice that had so often beautifully farewelled a fellow priest.

Cables were received from New Zealand from his friends there of Manly days, Bishop Liston (Auckland) and Monsignor Kennedy (Christchurch) who were fellow students and Bishop Whyte (Dunedin) who had been on the teaching staff in his time. Bishop Young, Auxiliary to Archbishop McGuire, sent Father Parker Moloney, Administrator of Yass, to represent him and the town of Yass, Monsignor Hartigan's birthplace.

He was buried at the little Catholic cemetery of North Rocks alongside his mother and father. This cemetery was originally the burial ground of the Sisters of Mercy of Parramatta. His sister Lily (Sister M. Gonzaga) was buried there in 1928 and his parents lie close to her.

The following week **The Catholic Weekly** contained a beautiful tribute to Father Hartigan from the gifted hand of his great friend, Monsignor (now Cardinal) James Freeman:

When Monsignor Patrick Hartigan died last Saturday week Australia

9. The Catholic Weekly, 8 January 1953.

319

*lost one of her most colourful priests, and thousands who never saw
him were suddenly aware of deep personal loss.*

*But his death meant more than that. He had grown up at the end
of epoch, at a time when the Catholic pioneers still rode in their
horse-drawn vehicles to the 'little church on the hill' and the Faith
was still building up in the lonely bush homes and under the roof of
the 'old bush school'.*

*He caught and held the spirit of those times in the things he wrote
until he himself became identified with it. He became a poetical
link between the past and the present. And now the link is broken.*

*Tall in stature, impressive in appearance and manly in everything,
he viewed the world of men and things with keen and kindly
observation and relayed what he saw with rare clarity in his speech
and in his writings. It did seem at times as though he viewed the
cavalcade of life from the sideline, as a sympathetic spectator rather
than a busy participant. The world fascinated him without absorbing
him; perhaps he lived in a world of his own.*

*To hear him talk when relaxed and at home was to get a better
appreciation of the man and of the things he wrote whether in
poetry or in prose. Without pretension or pedantry he spoke easily of
poets and poetry, art and artists, the country and its people,
automobiles and their parts. His conversation was charged with apt
quotation and yet he played his knowledge down so well that it was
only afterwards that you realised its breadth and its depth. He was
possessed of a droll and casual humour, which was keen without
being cutting and spontaneous to the point of surprise, and yet when
you learned to listen for it there was an underlying note of
wistfulness which disappeared as suddenly as it came only to linger
afterwards in the memory like the light of the retina when the flash
has gone. It would be inaccurate to describe him as a humorist
unless one had in mind that real humour which is only a step away
from a sigh.*

*He was a man of broad sympathy and a deep tender feeling while
contriving more or less unsuccessfully to conceal them both; but
basic emotions when they are strong cannot be hidden for long and
inevitably these things flowed over into his speech, his writing and
above all his actions. Today there are many people who for real
personal reasons will bless his memory with a prayer.*

*The sorrows of little children, the hardships of country people, the
generous sacrifice of nuns in primitive schools, the difficulties of
pioneer priests; these things were very real to him, and the evidence
of his feeling is easily detected.*

*It is true that he had his moods. Which of us is devoid of them?
Times when for a moment the humour and the buoyancy seemed to
disappear; and he withdrew more obviously into the world of his
own making, but they were like passing clouds on a bright summer's
day, and in the end they only emphasised the brightness. Above all,
he had the faculty of laughing at himself, which is in itself the badge
of greatness because it is indicative of humility.*

*The city clergy saw little of him in the days of his active ministry.
Occasionally he came up for clerical functions and at such times he
was always in demand as an after-dinner speaker. Never did he
disappoint. Those who heard him are not likely to forget the
impression he made nor can they fail to remember the originality,
the wit and the eloquence which were blended so impressively in
the things that he had to say. In his preaching he was not an orator
in the embellished sense of that word; partly because he was
diffident of ostentation and partly because his practical turn of mind
kept him close to reality when otherwise his imagination might
have tempted him to take flight. Yet to hear him preach was to get
an impression of solid piety, sound common sense and a sincere
preoccupation with the love of God. The pity is that he will be heard
no more and the spring is dry from whence the sparkling waters
came.*

*Shunning ostentation in his own life and being rendered uneasy by
its display in others, it followed logically that his own personal
devotion, for all its depth, was generally undemonstrative. But once
again to know him at all was to become keenly aware of the deep
spiritual currents that stirred in his soul; particularly his awesome
devotion to the Holy Sacrifice of the Mass and his tender affection
for the Mother of God. Right to the end, the prayers and liturgy of
the Canon[10] struck a note of wonder in his heart which was as
strong as on the day of his ordination.*

*I have used the word 'diffident' already in describing him and that
advisedly because I believe it contained a key to his character, but
never could this term be more aptly used than in describing his own
approach to his writings, particularly his poetry. He was naturally
pleased when people enjoyed his poems, but he stoutly refused to see
in them anything that approached excellence. He frequently spoke of
them as 'jingle' and that not with the attitude of a poseur who waits
for contradiction, but rather with the genuine humility of one who*

10. *Now more often called the Eucharistic Prayer, i.e. the central part of the Mass.*

sincerely depreciates his own work while admiring the talents of others. Moreover, he had grown up in the tradition of the old bush ballad and had lived long enough to see that medium give place to the abstract and impressionistic style of today. He respectfully saluted the change, though he never warmed to it, and he admitted it with his intellect though it did nothing to his heart. It would seem, too, that the change daunted him and sapped his confidence. In later years anything he wrote had to be literally wrung from him and even then he seemed to wait expectantly for the criticism he was sure would follow. Even today there still remain dozens of poems scribbled in idle moments on loose pieces of paper or between the covers of an old exercise book. He was loth to bring them into the light of day in his lifetime; perhaps, now that he has gone, there will come a harvester to gather the sheaves.

It was typical of the man that when at last he had to make a final break from his country home, from old associations and friends, he still contrived to build up new interests and new enthusiasms in the city, to fill up the gaps that the break had caused. The harbour and the sea for ever fascinated him. He watched their changing moods and colour with the air of one who is constantly making a new discovery, and the ships that passed by his Rose Bay home were the objects of his constant attention. He even made a study of the flags that flew at their mastheads and of the messages they had to tell.

But it did seem that even here his interest was wider than the object of his vision and that for him each ship told a story to which his imagination alone had the key. Old friends came to visit him while new friendships were building up, for he made friends without noticing it and retained them without effort. He probably died without knowing how many admirers he had.

When at last the signs of serious illness started to make their sudden and ominous appearance, he was intrigued by the mystery, but as usual he kept his concern to himself. Solicitous enquirers were greeted with that same droll whimsicality which betrayed so little while it hid so much. Then as apparent recovery was followed by further attack in stern regularity it was obvious to his friends that there was something seriously wrong, but to no one was it more obvious than to himself. What were his real thoughts during that period no one will ever know. Finally, when he was told with gentle discretion that his illness could only have one end, that, in fact, his days were numbered, he looked at death with the same calm detachment with which he had always looked at life. 'When a man has passed seventy', he said, 'he has had a good innings and he

shouldn't complain. At best, he could only have a few years more'.
So propped up on his pillows with his strength failing every day, he
waited for the end, serene and undisturbed, without any touch of
melancholy or regret—watching the lights go out one by one and
having no fear of the darkness because of the faith that burned
brightly in his soul. Never was his life so grand as in the days of its
passing.

He has gone now and his image will linger long in the hearts of
the thousands who revered him.[11]

The other beautiful tribute that appeared was in the pages of the
Messenger at the time, and was republished in that periodical in the issue
of January-February 1976. It was written by Father Owen Cosgriff who, as
curate at Ardlethan and elsewhere in the dioceses of Goulburn and
Wagga, knew Father Hartigan well.

It formed part of a continuing series, 'His Reverence', with a fictitious
Father Gilhooley as the principal character.

Father Gilhooley, having attained the right atmosphere, laid the
book on his knees. All he wanted to do now was to sit, think,
reminisce and wallow in Pathos. He began to wonder how many
others had heard of Monsignor Hartigan's death, and had reached for
the Boree Log to re-read the poems of the author, now dead. Then, the
undeveloped silence was shattered by the door-bell ringing.

It was old Dave Finnan. Now it was a toss-up whether Dave was
the personification of solidity or slowness. He was solid, physically,
mentally, as a citizen, as a Catholic and as a toiler; and his slowness
was just as comprehensive. He was not the type of conversationalist
Fr Gilhooley needed in his present mood, but he had to admit Dave.
Then, he had to settle down to hearing the preliminaries that Dave
always supplied before he revealed the actual purpose of his visit.
But Dave surprised him with a new technique.

'I've come', he said, 'to offer you my sincere sympathy on the
death of your old friend Monsignor Hartigan'. 'That's very nice of
you, Dave', replied a softened host. 'As a matter of fact, I've just had
the Boree Log out, going over the old poems, remembering old
times and recalling the days we had together. See—there's the
author's signature on my copy—P. Hartigan, alias John O'Brien'. 'I
wish I had his signature on mine, too', answered Dave, 'but I didn't

11. The Catholic Weekly, 15 January 1952.

*have to get the book out. I learnt all the poems years ago. I know
them all because I think John O'Brien was the greatest genius of
them all'. Fr Gilhooley indulged in a bit of appreciative thought
before he said, 'Yes, Hartigan was a mighty genius. Of course, Dave,
we never got around to calling him "Monsignor". When we were
talking to him he was "Paddy" and when we were talking about
him, somehow, he was always just "Hartigan"!'*

*'Like his "Hanrahan",' replied Dave, 'Do you know, Father, when
we read that Hanrahan poem the first time we all knew
"Hanrahan". We all knew dozens of "Hanrahans", but none of us
had the genius to take "Hanrahanism" and use it to emphasise the
marvellous goodness of God. Not one of us but "John O'Brien".'*

*'What's that?' asked Fr Gilhooley, wondering if he were really
listening to old Dave Finnan. And he was thinking that if Hartigan
could rouse the enthusiasm of Dave Finnan, well, he was a genius
all right.*

*'Oh, it isn't only Hanrahan', continued the inspired Dave, 'no
doubt you've read a good bit about the rosary?'*

'Yes, a goodish bit', agreed His Reverence.

*'How much of it could you understand?' asked Dave, and that
question made Fr Gilhooley realize that a spark could be struck even
from the stoniness that was Dave Finnan.*

*'Well,' he admitted, 'I haven't understood all of it, but you have
to make allowances for mystics, theologians, visionaries and deep
meditators'.*

*'Hmmmm' murmured the satisfied Dave, ' "John O'Brien" wasn't
a mystic, nor a theologian and he probably never had a vision, but
he was still able to pen the greatest memorial ever written to the
Rosary'.*

*'I beg your pardon'—from the incredulous priest, 'What's this
you're saying? Remember that some of the "also rans" to Hartigan
are saints and scholars, the cream of the centuries'.*

*Dave thought for a while, and then, headed for heresy or not, he
said: 'Who saw the toiler's hands so hard that the beads were not
felt and the kids had to yell: "Glory, Dadda, Glory—and he gloried
like a shot!" ' You've heard of people with their feet on the
ground—well—"John O'Brien" had his knees on the earthen floor of
a pioneer's shanty. He heard the exiles taking out their insurance on
their faith and their future. There is nothing mystical about simple
people talking to Our Lady in words of two syllables. And, Our Lady
liked it that way because they got "the bit of land"—"the hurted
hand", "the neighbour's troubles" and "the schooling", they were*

all "set right", and God knows how many mothers kneel to receive the blessing of an ordained son because "John O'Brien" wrote—"And little John, her pride, it was he who said the Mass in black the morning that she died". The old pioneers, they knew how to circle vocations with rosaries but we might have forgotten, had it not been for the Boree Logger.

Father Gilhooley was silent; impressively silent. Dave went on: 'A spiritual democrat, that's what John O'Brien was. He immortalised the people because it was the people who kept the faith for us, but he didn't stop there. Nothing was too unimportant for his kindly eye, and who else would have remembered the priest's gallant horse, or who ever thought before him of singing the song of the humble housekeeper?'

'Good on you, Dave', said Fr Gilhooley encouragingly, 'Tell me more; you know the real Hartigan'.

'I'll tell you more all right', said Dave, teething the bit, 'Take The Old Mass Shandrydan. It was a container for the poorest parishioners, the O'Briens—they got the dust from the gigs and buggies as the people who despised them hurried from their presence. Yes, they lumbered into Mass last, but bring out your theologians on the Mass, and see which one of them can tell a better story of appreciation of the Mass than "John O'Brien". He saw what it cost people to get to Mass, and it will not be his fault if the lesson is ever forgotten. Yes, he gave those people their due, and their glory'.

'Well, Dave', said Fr Gilhooley, 'You knew him, too. He was a simple man and modest. He loved the people, I remember him best as a yarnspinner. Many's the early night I've intended to have, and at 4 a.m. "Paddy" was still talking, keeping company with the glowing "boree". He had a habit of looking from the cigarette he was rolling to catch his listener's eye, and once fixed through those pince-nez glasses he used to wear, well, he could almost convince you that some of his yarns were true. He liked telling a yarn against himself, like the one from the time he was inspecting schools. On the black-board he wrote—"Jack buyed a horse",—turning to ask what was wrong with it. For a moment no response, and then a son of the Mulga puts up his hand and says, "Pretty rotten writing". Then, he was the grandest preacher. He'd preach on "Conway's cow", "Halloran's broken fence", "carting the wool" or "the sanctuary bell" and it was always the same: poetic and eloquent'.

'How did he die?' asked Dave. 'It was remarkable,' was the answer. 'All his life, Hartigan was scared of colds. They terrified *him, yet when he was told he had cancer it put a smile on his face. He was happy, yet he was facing death from an incurable disease. He was happier dying than he was living. He had not a bit of fear at all.' 'I'm glad to hear that', said Dave. 'I'm glad he felt that he was going home to the Blessed Lady for whom he did so much, home to the "Caseys", the "Hanrahans", to "Father Pat", and the myriad "Irish mothers", and the grateful "Josephines".'[12]*

Rev Dr John Harper, mentioned earlier in these pagers as Father Hartigan's companion for much of his trip in Europe in 1925, was ever a close friend and enthusiastic admirer of P.J.H. He very kindly volunteered these observations:

It is very difficult to convey to anyone who did not know him personally the essential personality and character of P.J.H. Those of us who knew and loved the man may list his gifts of mind and heart and yet fail to adequately convey the particular flavour of a unique personality.

His well-stocked mind was served by an eloquent and humorous tongue which made him the centre of any gathering he happened to be in. On many occasions I have been present at small gatherings of clerics where a couple of hours passed like so many minutes as we listened to the wit and wisdom accompanying the flood of anecdote and reminiscence. On one of those occasions the great Archbishop of Melbourne, Daniel Mannix, had to use his handkerchief to wipe away his tears of laughter.

Unrivalled as a conversationalist himself, he had the rare gift of drawing out others, even chance acquaintances, to speak of their personal interests; they immediately sensed that here was one who was personally and sympathetically interested in what they were saying.

His gift of communicating with others was quite extraordinary and knew no barriers of religious or social standing. An old pensioner who lived in a somewhat dilapidated shack near the railway bridge at Narrandera spoke glowingly of 'the fine man' who sometimes dropped by. Not a Catholic, she said, 'he just sits outside on a box and we talk rough'.

Writing under the name of John O'Brien, P.J.H. had an enormous success with two volumes of poetry, Around the Boree Log *and* The

12. Messenger of the Sacred Heart, *Melbourne, January-February 1976.*

Parish of St Mel's. *He always seemed to me to be genuinely surprised at their popular success and as edition followed edition remarked he was glad his 'jingles' apparently brought pleasure to many people. While somewhat better than jingles, as he called them, his verses couldn't be called poetry in the serious sense of the word.* But in the Boree Log *in particular, he expressed his admiration for the deep faith and warm hearts of the Irish pioneer Catholics of the bush, leaving an abiding memorial to them in felicitous and tuneful verse.*

However, it seems to me that his true ability as a writer is to be seen in his prose works. The most important of these was a series of sketches about the pioneer Irish priests of Australia called In Diebus Illis.[13] *There is nothing of the dry bones of history in those pages. They are living literary re-creations of the generous-hearted priests he so much admired. Those pioneer priests share with us a debt to the man who has left us human and unforgettable portraits of heroic priests worthy of the rough and hard times they endured. Maybe his real poetic gift is to be found in the pages of his prose, the balanced cadence of the sentences having some right to be called prose poetry.*

If ever a man deserved the somewhat trite description of 'being of childlike faith' it was P.J.H. His deep and simple faith was doubtless imbibed at the knee of that 'Little Irish Mother' and her 'Trimmings on the Rosary'. No theologian in the formal sense, he sometimes ruefully admitted that he just couldn't understand the higher flights of theological disputation. I remember his marvelling at an incident he read in Reminiscences of a Maynooth Professor *by Professor Walter McDonald. The professor gives a long account of himself defending a priest who had been cited in Rome because of some alleged false teaching with his 'kinetic theory of grace'. P.J.H. said to me, with genuine puzzlement, 'Fancy a man losing his soul because he was deemed heretical on the kinetic theory of grace!' Such heights of theological controversy were beyond him since his own certitude went straight to the heart of the matter with his abiding reverence for the Mass and the Mother of Christ. The parishioners of St Mel's, Narrandera, were indeed privileged to assist at the Mass and hear the golden words of a man who truly believed in what he was doing.*

As in so many other aspects of his activities, it is difficult to describe P.J.H. as preacher for anyone who hadn't the privilege of

13. *Later appearing in book form as* The Men of '38 and Other Pioneer Priests, *Lowden Publishing Co., Kilmore, Vic., 1975.*

actually hearing him. He practised none of the usual arts of oratory but his rather flat voice could hold a packed church spellbound as he preached the occasional sermon for some special function. He did this by the sheer poetry of his spoken prose and his always original approach to his subject. I well remember his doing just that when he preached the occasional sermon in Wagga Wagga Cathedral for the Jubilee of the diocese. The Australian Hierarchy were there and P.J.H. enthralled them and the packed Cathedral as the words of a literary artist joined the celebration of the moment to a fascinating account of the history of Cobb and Co's Coaches in the district! I can even remember one of the phrases when he spoke of a moment in our early history 'when convict hulks scarred the bosom of the fairest waterway in the world'.

As an after-dinner speaker he was unrivalled, particularly at clerical gatherings. Such speeches were constantly punctuated with laughter and applause. I remember an occasion at Bendigo, in Victoria, when P.J.H. and I arrived unannounced the evening before an Episcopal Consecration. [14] *The Administrator knew not P.J.H. and we could hardly complain when the reception given 'two blow-ins', as P.J. called us, was somewhat frosty. But wiser counsels apparently prevailed and the aggrieved Administrator asked P.J.H. to propose the toast of the Hierarchy at the luncheon following the consecration. It was an extraordinary performance 'off the cuff' and the clergy's appreciation of the humorous sallies that fell from his lips was heartily shared by the Bishops themselves. Before we left, the delighted Administrator thanked P.J.H. for playing such a great part in the success of the whole function.*

To ask what was the essence of the extraordinary charisma of P.J.H. is to pose a most difficult question. To reply that he was warm-hearted, had a great and sympathetic knowledge of human nature, and was eloquent, witty and humorous with words still doesn't fully convey the real picture of the man. But I think his warm-hearted sympathy and understanding of human beings was the main factor which brought instant rapport even when met by strangers.

Maybe a summing-up would be to say that he loved people, was always perceptively appreciative of their good qualities and passed no judgement on their folly or weakness. Small wonder that the thousands who met him over the years pronounce a smiling benediction on his memory.

14. *It was the consecration of Dr Hugh Ryan, Bishop of Townsville, on 18 October 1938.*

In the middle of January my mother and I set out for the Month's Mind at Narrandera. En route we stayed a couple of days at Yass, and I was able to say Mass in old St Augustine's there on 18 January, which was the golden anniversary of Father Hartigan's ordination. It was in this church that he had said his first Mass.

Bishop Young had an interesting account to give of his last visit to Monsignor Hartigan:

About ten days before the Monsignor's death I went to visit him in hospital to assure him of the prayers of the priests and people of his native parish. Monsignor spoke of old St Augustine's with affection and, although he was very weak, he was full of enquiries about the new St Augustine's. I asked him if he would write a few verses on the theme of the building of the new St Augustine's to take the place of the old. His eyes lighted with interest, he thought for a few moments and said: 'That would be a lovely subject; I'll do it for you'. God called him before he could take up his pen, however, it is good to know he was thinking of his beloved old church and parish during his last days. [15]

The Month's Mind was held in St Mel's, Narrandera, on Tuesday 20 January. His Lordship Bishop Henschke presided and preached. The celebrant of the Mass was Monsignor Harry Larkins, Vicar-General of the diocese, the deacon was neighbour and friend Dean Lacey of Leeton and the subdeacon was Rev Dr John Harper of Junee. Rev Michael Lane was master of ceremonies. The priests of the diocese were present in good numbers and a large crowd of parishioners and friends attended.

15. Focal News, 1, 3, St Augustine's Church, Yass, 1953.

Epilogue

There have been several developments since Monsignor Hartigan's death that require a mention to complete his story.

He had authorised me to gather together the poems that were unpublished and produce them as a collection entitled **The Parish of St Mel's.** Angus & Robertson were enthusiastic but at first they hesitated about the title. They argued that after his historical work **On Darlinghurst Hill,** a collection of poems with a parish title might be mistaken for another historical work. They even suggested as an alternative **Around the Gidgee Log.** When they realised that it was Father Hartigan who wanted St Mel's—that he wished thus to honour his old parish—they agreed and accepted the poems just as I presented them. The selection had been done in fact by Father Hartigan himself.

The book appeared in June 1954. The review in the **Australasian Catholic Record** was written by Monsignor Thomas Veech and it is a thing of beauty itself.

Once you open the book the old magic is at work, pulling at your heart, the song of HIS nightingales—the kookaburras, the magpie and the lonely curlew. In upon us crowd the Bush P.P., Old Sister Paul, Big Ned *and* Charlie Carter *who have the authentic tang of the bush Catholic about them . . .*

A superb example of 'John O'Brien' at his best is his account of the curse of saffron thistles and the advice of Ned Carter . . .

The great race of Bush P.P.'s, who, like Cobb's coaches, are getting forced further West, have found in 'John O'Brien' a pen to describe their deeds and dignity, even if the Code takes little notice of them. Then he brings wattle bloom to place at the feet of the Bush nuns, teaching the shy bush children, who dread the comings of school inspectors and bishops, the devoted women running the balls and socials ('For years herself and Mrs Bain'), the curates, the old people and the young. And every now and then a lovely line hurts you almost by its beauty:

And the wilgas wailed in the sobbing wind.[1]

1. Australasian Catholic Record *XXXI*, 4, 1954, pp. 352-5.

In 1975 THE MEN OF '38 was launched at St Michael's College, University of Sydney. With the author, right, are Father Tom Linane, centre, Monsignor John Harper, and John Lowden. The portrait of Father Hartigan in the background is by E.M. Smith. (Photo courtesy of Beth Henninger)

Other reviewers too were delighted with the book.[2] Father Hartigan
with his great respect for the Red Page of the **Bulletin** would have been
more than pleased with its critic's praise of his ability to sing the song of
the motor car:

*And as one who often bemoans the fact that there are so few ballads
about motor-cars, I can only say how astonished I am at the
mechanisation of these verses.*[3]

Frank Murphy in the **Advocate** (Melbourne) noted 'a deeper nostalgic
note, something of the sadness that the jester is said to feel'. He selected
'Old Sister Paul' as a favourite: 'It is a lovable, accurate portrait of a nun
who has spent herself in God's service'.[4]

The Parish of St Mel's was in fact a collection of verses from different
eras of John O'Brien's life. Perhaps half a dozen of the twenty-eight
poems in the book were written in later life, another half a dozen were
from his middle years and the rest go back to the time of the **Boree Log.**
The book was reprinted later in the year and 20 000 copies were sold.
Out of print for a long time, it has recently been reprinted.

In 1963, the Centenary of Narrandera was celebrated, and the Catholic
people erected a pulpit in the church in memory of Father Hartigan. In
1979 renovations to the church brought a new pulpit and it also was
dedicated to his memory. As well, the parish has a 'John O'Brien'
Memorial Hall, erected in 1972.

The publishing in 1975 of **The Men of '38**[5] was the achievement of
something that had been talked about for a long time, the collecting into
book form of the successful series of articles in the **Australasian Catholic
Record** with the title **In Diebus Illis.** Father Tom Linane put the
machinery in action by his reference to the articles and quotation from
them in his historical periodical **Footprints**[6] and he supplied the critical
notes for the book while I gave the biographical details in the
introduction; Cardinal Freeman contributed the foreword. The result was
a work that received a great welcome and has had good sales for that type
of writing. It received very favourable reviews, though naturally enough
some historians debated points here and there.

Following close on the heels of **The Men of '38** was the Australian
Broadcasting Commission's documentary **Behind the Boree Log.** Begun

2. E.g. The Catholic Weekly, *17 June 1954;* Our Cathedral Chimes, *Goulburn, 18 July 1954.*
3. Bulletin, *14 July 1954.*
4. Advocate, *Melbourne, 22 July 1954.*
5. *Lowden Publishing, Co., Kilmore, Vic.*
6. *July 1972, pp. 3-6.*

in 1974, it took eighteen months to produce. The idea of the documentary came from Patrick Kirkwood and the producer was Patrick Kavanagh. Very careful research was done, and the filming took place in various parts of the Riverina associated with Father Hartigan, the bulk of it naturally being done in Narrandera. Manly College and Rose Bay were the locale of some of the scenes. A wide spectrum of folk was used including a nonagenarian who, with humour and deep feeling, told of the wonderful generosity Father Hartigan practised and succeeded in hiding from the public gaze. This old man, Mr Perry, who died shortly afterwards, was a 'natural' for television—as Pat Kavanagh said: 'he leapt out of the television set at you'. The music was by Richard Connolly and it caught the mood very well. The program ran for 55 minutes.

It was rated a most successful documentary and public demand for it was such that after being shown nationally around Australia, there was an instant call for a second showing which took place later in that same year, 1976. A further request to show it to mark the centenary of the poet's birth in October 1978 resulted in its being shown again nationally on 18 December, and in 1979 it was shown on Irish television.

Literally hundreds of messages came in expressing appreciation of the documentary. Typical of them is the much-prized one from the retired Cardinal Archbishop of Sydney:

> *St John Vianney Villa,*
> *Randwick,*
> *13 March 1976.*
>
> *Dear Father Mecham,*
>
> *Permit me to thank and congratulate you on the Channel 2 production of 'Round the Boree Log'. I enjoyed every moment of the showing and liked everything about it.*
>
> *The management of Channel 2 deserves commendation for putting on the show and for the way in which it was done.*
>
> *Hoping that there will be more similar productions and renewing my thanks for this one.*
>
> *I remain,*
> *Yours sincerely,*
> *† N.T. Card. Gilroy.*

A very successful young Sydney artist Patrick Carroll was planning with Patricia Rainsford to have an exhibition of paintings at her galleries at Balgowlah. They were both devotees of 'John O'Brien' and decided to have his poems as the inspiration of the paintings. When consulting Angus & Robertson about the use of the titles of the poems they were told of the possibility of having both a new edition of the books illustrated by Patrick and an exhibition of paintings on **Boree Log** themes. Also, it was pointed out to them how apposite it would be to have the book and exhibition in 1978 to mark the centenary of Father Hartigan's birth.

I gladly contributed an introduction on the life of Father Hartigan and provided family photographs, and was happy that the centenary was being commemorated in these ways. This biography had originally been planned to mark the occasion but was not far enough advanced to make that feasible.

The book with its beautifully reproduced illustrations was an instant success, as was also the exhibition of paintings at the Rainsford Galleries. The paintings were snapped up immediately, and the book, in its edition of 6000, sold out in a few weeks. There were two reprints in 1979, making a total of 20 000 copies.

The reviews were flattering. Professor Patrick O'Farrell in the **Australasian Catholic Record** had this to say:

This is a presentation with such new dimensions as make the old completely and splendidly superseded. Full colour plates...
particularly the landscapes are strikingly beautiful in fashion of genuine Australian quiet, drowsy with brown heat, or blue with hint of evening cool.
When Polding dreamt of revealing to this land what he called the beauty of holiness he certainly had in mind other grander things. Yet here, in a uniquely Australian way is something of just that kind of beauty. Small, humble perhaps, but bringing to our lives, more than pleasure, an element of joy. And that being rare, is a matter for congratulation,—and gratitude.[7]

In March 1980 St Patrick's College, Goulburn, honoured Monsignor Hartigan with the **Age Quod Agis** award. This Latin quotation from the spiritual classic **De Imitatione Christi** is the college motto and means 'Whatever you do, do it well'. The award was a recognition of Father Hartigan as one who in his life fulfilled the implications of that quotation and contributed to the honour of the college and of Australia. Desmond Hartigan of Northwood, a nephew, and son of an old boy of the college, received the award on behalf of the family. Brother Marzorini, president of the college, spoke of the address Father Hartigan gave on the seventieth anniversary of the founding of the college[8] and described it as

7. Australasian Catholic Record *LVI, 2, 1979, pp. 212-13.*
8. *Reproduced above, pp. 246-259.*

among the finest he ever delivered.

These varied events since Father Hartigan's death indicate that he lives on in the hearts of the Australian people he loved so dearly, and all the time over the years **Around the Boree Log** has continued to be in demand. Reprints have followed one after another so that now the number of copies sold has exceeded a quarter of a million.

We can conclude the story of Father Hartigan with the closing words of Jim Kelleher's beautiful articles[9] in **The Catholic Weekly** of 1952: 'There is only one "John O'Brien".'

9. *Noted earlier on p. 94.*

Bibliography

Manuscripts

Papers of Father Hartigan held by the author at Holy Family Presbytery, Lindfield and letters kindly lent by friends.

Student Annals, Papers of Presidents and the Register of St Patrick's College Manly, all these in the College Archives. Papers of Dean O'Keefe in the possession of the Parish Priest of Yass. Diary of Bishop Gallagher, held at Canberra Archives of Archdiocese of Canberra and Goulburn. Parochial Registers at the Churches of Ballynacally (Irl.), Lisseycasey (Irl.), Yass, Albury, Berrigan and Narrandera. Material on Fathers Pat and Frank Hartigan held in Diocesan Archives at Wagga.

Newspapers and Magazines

The Advocate (Melbourne)

The Australasian Catholic Record (1st Series Sydney, 1895-1913, 2nd Series, Manly, St Patrick's College, 1924-   )

The Bulletin (Sydney)

Calamus Scribae (St Patrick's College, Goulburn)

Catholic Press (Sydney)

The Catholic Weekly (Sydney)

The Daily Advertiser (Wagga)

Daily Mirror (Sydney)

The Daily News (Albury)

The Far East (American Edition)

Focal News (Yass)

Footprints (Melbourne Historical Commission)

Freeman's Journal (Sydney)

The Gundagai Independent

The Herald (Melbourne)

Manly (Publication of the Manly Union)

Messenger of the Sacred Heart

Narandera Argus

The New Zealand Tablet

Our Cathedral Chimes (Goulburn)

The Pilot (Boston USA)

336

Smith's Weekly (Sydney)
The Sydney Morning Herald
The Tribune (Melbourne)
Yass Courier

Books

The Australian Encyclopaedia, Angus & Robertson, Sydney, 1925

The Catholic Church and Community in Australia, Patrick O'Farrell, Nelson, Sydney, 1977

Embrace the Past with Remembrance, Sr Bernadette Watson, PBVM, Summit Press, Canberra, 1975

The Emergence of an Australian Catholic Priesthood, 1835-1915, K.T. Livingston, Catholic Theological Faculty, Sydney, 1977

History of the Catholic Church in Australia, P.F. Moran, Oceanic Publishing Co., Sydney, n.d. (1896)

Life and Letters of Archpriest John Joseph Therry, Eris O'Brien, Angus & Robertson, Sydney, 1922

Poems, Maurice O'Reilly, Sands & Co., London, n.d.

Sands Directory of NSW, 1867

A Sketch of the Rise and Progress of the Yass Mission, Dr Morgan O'Connor, Chronicle Office, Goulburn, 1861

The Solid Mandala, Patrick White, Viking Press, New York, 1966

Centenary, Sisters of the Presentation of the Blessed Virgin Mary, compiled and edited by Bernard T. Dowd in association with Sheila E. Tearle, published by Presentation Sisters, Wagga, 1973

Index

Aborigines 15, 222sq, 225, 274
Adelaide 24, 42, 230, 238, 308
Adelong 10, 125
Albury 20, 38, 52-82, 87, 92sq, 98,
    105, 107, 111, 121, 242
  beginnings of 11, 118, 157, 223,
    228sq, 239, 254
  Convent of Mercy 17, 236
  St Patrick's Church 53, 236sq
  Thurgoona (Newtown) 56, 80, 93,
    138, 236, 239, 254
American interest in 'John O'Brien'
    166, 243sq, 292
Angus & Robertson Ltd 33, 42, 87,
    111, 133-136, 181, 223, 243,
    330, 333
Annerley 73, 181
Ardlethan 323
Around the Boree Log see 'John
    O'Brien', writings of
Around the Boree Log (film) 147-150
Around the Boree Log (music) 195
Auckland 315, 319
Australia 7, 49, 60sq, 76, 105, 113,
    126, 130, 136, 149, 168, 205sq,
    249, 254sq, 319
  beginnings of 8, 12, 60sq, 133, 153-
    157, 218-229, 232-235
  Catholic Education in 205-209, 247-
    259, 278
  First Plenary Council of 23, 239
Australian 39, 53, 55sq, 58-62, 76, 83,
    93-97, 99, 102, 112, 114, 121,
    126, 133, 141-144, 149-152,
    161-163, 179sq, 218, 226, 245,
    315
  Alps 93, 98-105
  Broadcasting Commission 172, 197,
    332sq
  Church, composition of 223-242,
    306-311
  literature, Fr Hartigan's views on
    58-62, 94-98
  vocations to the priesthood 20sq,
    53sqq, 181, 190-195

Badham, Professor Charles 33, 255
Bakker, Rev Harry 46
Balgowlah 20, 333

Ballarat 156, 252
Balldale 161
Ballybricken (Irl.) 249
Ballynacally (Irl.) 5
Balranald 233
Bantry Bay (Irl.) 8
Barnard, Marjorie 89
Barnawartha 38
Barry, Mgr Tom 284
Bartlett, Mgr Gerald 244, 292
Bathurst 8, 20, 148, 161, 230, 288,
    290
  St Charles' Seminary 46, 277
Bayliss, Henry 235
Beechworth 117
Behind the Boree Log (A.B.C.
    documentary) 172, 197, 332 sq
Benalla 225
Bendenine Station 96, 220
Bendigo 328
Benedictines 8, 156, 195, 232, 260,
    306
Bermingham, Rev Dr Patrick 11, 227,
    233-239, 241, 249, 254
Bermingham, Rev William 237, 241
Berrigan 107-113, 147, 271
Billabong Station 223
Binalong 97, 220, 223, 236
Black Andrew 221
Blackburn, Professor Bickerton 175
Blacklock, Fred 62, 87
Blakeney, Mgr Jim 246
Blaxland, Gregory 155
Blue Mountains 8, 155, 160, 288
Boldrewood, Rolf 233
Bombala Church, opening of 211-217
Bongiorno, Rev Sylvester 197
Boorowa *see* Burrowa
Boree Creek 238
Boree tree 123
Botany 9, 154
Bourke, Rev Pierce 14
Bourke, Rosie (Narrandera) 263
Bowna, St Francis de Sales' Church
    236
Bowning 11, 221, 223

Bracken, Thomas 95
Braidwood 29, 227
Breadalbane, St Brigid's Church 236
Brennan, Christopher 137
Brennan, Rev Michael 10, 223, 228, 247
Bridge, Rev Reginald 27, 31
Bringenbrong 98sq, 102
Brisbane 27, 73, 253sq, 261
Brodie, Bishop Matt 27, 152
Broken Hill 157
Brosnan, Rev John 29, 31, 43
Buckingbong 233
Buckley, Mgr Michael 241
Bulletin 15sq, 43sq, 62, 89, 104, 121, 133, 141, 144, 150, 152, 312, 332
Bullocks in early Australian transport 228sq
Bundidjarrie 233
Burke, Rev Dr Steve 49
Burrowa 14, 143, 229, 234
Burton, Rev Frank 27
Bushrangers 9, 116-118, 235
Butler, Rev Edmund 255
Bynon, Captain Thomas 238
Byrne, John ('Joker') 55sq, 72-76, 98-103, 110sq, 147

Cabarita 23
Caha Mts (Irl.) 8
Cahill, Rev William 112
Camden 224
Campbell, Rev John 194
Campbelltown 8, 225, 276, 288
Camperdown (N.S.W.) 23
Canberra 110, 119, 221, 296, 316
Canberra and Goulburn, Archdiocese of 47, 119, 133, 292sq, 319
Caringbah 19
Carlow (Irl.) 118, 157, 230, 235, 249
Carroll, Archbishop James 178
Carroll, Patrick 333sq
Carroll, Rev Thomas Joseph 118
Carson, Rev Frank 112
Cashel (Irl.) 230
Castlebar (Irl.) 104
Castlederg (Irl.) 146
Cattaneo, Archbishop Bartholomew 121, 181
Charleville (Irl.) 165

Chesterton, Gilbert Keith 150
Chisholm, Caroline 289 sq
Christchurch 319
Christian Brothers 34, 42, 205, 234, 241sq, 248sq, 257sqq, 278
Clancy, Archbishop Edward 178
Clare (Irl.) 5, 12, 14, 83sq, 165
Clark, Mgr William 179, 181
Clarke, Marcus 60, 141
Clarke, Rev Owen 120, 284
Clifton Gardens 44, 168
Clontarf (Irl.) 5
Clune, Frank 88sq
Clune, Bishop Patrick 114, 242
Cobar 157
Cobb & Co., Coaches 11, 158, 232, 237, 328, 330
Coen family 15, 22, 36, 163, 280, 316
Coffey, Rev Michael 248
Cogeldrie 233
Collins family 8, 17
Collins, Rev Neil 27
Comins family (Yass) 15, 143
Conaghan, Mgr Denis 46sq
Concord 43
Condobolin 118
Coningham, Arthur 48
Connolly, Richard 333
Conolly, Rev Philip 155, 260, 306
Conroy family 11, 97, 222sq
Conscription issue 113sq
Coogee 23
Cook's River 9
Coolac 8, 279
Coolamon 237
Cootamundra 125, 175sqq, 254
Cork (Irl.) 8, 114, 165
Corowa 107, 116sq, 197
Corryong 105
Coughlan family (Narrandera) 197
Crashaw, Richard 316
Crennan, Mgr George 312, 316
Cronulla 19
Crookwell 116
Cullinane family 44, 118, 178
Cunningham, Allan 155
Currie, Captain Mark 220

Daley, Victor 61
Dalley, Hon. Bede 23, 33

339

Daly, Rev Dr Richard 37, 121
Darling River 22
Darlinghurst 26, 47, 312sqq, 316
Daughters of Charity 176sqq
Delaney, Rev James 31, 309
Deniliquin 295
Dennis, C.J. 119, 135, 141sq
Denny, Rev Richard 47
Desmond, Rev Thomas 197, 313
Devine, Mgr Harold 54sq
Dickens, Charles 61
Dixon, Rev James 260
Doherty, Rev Patrick 46
Dolan, Rev Michael 28
Donegal (Irl.) 14, 236
Donnelly, Rev Hugh 243
Dookie 48
Douglas Park 20
Douro Station 9, 220sqq
Dowling, Rev Vincent Christopher
    O.P. 306
Dowling, Rev Patrick 38, 43
Drummoyne 318
Dublin (Irl.) 16, 118, 161, 166, 306
Duck, Rev Norman 245, 263
Dunedin (N.Z.) 29, 31sq, 42, 89, 95
Dunne, Bishop John 14, 241
Dunne, Mary (Mother M. Stanislaus
    P.B.V.M.) 124, 128
Dunne, Rev Patrick 33, 80, 239, 252-
    255
Durkin family (Devonport) 317sq
Dwyer, Bishop Joseph 38-41, 56, 81sq,
    121sqq, 125sq, 128sq, 146,
    161sqq, 197sq, 202, 229, 238,
    241sq, 272
Dwyer, Bishop Vincent 24, 121

Eastwood, St Catherine's Villa 175,
    177
Education, Catholic 205, 247, 249sq,
    252, 254-259, 278, 305, 309sq
Egan, Rev John 27
Elizabeth Bay 274
Emmet, Robert 288
England
    Fr Hartigan's appreciation of 76sq,
        245, 268, 271
    strife with Ireland 114, 136, 245
English influence on Australian
    literature 60sq, 94-97, 144

Ennis (Irl.) 5sqq
Essendon, St Columban's 243

Fiesole (Italy) 164sq
Fitzpatrick, Mgr John 10, 14, 223,
    228sq, 231
Flanagan, Mgr Edward 277
Flemming, Rev Michael 28
Flynn, Rev Dr Frank 45
Flynn, Louis 24
Forest Lodge 292
Forrest, Rev Dr John 231
Fox, Bishop Thomas 242
Franklin, Sir John Myles 226
Franklin, Miles 88sq
Freeman, James Cardinal 279sq, 315,
    319-323, 332

Gallagher, Rev Bert 197
Gallagher, Bishop John 21, 24, 29, 33-
    37, 40, 49, 52sq, 80sq, 116,
    119sqq, 130, 143, 145sq, 150,
    195, 237, 239sqq, 255sqq
    esteem for Fr Hartigan 37, 80sq,
        130, 145sq
    Fr Hartigan's tributes to 33-37,
        239sqq, 255sqq
Galong 41, 195, 222, 277
Ganmain 56sq, 120, 125, 237
Geoghegan, Bishop Patrick 252
Gilchrist family (Mosman) 20, 175
Gillenbah 115
Gilroy, Cardinal Norman Thomas
    177, 181, 262, 279, 284, 319,
    333
Glengariff (Irl.) 8
Golden Grove 19
Gulgong 237
Gundagai 11, 14, 112, 115, 224, 226,
    233, 236, 254, 279, 290
Gundaroo 96
Gunning 9, 112, 220, 233, 236

Haberfield 123, 160, 162, 174-177,
    187, 277
Hand, Rev John 306
Hankinson, R.H. (Narrandera) 264
Hanly, Rev James 10, 14, 261
Hanrahan, Rev Patrick 147, 187sqq
Harden 21
Hardwicke Station 9

Hargraves, Edward Hammond 156
Hartigan family 5-8, 12-14, 16-21,
163, 175, 285, 319
Hartigan, Rev Patrick Joseph *see also
under* 'John O'Brien'
ability in sketching 63-71, 150
against snobbery 277, 284sq, 326
appreciation of nature 57, 60sq,
75sq, 100, 141, 143sq, 218,
220, 320sq, 324sq, 326sqq, 330
Australian patriot 58-62, 114, 141,
143, 161, 165sq, 168, 181,
218sq, 245, 267sq, 311
birthday 17
Diocesan Consultor 121, 123, 273
Domestic Prelate (Monsignor) 271,
282-285
ecumenical spirit 69, 76-79, 81sq,
126sq, 269
faith and piety 318, 321, 323, 327
fond of ships 32, 276, 322
guest-speaker 81, 179sq, 244, 246-
259, 265-271, 321, 328
his cars 86sq, 112, 166sq, 168,
176, 198-201, 277, 320
historical sense 93, 218, 232, 260sq,
276sq, 312-315, 327
Inspector of Schools 80-87, 93, 107,
119, 121, 125, 150, 276, 281
interest in coaching days 11, 158,
232, 237, 328
knowledge of horses 57, 62, 98,
100-105, 161, 228, 235
love of Manly College 21, 43, 49,
179sqq, 281sq, 304-311, 318
on Australian literature 58-62,
94-98
pastorate in Narrandera 169, 195,
197sq, 245sq, 263sq, 269sq, 277
preacher 10sqq, 14sqq, 21sq, 38-42,
49sqq, 52, 76sq, 110, 126sq,
152-159, 187-195, 202-217, 232-
242, 278, 285-311, 321, 325,
327sq
reverence for the priesthood 39, 42,
50sq, 152, 159, 180sq, 187-195,
229-243, 260sq, 273
writings *see* 'John O'Brien',
writings of
Hartigan, Thomas (Commissioner of
Railways) 7
Hartley 230
Hay 220, 223, 229, 233
Hayden, Mgr Thomas 21, 24sqq, 31,
43, 152

Hennessy, Rev Aeneas 119sq
Henry, Mick 75sq
Henschke, Bishop Francis 202, 218,
232, 242, 271sqq, 281, 284,
313, 319, 329
Herbert, Sister Annette O.L.S.H. 82-
85, 316
Hobart 114, 222
Hogan, Rev Arthur 46
Hogan, Rev Jeremiah S.J. 312
Holbrook 190, 194
Homebush 95
Howlong 224, 228
Hughes family (Elizabeth Bay) 227,
274
Hume, Hamilton 10sq
Hunt, John Horbury (architect) 276
Hurstville 130

Illawarra 225
Immigration 226sq, 252sqq, 289sq
Indi River 100
Ireland
Fr Hartigan's impressions of 165sq
of last century 5, 7, 154
Irish
background of the Hartigans 5-8
content of early Australian Church
8, 14sq, 38, 55, 108, 154-159,
223-239, 252sqq, 260, 307
influence on 'John O'Brien' 22, 38,
83, 112, 114, 130, 165sq
interest in 'John O'Brien' 89, 133,
145sq, 333

Jamestown 202
Jerilderie 11, 53, 116sq, 118, 160
Jesuit Fathers 153, 242, 252, 273, 278
Jingellic 98
'John O'Brien', origin of the name 89
'John O'Brien', writings of
Around the Boree Log
original edition 73, 75sq, 107,
109, 110sq, 130, 133-147, 150,
162, 166, 176, 323, 326, 335
first illustrated edition 150
American edition 243sq
illustrated edition 1978 243,
333sq
origins of individual poems 42,
92, 108sq
Australian Born (novel) 93

Father Brendan's Christmas Day (short story) 181-187

His Little Irish Mother (short story) 187

In Diebus Illis 261sq, 276sq, 327, 332

The Man from Snowy River 94-104, 150

The Men of '38 and other Pioneer Priests 10, 33, 116, 150, 231, 242, 253, 261, 322

On Darlinghurst Hill 26, 47, 312, 316, 330

The Parish of St Mel's 327, 330, 332

origins of individual poems 62-71, 85sq, 109, 130, 137, 150, 181, 316sqq, 330, 332

A Plea for Australian Literature 59-62

Unpublished poems 43sq, 57sq, 73, 90sqq, 111, 130sqq, 138-141

Johnson, Ben 47

Jugiong (earlier, Thugiong) 11, 14, 156, 221, 233, 236

Junee 85, 121, 152, 158, 237, 319, 329

Kavanagh, Rev Michael 227

Kavanagh, Patrick 333

Kelleher, Jim 43, 109, 112, 135, 313, 335

Kelly gang (bushrangers) 116sqq

Kelly, Mgr Jim 46, 75, 181

Kelly, Rev Vincent 318

Kendall, Henry 60, 95

Kennedy, Mgr James 309, 319

Kenny, Rev James Aloysius 31

Kenny, Judy 316

Kenny, Rev Patsy 87

Kensington 20

Khancoban 100sq

Kidman, Jimmy 95

Kiely, Rev Richard 116sqq

Kieran, Dr John 174

Kilkenny (Irl.) 43

Killarney (Irl.) 165

Kilmore 33, 116, 150, 261, 327

Kilrush (Irl.) 7

Kincoppal 274

King, Mafe (Mrs Sorrell) 169-172

King, Mgr Tom 51

Kinnegad 14sq

Kipling, Rudyard 167

Kirkwood, Patrick 333

Kogarah 125, 129

Kosciusko 98, 103

Kyneton 31

Lacey, Dean Gus 194

Lachlan River 9, 115, 218, 233, 237, 248

Lake George 227

Lane, Mgr Michael 329

Lang, Dr John Dunmore 10

Lanigan, Rev Patrick 248

Lanigan, Bishop William 14, 33, 53, 116, 118, 237, 250sq, 254, 295

La Perouse, Jean-Francois 155

Larkins, Mgr Harry 329

Lawless, Mgr James 48, 198

Lawson, Henry 60sq, 93, 135, 141, 225

Leeton 119

Leonard, James 24, 29

Lewisham 20, 73, 80, 105, 163, 197, 280, 312, 315, 318

Limerick (Irl.) 5sqq, 230

Linane, Rev Tom 150, 331sq

Lindfield, Holy Family Church 51

Lismore 20, 80

Lissycasey (Irl.) 5sqq, 12, 165

Liston, Archbishop James 28, 32, 152, 308, 315, 319

Little Company of Mary 163sqq, 238, 318

Liverpool (N.S.W.) 9, 224

Livingston, Kevin 23, 31

Lloyd, Rev Frank 46

Lockhart 147, 187, 237

Long, Rev Thomas 238

Longford (Irl.) 28, 118

Lovat, Rev Charles 10, 230, 236, 261

Lynch, Dean John Thomas 230

Lyons, Dame Enid 317

Lyons, Bishop Patrick 309

McAlroy, Rev Michael 10, 33, 222, 232-237, 239, 249sq, 252

McAlroy, Rev Peter Paul 53

Macaulay, Lord Thomas Babington 59, 96

McCarthy, Rev Patrick 27

McDermott, Rev Hugh 21, 24, 31, 43, 49, 54sq
McDonald, Rev Walter 327
McEncroe, Archdeacon John 249, 278
McEvoy, John Shiel 147
McEwan, Rev Sydney 280
McGaurin, Anthony 248
McGuinness, Mother Dorothy R.S.C.J. 263, 276, 316
McGuire, Archbishop Terence 31, 47, 49sqq, 146, 181, 246, 259, 281sq, 292-296, 319
Maclean 317
Macleay family (pioneers) 220
Maclure, John 57sq
McMahon, Sister Betty R.S.C.J. 316
McMahon, Sister Patrick P.B.V.M. 110
Macquarie River 115, 227
Madden, Sister Mary P.B.V.M. 175
Mahoney, Dean Edmund 230sq
Maitland 24, 230sq, 238, 252, 277, 319
Malvern 316
Mangan family 4, 92
Mangoplah 101
Manly 20sq, 29
    St Patrick's College 23-33, 37, 40, 42-51, 53sqq, 79, 95sq, 105, 120, 152, 178-181, 198, 277, 281, 304-311, 317sqq, 313
    Union 45, 55, 150, 160, 179sqq
Mannix, Archbishop Daniel 48, 113sq, 147, 161sq, 165, 326
Marella, Archbishop Paul 319
Marsden, Rev Samuel 225
Marsfield, St Anthony's Church 178
Martin, Rev Denis 253
Marulan 295
Mary Ann (early nom-de-plume) 43sq, 62, 89, 150
Marzorini, Brother Francis Daniel C.F.C. 334
Mauritius 260
Maynooth (Irl.), St Patrick's College 116, 146, 327
Mayo (Irl.) 104
Meath (Irl.) 24
Mecham family 105, 163, 172-178, 277sq, 315, 319, 329
Millet, Jean Francis 296sq, 303
Mitchell, Major Thomas 223sq
Mittagong-Bowral 114

Moloney, Rev Parker 319
Moloney, Rev Patrick M.S.C. 108sq, 163
Monaro 101, 220
Moran, Cardinal Francis Patrick 16, 23, 29, 31, 46, 155, 239, 242
Moran, Bishop Patrick 95, 307, 308, 310
Morris, Bishop William Placid 260
Morundah 197, 264, 272
Mosgiel (N.Z.) 43, 308
Mosman 20, 132, 285
Mudgee 277
Muldoon, Bishop Thomas 318
Mulligan, Rev Peter 53
Mummel 226
Mundarlo 233
Mungabareena 223
Murphy, Bishop Francis 230
Murphy, Frank 332
Murphy, Bishop Patrick 27
Murphy, Rev Dr Patrick 43sq
Murray, Archbishop Daniel 230
Murray, Bishop James 332
Murray River 11, 38, 98, 100, 104, 156, 218, 224, 228, 288
Murrumbidgee River 9sq, 115, 156, 218sqq, 224, 233
Muttama 225, 227

Narrandera 5, 7, 51, 112sq, 115 sq, 118-121, 123sqq, 127, 160sq, 165, 168-174, 179sq, 195-202, 233, 237, 244sqq, 272sq, 327, 329, 333
    beginnings of 115-119
    Convent 118, 169, 173sq, 271
    Fr Hartigan's first years in 119sqq, 123sqq
    his last days there 261-273
    his nostalgia for 265, 277, 279, 315
    St Brigid's Church 116, 118
    St Mel's Church and Parish 106, 118, 123, 150, 245sq, 268, 329
Nevin, Mgr John 181
Newcastle 143
Newman, Cardinal John Henry 33, 281
New South Wales 75, 87, 115, 221, 249sq
    South West 11, 157, 218-242, 244
Newstead 317

New Zealand 27sqq, 43, 95, 105, 145, 150, 152, 264, 308, 319
Nolan, Mgr Tom 46
Northern Ireland 53, 113, 146, 226
North Rocks cemetery 178, 187, 319
Northwood 7
Norton, Bishop John 209

O'Brien, Cornelius 222
O'Brien, Archbishop Eris 133, 146, 155, 223, 281, 319
O'Brien, Florence (Sister M. Regis P.B.V.M.) 17
O'Brien, Henry 9sqq, 220sqq
O'Connell, Daniel 227
O'Connell, Mgr Tim 152-159
O'Connor, Dr Morgan 9, 235
O'Donnell, Mgr Edward 260, 277
O'Donoghue, Rev John 38
O'Farrell, Bishop Michael 161
O'Farrell, Professor Patrick 113, 334
O'Flynn, Rev Jeremiah 155, 260, 287, 306
Ogilvie, William Henry 60sq
O'Grady, Rev Harry 31
O'Hanlin, Rev Joseph 47
O'Haran, Mgr Denis 23sq, 48
O'Harris, Pixie 94
O'Hurley, Rev Dermot 14
O'Keefe, Rev Patrick Francis Capistran O.F.M. 14sqq, 143, 242
O'Mara family 280sq
Omeo 104
O'Neill, Rev Harold 260
O'Neill, Rev Patrick 32, 309
O'Neill, Rev Thomas 234
Orange 118
O'Reilly, Rev Maurice C.M. 89, 114, 137sq
O'Reilly, Rev Michael 230
O'Reilly, Rev Patrick 197
O'Sullivan, John 222
O'Sullivan, Mgr Timothy 31
Ournie 100
Ovens, Major John 220
Ovens River 228
Oxley, John 155

Parkes, Sir Henry 15, 248

Parramatta 9, 16sq, 19, 129, 187, 221, 230sq
Partridge, Brigid, (Sister M. Ligouri P.B.V.M.) 125-130
Paterson, Andrew Barton ('Banjo') 60sq, 89, 93, 96, 103sq, 141, 222
Penola 205
Penrith 8, 134, 224, 230sq
Percy, Rev Arthur 54, 105
Perry, William 333
Perth 114, 242, 308, 315
Phelan, Rev Michael 242
Phelan, Bishop Patrick 242
Phillips, Stephen 92sq
Picton 224
Pitt, Marie 103
Poe, Edgar Allan 60, 144
Polding, Archbishop John Bede 8, 10sq, 23, 46, 156sq, 205, 222sq, 231, 242, 249, 260, 306, 334
    Fr Hartigan's tribute to 250
Port Hacking 19
Port Macquarie 290
Port Phillip 9, 10sq, 156, 220, 252
Port Pirie, diocese of (earlier, Port Augusta) 31, 202
Powell family (Berrigan) 109sq
Power, Rev Daniel 306
Presentation Sisters 17, 125, 128sq, 175, 205, 227, 241
    beginnings in Wagga 237sq, 249, 252
Preston 198
Pyrmont 276

Queanbeyan (earlier, Limestone Plains) 227, 229
Queensland 75, 81, 160, 178, 245, 252sqq
Quinn, Bishop James 254
Quinn, Bishop Matthew 238, 252
Quinn, Roderick 61, 137

Rainsford, Patricia 333
Randwick 149
Rawlings, Emeritus Archdeacon 264
Receveur, Pere Louis O.F.M. 155
Redemptorist Fathers 195, 254
Redfern 27
Redwood, Archbishop Francis 121

Reidy, Rev Patrick 119, 189sq
Religious life 202-211, 278, 309sq
Religious of the Sacred Heart 262sq,
    274-277, 280, 284sq, 315sq
Renno, Mary 148
Rice, Edmund Ignatius 205, 278
Rigney, Rev John 230, 261
Riley, Jack (of Snowy River) 98-105
Riverina 158, 218-229, 239, 249, 253,
    261, 271, 333
Roberts, Sister Veronica P.B.V.M.
    175
Robertson, George 134-137
Robertson, Sir John 11, 23, 115
Rochfort Bridge (Irl.) 15, 21sq
Rome 16, 27, 31, 42, 49, 153, 161-
    165, 177, 239, 293, 308, 319
Roscommon (Irl.) 226
Rose Bay, Covent of the Sacred Heart
    176, 200, 262, 271, 273-285,
    316
Rossi, Captain Francis 231
Rourke family (Narrandera) 165
Rutherglen 48, 198
Ryan, Bishop Hugh 328
Ryan, Tighe 72
Ryan, Rev Tom 38-42, 46sq, 49, 121
Ryde 19

St John's College (University of
    Sydney) 35, 89, 138, 231, 240,
    252
St Mary's (Western Line) 134
Sandgate 254
Sevenhill 252
Shane Park (near Penrith) 224
Shanley, Rev Thomas 245
Sheehy, Rev Patrick 79
Sheen, Bishop Fulton 243, 292
Simonds, Archbishop Justin 31, 319
Singleton 261
Sisters of Charity 20, 205, 278
Sisters of the Good Samaritan 205
Sisters of the Little Company of
    Mary 164
Sisters of Mercy
  Albury 17, 56, 105, 249
  Goulburn 52, 175-178, 249
  Parramatta 16sq, 19, 178, 187, 319
  Yass 14-17, 21sq, 27, 52, 243, 249,
    252

Sisters of Our Lady of the Sacred
    Heart 82
Sisters of St John of God 7
Sisters of St Joseph
  Goulburn 118, 169, 194, 202-211,
    246, 249, 263sq, 280sq
  Tasmania 317
Sisters of St Joseph of the Sacred
    Heart 195
Slattery, Rev Michael 52, 116sqq
Slattery, Dean Thomas
    (Warrnambool) 230
Slattery, Rev Thomas (Goulburn
    Diocese) 121
Slattery, Bishop William 230
Slattery, Rev William 271, 284
Smith, Edward M. (artist) 281
Snowden 57, 100, 235
Sowerby, Rev Dean W. 231
Springwood, St Columba's College 45,
    74, 178, 260, 277, 304
Stanmore 19, 51
Sturt, Charles 115, 156, 220sq, 223,
    232
Sullivan family (Coolac) 8, 52, 112,
    175, 279
Summer Hill 20, 105
Surry Hills 18, 133
Swinburne, Algernon Charles 144
Sydney 5, 8sq, 17, 20, 33, 77, 129,
    148, 178, 262, 276
  Archdiocese of 28, 38, 262, 319
  early Catholics in 8, 12, 33, 104,
    287sq
  Fr Hartigan's visits to 51, 87, 112,
    136, 138, 179sq
  last century conditions 8sq, 156sq,
    220, 225, 252, 260, 274, 287,
    290
  St Mary's Cathedral 8, 12, 31, 43,
    48, 181, 262, 278, 285, 296,
    319
  University 33, 35, 175, 225

Tangmangaroo 143
Tara (Irl.) 156
Tasmania (earlier, Van Diemen's
    Land) 105, 260
Tearle, Sheila 129
Temora 116, 229, 237
Therry, Archpriest John Joseph 10,
    155, 157, 220, 223, 225, 260,
    288, 306

Thompson family (Narrandera) 200sq
Tipperary (Irl.) 118
Tocumwal 107, 112sq, 146, 161
Tom Groggin River 100, 102
Toohey, Bishop John 319
Tooma 100, 160
Toowoomba 75
Touchell, Rev William 125-129
Townsell (or Trousdell) family 7,
    12sq, 16, 165, 187
Towong 100
Treacy, Brother Ambrose 257sq
Trollope,Sir Anthony 233
Tuamgraney (Irl.) 5
Tullamore (Irl.) 14, 252
Tumbarumba 261
Tumut 10, 11, 14, 118, 223, 227,
    229, 236
Tuomey, Mgr Patrick 5, 114, 165

Ullathorne, Bishop William 223, 230,
    260, 307
Urana 11, 237, 264

Vaughan, Rev Arthur 108sq, 162
Vaughan, Cardinal Herbert 223
Vaughan, Archbishop Roger Bede 238,
    250, 255
Veech, Mgr Thomas 281, 330
Vercruysee, Mother Sebronie R.S.C.J.
    274, 276
Verdon, Bishop Michael 24, 27sqq,
    31, 33, 37, 42, 308
Victoria 38, 48, 75, 81, 115, 223, 252,
    318, 328
  early settlement in 223sq
Vincentian Fathers 160

Wagga 29, 107, 147, 161, 175, 229,
    257, 260, 271
  beginnings of 115, 118, 158, 222,
    224, 232, 237
    St Michael's Cathedral 38sq, 123,
    128

Wallace, Mgr Thomas 195, 284sq,
    312, 315, 319
Walsh, Rev Denis 249
Walsh, Philip K. 147sq
Walsh, Rev Richard 248sq
Wangaratta 158
Warrnambool 230
Waterford (Irl.) 249
Watson's Bay 276
Wentworth, William Charles 155,
    274
Wentworth Falls 160
Werribee, Corpus Christi College
    308, 318
Westmeath (Irl.) 252
Westport (Irl.) 249
Wilcannia 118
Wilcannia-Forbes Diocese 233
Windsor 225
Wodonga 45, 223
Wollongong 230
Woodlock, Mother Margaret 316
Woods, Bridget 163, 165
Woods, Rev Julian Tenison 205, 207
Woollahra, Holy Cross Convent 19
World War I 48, 51, 123, 171, 198,
    268
World War II 198, 244sq, 269sq
Wyalong 237
Wymah, St John's Church 236

Yamba Station 7
Yarrabee Station 197
Yass 9-22, 38, 47, 96sq, 112, 218,
    220, 223, 225, 227, 230, 233,
    236, 249, 260, 319
  early families 15, 143, 163, 220,
    225, 280
  Mount Carmel Convent 10, 14, 22,
    27, 52, 82, 175, 230
  St Augustine's Church 10sqq, 52,
    222, 229, 329
Yeomans, John 318
Young 53, 118, 175sq, 253
Young, Archbishop Guildford 329